Applied Community Policing
in the
21st Century

Dennis J. Stevens

University of Massachusetts Boston

Boston   New York   San Francisco
Mexico City   Montreal   Toronto   London   Madrid   Munich   Paris
Hong Kong   Singapore   Tokyo   Cape Town   Sydney

Series Editor: *Jennifer Jacobson*
Editorial Assistant: *Tom Jefferies*
Marketing Manager: *Judeth Hall*
Cover Administrator: *Kristina Mose-Libon*
Composition Buyer: *Linda Cox*
Manufacturing Buyer: *JoAnne Sweeney*
Production Editor: *Christine Tridente*
Editorial-Production Service: *DMC & Company*
Text Design: *Donna Merrell Chernin*

For related titles and support materials, visit our online catalog at www.ablongman.com.

Between the time Website information is gathered and then published, it is not unusual for some sites to have closed. Also, the transcription of URLs can result in unintended typographical errors. The publisher would appreciate notification where these errors occur so that they may be corrected in subsequent editions.

Library of Congress Cataloging-in-Publication Data
Stevens, Dennis J.
    Applied community policing in the 21st century / Dennis J. Stevens.-- 1st ed.
        p. cm.
    Includes bibliographical references and index.
    ISBN 0-205-33222-6 (pbk. : alk. paper)
    1. Community policing--United States. 2. Police-community relations--United States.
    3. Police administration--United States. I. Title.

HV7936.C83 S737 2002
363.2'3--dc21

                                                                            2002018468

Printed in the United States of America

10 9 8 7 6 5 4 3 2 1   RRD-IN   08 07 06 04 03 02

Dedicated to my children
David D. Stevens
Mark A. Stevens
Alyssa P. Stevens

Other Books by Dennis J. Stevens

Case Studies in Applied Community Policing (2003) Allyn and Bacon
Case Studies in Community Policing (2001) Prentice Hall
Policing and Community Partnerships (2002) Prentice Hall
Inside the Mind of the Sexual Offender: Predatory Rapists, Pedophiles,
  and Criminal Profiles (2001) Author's Choice
Inside the Mind of the Predatory Rapist (1998) Austin Winfield
Corrections Perspectives (1997) Coursewise

Contents

9 *Testing Police Performance in Boston and Columbus* **157**

10 *Problem-Oriented Policing* **176**

12 *Family and Domestic Violence and Sexual Assault* 212

13 *Youth, Drugs, and Alcohol* 226

14 *The Fear of Crime and Homicide* 248

Preface

The centerpiece of this work relates to the new challenges facing police, partly due to America's cultural changes and the terrorist alerts. These challenges put Western European tradition linked to police policy on notice. Community-policing strategies can be tailored to meet these new challenges. To help guide this process, 2,010 surveys and 76 interviews were conducted in eight cities across the US in English, Spanish, and Chinese.

This work contains the principal concepts of community policing linked to clues about culture, communities, and social order which in turn are linked to ways of looking at behavior. These ideas are presented in terms of police strategies such as problem-solving, curbing violence, and controlling drugs and juveniles which, in turn, are linked to ways of evaluating performance, and finally, to measuring the performance of police efforts across America.

In what way is this work unique? Largely, most police textbooks authored by an academic are long on theory, and when penned by a practitioner, are detailed in police icons. While both approaches make a significant contribution, they tend to be short on real-life expectations of people who experience various forms of community police efforts every day and want to talk about it. There is a tendency for basic textbooks to offer idyllic explanations and strategies implying that those explanations and strategies work. This textbook explains strategies and asks police agencies what services they provide, while also explaining behavior and asking community members what they think of police service.

Policing in a democracy creates real problems from the get-go. Profiling, detaining, and intrusions upon specific groups of people in specific neighborhoods can represent a denial of due process guarantees, and this issue is one that America has fought wars over. It is time the American police and the communities they serve discard myths of academic theory and consider some of the realities of various police strategies and hear the impact those strategies have on American neighborhoods. Emerging from this work are also the expectations community members have of municipal services from garbage pickup to business license revocation, since they see police service and municipal service as related issues that impact their quality of life.

At the core of this work are three central issues: America's population is more culturally diverse than ever; the community is not willing to accept choices made by public agencies; and community members, including individuals of color, are voicing their opinions on the difference between police rhetoric and police practice. At the core of this investigation lies the official rhetoric of a police agency versus actual practices from the perspective of their constituents.

In light of the women's movement, civil rights, and a war the public didn't sanction, it should be clear that the American public wants to be involved in the decision-making processes that affect their lives regardless of the language they speak or country of their birth. They want to know how things work, who lives next door, and what governmental agencies are going to do for them.

It is suggested that you obtain a copy of the accompanying evaluations of eight jurisdictions that were surveyed as part of this textbook: *Case Studies in Applied Community Policing*. This companion text contains specifics that relate to this textbook. The jurisdictions evaluated were Alexandria, Boston, Columbia, Columbus, Miami-Dade County, Midland, Palm Beach County, and Sacramento.

This work should not be considered a final word on public order, communities, and cultural diversity, or police and policing strategies. Rather, it should be looked upon as a working draft, and as such it can act as a guide for students researching policing and municipal service outcomes. It can also act as a guide for police and municipal agencies to better understand community perspectives since this work deals with real experiences of people in the twenty-first century.

Dennis J. Stevens
Boston

Acknowledgments

There are always many to thank. Professors Nina Silverstein, University of Massachusetts Boston, College of Public and Community Service, and Xiaogang Deng, Department of Sociology, reviewed chapters on measuring policing performance. Ramona Hernandez, College of Public and Community Service, translated the survey from English to Spanish. Cuff Ferguson, College of Public and Community Service, helped write the section on Columbia, South Carolina and Richard Hines of the Columbia South Carolina Police Department contributed to this text as well.

The following colleagues reviewed the social instrument prior to distribution: Jill DuBois at Northwestern in Chicago; Captain Michael Masterson at Madison Police Department; and Kurt Kerley, University of Tennessee in Knoxville. The following individuals helped distribute surveys and/or provided information: Lt. Stephen Dickinson at Palm Beach Sheriff's Department; Lt. Gerald Rudoff at Miami-Dade Police Department; Professor Ellen G. Cohen Florida International University; Elizabeth Wright, Alexandria, Virginia; Captain Robert Dunford, Commander, Dorchester Boston Police Department; Chief Charles H. Ramsey Metropolitan Police, Washington DC; Commander Kent

Shafer at the Columbus Ohio Police Department; Chief Francis D'ambra at Matino North Carolina Police Department; Captain Ben Dickie at Metropolitan-Nashville Police Department; Sutham Cheurprakobkit at the University of Texas Permian Basin at Odessa; Professor Robert Peetz, Midland College; Mike Schneider, Midland College; Midland Hispanic Chamber of Commerce; Jane Hellinghausen, Midland College; Captain Steve Segura and Nancy Boemer-Otis, Sacramento Police Department.

Ten University of Massachusetts Boston students interviewed 76 participants in Boston. Hector Ruiz interviewed 21 immigrant Latinos who were from many countries including Mexico, Colombia, Panama, Guatemala, Brazil, El Salvador, Honduras, Venezuela, and Peru. They attended an English as Second Language course at Centro Presente in Cambridge, Massachusetts. Antonio Vera-Cruz conducted 12 interviews of Cape Verde families. UMass Boston students who were also Latino Boston Police Officers, Maria Gonzalez and Debra Blandin, assisted by Damaris Otero, and one other female officer who wanted to remain anonymous interviewed 17 community members in Spanish, Portuguese, and French Creole in their police districts of Boston and distributed and collected surveys. UMass Boston students and Boston Police Officers, Sergeants Roy Chambers and Stanley Demesmin, attended several of the community meetings in Boston, distributed surveys, and conducted 16 interviews for this study. Lynda McGann, a UMass graduate student, partnered with Sergeant Robert Young, Sr. in South Boston and interviewed 10 individuals of color.

UMass Boston students Officer Nadya Marino from Martha's Vineyard PD, Melissa Driscoll, and Caroline Randall, and Boston University graduate student Danka Charland served as readers, distributed and collected surveys, and/or keyed data from surveys into a computer grid.

Sociology and criminal justice students from the following universities also deserve mention: California State University Sacramento; Columbus State Community College; University of Massachusetts Boston; Boston University; Harvard University; Midland College; University of Texas Permian Basin, Odessa, Texas; University of South Carolina; and Ohio State University. Also, there were numerous others who wished to remain anonymous, including some involved in neighborhood associations.

I would also like to thank the following reviewers: Thoman E. Drerup, Clark State Community College; Deborah L. Dwyer, University of Arkansas, Little Rock; David N. Falcone, Illinois State University; Susan V. Pons, Guilford Technical Community College; Gregory B. Talley, Broome Community College; Robert P. Weiss, SUNY, Plattsburgh.

Personal contributions were made by Wesley Skogan, Lawrence Sherman, Herman Goldstein, David Carter, and Carl Klockars. I would also like to thank Donna Chernin and DMC & Company, who edited and enhanced this work above and beyond the call of duty. Finally, with the inspiration of my friend and colleague, Frank Schmalleger, completing this work was made a little easier.

Foreword

At the dawn of the twenty-first century, police and the public find themselves joined together in a dance, and they both have sore toes to show for it. They need each other, but are afraid of getting too close, and they don't yet have enough practice to bring off the performance smoothly. They are used to being soloists, and find that in order to keep in step, they still must warily watch each other's feet.

Most residents of high-crime areas would like to form a long-term relationship with the police who serve their community. Plagued by street drug markets, loitering gangs, and the sound of gunfire at night, they know they cannot get by without a partner. But too often there is a long history of broken promises and even abuse that needs to be worked through, and this takes a great deal of honest communication.

Families with a young male at home have heard tales of harassment, and worry about what might happen to their sons in a "profile" stop. Police who work their neighborhood all live in the suburbs, and know the community mostly through the troublemakers they haul in. The groups that represent the area, especially those claiming "grass roots" connections, have long built their base by challenging police. They rallied their followers around complaints about excessive force and racial or cultural insensitivity on the part of neighborhood officers, and they and the police are on unfamiliar ground when they meet to discuss joint action plans.

On their side, police have come to recognize that going through the motions without a partner cannot continue. Having a partnership with the community certainly can be aggravating at times, but the taxpayers who pick up the check have developed romantic expectations about their potential relationship with the police, and expect the new model of community policing. For the police, this means that they have to listen to seemingly endless complaints about a broad litany of neighborhood problems, and they are mystified about how they could possibly do anything about them. They fret that local loudmouths will take over, and try to use the police for their private purposes. The many new things that they are being asked to do bring with them new pieces of paper that must be filled out. They fear that the many hours they are spending on "soft" policing means that they won't "make their stats" with enough arrests or gun seizures, and that they won't make detective as a result. They just want to do what they signed up for, and hope that after the next election this latest fad will fade away.

All of this misunderstanding is compounded by the changing complexion of American cities. The most rapid growth—and often the only population growth at all—is among groups that do not speak English as their first language. These newcomers generally avoid established community churches, and they have difficulty recognizing the value of existing neighborhood organizations. Many come from places where police officers were not the friend of common people, and in fact were often corrupt and incompetent. They stick to themselves and try to deal with everything on their own. Their children quickly adopt alien ways of life, and risk getting involved in difficulties their parents could never imagine at home. Somehow, police department recruiters never manage to attract them to the force.

This book addresses all of these issues. It roots the practice of community policing in the communities where it has to work, and takes an analytic view of the difficulties involved in making that happen. It is an important link in a grand experiment that the country is undertaking, for it ties the arm-chair theories of policing being promoted by federal funds to the actual work of officers on the street. There are specific lessons that the reader can carry away from this important work on communities and the concept of community policing from an applied perspective that was crafted by my colleague, Professor Dennis J. Stevens, while still keeping their eye on the big picture.

Wesley G. Skogan
Institute for Policy Research
Northwestern University

1

Police History and Community Policing

"To succeed in the world it is not enough to be stupid, you must also be well-mannered."

Voltaire (1694–1778)

Key Terms _____

Community Policing	Local Law Enforcement	August Vollmer
Decentralization	Paradox	Wickersham Commission
Fragmentation	Police Power	

Key Topics _____

- Historical background of policing.
- Comparison of early English and early American police practices.
- Development of American policing in the twentieth century.
- Definition, critique, and future of community policing.

Introduction

Community policing and the role of police in the United States is largely affected by the changing demographics of the American community. The objective of community policing—to maintain a partnership with the community while protecting public safety—is an enormous challenge, due to advances in technology, sophistication of criminal activities, uncertainties about new responsibilities mandated by law, a due process revolution, and, most recently, terrorist attacks on the United States.

Applied Community Policing in the Twenty-First Century identifies, describes, and evaluates a police strategy referred to as *community policing* in many jurisdictions across America. This work describes community dynamics such as social class, culture, and social order. Research included a survey of 2010 people and 76 interviews, asking the question: Does police practice enhance neighborhood safety issues and provide social order or stability? It was believed that community police strategies give rise to crime control, reduction in the fear of crime, and enhancement in the community's quality of life. It was assumed that if community members, especially culturally diverse members, influenced the decisions of the police, the greater the likelihood that public safety and lifestyle experiences would be enhanced. The results of this survey are discussed in detail in *Applied Community Policing: Case Studies* (2003).

This book explores ideas about behavior and offers a way to measure police practices. Various police strategies are examined and, to better understand policing strategies firsthand, performance tests were conducted in nine police jurisdictions by their constituents.

At the conclusion of this book, you should have a practical as well as a logical grasp of the experiences of diverse communities and police efforts to maintain public safety, reduce the fear of crime, and enhance the quality of life within communities. You might conclude that one strategy well suited to twenty-first century America is the concept of community policing. Also, you should have developed an informed perspective about community police partnerships and their links to social order.

The companion book, *Case Studies in Applied Community Policing (2003)*, Allyn and Bacon, gives findings of eight jurisdictions, which are individually discussed using techniques developed from this textbook. Some of those findings are referred to in this work, but for a broader picture of what is working in all eight jurisdictions, refer to that publication. Those jurisdictions include Alexandria, Boston, Columbia, Columbus, Miami-Dade County, Midland, Palm Beach County, and Sacramento.

History of Policing

The term *police* was derived from the Greek word *politiea* relating to the concept of government citizenship or *polis* for city, and both Greek words applied historically to the exercise of civic or collective authority including the word *politics*. For most of the past one thousand years, Britain barely had a visible police agency. France processed a central police agency in the early part of the eighteenth century. American policing is a product of English heritage brought here by the colonists as part of their culture, which probably included English common law, the court system, various forms of punishment, and law enforcement ideals.[1] Many colonists departed England to escape an often-tyrannical government and they valued individual freedom, discretion, and participation in governmental decisions.[2] Therefore, an organized police force in early America (and in England) was viewed with a great deal of suspicion due to "its potential for despotic control over citizens and subjects."[3] This thinking is explored further in the chapter.

Some ideals held by the early colonists were no doubt influenced by traditional notions developed by Alfred the Great's (870–901) institution of a system mandating citizens as being responsible for their own conduct and the conduct of others. Citizens during his reign were expected to apprehend offenders, and if they did not, they were fined. Edward I (1272–1307) created the first official police force in large English cities to protect property, and Edward II established the Justice of the Peace Act of 1327 to assist the sheriff at enforcement.

Other influences might have included the use of frankpledges which compelled all males twelve years of age and older to serve in a quasi-police role (Blakely & Bumphus, 2002; Uchida, 2002). Each individual was sworn to protect other citizens and as part of their duties, held official authority to hold an offender in custody while awaiting trial.[4] These individuals formed a group of nine or *tything*; ten tythings were grouped into a hundred, and took direction from a constable appointed by the local nobleman. The constable can be considered the first official with law enforcement responsibilities in England. If any member of a tything failed to perform, all the members of the tything were levied severe fines. Citizen groups were obliged to control any group member committing an unlawful act. This style

---

[1] See Samuel Walker (1998) and Walker and Katz (2001) for more detail on this perspective.

[2] For a closer look at these dynamics, see Curtis R. Blakely and Vic W. Bumphus. (2002). American criminal justice philosophy: What's old—what's new? In Wilson R. Palacios, Paul F. Cromwell, and Roger G. Dunham, (pp. 16–24), *Crime & justice in America*. Upper Saddle River, NJ: Prentice Hall.

[3] See Craig D. Uchida. (1993). The development of two American police: An historical overview. In Dunham and Alpert (Eds.) *Critical issues in policing*. Prospect Heights, IL: Waveland Press.

[4] See Craig D. Uchida. (2002). The development of the American police. In Wilson R. Palacios, Paul F. Cromwell, and Roger G. Dunham, (pp. 87–101), *Crime & justice in America*. Upper Saddle River, NJ: Prentice Hall.

of controlling criminal activities was predominant in England after 1066 due, in part, to the Norman Conquest (Uchida, 1993).

As early as 1684, organized policing concepts did exist in early America, but it was often an incompetent night-watch system limited to urban communities such as in Boston, Philadelphia, and New York City (Carter & Radelet, 1999; Uchida, 2002). Night watch was exactly that in most cases—nighttime surveillance of "fires, suspicious individuals, riots, and other incidents requiring immediate attention" (Blakely & Bumphus, 2002, p. 17). They also "raised the hue and cry" and maintained street lamps (Uchida, 2002). The night-watch system eventually included day-watch activities, and some scholars suggested that this system of watching out for the community was preventive in nature and the forerunner of the modern police department. Population increases by the mid-eighteenth century continued to show that this system was ineffective and encouraged the rise of bounty-hunting private detectives. Additionally, in England, despite all the suspicion surrounding the issue of public safety versus individual liberty, Parliament approved the London Metropolitan Police Act in 1829 (Uchida, 2002). A large uniformed patrol force was established in London and cities in the United States (such as Boston) followed, in part, London's model of policing.

Suspicion and Police Authority

Police drew authority from the power of the state rather than the authority of the law. Early eighteenth-century accounts of the police in both England and France showed that policing was viewed with the utmost suspicion, like that of a sinister force (Manning, 1997). One widely held perception was that the police were secretly surveying and controlling citizens. Therefore, some influential British writers advanced the idea that the police should be restrained and their focus should be limited to civil preventive actions having justice and humanity as its core, and the general security of the state and its individuals as its ultimate object. As a result, police control was a key issue since police were an available extension of the rights and obligations of the citizen under English common law. It appears to have been a trade-off suggesting that since constables held a "legal monopoly on violence," as Max Weber might explain, their arrest powers had to be regulated, they had no power to bring charges against individuals, and they could not decide the outcomes of those individuals whom they arrested (Manning, 1997). This notion is in part consistent with the sanctions and issues shaping contemporary American policing.

Nonetheless, by the early nineteenth century the old systems in England collapsed. London had grown into a large industrial city. Unfortunately, industrial progress tends to promote crime, poverty, and conflict between social classes comprised of what can be referred to as the "haves" and the "have-nots." In 1780 for example, the Gordon riots, a clash between Irish immigrants and English citizens, provoked a 50-year debate over the need for social control. Consequently, the government created the London Metropolitan Police, founded by Sir Robert Peel in 1829 (from whom the term *bobby* originated). Peel established nine police principles:

Police Principles of Sir Robert Peel

1. The basic mission for which the police exist is to prevent crime and disorder as an alternative to the repression of crime and disorder by military force and severity of legal punishment.
2. The ability of the police to perform their duties is dependent upon public approval of police existence, actions, behavior, and the ability of the police to secure and maintain public respect.
3. The police must secure the willing cooperation of the public in voluntary observance of the law to be able to secure and maintain public respect.
4. The degree of cooperation of the public that can be secured diminishes, proportionately, the necessity for the use of physical force and compulsion in achieving police objectives.
5. The police seek and preserve public favor, not by catering to public opinion, but by constantly demonstrating absolutely impartial service to the law, in complete independence of policy, and without regard to the justice or injustice of the substance of individual laws; by ready offering of individual service and friendship to all members of the society without regard to their race or social standing; by ready exercise of courtesy and friendly good humor; and by ready offering of individual sacrifice in protecting and preserving life.
6. The police should use physical force to the extent necessary to secure observance of the law or to restore order only when the exercise of persuasion, advice, and warning is found to be insufficient to achieve police objectives; and police should use only the minimum degree of physical force that is necessary on any particular occasion for achieving a police objective.
7. The police at all times should maintain a relationship with the public that gives reality to the historic tradition that the police are the public and that the public are the police; the police are the only members of the public who are paid to give full-time attention to duties that are incumbent on every citizen in the interest of the community welfare.
8. The police should always direct their actions toward their functions and never appear to usurp the powers of the judiciary by avenging individuals or the state, or authoritatively judging guilt or punishing the guilty.
9. The test of police efficiency is the absence of crime and disorder, not the visible evidence of police action in dealing with them.[5]

Comparison of Early English and Early American Police

American law enforcement tried to replicate English police concepts; yet there were distinctive differences. American society from the beginning was far more violent than most European countries (Carter & Radelet, 1999). This trend continues into the twenty-first century. Early American police were public servants with duties pertaining to public health, clean streets, and slave patrols (Carter & Radelet, 1999; Williams & Murphy, 1999). In the eighteenth century, private agencies in America, such as Wells Fargo, were primarily hunting down offenders

---

[5]See W.L. Melville Lee. (1901). *History of Police in England*. London: Methuen. Chapter 12.

while the police dealt with menial tasks, producing an impression that a police officer was a backward character, more or less a simpleton, explains Carter and Radelet (1999). This character can be seen in Barney the deputy as depicted on the popular television Andy Griffith show. In the 1840s, police were often unarmed watchmen and in many of the large cities, the police helped with overnight lodging services, supplied coal for the poor, soup kitchens for the hungry, and jobs as domestics to keep girls away from prostitution (Carter & Radelet, 1999). Eventually, organized charities felt it inappropriate for the police to engage in these social service activities. At the turn of the century, maintenance of order became the primary function of the American police. But two influences shifted emphasis away from maintaining order to that of law enforcement: prohibition and the Great Depression of the 1930s.

Generally, American departments were decentralized, under the authority of the municipality and often appointed by politicians, while in England central authority was appointed by the Crown (Kelling & Moore, 1999). English police chiefs had the authority to fire and discipline their officers. Their American counterparts did not have this authority, a situation that resulted in corruption and incompetence. British policing emphasized crime prevention and the maintenance of peace. American policing emphasized the protection of security and the enforcement of law, at least until the emergence of community policing strategies.

English tradition had inspired American policing to develop two themes that are prevalent in American policing: (1) an emphasis on protecting individual liberty as defined in the Bill of Rights and (2) local control of policing authority.

Themes of American Policing

1. A high premium on protecting individual liberty as found in the Bill of Rights.
2. Local control of policing authority as opposed to centralized national police agency.

English law does not provide its citizens with the equivalent of the Bill of Rights; therefore, any comparison between the two countries concerning arrest practices is probably inappropriate. Furthermore, local control versus national control produces a decentralized and fragmented system of policing. Many European countries, as well as Asian, African, and South American nations tend to have centralized agencies. England, a country that is one-fourth the size of the U.S. has 43 police departments: 41 provincial departments and 2 police forces with broad authority in contrast to America's more than 18,000 police departments and almost 700,000 sworn officers with less authority. All 43 English agencies are under the supervision of the Home Secretary, one of the top officials in the national government, who has the power to issue administrative regulations on personnel and police decisions. Each provincial department answers to a local police commission.

In America, contemporary policing is under local political control. It is decentralized and responsibility for its operation rests with local government: city, county, and state.[6] As a result, American police agencies are fragmented.

---

[6]Excluding federal law enforcement agencies.

Fragmented

Fragmented: lacking coherence: made up of disconnected parts or elements.[7]

There are no formal centralized systems in place that direct, regulate, or coordinate the efforts of each and every police agency. But, there are some federal and state regulations that affect police at the local level. This fragmentation produces variety at all levels of policing. For instance, agencies at each level (city, county, state, and federal) have different roles, level (city, county, state, and federal) have different roles, different responsibilities, different personnel, different experiences, different external and internal methods of control, and different methods of delivering police services. As a result, it is difficult to generalize about policing, especially community policing. Many agencies have some characteristics in common but most generalizations about a "typical" agency meet with suspicion.

American Police Experiences

One explanation on policing in the United States for the past century is offered by George Kelling and William Moore (1999) who divided police experiences into three eras: the political era, the reform era, and the community-policing era (see Table 1–1).

The Political Era

In the first quarter of the twentieth century, when modern policing was being developed in the United States, police chiefs were appointed by local politicians, which often resulted in a mutual system of political favors.

The Political Era

Police officers owed their jobs and their loyalties to local political leaders.

This was referred to as a *patronage system*. Police chiefs had little authority over police officers; consequently some officers were involved in inefficient and sometimes corrupt conduct. Since foot patrol was the most common police strategy used in America, officers knew the people in the community. With the legitimate authority of arrest, search, and seizure vested in police officers, also came the illegitimate authority of false arrest, unwarranted search, and unlawful seizure. The "spoils era" of politicization promoted reciprocal political favoritism more often than crime control. Prohibition, fueled by organized crime, is one example pointing to the abuses of political authority produced by the link between politics and police. As a result, in 1931 President Hoover appointed General George Wickersham to

[7]Encarta® World English Dictionary [North American Edition] © & (P) 2001 Microsoft Corporation. http://dictionary.msn.com/

head a committee known as the National Commission on Law Observance and Enforcement to look into the matter. The Wickersham Commission considered both police and politicians as principally blameworthy for corruption and incompetence, and reform became the slogan leading to the reform era.

The Reform Era

One finding of the Wickersham Commission was that the rise of crime meant police were not or could not do their job. In part, one of the obstacles to quality police service, the Commission implied, was the link between officers and local politicians. Police work that did not relate directly to "crook catchers" was suspect. It was also believed by some sources that police manipulated crime reports in order to appear to fit the expectations of the public (Carter & Radelet, 1999, p. 118).

August Vollmer and O.W. Wilson are attributed with advancing a reform movement that called for a drastic change in the way police agencies did business. Vollmer was the police chief at Berkeley, California. He started the first college education and training program at the University of California at Berkeley. Vollmer, known as the father of American policing called for police to:

- Enhance accountability for actions and behaviors to the public.
- Ensure impartiality in law enforcement activities by not favoring (or disfavoring) any group regardless of their social or political position.
- Increase the honesty of all police officers by attempting to rid the police service of corruption and political influence.

Chicago Police Department Superintendent O.W. Wilson (and former Chief of Police in Wichita, Kansas) heightened reform efforts and increased the movement's visibility throughout law enforcement. His national leadership changed the face of policing by raising the reform movement to a higher plateau.

The Reform Era

Reformers rejected politics as the basis of police legitimacy.

Replacing politics as the basis of police legitimacy, reformers wanted to professionalize the police in order to become more effective in dealing with crime and to curb their own widespread involvement in it. The police tried to gain control of their destiny, develop policy, and organize their diverse responsibilities around police services. The organizational form adopted by police reformers reflected the scientific or classical theory of administration advocated by Frederick W. Taylor during the early twentieth century. Taylor's perspective made two assumptions: (1) workers are inherently uninterested in work and if left to their own devises, will avoid it; (2) workers have little or no interest in the substance of their work and the sole interest between workers and management is found in economic incentives for workers. These two principles produced a division of labor and unity of control within policing. Specifically, police work was broken down into smaller components and a centralized hierarchy of command was established. Police leaders redefined the nature of a proper relationship between police and constituents and determined that the new model demanded an impartial officer. A professional distance assumed that the role of police constituents was to be passive recipient of a professional crime control provider.

? *Something to Think About*

While professional growth occurred within a police agency, the officers became isolated from the community.

Professional distance or what some call isolation was also an outgrowth of accelerating police services through the use of patrol cars, radios, and differing strategic approaches to unique police problems. It comes as no surprise that during the reform era the concept of the *thin blue line* developed as it refers to the line that separates law-abiding, peaceful citizens from the predators, and police from the public they serve. The thin blue line, as noted by Kelling and Moore, "connotates the existence of dangerous external threats to communities, portrays police as standing between that danger and good citizens, and implies both police heroism and loneliness" (Kelling & Moore, 1999, p. 12).

As Kelling and Moore note, other problems surfaced for police during the reform era:

- Police failed community expectations to control crime.
- Fear of crime continued, and since fear is linked more often to social disorder than crime itself, social disorder continued.
- Impartial treatment was not experienced by all citizens.
- Civil rights and antiwar movements challenged police practice and policy.
- "Crime fighting" was an activity that was practiced less among police officers than expected.
- Reform ideology was largely at the police management level and failed to rally line officers.
- Police lost a significant portion of their financial support as cities found themselves in fiscal difficulties.
- The rise of private security was competing with public officers.

American culture, however, was moving faster than the police were able to respond. Considering events in the 1960s and 1970s that reshaped both police and society, police managers realized that more than reform would be necessary to control crime.[8] For instance:

- U.S. Supreme Court decisions, under the leadership of Chief Justice Earl Warren, significantly changed criminal procedure and police policy.

---

[8]See David L. Carter and Louis A. Radelet. *The Police and the Community*. Upper Saddle River, NJ: Prentice Hall. Chapter 1 presents an in-depth look at some of these thoughts.

- A "counterculture" movement was characterized by recreational drug use and sexual promiscuity.
- The National Guard at Kent State University killed students as they protested the Vietnam War.
- President Richard Nixon resigned as President of the United States.
- The Civil Rights Movement, Vietnam War protests, and the "counterculture" produced riots in many of the nation's cities and on college campuses.
- Technological advances changed police responses.
- Media coverage of police practices influenced public sentiment, which in turn shaped policy and funding decisions. For instance, Chicago Police actions were recorded on film and shown to the nation on news programs during the Democratic National Convention in 1968.

Although these events might seem like small isolated problems, putting them together, implies the following:

- The public did not trust the police.
- The public did not support the police.
- Police organizations and practices were outdated.
- Training was inadequate for the times.

These factors were compounded by a paradox: The rigid organizational controls that were necessary to overcome corruption and political influence characteristic of the spoils era, became problematic during the 1960s because they institutionalized police responses and attitudes. Facing new demands, the police were "inflexible, cloistered, and resistant to external influences of change."[9]

In 1967, the findings of the President's Commission on Law Enforcement and Administration of Justice were released. This landmark commission's multi-volume report addressed a continuum of issues facing police agencies. In 1963, the two additional reports were issued by federal agencies: the National Advisory Commission on Civil Disorders and the National Commission on the Causes and Prevention of Violence. Although the inherent focus of these three federal agencies was somewhat different, the findings and the recommendations were similar with respect to the police. One commonality among all three reports suggested that the police required open communication and should develop a greater empathy with the community, which might lead to controlling civil disorder and violence.

The Community Problem-Solving Era

During the late 1970s and 1980s, some of the practices and experiences of police service provided public safety to constituents. For instance, foot patrol remained popular and in some cases citizens voted to increase taxes in order to fund it. Foot patrol was linked to order maintenance and citizen fear of crime levels. Somehow, visibility of officers made the general public feel safe. Many studies were conducted about police service and some of those studies provided meaningful ideas

[9]Carter and Radelet, 1999, p. 16.

about police practice. For instance, it was suggested that "information" could help police enhance arrest records. That is, if information about crimes and criminals could be obtained from residents by police, primarily patrol officers, and could be properly managed by police agencies, investigative and other units could increase their effect on decreasing crime.[10] These findings led to new opportunities that eventually shaped what appear to be community police initiatives and problem-solving strategies.

Table 1–1 describes the three eras of police experiences. Twenty-first century community-policing strategies were added to show you where community policing is presently headed, based on evidence from public records and conversations with community police officers as of the year 2001. These findings are linked to leadership, objectives, organization design, relationship to the community, demand, tactics, expectations, and outcomes much like the political, reform, and community police eras. Although Kelling and Moore describe police history through the 1990s, adding twenty-first century community-police expectations helps define the dynamics of police service.

A Critical Review of Kelling and Moore's Account

Among others, Hubert Williams and Patrick Murphy (1999) take issue with Kelling and Moore's (1999) historical perspective of American policing. Williams and Murphy felt that Kelling and Moore's interpretation is inadequate—it fails to take account of how slavery, segregation, discrimination, and racism affected the development of police strategies, and how these strategies affected police response to minority communities. Williams and Murphy argue that legal order may have encouraged slavery, segregation, and discrimination. The task of the police was to keep minorities under control with little incentive to protect them as individuals from crime within their communities. Members of minority groups benefited less than others from advances made by the police. Furthermore, during the political era, Williams and Murphy suggest that Kelling and Moore neglected to consider the effects of the Reconstruction period upon minorities. There existed a legal and a political powerlessness among minority communities in both the North and South and police response did little to empower those communities in public safety. According to Williams and Murphy, lower-class communities may have been over-represented in police response accounts, therefore much might be missing from Kelling and Moore's study.

Williams and Murphy argue that Kelling and Moore's analysis of policing was largely based on the northeastern United States. For instance, southern slave patrols and racially biased laws were never mentioned. Most of their ideas seem centered in early American history but reflect a white, twentieth-century bias toward northern, urban white conditions such as those in Boston, Chicago, Detroit, and New York City. However, the minority community played a key role in initiating the era of community policing.

[10]Kelling and Moore, 1999.

TABLE 1.1 *The Three Eras of Policing and Twenty-First Century Policing*

	Political Era 1840s to 1930s	*Reform Era 1930s to 1980s*	*Community-Policing Era 1980s to 1990s*	*Twenty-First Century Community Policing*
Leadership	Primary political	Law and professionalism	Community support (political), law, professionalism	Facilitative
Objectives *ranked priority	Crime control,* order, maintenance, broad social services	Crime control, isolate from politicians, expected community passiveness	Crime control, crime prevention, problem solving	Crime prevention, crime control, problem solving
Organizational Design	Decentralized geographical	Centralized, classical	Decentralized task force, matrices	Level task force
Relationship to Community	Close and personal, face to face, intimacy	Professionally remote	Consultative police defend values of law and professionalism, listen to community concerns	Partnerships
Demand	Managed through links between politicians and precinct captains	Channeled through dispatching activities	Channeled through analysis of underlying problems	Problem-oriented policing
Tactics	Incident driven foot beat patrol rudimentary investigation	Preventive patrol, rapid response	Foot patrol, problem solving	Reorientation of patrol, organize community, empowerment, participative management
Expectations	Maintaining citizen and political satisfaction, neighborhood norms	Number of arrests, response time, number of passings:* crime rate	Quality of life citizen satisfaction, order maintenance	Quality of life, resident satisfaction, officer satisfaction, social order
Outcome	Political satisfaction, discrimination, police corruption, lack of agency control	Crime rose, fear of crime rose, unfair treatment, lost financial support	Quality of life and community satisfaction	Quality of life

*Number of times a police car passes a given point of a city street

Some of Williams and Murphy's observations are consistent with writers such as Randall G. Shelden (2001). Shelden argues that the formation of the Metropolitan Police Act passed in 1829 in England was without serious opposition. Both the passage of the act and the formation of the London police represented the foundation of the centralization of state power led, in part, by wealthy business and landowner interest groups such as Sir Robert Peel (who was also the son of a wealthy manufacturer). The early primary mission of English policing practices was control of the "masses," Shelden (2001) emphasizes. Peel "sought to legitimate his police force in the eyes of the people by arguing the police would serve the interests of all people" (p. 76).

Whatever your views on Kelling and Moore's work, be mindful that policing has changed drastically in the past twenty years. And it is likely that changes will continue throughout the next twenty years. These changes include responses of the justice community toward targeted groups in the name of national security after events such as the destruction of the World Trade Center on September 11, 2001. As might seem apparent, the police must find a balance between prevention practices such as in the conceptual police strategy of community policing without compromising enforcement practices, American liberty, and the new responsibilities of aiding national security.

Community-Policing Strategies

Community policing is a conceptual police strategy that can be described as an outreach by a police agency to the community. The purpose of this outreach is to enhance public safety, reduce the fear of crime, and to improve quality of life experiences through an empowered partnership with the community. At the core of this relationship lie problem-solving strategies of social problems linked to crime.

What is Community Policing?

> Community policing is a preventive approach through an empowered problem-solving partnership of police and community to control crime, reduce the fear of crime and enhance lifestyle experiences of all community constituents.

Community policing expands the responsibility for crime control to the community at large and through this association, it takes a preventive approach to crime by solving community issues and problems that lead to crime. To accomplish this goal, a police agency decentralizes its authority and empowers both community members and rank-and-file officers so that they can make the decisions bringing them closer to solving community problems linked to potential criminal activity. "Community policing is a way of conducting business—a department-wide philosophy."[11]

Because each police agency is as different as its constituencies—due to location, history, budget, cultural nuances, community demographics, and authority—

[11]See Dennis J. Stevens (2001a). *Case Studies in Community Policing,* p. 7.

community police strategies are different, too. What works in Boston's North End will not necessarily work in Miami's North Side, or Chicago's West Side. In an earlier study of nine police agencies across the United States, one point that was clarified about a community police model was that each agency possessed its own brand of community policing that may or may not work in a similar jurisdiction (Stevens, 2001a).

It could have been the "broken windows theory" of crime that described urban deterioration as promoting an environment conducive to confront criminal behavior. This perspective may have provided a basis for the adoption of community-oriented policing programs and the establishment of various strategic and neighborhood-oriented policing methods in those lower-class communities.[12] One assumption of this perspective is that criminals require opportunity to commit crime, and opportunity is perceived in a neighborhood where no one seems to care if homes have broken windows, cars are abandoned, and scattered trash abounds. The community and the police take a preventive measure against potential crime and work together to repair "broken windows" in the neighborhood, thereby reducing the opportunity for the criminal (Stevens, 2001). Therefore, a focal point of community policing is proactive (prevention) strategies that are defined as: "a collaboration between the police and the community that identifies and solves community problems" (Bureau of Justice Assistance [BJA], 1994). The collaboration, however, is not necessarily an equal relationship, rather the police must play the role of a facilitator in a two-way relationship with the public in order to address and solve public problems. However, the mission of recent community-policing projects is to primarily enhance the quality of police service while older community-policing projects used community policing as a means of giving the community more direct control over police operations (Goldstein, 1987). Nonetheless, the Community Policing Consortium (CPC), 2000,[13] argues that at the core of community policing, there are essential and complementary components. Largely, community-policing programs as described by the CPC (2000) and others, have the following characteristics:[14]

- Permanent assignment of officers to specific duty assignments and often geographical areas.
- Significant decentralization of authority and responsibility.
- Empowering officers and community members with decision-making authority although limited.

[12]See Oliver, 2000; Stevens, 2001a; Wilson & Kelling, 1982.

[13]The Community Policing Consortium is a partnership of five of the leading police organizations in the United States: International Association of Chiefs of Police (IACP), National Organization of Black Law Enforcement Executives (NOBLE), National Sheriffs' Association (NSA), Police Executive Research Forum (PERF), Police Foundation. These five organizations play a principal role in the development of community-policing research, training and technical assistance, and each is firmly committed to the advancement of this policing philosophy. The Community Policing Consortium is administered and funded by the U.S. Department of Justice, Office of Community Oriented Policing Services (COPS).

[14]See DuBois and Hartnett, 2002, Goldstein, 1987, Manning, 1984, and Skogan, Hartnett, DuBois, Comey, Kaiser, and Lovig, 1999 .

- Community member participation in decision-making processes that can include identification and prioritizing of social issues that impacts their community.
- Partnerships with public and private institutions and agencies.
- Adoption of a problem-solving approach to the daily work of the agency.

Community policing is a fundamental shift in authority, obligations, and decision-making responsibilities and expectations from the traditional chain-of-command organizational control: top-to-bottom; to a contemporary method of control to fit a community-policing philosophy: bottom up, turning an organization upside down (Wycoff & Skogan, 1998). Expressed another way, a community-policing strategy is the community's obligation and responsibility, in partnership with a police effort to control crime. Nonetheless, while the police are busy with preventive measures, day-to-day crime produced by yesterday's broken windows, for example, continues. How does an agency effectively split its limited resources consisting of work force, budget, and policy to operationalize a community-police strategy and would it take the place of the day-to-day operation of an agency? This is in part a piece of the balancing act that police agencies are attempting to address. If a police agency neglects daily crime in favor of committing most of their resources to a community-policing strategy, more than likely the frequency of crime will increase, as will its intensity.

Turning community policing upside down, one study evaluating community-policing efforts in eight cities learned that most of these cities experienced extreme difficulty in establishing a solid community infrastructure in order to build their community policing programs (Sadd & Grinc, 1994). The writers concluded that of all the implementation problems encountered by community policing efforts the most difficult problem was the inability of a police agency to organize and maintain active community involvement in their partnership.

In fact, others have advanced the perspective that community support must be won (DuBois & Hartnett, 2002). It cannot be assumed that community support will automatically be produced because police promote a program. Initially, residents resist change, which suggests that recruiting community members may not be as productive as expected. An organized community, trained in community-policing initiatives, is as critical for the community as it is for the police (DuBois & Hartnett, 2002). Also, these writers suggest that there is a real risk of inequitable outcomes. That is, the most advantaged members of the community will accept community policing naturally, but those who really need it may be last to come on board—if they come on at all. Therefore, gaining community support and maintaining it may be a lot more work than expected.

Police Critics

There are critics who suggest that community policing can be a method to increase police intervention through arrest by using the community to identify, locate, and detail illegal activity (DeLeon-Granados, 1999). Also, inappropriate community-policing practices can create limited roles for officers and community members.

One effect of limited roles can be found in ineffective crime control models that disturb community ecology more than stabilize it. It can also hold officers back in fully managing cohesive resourceful community networks, in favor of surveillance, crackdowns, sweeps, arrests, and problem obliteration. It can also support some notions that community policing may exist more in rhetoric than in reality.[15] Limited roles may even further misconceptions that community-policing concepts are "simply inflated promises" (Albritton, 1999). Specifically, Albritton says, "I am convinced that the movement has missed some crucial and determining points in the analysis of the relationship between police and society" (p. 221). Clearly, observational case studies on police agencies, including some conducted by this author, describes struggles and failures to introduce changes in police organizations, which reported widespread resistance to change from the police culture, numerous organizational barriers, and a desire by stubborn personnel to "weather the storm" (that is, to outlast the current administration) (DuBois & Hartnett, 2002; Stevens, 2001). However, in the final analysis, community policing exists. Its promise is still uncertain, despite many success stories as well as stories of failure. Many hard-working men and women in police agencies, school systems, churches and temples, and in homes of children at risk continue to work and pray that community policing or some element emerging from it will enhance public safety, improve quality of life standards, and give children an opportunity to become safe and contributing law-abiding adults.

Planning for the Future

David L. Carter offers some insight into the future of policing strategies, particularly about an important aspect of long-range planning in police management.[16] Carter developed a comprehensive self-assessment through a three-staged approach that includes refocusing, refining, and reallocation of police perspectives for the future:

- Refocusing would involve re-examining an agency's mission, goals, and objectives and redefining their significance. The activities and services an agency provides in the future must be articulated in written form.
- Refining occurs after an agency's direction is refocused. At this point, policies, procedures, job descriptions, personnel evaluations, and training must be adjusted to match the new mission.
- Reallocation of agency resources (people, budgets, equipment) is required to meet the needs of a newly defined agency direction.

Future problems can be addressed by building an adequate foundation for change through thoughtful planning and the development of a strong vision.

---

[15]See Albritton, 1999; Eck and Rosenbaum, 1994; Kraska and Kappeler, 1997; Maguire, 1997; and Moore, 1994.
[16]See David L. Carter's website at http://www.ssc.msu.edu/~cj/cp/cpmeasure.html

Contact with police can affect the attitudes of individuals toward the police, regardless of their perspective. The literature is replete with evidence that contact and experience with the police are the greatest determinants of successful police-community relationships, greater than any other set of variables.[17] For instance, receiving a traffic citation can be stressful because of the financial obligations towards the court and possibly your insurance company. But a real negative attitude can develop if the officer's intervention is less than professional. That is, getting a moving violation is not the determining agent that produces the negative attitude. Respondent perceptions and evaluations during the intervention of the speeder and the officer shaped negative or positive attitudes about the police (Cox & White, 1988). Getting the speeding ticket is one thing, but getting it from a rude police officer can be another thing. To build a positive relationship with community members, police must be mindful that their behavior during every intervention will impact community respect.

? *Something to Think About*

It isn't that the police make an arrest, it's how they do it that counts.

That is, people accept the idea that an officer's job is to issue a traffic citation or take a violator into custody. It's not what an officer must do—it's how an officer performs his or her job that counts. The style of an officer is measured by community respect rather than the ability to make arrests.

The finest professional management program available, delivered in an unprofessional way, will produce unprofessional results—no matter how sound the program. Many of us listen to the way a message is delivered, before we make a decision about the message. This advice seems to fit with Voltaire's message at the beginning of the chapter.

Summary

We examined policing from its origins in England through its development in the United States. Legitimate police authority was described and the principles of policing were highlighted. A brief comparison was offered between English and American police systems, and American police experiences were characterized into three eras: political, reform, and community policing. A critical review of the three eras was followed by a description of community-policing strategies. Finally, a brief critique of community policing was discussed and future thoughts on community policing were emphasized. A theme was introduced in this chapter, namely that the style in which the police perform their job may be as relevant as the laws they are expected to enforce This theme sets the stage for the chapters ahead and suggests that if policing is to remain a vital part of the American culture, it might consider polishing its performance.

[17]See Cheurprakobkit and Bartsch, 1999; Cordner and Jones, 1995; Cox and White, 1988; Lasley Vernon, Dery III, 1995; Zevitz and Rettammel, 1990.

Do You Know?

1. Describe at least two historical experiences of policing that can be linked to contemporary policing in the United States.
2. Describe some of the reasons why there was a great deal of suspicion surrounding police empowerment in England and in the United States in its early history. In your opinion, in what way were those suspicions justified?
3. Identify five of the principles of Sir Robert Peel and explain in what way at least two of them might have shaped contemporary policing strategies in America.
4. Compare and contrast the English police system to the American police system. Which part of the English police system is found in the American system? Which part of the American police system is most atypical of the English police system?
5. Describe the primary characteristics of the political era of policing.
6. Describe the primary characteristics of the reform era of policing.
7. Describe the primary characteristics of the community-policing era.
8. Characterize the primary principles of community policing. Of those characteristics, which one would be the easiest to accomplish and which one might be the most difficult to accomplish? Explain your answers.
9. Identify the major criticisms of community-police strategies.
10. Describe the future of community policing.
11. The author suggests that police as an institution could be short lived unless it polishes its performance. In what way should an agency polish its performance? Why do you agree and disagree with that statement?
12. Identify the three-staged approach of David L. Carter that police agencies should focus on in the future. Add the fourth suggestion recommended and explain why you think that idea might be equally important if not more important than the other perspectives.
13. In what way does Voltaire's statement apply to the idea of police performance? "To succeed in the world it is not enough to be stupid, you must also be well-mannered."

Recommended Readings

Barker, T., & Carter, D.L. (1994). *Police Deviance.* Cincinnati, OH: Anderson Publishing.

Oliver, W.M. (2000). *Community Policing: Classical Readings.* Upper Saddle River, NJ: Prentice Hall. This work contains both a classical and contemporary collection of articles that helped shape community policing initiatives more than any other articles. The writers are on the "must read" list and include: James Q. Wilson, George L. Kelling, Herman Goldstein, Mark H. Moore, Robert C. Trojanowicz, and Lawrence W. Sherman.

Police Executive Research Forum. (1996). *Themes and variations in community policing: Case studies in community policing.* Washington DC: Police Foundation. Probably one of the best accounts of community-policing implementation and maintenance from an applied perspective offered through policing manager practitioners.

Skogan, W.G., Hartnett, S.M., DuBois, J., Comey, J.T., Kaiser, M, & Lovig, J.H. (1999). *On the beat: Police and community problem solving.* Boulder, CO: Westview Press. This work contains a detailed method of recruiting and maintaining community members to advance community-policing initiatives. It also contains a detailed account of how the Chicago police utilizes SARA in problem solving skills to help solve social issues that lend themselves to quality of life matters.

Stevens, D.J. (2001). *Case Studies in Community Policing.* Upper Saddle River, NJ: Prentice Hall. Case studies of nine police jurisdictions across the United States including Broken Arrow, OK; Camden, NJ; Columbus, OH; Fayetteville, NC; Harris County Precinct 4 Constable's Office, Spring, TX; Lansing, MI; Nashville, TN; Sacramento, CA; and St. Petersburg, FL. These case studies were from the perspective of the agencies and media involved.

Stevens, D.J. (2002). *Communities and Community Policing.* Editor. Upper Saddle River, NJ: Prentice Hall. Articles both empirical and impression about community policing authored by scholars, practitioners, and researchers. Grass roots organizational methods, police strategies, and investigative methods of evaluation are topics in this work.

2

Police Power, Order and Law, and Police Response

"If one morning I walked on top of the water across the Potomac River, the headline that afternoon would read: PRESIDENT CAN'T SWIM."

Lyndon B. Johnson

Key Terms

Crime	Democratic Policing	Pyrrhic Victory
Criminal Justice Community	Due Process	Social Disorder
Criminalization of Poverty	Judiciously	Social Order
Cultural Diversity	Law	
Culture	Police Power	

Key Topics

- How a police agency gains acceptance within the community it serves.
- Police response to political changes, ideals of due process, social order, and the law.
- Distinction between order and disorder.
- The nature of crime and its consequences.
- The relationship between fear of crime and social disorder.
- Dynamics and effects of quality police service and community lifestyle experiences.

Gaining Community Acceptance and Professional Status

Through the eyes of the American public, police, as a whole, may not be regarded as highly as their responsibilities. The American public wants change, yet there seems to be disagreement about what change might be required. That might be partially due to a lack of knowledge about police work since often the media tends to offer their own version of it, which can amount to good entertainment.[1]

Then on the other hand, it's said that there is an important distinction between the self-image of police and day-to-day reality of routine policing (Goldstein, 1977; Walker, 1984). The emphasis on crime control, some writers argue, has been largely a matter of what the police say they are doing about crime (Walker, 1984). National surveys suggest that the public tends to trust the police far less than expected. There are thoughts that some police agencies might manipulate community-policing efforts in order to advance professional and political autonomy (Manning, 1997; Walker, 1984). In that regard, it is often implied that police agencies establish community-policing agendas merely to receive federal funding (Kerley, 2002). Ultimately, how quickly the police are raised to a professional status will depend on how they are perceived by the community, especially those parts of the community where the police are most active (Trojanowicz & Dixon, 1974; Stevens, 1999j; 1998b).

The public will perceive the police as professional and comply with their directives when the police utilize their legally mandated prerogatives such as

[1]See Dennis J. Stevens. (2002). Civil liabilities and arrest decisions. In Jeffrey Walker (Ed.) (2002). Civil liabilities and arrest decisions. In Jeffery T. Walker (Ed.), *Policing and the Law,* (pp. 127–141), Upper Saddle River, NJ: Prentice Hall. And, Dennis J. Stevens. (2001, May). Civil liabilities and selective enforcement. *Law and Order,* 49(5), 105–109.

discretion, use of force, and community-policing strategies as objectively as circumstances permit. That is, an agency must handle most situations "judiciously" (Trojanowicz & Dixon, 1974, p. 147).

Judiciously

Judiciously: Sensible and wise. Showing wisdom, good sense, or discretion, often with the underlying aim of avoiding trouble or waste.

When police practice meets community standards judiciously, the community is generally satisfied and most community members attempt to comply with standards and the directives of the police. Simply put, the community will support the police when the community feels police power mirrors their own ideals. The result? Law and order is upheld without the use of force and the police will no longer be viewed "as the most visible symbol of the most negative elements of government."[2]

? *Something to Think About*

The greater the legitimacy of a police agency, the fewer the violators, and the less coercion or force required by the agency.

Trojanowicz and Dixon (1974) ask which came first: professional status or professional conduct? One way for the police to boost their status in the eyes of the public is to develop a more objective method of evaluating police performance—one of the reasons this text is being written.[3]

A police officer is an individual commissioned by the community to protect and enforce constituent standards, often through the threat or use of force (Trojanowicz & Dixon, 1974). The authority an agency has as a representative of a government "by the people" gives police officers both moral and legal justification for *police power* that includes detainment and use-of-force practices.[4]

---

[2]See Trojanowicz and Dixon, 1974, p. 147.

[3]As one student stated in a classroom of the writer, "I don't understand why a first grade teacher in a public school requires an appropriate college degree, certification, and a host of other documents when often, becoming a police officer in many jurisdictions requires, a valid driver's license, high school or a GED, and be at least 21 years of age." This thought may have merit in the sense that there are many opportunities for new community college graduates in policing. And those individuals who advance their education, too, will bring a wealth of resources to any police agency. For a closer look at college education pursuits when an officer is a student, too, see: Dennis J. Stevens, (1999a). Do college educated officers provide quality police service? *Law and Order*. December, 47(12), pp. 37–41.

[4]For a closer look at this perspective see Peter K. Manning, 1997, Police Work: The social organization of policing. Prospect Heights, Il: Waveland Press. pp. 97–101. For instance, Manning argues that it is a contradiction that "the police are, in symbolic terms, the most visible representation of the presence of the state in every day life and the potential of the state to enforce its will upon citizens," p. 97.

Police Power

> **Police power** The power of a government to exercise reasonable control over persons and property within its jurisdiction in the interest of the general security, health, safety, morals, and welfare except where legally prohibited (as by constitutional provision).[5]

A police department requires legal authority, power, and popular morality to effectively provide police services without the overburden of enforcement. There are two other important considerations:

1. As metropolitan communities change demographically, there is disagreement about the definitions of judicious police service and social order.
2. Some police agencies might not recognize all of the alternatives because they have difficulty relating to certain segments of the community.

There is another important issue so often overlooked suggested by Chief Finney (2000, p. 4) who adds, "We also recognize that sometimes, certain people must be policed." With all those ideas in mind (and others unintentionally neglected), the point is that police service is not the goal itself.

? Something to Think About

> Policing is a means to justice and to the sanctity of individual liberty.

Through law and order, a government gains legitimate power over the people it governs. How do police define social order? What conditions must be present to determine that social disorder exists? What action should be used to restore order and are those methods consistent with the law? Herein lie the central issues of many discussions on the subject of police power. It is believed that policing in the twenty-first century should professionally facilitate community response to social order couched in a mutual partnership through a democratic policing effort.

Community policing can be described as compliance-based policing through facilitation since one of its goals is shifting responsibility to the community through outreach strategies. This idea is consistent with that of Richard Ericson and Kevin Haggerty (1997), who add that police can be a powerful proactive force in making communities better and safer. Robert C. Trojanowicz (1982), one of the architects of community-policing initiatives, suggests that police officers can provide catalytic assistance and expert advice to neighborhood associations for the purpose of winning their support and ultimately, compliance. It is easier to protect people when they rule themselves than when they are ruled—self control versus institutional control—government for the people by the people. The spirit of the law that provides the authority for police to perform the task of policing also provides the authority of the people to govern police performance.

---

[5]Find Law for Legal Professionals. www. Findlaw.com

"We the People of the United States, in Order to form a more perfect Union, establish Justice…"

One idea is to bridge differences between cultural diversity and police practice so social order can be defined in a realistic fashion in keeping with Constitutional guarantees and the community in order to enhance the quality of life experiences for all residents. If the American police don't defend their constituents, who will?

Grass Roots Politics

The mass demonstrations linked to racial and gender civil rights issues of the past decades along with the serious concerns of an unpopular war in Southeast Asia presented an untenable position for the American people and their leaders concerning political stability. From the denial of due process in the name of social control and national security, a clear message resonated for targeted groups: the seats of power were remedies to *due process* issues[6] and power was centered squarely in community participation.

Due Process

Due Process A requirement that laws and regulations must be related to a legitimate government interest (as crime prevention) and may not contain provisions that result in the unfair or arbitrary treatment of an individual.[7]

No person shall . . . be deprived of life, liberty, or property, without due process of law.

Unlike national elections that reflect an increase in voter apathy, local elections and campaigns produced many changes in the voting patterns of the American people. It became evident with the wave of the new political power base across the nation that lifestyles and personal choice, and ultimately the way

[6]As suggested above, due process means that statutes may not be defined or enforced in an unreasonable, capricious, or arbitrary manner; targeting specific groups of people in justice's name compromises equal protection provisions found in the Constitution of the United States. That is, equal protection means that no person or class of persons may be denied the same protection of laws that is provided to other persons or classes of persons (Reid, 2001, p. 21).

[7]Find Law for Legal Professionals. [On-Line], Available: www.Findlaw.com. Note: The guarantee of due process is found in the Fifth Amendment to the Constitution, which states "no person shall . . . be deprived of life, liberty, or property, without due process of law," and in the Fourteenth Amendment, which states "nor shall any state deprive any person of life, liberty, or property without due process of law." The boundaries of due process are not fixed and are the subject of endless judicial interpretation and decision-making. Fundamental to procedural due process is adequate notice prior to the government's deprivation of one's life, liberty, or property, and an opportunity to be heard and defend one's rights to life, liberty, or property. Substantive due process is a limit on the government's power to enact laws or regulations that affect one's life, liberty, or property rights. It is a safeguard from governmental action that is not related to any legitimate government interest or that is unfair, irrational, or arbitrary in its furtherance of a government interest. The requirement of due process applies to agency actions.

the police safeguard those lifestyles and choices must change, prepared or not. For instance, due process safeguards applied to school bussing and affirmative action that often produced anger, uncertainty, and violence on all sides. While political leaders, including the President of the United States, were involved in criminal and suspect activities, an immediate availability of illicit drugs, rise of juvenile violence, and breakdown of the traditional American family added to the despair of many Americans.

These experiences paved the way for many political changes at that time. For instance, in 1973 labor unions, student coalitions, and community groups in Madison, Wisconsin elected a student activist to the first of three terms as mayor. Throughout the 1970s African American candidates scored impressive political victories across the nation.[8] The newly elected African American mayor of Atlanta, Maynard Johnson, said that politics was the civil rights movement of the decade—a point confirmed in 1978 by the 2,733 African Americans elected to offices in the South (a gain of ten times the number compared to the previous decade). African Americans were elected as mayors of major cities such as Chicago, New Orleans, Detroit, Gary, and Los Angeles. Other diverse groups such as Mexican Americans, Asian Americans, and Puerto Ricans also elected officials in San Antonio, New York City, and Hawaii. With those changes and many more, the elected official (along with support from others) began to resemble the cultural appearance of the people served by the governmental agencies.[9]

Groups with less political power such as women, Latinos, and Asian Americans remained under-represented in powerful positions in government, business, and institutions of higher learning until the latter part of the century. A study by the American Council on Education reports that the number of university and college presidencies held by women doubled from 1986 to 1998, and that the number of African American, Latinos, Asian American, and Native American college presidents rose by a total of 40 percent (Lively, 2000). Changing the seat of power for other groups is taking more time. Enormous political instability was experienced after the terrorist attack on the World Trade Center in New York City on September 11, 2001. In the name of national security, denial of due process guarantees were pervasive among many enforcement agencies modeled after the Federal Bureau of Investigation. Outcomes arising from this new set of responsibilities for local police agencies have yet to be determined, but it appears that freedom of individual movement and definitions applying to social order within the U.S. changed forever.

For example, in early 2002, the federal government in keeping with the USA Patriot Act of 2001, can, among other things, enter offices and homes of an individ-

---

[8]For a closer look at this perspective and a better review of a history of the American people see Faragher, Buhle, Czitrom, and Armitage, 2000, p. 927.
[9]However, social class and physical characteristics of a cultural group might still remain at odds. That is, it is unlikely that lower class representation in American government mirrors the lower class population.

ual who might simply have the physical characteristics of a terrorist to conduct a secret search, detain him for an unreasonable period of time, and interrogate him. Apparently due process or equal protection of the law does not apply to even an American citizen who resembles a terrorist. Thus, some might question that while the tragic death of innocent people at the World Trade Center is unacceptable and calls for an immediate response, does that response imply that individual rights and guarantees of the U.S. Constitution no longer apply? Should local police attempt similar behavior, they would meet immediate litigation challenges and community responses that easily become a riot, as American history supports. A strong police-community relationship will help America survive both the terrorist invasion from outside and a federal invasion of personal rights from inside.

Defining Social Order

One way to define social order is that it is the smooth functioning of social institutions, such as the police department and water department, the existence of positive and productive relations between individual members of society, and the orderly functioning of society as a whole.[10] Think in terms of predictability and reliability. For instance, the city bus will stop at specific points along the way at twenty-minute intervals between the hours of 7AM to 10 PM. We are connected to each other through social institutions such as the economy, education, and religion, which are also connected to each other, and many social institutions help shape the set of choices available to each of us, individually. Social institutions guide social order. Social order can also be defined as a condition of social stability and certainty.

Social Order

Social order has many meanings but loosely defined it can mean public safety.

However, whatever definition you give to social order will be revisited many times and might even become the rallying point of this work since ideas about public stability depend on who is defining it, the police or the public.

Most societies recognize that both law and order are essential to survival. We associate social order with a form of social control that usually involves some kind of police agency.

? Something to Think About

A position that arises about policing in a democratic society is the means necessary to maintain social order.

---

[10]See Frank Schmalleger, 1999b. p. 754.

The police are thought to be America's first line of defense against crime, and crime is one result stemming from social disorder. The resulting paradox is that the primary responsibility of the police is to protect our democratic values—and by law, the police have an obligation to exercise coercive power that can compromise those same democratic values. Herein lies the central issue of American policing.

? *Something to Think About*

The same authority that protects freedom, can take it away.

What stands between a lack of freedom or disorder is law, and fundamental law relates to equality. Therefore, the primary mission of a police agency is to ensure equality of the law, in this case, democracy, which in turn promotes social order.

The Emergence of Law

In primitive societies, small bands of individuals living together behaved pretty much as they were expected to, without any type of direct intervention of "any centralized political authority."[11] To a large extent, gossip, criticism, fear of supernatural forces, loss of respect and status, and physical or social isolation served as an effective method of social control in those societies. Even today, in a small town or community where everyone knows everyone else (including everyone else's business), when scandal involving morality has taken place, townspeople stop each other on streets and in the food stores to talk about it. "A common indignation is expressed."[12] The sentiment or a "common consciousness" of society can affect an outcome, according to Durkheim (1984–1933). The fear of community sanction can, under certain circumstances, impact individual behavior. Can you think of some incidents in your daily life where "talk" had something to do with your feelings of discomfort or motivated you to do something you might not have done under other circumstances?

You might agree that formal enforcement of laws might not be necessary when behavior can be regulated through informal methods of social control. For some of us, this single idea might characterize the centerpiece of community policing rationale. Indeed it is possible that people who govern themselves tend to follow the rules more often than people who are less self-governed.

From infancy to childhood to adulthood, behavior learned through families and other social institutions that influence us, has a lot to do with decisions we make. Control through values deeply internalized in the minds of individuals can be referred to as *cultural controls* (Haveland, 2000). This will be discussed in a future chapter.

---

[11]An detailed report can be found in William A. Haviland (2000). *Cultural Anthropology.* NY: Harcourt, pp. 357–387.
[12]See Emile Durkheim, (1984–1933). *Durkheim: The division of labor in society.* Translated by W.D. Halls. NY: The Free Press, pp. 58–65.

As populations increase and individuals become less influenced by family or cultural controls, face-to-face methods of controls are no longer as effective, particularly if laws are formalized and complex. As a result, conflicts arise among individuals and between various institutions and "a more formal, rationally thought-out method of social control is necessary" (Reid, 2001, p. 3). External social controls are designed to encourage conformity.[13] Whatever form a society's political organization, from chiefdoms to states, social stability has been one of a political organization's primary missions. Formal controls to resolve conflict that produce social disorder are called *laws*.

Law

Law: Old English lagu, of Scandinavian origin.[14]
1. A rule of conduct or action prescribed or formally recognized as binding or enforced by a controlling authority: as
   a. a command or provision enacted by a legislature.
   b. something (as a judicial decision) authoritatively accorded binding or controlling effect in the administration of justice.
   Example: that case is no longer the law of this circuit
2. A body of laws
   Example: the law of a state

The maintenance of social order requires an "institution that can enforce the legal rules created by the state," argues Robert Michalowski (1985, p. 32). There are three related tasks of law enforcement which are exercised through the community justice community:

- Police Bring Suspects to Justice (among other tasks)
- Court Passes Judgment on Suspects (among other tasks)
- Correctional Systems Carry out Sanctions of the Court (among other tasks)

The Criminal Justice Community

Criminal Justice Community is largely comprised of the police, courts, and corrections. The justice community as a whole secures compliance with law, passes judgment, and punishes those found guilty. Among law enforcement institutions, the police have the delegated role and authority to bring suspects to justice. Justice is the task of the court, and correctional and jail systems carry out sanctions or penalties (excluding fines and maybe community services) adjudicated by the court.

---

[13]A few paragraphs can provide a thumbnail view on the emergence of law, however, for a full account see Sue Titus Reid (2001) Criminal Law, NY: McGraw Hill, pp. 1–5.; Raymond J. Michalowski (1985), Order, Law, and Crime. NY: McGraw Hill, pp. 22–38.
[14] Source: Findlaw Dictionary. www.findlaw.com

Ultimately, one purpose of the criminal justice community is to control behavior and to protect the interests of the individual and society. That is, to maintain social stability in keeping with collective ideals and beliefs—by the people, for the people!

Social Order and Change

Social order as linked to policing has not been studied extensively, especially taking into consideration the changes in the twentieth century and the urgent demand of the people. Nearly every country registered significant transformations in their definition and handling of public order as they experienced the transition from a pre-industrial society to an industrial society.[15]

A society must provide social order before it can enjoy prosperity. For instance, in the early nineteenth century, the capitalist class in London and Paris prospered, but their property needed to be protected from the "dangerous class" of citizens, that is, those in poverty (Gatrell, Lenman, & Parker, 1980). Those in power accepted the rationale concerning the dangerous class because if the dangerous class escalated their criminal activities to the point of anarchy, state power might be curbed and what would become of their personal property? It was the state that supported personal property. Therefore, if the state fell into anarchy or lawlessness, then what happens to property values?

However, the centrality of law and order to the processes of economic growth is questionable for several reasons: that idea is based on a serious misrepresentation of most pre-industrial societies.[16] Petty thievery, violence, and warfare were pervasive during the Middle Ages in Western Europe. Yet, were those societies undisciplined or anarchic? Records suggest that European societies including Upper Bavaria, England, France, Spain, and Italy were under extremely strict social sanctions.[17] Scotland, for instance, boasted some 3,000 lay and ecclesiastical courts by the end of the seventeenth century, "dedicated to enforcing on the million or so inhabitants of the kingdom the moral standards of Protestant Christianity" (Gatrell, Lenman, & Parker, 1980, p.6). The United States is a highly progressive and successful industrial nation; yet it has always been a country of crime and violence with an alarmingly high homicide rate, widespread larceny, and pervasive racketeering and corruption (Gatrell, 1980). Order and industrial progress might not be as related as we have been led to think. Disorderly communities are generally poor and unstable. In fact, one of the strongest correlates of disorder, argues Wesley Skogan (1997), is area poverty. If social order fills a function in a society, then what function does poverty and policing fill?

Racial and ethnic differences have been considered major factors in developing attitudes toward crime and the law. However, beliefs are formed by neigh-

[15]For a closer look see Chesney, 1970; Lenman and Parker, 1980; and Weisser, 1980.
[16]See Gatrell, Lenman, and Parker, 1980; Lenman and Parker, 1980.
[17]See Chesney, 1970; Lenman and Parker, 1980; McMullan, 1984; Schulte, 1989.

borhood context, not race. Blacks and whites view the law similarly after neighborhood disadvantage is taken into account.[18] There were no tests on Latinos or other cultural groups available (Skogan, 1997).

Responses of the Criminal Justice Community

Some might say at this point, "So, should we let offenders do whatever they want?" No, but this problem needs focus. If officers did not respond to a domestic violence call for help, a gun battle, a gang fight, or a drug sale that went bad, what chaos might result? However, there is something unsettling about advice found among many popular writers, fear-peddling entrepreneurs, and bleeding-heart liberals who proclaim rehabilitation is achievable for every serial murderer, chronic pedophile, and spouse basher. When police look the other way, what are the results?

In Philadelphia in the latter 1990s, serial rape reports were ignored by police.[19] "Over nearly two decades, thousands of women who have gone to the Philadelphia police to report sexual assaults have been dismissed as liars or had their cases dumped in bureaucratic limbo," Inquirer reporters wrote.[20] Compelling evidence indicates that one result of the police ignoring rape was the murder of Shannon Schieber by the offender known as the Center City Rapist. Police fail to understand that chronic offenders read newspapers and have a good sense about agency priorities. Where better to attack women than where those attacks are rarely investigated?

On the other side of the coin, the police, from their own testimony, which is consistent with government statistics, suggest that they do not control the mean streets of many cities.[21] Furthermore, one assumption a civilized society can make is that the severity of punishment has not always guaranteed the results sought: justice and efficient crime reduction.[22] Yet, the federal government reports a decrease in crime in the early twenty-first century. However, every twenty seconds someone in America is arrested for a drug violation.[23] Every week, on average, a new jail or prison is built to lock up more people in the world's largest penal system (Egan, 2000). There is a mystery linked to this finding since prison seems not to be a crime deterrent for many offenders (Stevens, 1992a, 1992b). In

---

[18]For a closer look see R.J. Sampson and D.J. Bartusch (1999). Attitudes Toward Crime, the Police, and the Law: Individual and Neighborhood Differences.

[19]See *Philadelphia Inquirer*. Women victimized twice in police game of numbers. October 17, 1999. http://www.philly.com

[20]Ibid.

[21]For more detail see studies with police officers from many jurisdictions conducted by Dennis J. Stevens, 1999c; 1999d; 1999f; 1998a; and BJS, 2001.

[22]For a good look at this perspective see Daniel Glaser (1997). *Profitable penalties: How to cut both crime rates and costs*. Thousand Oaks, CA: Pine Forge Press.

[23]Those crimes counted and perceived as most critical might be down as each year's count is taken, yet there are some concerns that predators, white collar crime, and family and school violence are out of control.

fact, it is possible that policy makers and the public have been misinformed about the effects of incarceration. Policy makers should concentrate on reducing prison terms, implementing cost-effective intermediate sanctions, and redeploying resources earmarked for imprisonment to crime prevention strategies that adequately protect the public while offering more hope for long-term reductions in crime (Irwin, Austin, & Baird, 1998; Stevens, 1997c, 1997d).

Furthermore, some writers advance the idea that the criminal justice community must actually fail, in order to succeed. This idea suggests both a conspiracy and the incompetence of the criminal justice community's personnel and volunteers, many of whom work hard with the compassion and dedication of Mother Teresa, but their rewards are few and far between. Jeffrey Reiman (1995) explains criminal justice outcomes through what he calls the *Pyrrhic defeat theory.*

> A Pyrrhic victory is a military victory purchased at such a cost in troops and treasure that it amounts to a defeat. The Pyrrhic defeat theory argues that the failure of the criminal justice system yields such benefits to those in positions of power that it amounts to success…. from the standpoint of those with the power to make criminal justice policy in America: nothing succeeds like failure (pp. 4–5).

Reiman implies that if the police were successful, they would not continue to arrest the same individuals over and over again. If corrections were successful, recidivism rates would drastically drop; and if the courts were successful, there would be respect and applause for their verdicts. One assumption is that the police have failed.

This notion of failure goes further. Some writers think that American democracy is in trouble and that residents lack confidence in democratic institutions, including the police (Elshtain, 2000; BJS, 2000). There is a feeling that authority no longer exists in the modern democratic world, because of a loss, in particular, of authentic and indisputable experiences common to everyone, or can be called solidity.[24] In the twenty-first century, some Americas think we are faced with only two world views: (1) reaffirming traditional faith in authoritative norms (self-evident truths) that many see as arbitrary or coercive, or (2) having so little confidence in authority that "nearly everything at every moment is up for grabs," Elshtain (2000, A14) writes.

Another example supporting Elshtain and Reiman's perspective relates to politicians and the media. It appears that crime is often politicized and its meaning is different than its reality. For example, Baltimore's mayoral candidate Martin O'Malley, a middle-class professional, ran for office on a zero-tolerance

---

[24]Actually, these are Hannah Arendt's assertion's which were evaluated by Elshtain (2000) who focused on the crisis in democratic authority. "Today," Elshtain writes," it seems, we are stuck between two options: reaffirming traditional faith in authoritative norms—self-evident truths—that many see as arbitrary or coercive, or having so little confidence in them that "nearly everything at every moment is up for grabs" (p. A14). Elshtain calls for a renewal of democratic authority and warns that "unless citizens or would-be citizens are able to repair to some shared political and normative vocabulary, a democratic society cannot sustain itself over time.

(no warnings, only arrests) platform against 27 other candidates and won the election. African American voters determined the outcome (Khan, 1999). Yet, one of four Baltimore residents lives in poverty and most of them are African American; one in eight is addicted to drugs, and an estimated 1,000 middle-class residents flee the city each month for the suburbs (Khan, 1999). The Center for Disease Control reported that Baltimore has one of the highest syphilis rates in the country. Clearly, Baltimore has more complicated problems than a zero-tolerance platform can resolve, but politicians influence voters in determining what is significant in their community, and they misguide the public into a false sense of security (Khan, 1999). Many individuals in the seats of power give meaning to crime and social order that is far different than the actual experiences of a population resulting in the further exploitation of that population.

Community Changes and Police Practices

Social order is defined differently by different people. Community-policing initiatives are as unique as the diverse communities and jurisdictions they serve. One of the major issues addressed in this text is that in the twenty-first century, both the community and the police have been reconstructed, altering every definition of social order. This is an important point, yet equally important is that neither of the two entities, the community or the police, is aware of the changes and nuances of the other.

There are two points that should be examined: First, the social demographics of most major regions throughout the United States now reflect cultural diversity through multiple immigration on a scale never previously experienced by any industrialized country at any time. When immigration is taken into account, for example, about one million people are added to the population of the United States every year. While the number of European immigrants to the United States has declined over the years, migration from other regions of the world has steadily increased. These newly arrived individuals tend to locate themselves where there are people with similar backgrounds. In most cases, they settle in urban communities. One result of this recent development is that America's new residents are helping to shape a distinctly different culture in American cities, away from the traditional Euro-American culture (Kabagarama, 1997). How well do the American police relate to those communities and what path do they follow to facilitate social order?

Secondly, the responsibility of police agencies has changed to reflect community input as one method of maintaining social order, yet social disorder continues to be measured by traditional methods of police productivity, such as crime rates, response time, and citizen complaints. Therefore, since government statistics reported crime rates in the early twenty-first century have declined, does it necessarily follow that social order exists? This book argues that this position is untenable, due in part, to the demographic changes in American communities, which tend to rely less on American policing for services. Since diverse communities hold a different perspective about social order than previous populations, one response by the police is to see these diverse populations as invisible, yet annoying, due largely to the police's lack of resources and high demand by other segments of the population.

In one respect, the traditional American public is drowning the police in 911 calls for service and in another respect, some officers are denying due process guarantees to some segments of the American public.[25] Once we can accept the notion that there is a difference between social and physical disorder, we need to consider that there is also a different cure for each. However, both disorders might produce a similar result, fight or flight, argues Skogan (1990).

For instance, 82 percent of Camden, New Jersey's residents received some form of public assistance in 1998. Sixty-nine percent of the city's households received assistance from Aid to Families with Dependent children (AFDC). More than 12 percent of Camden's housing units are vacant, creating a dismal atmosphere where abandoned houses have caught fire, leaving piles of ruble in their wake. Camden experienced a record number of homicides, increasing 88% between 1988 and 1992, many of them drug-related. The city has 12 percent more children than the state percentage, and is called by some a "city of children." Almost one-third of all births are births to children themselves. With these deep-seated economic and social problems and the negative image surrounding the city, it will take more than a community-policing effort to restore the city. In July 2000 the state government of New Jersey took control of the city government, including the police department.

Social Disorder

One idea is that "order is defined by norms about public behavior and these norms are only a subset of the manners and morals of the community" (Skogan, 1990, p. 4). How do cities like Camden and Baltimore define social order? Do communities, especially culturally diverse communities, define social order differently than, say, the police?

Wilson and Kelling's (1999) broken-window theory described urban deterioration as fostering an environment favorable to criminal behavior. The condition of a building leads to crime! In this sense, some people like to bring up a study conducted some time ago suggesting that inhibition level may vary by neighborhood. For example, to test this idea, similar cars were "abandoned" in New York City and near Stanford University campus in California. Anonymity provided by the size of New York City encouraged rapid destruction of the car after it was initially spoiled by removing its license plates and leaving the hood raised. But the destruction of the other auto, near the Stanford campus, took longer and took more extreme releaser cues, smashing it a bit more (Zimbardo, 1970). It didn't

[25]For instance, calls for service have doubled for most police departments from 1990 to 1999 and bringing evidence to that findings, reported in a case study of nine departments across the US, Fayetteville, North Carolina Police, typically reported that calls for service have risen from 110,116 to 167,564 during that time period (BJS, 2000; Stevens, 2002).

take long before both vehicles were eventually destroyed. Similarly, a building with broken windows will eventually be seen as abandoned property. There appear to be links between deterioration and crime, in the sense that an abandoned building might be perceived as an opportunity for things to happen. If the onlooker has the intention to commit a crime, the chances are greater that it will be attempted.

Social disorder, Wesley Skogan (1990) argues, is an outcome of conduct and can be seen (public drinking, or prostitution), experienced (catcalling, or sexual harassment), or noticed (graffiti, or vandalism). Physical disorder involves visual signs of negligence and unchecked decay: abandoned or ill-kept buildings, broken streetlights, trash-filled lots, and alleys strewn with garbage and alive with rats. By and large, physical disorder refers to ongoing conditions, while social disorder appears as a series of more or less episodic events. Social disorder and physical disorder are different problems with different cures. Both might produce feelings of fight or flight and while disorder is clearly associated with common crime, the two turn out to be distinct issues (Skogan, 1990). Disorder violates widely shared values, but there is disagreement about what social order is, argues Wesley Skogan (1990).

An abandoned car or a neglected building are conspicuous objects that can lead to deterioration and eventual criminal activities. What about things in our society that may not be so conspicuous? Does deterioration mean population shifts from Western Europeans to people of different origin? There are many American cities where Western Europeans are declining in the population. How does that impact a police department's definition of social order when policy and perceptions of law and order are focused on Western European values? St. Paul Minnesota police chief, William Finney (2000, p. 4) offers the following:

> ...for many years, my perspective, both as chief and throughout my law enforcement career, has been that both functions (policing diverse communities and maintaining positive relations with communities of different cultural and racial backgrounds) set up a problematic dichotomy that may likely be the cause– rather than the cure—for prejudicial and unjust application of police authority in minority communities (p.4).

Many newcomers to the United States tend to live in urban environments where others like themselves seem to live and those parts of the city are often perceived as lower-class sections of the city (Portes & Rumbaut, 1996). One implication of Wilson and Kelling's broken window theory is that crime is greater in communities where more broken windows exist. In what part of the city are most of the windows broken? One answer is that there are many broken windows in lower-class neighborhoods. Therefore, immigrants and people at the lower economic levels of our society tend to receive police attention including community-policing initiatives more often than other groups of people.

It is also clear that while many residents want community change, few want to become involved (Stewart-Brown & Rosario, 2001). Many say they are held back by a lack of trust between themselves and the police or by a fear of retaliation from criminals. This thought is consistent with the results of the investigation conducted for this textbook among 2,086 participants in eight jurisdictions.[26] That is, they want change, they may even attend meetings, but offer little genuine support to help meet the objectives.

Nonetheless, it is clear that social disorder plays an important role in urban decline (Skogan, 1990), but it is not clear that social order is absent in poor neighborhoods. Public gambling and drinking, prostitution, and the sale of narcotics are illegal, but violations of other widely approved standards of public conduct are not as clearly illegal, for example, noisy neighbors, accumulating trash, poorly maintained buildings, and congregating bands of youth. It could also be said that nonwestern European populations demonstrate behavior that tends not to fit with the Western European notions of social order.

Other forms of disorder seem to present intractable enforcement problems despite their unlawful status, resulting in ambiguous legal categories such as disturbing the peace, loitering, and vagrancy. But this raises a different set of questions: Does the concept of social disorder represent anything other than intolerance for all but conventional middle-class views of behavior? How often does the definition of social disorder justify police action, including suspect police activity and corruption in less affluent or "different" communities? Would the rhetoric of community-policing's proponents create expectations that are impossible to meet (Klockars, 1988)? Does order mean controlling the economically deprived or the lower classes of America while those with resources avoid police scrutiny?

When law breaks down or doesn't represent the predominant or collective thoughts of the people it regulates, social order can deteriorate. Recall South Africa, Kosavo, and numerous other places (since recorded history began), where groups are targeted and labeled by those in power as "problematic" or criminal. Targeted individuals in some cases can be labeled criminals simply because of their biological features or their beliefs or the way they prayed. This targeting can be rationalized in many ways, for instance in Nazi Germany, Jews were targeted because they were different from the general German population and used as scapegoats for the ills of the country. In America, after the destruction of the World Trade Center, wasn't there a group of people automatically targeted as the enemy? Americans who biologically resembled the enemy were targeted and their lives were disrupted. In this case, President George W. Bush delivered several speeches on television urging everyone to be patient. The President said that the individuals responsible for the terrorist acts against the U.S. would be brought to justice. He invited religious leaders including Buddhists, Catholics, Jews, and Moslems to appear together in a televised event to demonstrate unity. Targeting specific groups is a normal reaction by people who are trying to understand incidents that might be tied to tragic experiences such as terrorist attacks or poverty.

Then, too, when a group of individuals are targeted as criminals, their behavior tends to be defined as a form of social disorder and their individual

[26]There were 2010 survey participants in eight jurisdictions and 76 participants were interviewed only in Boston.

lifestyles are explained as self-directed. For instance, the view that poverty is the result of personal inadequacy and that it leads to social disorder is still widely accepted in middle America. One strange side to this thought is that poor people tend to share the perspective that they're inadequate, too. Because poor people cannot live up to social expectations of the middle class, many disadvantaged individuals are easily manipulated and used by unscrupulous (or ignorant) individuals or institutions within the criminal justice community. The *criminalization of poverty* might be one way to describe this targeting perspective.

Today, many police executives continue to rely on targeting and antiquated methods of control, such as use of force and zero tolerance, with little room for debate. One example comes from Chief Emmett Turner who announced in early 2000 that the Metropolitan Nashville Police Department (Metro) would "embark on a sweeping, comprehensive plan to attack violent crime throughout Davidson County, Tennessee" (Stevens, 2001a, p. 83). The chief's intentions were honorable, yet flawed. The plan enlisted the assistance and support of all police personnel and resources, as well as a host of other law enforcement agencies, including the Tennessee Highway Patrol; Bureau of Alcohol, Tobacco, and Firearms; Federal Bureau of Investigation; Drug Enforcement Administration; Immigration and Naturalization Service; and the Secret Service. The chief said, "I am very serious about ridding our neighborhoods of the gun-toting drug dealers, thieves, and other criminals who are terrorizing innocent citizens. The plan I am announcing today sends a clear message to law breakers that the war is on, and we intend to win" (Stevens, 2001a, p.82). Metro's violent crime strategy, like that of many other police agencies, consists of several elements: targeted hot spots, policies aimed at the prevention of retaliation in homicide and aggravated assault cases; undercover buy/bust operations; reverse drug stings; undercover prostitution operations; reverse prostitution stings; enforcement roadblocks; saturation patrols; and enforcement of quality of life laws. The chief said:

> "Officers must address all violations of the law. They should be willing to prevent and enforce such issues as; prostitution, littering, open container, loud music, rock throwing, panhandling, etc. While these may seem trivial, they have a direct effect on a neighborhood and affect the quality of life in a neighborhood. . . . allowing minor infractions to go unchecked paves the way for more serious violations to occur" (Stevens, 2001a, p. 86).

We all applaud these tactics. However, some parts of Davidson County and Nashville are under an "occupational authority" or as can be implied by one critic, "an army of occupation" (Bayley, 1991, p. 229), while other sections of the city might rarely see a police officer drive by their home.

Continuing along this line of reasoning, earlier investigations suggest that many officers are reluctant to make a lawful arrest of youths, especially females. Officers are reluctant to intervene in domestic violence disputes, and officers are reluctant to provide appropriate police protection to urban African American populations. One product of police reluctance, each investigation concludes, is that many individuals, especially law-abiding individuals, developed the idea that a violent response, including murder, was appropriate against others who might attack them because the police failed to do the job of protecting them.[27] In fact, other research suggests that officers tend to overlook violators if the officers fear the threat of a civil suit (Stevens, 2001b). One implication can be that some officers are more concerned with CYA[28] than controlling public order.

Yet, it is here that the American police take their stand. It can be argued that if all police agencies reject Constitutional guarantees and fail to provide public safety, would the U.S. be as strong a nation as it is presently? Clearly, many agencies perform in the best interests of Constitutional guarantees and in fact, officers across the country help many individuals but, alas, that doesn't sell newspapers. Think of all the hard, even life-threatening, work New York City officers and firefighters performed after September 11, 2001. There are small non-fatal incidents happening across the country every moment, and police officers are the individuals called upon for help. As one officer commented, "Helping others is the reason I became a cop."

Furthermore, through community-policing strategies such as problem-solving partnerships with the community, making good decisions about police service with an eye on Constitutional mandates should become a national reality.

Support for this basic ideal comes from Chief Charles Ramsey of the Metropolitan Police, Washington DC. The chief argues that "if history tells us anything, it tells us that if calls for these types of actions should occur in the future, we the police must be the first and the loudest to speak out" (Milofsky, 2000, p. 1). The chief was referring to the orders directed to the German police officials under the Nazi regime.[29] The chief questioned why German police officials had conducted themselves in practices that were morally wrong. Chief Ronald Hansen, Fayetteville, North Carolina furthers this thought suggesting the "protector of due process and guardian of the American spirit of democracy is the responsibility of every police officer and every police agency in America" (personal communication, 2000). Those rights are guaranteed by the U.S. Constitution and enforced by over 700,000 sworn officers employed by over 18,000 police agencies. Protecting individual rights is woven into the responsibility of policing. Of course, there are always other views about what fuels police intention as an institution, but the fact remains that America has always been a violent nation and continues along that path. Without a professional police presence, how much more violent might those who favor violence, become?

---

[27]See Dennis J. Stevens, 1999j, 1998b, and 1998c. Of particular interest is 1998c. Mandatory arrest, spouse abuse, & accelerated rates of victimization: Attitudes of victims and officers. *The Criminologist.* It was learned that in a state with mandatory arrest policies in place for all domestic violence calls, that high percentage of officers did not make an arrest for two primary reasons: 1) the officers felt that it sometimes took "two to tango" in issues relating to domestic violence and the relationship was linked to continual conflict. That is, the partners sought conflict in their lives. "The partners are on a suicide mission," one officer said. And 2) The justice system removed officer discretion in dealing entirely with a police matter.

[28]CYA, can be explained as "cover your ass," one officer privately communicated with the writer. "It means take steps to ensure yourself that possible political harm cannot befall you or your job," she added. "Do your job by the book," another officer communicated.

These ideals have critics (and rightfully so) who might describe these notions as lofty in nature and/or suspect the relevance of Chief Ramsey's and Chief Hansen's positions. But solid evidence supports the idea that community-policing initiatives grounded in the intention of delivering quality police service and servicing diverse communities has produced police officer resistance from police recruits, commanders, and local politicians (Stevens, 2001a). If something is good for the community, why would there be resistance on anybody's part? Maybe those individuals don't want to help or don't understand the nature of crime.

The Nature of Crime

When people talk about crime, they are usually talking about an event or an outcome resulting from an action that they are equally concerned about and that they expect some kind of action taken against.[30] Someone's conduct can become a social problem when individuals take "collective action" to do something about it.

Crime

Crime is the commission of an act prohibited by criminal law or the failure to act as required by criminal law.[31]

"Implicit in this definition is the power of the government to impose sanctions or penalties" (Reid, 2001, p. 11). Two principles contribute to our understanding of crime in America:

1. Government cannot punish unless there is a law (statutory or common) providing that an act (or a failure to act) is a crime.
2. There is no crime without punishment.

These two provisions suggest that unless the state (or federal government) defined an act or omission as a crime and provided sanctions, punishment cannot be inflicted just because the act is harmful to others (Reid, 2001).

Most of us agree on the definition of straightforward street crimes, such as murder, rape, robbery, burglary, and theft and we tend to view street crimes as a greater criminal problem for the public than all the deadly and costly crimes of corporate and political enterprise.[32] Perhaps street violators are easier to appre-

---

[29]Chief Ramsey made that statement after touring the United States Holocaust Memorial Museum. One result was that the Metropolitan Police embarked on a training program that includes a tour of the museum by all police recruits to examine the issues of police community relations, personal responsibility, and protection of individual rights through a new lens (Milofsky, 2000).

[30]See Richard L. Henshel, (1990). *Thinking about social problems.* San Diego: Harcourt Brace Jovanovich Publishers. Chapter 3. And, David R. Simon. (1995). *Social problems and the sociological imagination.* NY: Mc Graw-Hill. Chapter 2.

[31]See Sue Titus Reid (2001). *Criminal law.* Fifth Edition. NY: McGraw-Hill. p. 11.

[32]See Jeffrey Reiman. (1998). *The rich get richer and the poor get prison.* Boston: Allyn Bacon. Pages 101–116. Randall G. Shelden. (2001). *Controlling the dangerous classes.* Boston: Allyn Bacon. pp.131– 148.

hend, especially in light of the limited training police officers receive in the other areas of criminal activity and cultural diversity.[33] Traditional criminologists argue that crime is really behavior in violation of the serious or violent crime perceptions of law. It may be for those reasons that *crime* can be defined as a violation of whatever appears on the statutes at a particular time and place—it is whatever the law says crime is.[34]

There is a "politics of crime" that some might argue has to do with those who have the power to define crime, which helps shape policy. For example, crime may be depicted as evidence of the breakdown of law and order, of the demise of the traditional two-parent family, or of social and economic inequality. Crime-related issues are thus socially and politically constructed, argue Beckett and Sasson (2000). That is, crime acquires its meaning through struggles over interpretation and representation; depending on whose definition dominates, policy can follow. For example, to the extent that crime is seen as a consequence of lenience with the criminal justice system, "get-tough" policies were implemented. Definitions that depict crime as an outcome of poverty, unemployment, or inequality may help form social and economic policies. Definitions that portray crime as a consequence of alcohol, led to the establishment of Prohibition Laws. However, behavioral expressions include panhandling and sidewalk solicitation by individuals that make residents feel unsafe. By increasing fear, these expressions of disorder are presumed to weaken the informal community controls that prevent crime (Beckett & Sasson, 2000). The fear of crime plays a major role in social disorder.

The Fear of Crime and Social Disorder

How closely linked are crime, the fear of crime, and social disorder? James Q. Wilson and George Kelling (1998) maintain that disorder spawns serious crime. They suggest that a sequenced progression follows disorder. For instance, unchecked rule-breaking invites petty plundering; gambling and drinking lead to robberies and fights; prostitution and drug sales draw those who prey on consumers of vice (Skogan, 1990). Wilson and Kelling suspect that a concentration of supposedly "victimless" disorders would deluge an area with serious, victimizing crime. Skogan's evaluation of that progression is challenged on the precise relationship between crime and disorder. Where disorder is visible and frequent, and no one steps in to alter that trend, criminals feel uninhibited in criminal conduct. However, "small shifts in levels of reported crime simply have no practical impact on the vast majority of citizens" (Kelling & Coles, 1996, p. 37).

What does have a major effect on residents seems to be the fear of crime. There is a strong link between the fear of crime and the decisions individuals make

---

[33]See Ronald D. Hunter (1994). Who guards the guardians? Managerial misconduct in policing. In Thomas Barker and David L. Carter (Eds.) Pages 169–184), *Police Deviance.* Cincinnati, Ohio: Anderson Publishing Company. And, Katherine Beckett and Theodore Sasson, (2000). *The politics of injustice: Crime and punishment in America.* Thousand Oaks, CA: Pine Forge Press. pp. 32–39.

[34]See Richard L. Henshel. (1990).*Thinking about social problems.* San Diego: Harcourt Brace Jovanovich Publishers. pp. 36–37.

about their lifestyles. For instance, the randomness of violence beyond high-crime areas makes people anxious, argues Robert Blendon, who tracks public opinion surveys for Harvard University's School of Public Health.[35] Those incidents send a symbolic message to people indicating that crime is out of control. For instance, using an extreme example to help make the point: after the destruction of the World Trade Center, some people felt at risk even when they took precautions, and they felt that the safest place could turn into the most dangerous place without any warning. The point is that behavior is different when people feel threatened. Fearful people make lifestyle decisions that often place themselves smack in the center of criminal activity. They buy guns or engage in compulsive aggressive behavior with others, including family members and strangers.

Residents, Fear of Crime, and Outcomes

In communities where the fear of crime becomes a way of life, some residents flee. Middle-class families leave first (Skogan, 1990). Those families are often replaced by unattached and transient individuals. Those who cannot leave withdraw psychologically producing a reduction in supervision of youth and less participation in community issues. Deterioration of local housing and business conditions become evident and fewer individuals want to shop or visit the community. As isolation sets into the neighborhood, these problems, Skogan (1990, p. 13) states, "feed upon themselves, and neighborhoods spiral deeper into decline." In a twenty-year study in Los Angeles crime shifted from being an effect of social and economic conditions to being a cause of those conditions (Skogan, 1990).

The idea that the fear of crime exists and motivates behavior can be found among police officers, too, in the sense that when they feel threatened by a civil lawsuit, for example, they make fewer probable cause arrests.[36] On the other hand, when the police attempt to "cure" a neighborhood of "disorder" through aggressive intervention, their attempts could produce an increase in the fear of crime. For instance, George Kelling and Catherine Coles (1996) suggest that one product of aggressive police intervention can be perceived as a direct challenge to the legal and constitutional protections of fundamental liberties, including due process guarantees. That is, citizen demands are based on their experience in public spaces with what they believe are the precipitating signs of crime—disorder and media coverage of crime—daily "in your face" street experiences. For instance, during the early 1990s businesspeople from the Upper West Side of Manhattan requested a meeting with both their police precinct commander and a representative of the district attorney's office to voice their objection to police placing a high priority on robberies resulting in neglect of illegal vending (Kelling & Coles, 1996). Illegal

[35]Comments made during a presentation on the fear of crime, Harvard University, Spring, 2001.
[36]See Dennis J. Stevens. (2002). Civil liabilities and arrest decisions. In Jeffrey Walker (Ed.), *Policing and the Law*, (pp. 127–141), Upper Saddle River, NJ: Prentice Hall. And, Dennis J. Stevens. (2001, May). Civil liabilities and selective enforcement. *Law and Order*, 49(5), 105–109.

vending was less the problem than were drug users, who were selling "hot" merchandise to the illegal vendors, "hanging out," using drugs, panhandling, and harassing shoppers and pedestrians. Business owners made it clear that while they feared robbery, robberies could be managed through security, control of merchandise, and control of cash flow. They could not survive if shoppers were unwilling to cross the "phalanx of importuning street people," for business would languish and ultimately fail—a personal financial loss to the merchants, but a loss to the neighborhood too.

In the final analysis, crime and disorder are related issues and tend to influence each other but, crime and disorder might be perceived by the community as a different experience with a different set of expectations for constituents than the police expect. Additionally, some argue that the very process of social control directly triggers violations. That is, should priorities move to less serious crimes, if there is such a thing, Gary Marx (1999) postulates that more police involvement in otherwise less prioritized conduct, we can expect that conduct to escalate. Think of it this way: where would drug abusers go for help if the community is engaged in a war against them? Because the problem-solving repertoire of the police depends heavily on arrests, community members who otherwise might come forward as potential offenders in order to seek preventive community support, remain silent (DeLeon-Granados, 1999).

Summary

A police agency and their officers should use their legal and moral prerogatives to gain professional status and community respect, which could easily aid in community compliance to laws and cooperation. We discussed political changes; examined ideals of due process, social order, and the law; and described practices or responses of the police linked to these ideals. Some responses included targeting of populations as evident by the example from Nashville, Tennessee. One point made was that law and police practice, although they play a large role in social order, are methods leading to order, not a goal themselves. Criticism was offered about police responses, and distinctions between order and disorder were characterized, suggesting that definitions depend on who is doing the defining. The nature of crime was discussed, suggesting that most crime is a result of living conditions, relationship expectations, pure selfishness, and a lack of self-control. The notion of the "criminalization of poverty" was offered as one explanation of targeting the lower class as criminals. An implication arising from that finding is that crime isn't the business of the police but of other institutions. Finally, the relationship between fear of crime and social disorder were revealed, suggesting that fear alone can have a greater impact on the behavior of community members than arrest rates. And here, too, the police have less to do with peddling fear than other institutions.

Do You Know?

1. The public will perceive the police as professional when the police utilize their legal and moral prerogatives. Define those prerogatives and explain why you think they are important to the public.
2. In what way are police officers representatives of the government?
3. Define police power and what an agency requires from the community to effectively exercise its power without the overburden of enforcement.
4. In what way have most societies recognized that law and order are essential to the society's survival?
5. If the police ignore routine daily crime and concentrate on preventive measures, what results might occur, according to the author? In what way do you accept this perspective? What, if anything, has the author neglected in his answer?
6. Describe the Pyrrhic defeat theory and explain how it applies to criminal justice outcomes. In what way do you agree and disagree with this viewpoint?
7. Describe the conditions in Camden, New Jersey that led to its failure to implement community-policing initiatives. Can you offer any advice to Camden policy makers?

8. Describe how public order should be defined and the way it is generally defined, from the perspective of the author. In what way do you agree with the author's perspective? In what way would communities be affected if public order were defined differently?
9. Define law and its function in the American society.
10. How are crime and social disorder linked?
11. Define targeting as used in this chapter and identify past and present methods of official targeting and their effects. In what way do you agree and disagree with targeting techniques in policing?
12. What is the primary function of the American police, using the interpretations of Chief Charles Ramsey of Washington, DC, and Chief Ronald Hansen of Fayetteville, NC?
13. President Lyndon Johnson said, "If one morning I walked on top of the water across the Potomac River, the headline that afternoon would read: PRESIDENT CAN'T SWIM." How do his thoughts fit this chapter? Hint: There is always more than one way to look at everything.

3

Culture, Social Class, and Population Change

"If a free society cannot help the many who are poor, it cannot save the few who are rich."

John F. Kennedy (1917–1963)

Key Terms

Census 2000	Ethnocentrism	McDonaldization
Culture	Eurocentrism	Melting Pot
Cultural Diversity	Immigration	Social Class
Cultural Pluralism	Instincts	Stratification

Key Topics

- The social influences that impact American lifestyles.
- Discussion of cultural diversity and cultural pluralism
- Effects of population and immigration changes
- Perspectives on poverty
- How Eurocentrism affects criminal justice response in the United States

Introduction

Understanding how social influences—culture, class, population and immigration, poverty, and Eurocentrism—affect the justice system in America is a lot to cover in one chapter. Be prepared to supplement this information with your own experiences and knowledge. How people treat you might have a lot to do with your cultural heritage and where you are in your social structure, often referred to as *social class*.

We will see how these cultural factors influence police service and community response to police service. It is helpful to know that each of these influences is linked with and shaped by one another, along with a number of other social influences, some of which are briefly mentioned here. Socio-cultural influences impact most aspects of our lives, including the following:

- Beliefs: things we value and our ability to distinguish right from wrong.
- Opportunities: individual chances to grow and be safe.
- Limitations: things that stop us from getting what we want, such as economics, age, education, skills, and physical capabilities.
- Expectations: our hopes and dreams.

What shapes our beliefs, opportunities, limitations, and expectations? Among other things, our cultural heritage (no matter where we live now) and our social class heavily influence our decisions.[1] They also impact decisions other people make about us. If you're getting the idea that law and order's response toward you and your family might depend more on your culture and social class than on your actual behavior, you're probably more right than wrong.

[1] While this idea might seem novel, it was Durkheim's (1858–1917) study of society whose notions included an analogy of the human body to explain society. There was the suggestion that there are many parts to society and that no one part is greater than the whole. At the core of his perspective was the idea that it requires all the body parts, to make one complete body. Just as it take culture, diversity, community, change and crime to make one complete society. Each part serves a function within a society contributing to the whole.

Keep in mind that American society is constantly changing and those changes include more than an increase in actual numbers. They include a change in cultural perspectives, too.

Culture

What do you think when you hear the word *culture*? We may associate the term with art forms such as literature, music, and dance. Describing someone who attends the opera, for instance, seems to elicit the comment, "She has culture," suggesting someone appreciates the "finer things in life." On the other hand, those of us who find opera boring supposedly have little appreciation for culture.

Culture does not specifically refer to upscale or refined lifestyle. Culture is usually taken for granted because it has been with us prior to our birth, and will remain long after our departure. From birth to death, we are influenced by cultural pressures telling us among other things, how to eat, sleep, work, live, play, and even how to feel good or how to feel bad about ourselves and others.[2] Culture informs us about what type of person would be appropriate to date including his or her age, race, and gender and it advises us how to care for our children.

Culture

Culture is a shared lifestyle.

As we interact with our social environment, decisions about how to act and how to treat others are shaped in concert with our cultural context. Yes, we are free to choose how to respond, but those choices are often dictated by our cultural perspective. Culture consists of abstract values, beliefs, and perceptions of the social world that and are reflected by behavior (Haviland, 1999; Kabagarama, 1997). Culture can represent social agreement or a collective ideal and it may contribute to social stability (Durkheim, 1984, 1933). Not accepting your culture's shared ideals or standards presents problems for the individual. Let's illustrate this point with a discussion about dating someone from another culture. Your friends may respond to you differently than you expect if you date someone from another culture. How would your parents (or your children, if you had been previously married) respond toward the new love of your life? Now, connect some of these answers to police response toward a different cultural group.

When an individual is observed by others of the same cultural group, behavior is judged on the basis of the shared culture, regardless of where those individuals are observed (Haviland, 1999). When a Haitian living in Boston is encountered by other Haitians, the Boston Haitian's behavior is judged not by Boston standards but by Haitian standards. Most of us recognize that when

[2]For a closer look at culture, see D. Kabagarama (1997). *Breaking the ice: A guide to understanding people from other cultures.* Boston: Allyn and Bacon.

Haitians move to Boston, they must learn how to appear to conform to the culture of Boston for the sake of survival, and at the same time, satisfy their birth culture. If they don't, they are subject to isolation from friends and criticism from family members (Haviland, 1999). Americans or members of other cultural groups might, when encountering a Haitian in Boston, criticize the Haitian's "American behavior" if the Haitian forgets his or her previous culture, and may even bring sanctions against the Haitian. In some cultures it is not okay to neglect your birth culture. That may not always be the case, but there was strong agreement to this statement by many of the respondents who participated in the survey conducted for this textbook.

Instincts Versus Culture

Because we are so vulnerable at birth, dependence is part of being human and cooperation of others is necessary to maintain life. We form groups in an attempt to meet our needs, including food, shelter, and safety. Compared to many other creatures on this planet, human beings are weak when they stand alone. Thinking about electricity, water, and food tells you that we need others in order to comfortably survive. Other creatures cooperate with each other, such as ants, and through genetic programming, construct nests, follow dictates, and do battle without training. Humans cannot live in isolation and build a home similar to their parents, without having access to blueprints. Ants, birds, and other creatures can and do many things without the benefit of learning. Mankind is not so lucky. And of course, as history proves, it is not a given that humans automatically cooperate with each other.

What is natural in human behavior is that we have a capacity to create culture in our lives. Every other form of life, from ants to zebras behave in a uniform, species-specific style. While human behavior varies across the globe, the behavior of a dog, for instance a cocker spaniel, remains fairly consistent. In fact, the conduct of cocker spaniels throughout history is probably similar to contemporary cockers. One reason for this is that animals possess *instincts*.

Instincts

Instincts can be defined as biological programming over which animals have little control.

We could argue with some degree of confidence that animals tend to behave in a similar way under similar conditions throughout their existence. And animals never lie, nor do they join a religious group.

Humans on the other hand, have the ability to behave in a variety of ways regardless of the environmental conditions because in part, most human behavior is a learned process or what can be called social heredity through culture. An argument offered as proof that humans have instinct is based on the idea of survival instincts. Put a gun to a person's head and he or she will do whatever it

takes to conform to the wishes of the gun holder. But the truth is that many people will still perform certain behavior regardless of imminent danger. Can you
think of some scenario or situation where individuals have not carried out some
specific directives even when threatened with harm? The truth of the matter is
that suicide, hunger strikes, religion, and killing oneself or others over principles
alone is hardly within the range of choices of any animal.

Learning Culture

Because we are not genetically programmed to accept and follow rules, each generation must be taught the principles of their culture. We are not controlled by our
genetic makeup as other creatures are and that is why we have rules to follow
instead. However, each of us is caught inside our own biology and awareness, and
no human being is directly able to experience the consciousness of another human
being. Therefore, we need to learn cooperation through culture, especially by
growing up with it; in sociological terms, this is a lifelong socialization process.

The process whereby culture is transmitted from one generation to another
is called *enculturation* (Haviland, 2000). Through enculturation we learn culturally appropriate ways to satisfy our biological needs. There are distinctions from
one cultural group to another. For instance, Irish Bostonians have eating habits far
different than the eating habits of typical Asians or Ethiopians. Differences were
learned through enculturation. Among cocker spaniels some can learn tricks, but
that behavior is reflexive, the result of conditioning by repeated training, and not
the product of culture, enculturation, or individual choice (Haviland, 2000).

Material and Nonmaterial Cultural Components

Culture consists of two components: material and nonmaterial. The former refers
to tangible items such as cars and the latter is comprised of intangible elements
such as values and beliefs. Culture plays a significant role in that it may be perceived as the springboard of human activity. On a basic level, culture facilitates
the production and distribution of goods and services that are necessary for survival. It is no wonder that there are so many methods of production in operation
all over the world (Kabagarama, 1997).

Culture has fundamental characteristics such as symbols, language, values,
norms, material goods, and goals that distinguish it from other concepts. It
processes its own belief systems of right from wrong, of comfort and discomfort,
of strong to weak, and of life and death. Although culture is complex with many
parts that seem unrelated, every part of culture is shaped and linked with every
other part (Kabagarama, 1997). It is, for example, difficult to separate the role of
education from that of governance, family, health, and economic activity. Culture
is learned in a variety of ways from one generation to the next and lends itself to
cultural survival in the sense that humans developed the mental power to fashion
the natural environment for themselves. Yet, as human groups made and remade
their world, it is easy to understand how cultural diversity came into being.

World Culture

Among other things, with the rise of the multinational corporations, the world's resistance to political integration seems possible. The worldwide spread of products such as Pepsi®, Coca Cola®, and McDonald's® might be taken as a sign that a homogeneous (similar) world culture is developing.[3] There is a trend toward the McDonaldization of human experience in every quarter of life (Ritzer, 1993).

McDonaldization

McDonaldization of society relates to a global trend of modeling many aspects of life on the organizational principles that underlie McDonald's fastfood restaurants, such as efficiency, calculability, uniformity, and control.[4]

However, the future of the human species is centered in culture since people solve their problems of existence and determine the level of participation through it. Of course, some would argue that there is a trend suggesting that the problems of human existence seem to be outdistancing culture's ability to find solutions. Nonetheless, the idea that we have a one-world culture seems to be supported by the observation that communication, transportation, and trade link the peoples of the world and as a result, many people across the globe wear similar clothes, eat similar food, and watch similar television shows (Haviland, 2000). It is striking that many people resemble other people, but do they think alike?

There is evidence that an equal percentage of American citizens and immigrants obtain college degrees. The average individual who leaves his or her homeland for another country is not a typical individual, and they tend to possess high life aspirations and expectations.

---

[3]One perspective is that with thousands of McDonald's restaurants dotting America and the world landscape, there is a new trend underway. It's more than hamburgers and fries. McDonaldization of society refers to the increasing rationalization of the routine tasks of everyday life. The principles of Henry Ford have been applied to preparation and distribution of food. In a like sense, McDonald operators are told how to draw milk shakes, grill hamburgers, and fry potatoes. Specified cooking times, exact temperatures, fixed portions including condiments (i.e., onions, pickles), cheese slices (32 slices per pound of cheese), and fry size (nine-thirty-seconds of an inch thick). Hamburgers are placed on the grill from right to left creating six rows of six patties each. And because the first two rows are farthest from the heating element, flip the third row first, then the fourth, fifth, and sixth before the first two. This process is promoted in many quarters of society. For more detail see George Ritzer (1993). *The McDonaldization of Society.*

[4]For a closer look, see George Ritzer (1993), *The McDonaldization of Society.* Efficiency refers to marketing the idea of fast is good; calculability refers to mass produced uniformly according to a standard plan; i.e., McDonald's operating manual declared the weight of a regular raw hamburger to be 1.6 ounces, its size to be 3.875 inches across, and its fat content to be 19 percent. A slice of cheese weighs exactly half an ounce, and fries are cut precisely $9/32$ of an inch thick. Uniformity and predictability refers to an individual who can walk into a McDonald's anywhere in the world and buy the same sandwich, fries, and coke; control through automation refers to automated equipment that cooks food at fixed temperatures for set lengths of time.

The view of the world used to be vertical. It used to come from the past, or from the hierarchy of heaven, earth, and hell.[5] Today, it is horizontal, made up of an endless multiplicity of events going on at once and pressing at each moment. Evidence? Watch a cable new's show or carefully read a major newspaper. People living in America want to live here regardless of where they were born and they want and should have the Constitutional mandates available to them.

The discovery of each new layer of our society can change the perception of the whole picture. Of course, different individuals have different ideas about social order and the function of the American police. However, some of our comfortable lifestyles (whether we want to admit it or not) has an effect on something else: poverty, ignorance, hatred, discrimination, and criminal activities.

Cultural Pluralism

Many people in Boston share similar services, products, and even employment; yet the differences between them are still evident by their cultural norms and expectations. True, there may be a superstructure in place that many give lip service to in order to fulfill goals, but when it comes to specific group lifestyles, clearly there are divisions in thoughts, words, and deeds. For example, in Houston's Vietnamese neighborhoods, with their distinctive cultural traditions and values, people exist side by side with other people. However temporary for these Vietnamese people, they still have their own language, music, religion, food, and history. As we look at other cities such as Chicago where generation after generation of Polish Americans have resided in a specific section of the city, there is a continuation of strong ties between them and the city of Chicago. In New York City's Little Italy section, Italians continue to reside there, and in Chinatown of Los Angeles, 60 percent of the businesses in the neighborhood are owned by Chinese people.

Maybe some groups will become Americanized or take on an entirely different culture after a few generations or even after the first generation, but it is more likely that America will remain a pluralistic society.

Cultural Pluralism

Cultural pluralism is when more than one culture exists in a given society.

Pluralistic societies such as the United States are multicultural and could not have existed before the first politically centralized states arose some five thousand years ago (Haviland, 2000). In part, with the rise of the state, independent societies each with its own culture, could politically unify, thereby creating what amounts to a higher social order that transcends the theoretical one-culture one-society linkage (Macionis & Parrillo, 1998). This union creates many advantages for those societies that politically merged, which include a higher quality of life

[5]See DeCourtivron, I. (2000, July 7). Educating the global student, whose identity is always a matter of choice. *Chronicle of Higher Education.* (On-Line), Available: http://chronicle.com/search97cgi/s97_cgi

for all concerned. However, the other side of pluralism takes us to the heart of the problem in many community-policing initiatives: the cultural groups within that union by virtue of their high degree of cultural variation, are essentially operating by different sets of rules (Haviland, 2000).

In a culturally pluralistic society, it is difficult for the members of any one subgroup to comprehend the different standards motivating the others. At the least, this can lead to major misunderstandings and even death. Using history to make a point, consider the former European nation of Yugoslavia. The recent civil war there was fueled by cultural diversity. This one small country made use of two alphabets, embraced three major religions, spoke four major languages, contained five major nationalities, was divided into six separate republics, and reflected cultural influences of the seven countries that surrounded it. Cultural conflict that plunged this nation into disorder at a catastrophic level shows that subcultures are a source not only of pleasing variety but also of tension and outright violence (Sekulic, Massey, & Hodson, 1994). Some individuals view the U.S. as a *melting pot*, where many nationalities and ethnic groups blend into a single American tradition.

Melting Pot

Melting pot can be defined as the traditional term for the assimilation of racial and ethnic elements in large urban centers.[6]

These traditional pursuits ring clearly with Western European belief systems. If the U.S. does not return to its previous pursuits, these advocates suggest we are destined to find ourselves in a state of anarchy. *E Pluribus Unum,* the Latin phase on the U.S. coin means: "out of many, one." Has the U.S. melted into one culture?

Taking a moment to reflect on what we know about our country, we see that many people maintain individuality while still associating with others, but those others tend to be from similar cultures as themselves. Could current affairs lead the U.S. to become another Yugoslavia?

? Something to Think About

In a pluralistic democratic society, the question arises: Whose perspective of public order will prevail?

In the press, on television, and in classrooms, we often hear the term *cultural diversity.* Despite the fact that each year diversity in the United States increases by almost one million people from other lands, the reality of this event seems to be poorly understood by Americans (Portes & Rumbaut, 1996). Today, a spirited

---

[6]This thought became popular in the successful drama, *The Melting Pot,* by Israel Zangwill, produced in 1908.

debate asks if English should be the only language spoken in our classrooms, and if historical Anglican traditions should be taught in American history courses (Orwin, 1996).

As you look around your city, your school or your hometown, exactly how well has the U.S. population melted? Early in American history, the English formed a majority of the elite that controlled a large chunk of U.S. wealth. And people of other backgrounds were advised to model themselves after "their betters," so that the "melting" was more accurately a process of Anglicization—adapting English culture and goals. This notion is alive today as evidenced by the media's coverage of the tragic death of Princess Diana. Other individuals who died had far less coverage in the news, including people who really made a difference in the lives of others such as Mother Teresa (who died a few days after Princess Diana). That is, culture when linked to Western European political beliefs is of crucial importance in the shape of many patterns of American social life, but can those patterns continue to control crime, reduce the fear of crime, and enhance the lifestyles of most people living in the U.S.?

Ethnocentrism

Simply understanding that more needs are met in a stable cooperative environment than in an unstable one, should give you insight into human behavior. Stable or fixed conditions might include both our physical and social environments as well as our cognitive or emotional condition. Stability can mean more than personal comfort and safety; it means predictability. That is, since stable environments or conditions are somewhat unchanging, it is easier to figure out what will happen next. Recall how you felt about your future when the World Trade Center was attacked? What were the many thoughts running through your mind about your family, yourself, and your country? If you were like most of us, you really weren't sure what would happen next. One way to understand culture is to realize that it conveys the feeling that it is a "naturally" shared lifestyle among a group of individuals.

What is meant by the term "naturally"? No single cultural trait is inherently "natural" to a group of individuals even though most people view their own way of life as being "best" or "normal." Given that a particular culture meets our needs in a number of ways, it also is the basis for our interpretation of reality. Therefore, it is not surprising that people everywhere exhibit an ethnocentrism.

Ethnocentrism

Ethnocentrism can be defined as judging another group or culture by one's own standards.

One problem of ethnocentrism is that it can generate misunderstandings and conflict, especially if individuals feel their standards are the only correct standards. For instance, when police personnel serve a culturally diverse community, whose standards of right and wrong prevail? Most of us rely on ethnocentric perspectives and practices when dealing with each other. Two points: (1) It is human or natural, if you will, to use our own ideas as being "best," and (2) We need to set aside our judgments when evaluating others.

Furthermore, although ethnocentrism is common and universal, it can be suppressed with *cultural relativism*, the belief that a culture must be understood on its own terms. By looking at cultures and people on their own terms, we can better understand their behavior. For instance, when a police agency and a culturally diverse community group are engaged in resolving serious neighborhood problems through problem-solving strategies, officers would produce greater cooperation with community members if they looked at the neighborhood problems through the eyes of the community.

Social Class in a Stratified Society

Social class is tied to the highbrow and lowbrow ideas. Whether you accept social class as relevant, it is a basic part of life in America and throughout the world. Each of us has an image of society. Each of us has thought about our place in our social world. Some of us think about it more often than others, and many of us see differences between where we are and where others are. These differences are properly called a hierarchical system. Good is up; bad is down. There might be a definite line separating people. And many of us see different people at different levels and for some reason, we envision those levels as being linked with social order. The lower the level, the less social order and of course, the higher the level, the more social order. We may see those above us and those below us in terms of class issues. One writer explains it this way: "It includes the necessity to place oneself in the social universe of reference" (Dahrendorf, 1959, p. 234). Therefore, *social stratification* can represent a system of social inequality based on hierarchical orderings of groups according to their members' share in socially valued rewards. These rewards vary from society to society, but usually consist of wealth, power, and status. Thus, in a community meeting, does this suggest that those with the most wealth, power, and status tend to be heard most often? And if those individuals are perceived as the police, it is a safe bet that few of the views of the community are earnestly discussed unless the police have received training in facilitative practices.[7]

Class plays a huge role in the ways in which we define ourselves and how others define us. It also might determine how we behave and how others behave toward us. That is, a different set of interactions, interventions, and/or access to various opportunities are linked to one's social class. In a final investigation, class is behavior (both expected and actual behavior). Social class—much like race,

[7]For a closer look see Dennis J. Stevens (2001). Community policing and managerial techniques: total quality management techniques. *The Police Journal*, 74(1), 26–41. And Dennis J. Stevens (2000, October). Improving community policing: Using managerial style and total quality management. *Law and Order*, 197–204.

gender, and ethnicity—plays a major role in defining power relations. Thus, it is a compelling framework for analysis.

Social Class

Social class is merely a category of people who have been grouped together on the basis of one or more common characteristics, which are viewed in an hierarchical stratified social structure.

Since traces of class exist worldwide, there are many common characteristics of social class that can be seen among, for instance, the highbrows of Sudan, Iran, and Cape Cod. Class is a force that unites individuals into groups who culturally differ from one another by overriding those cultural differences between them.

In one way, a social system with a pecking order aids public order and movement or mobility into other classes. Dennis Gilbert and Joseph A. Kahl (1987) argue the criterion of social class can include the following nine variables:

1. Occupation
2. Income
3. Wealth (net worth)
4. Personal prestige
5. Association (networks—who we know)
6. Socialization
7. Power (what we control)
8. Class consciousness
9. Mobility

Not everyone will readily accept these categories, and some individuals might offer sound arguments in other directions. For instance, income, associations, and personal prestige can define social strata but not class, Dahrendorf (1959) might argue. What about lifestyle or motivation? Certainly, the way we live or how motivated we are to pursue the good things in life should be part of a definition of class, and some of us believe they are. What about education? Although we can present arguments rejecting or adding to these ideas, they give us an opportunity to think in terms of a number of elements comprising social class as opposed to one or two components. Class criteria have to work together, too. For instance, making a lot of money as a truck driver might not qualify an individual for an upper-class position since occupation, wealth, and associations might be important components.

Karl Marx (1818–1883) argued that there were two social classes—owners of labor and labor—or expressed another way, the owners of capital and everybody else,[8] and that this disparity in property ownership produced conflict. Max Weber (1864–1920) agreed with Marx, but added, status or social prestige and power. For

---

[8]For more detail, see *The Marx-Engels Reader*. Edited by Robert C. Tucker. NY: W.W. Norton.

instance, a local official might wield considerable power yet have little wealth or social prestige. Weber's concern was to explain layers of society based on power, whereas Marx saw power only in the hands of those who owned the methods of production or factories.

Contemporary writers see three social classes: upper, middle, and lower class, and each of these three classes possess an upper, middle, and lower component: i.e., upper-middle class, middle-middle class, and lower-middle class. A class system in the United States is founded on two primary influences: birth and achievement. However, some see race as a factor in class issues, too. Birth suggests who your parents are, and achievement relates to people such as Michael Jordan, Madonna, and Bill Gates.

The United States is a stratified society, meaning it is layered and grounded in those layers are traditions, values, norms, expectations, and goals, or what can be called culture. It could be suggested that each class possesses a different culture.

Class impacts the criminal justice community in that there is evidence suggesting that class can be linked to police service, offender apprehension, and conviction sanctions. O.J. Simson's trial suggests that his class position might have been on trial more than the murder of his former wife and another individual. Also, where a person is located within the class structure might depend on the quality of police service he or she receives or doesn't receive. In one study, law-abiding individuals belonging to the lower class tend to see violence as an appropriate response when they are attacked due to a lack of quality police service (Stevens, 1998b). "The police don't protect me, so I protect myself," some of those individuals might say. One implication of this perspective is that American blacks kill American blacks at a higher ratio than American whites kill American whites (Stevens, 1998b). Can you think of some characteristics or values that might be specific to the middle class and some that might be more specific to the lower class? (Hint: Middle class, especially affluent upper middle class America is mobile; they move with the job. Therefore, their community roots and involvements might be different than people who don't move. What are the consequences for the community?)

Class and Crime

It isn't difficult to see the connection between American law, police service, and Western European cultural beliefs, norms, and values. Cultural beliefs justify and reinforce American stratification levels or social class. Beliefs—for example the idea the rich are smart and busy while the poor are stupid and lazy—are woven into cultural belief systems. On the other hand, the U.S. stratified society could well have a beneficial consequence for the operation of a specific culture. For instance, the greater the functional role of a job, the greater the rewards. Highly specialized positions, such as medical doctors, are generally better rewarded with power, income, professionalism, and status than a less specialized position such as a farmhand or car salesperson. It would follow that those individuals should receive a higher quality police service than others. People will work harder to get those rewards. Therefore, it could be said that only hard-working people will make it through medical school. This strategy promotes productivity, since rewarding important work in many ways encourages people to advance themselves and to work harder and better and longer than others.

? Something to Think About

Unequal rewards are one key to a more productive society.

The streets are stereotyped as beehives of crime. But the truth of the matter is that confidence men on Wall Street steal more money than all the youthful offenders breaking into businesses and homes. Financial cost of white collar and corporate crime is probably several times as great as the financial cost of all the crimes that are customarily regarded as the crime problem.[9] It is interesting that white-collar criminals are motivated by the same forces that drive street criminals: self interest, the pursuit of pleasure, and low self-control (Gottfredson & Hirschi, 1990; Schmalleger, 1999). There is a focus on street crime and notions of public disorder linked to lower-class individuals as opposed to other types of crime committed by the middle-class and upper-class Americans. In this analysis, crime can be identified by actions of the ruling or elite class who also define as criminal, activities that contravene the interests of the rulers. At the same time, members of the ruling class will inevitably be able to violate criminal law with impunity because it is their own creation (Chambliss, 1975; Schmalleger, 2000).

Because of differences in perception about certain aspects of reality, it is easy to misinterpret human behavior. For instance, African American speech patterns and Caucasian speech patterns are different. On observing a meeting between African American leaders and academic faculty representatives in Chicago, the two groups hardly understood one another's speech pattern. While the behavior of community leaders did not meet faculty requirements for rational discussion and the meeting was called a "Baptist revival meeting," or "pep rally," the faculty were considered lacking in sincerity, honest conviction, and were even viewed as sometimes devious (Kabagarama, 1997). Let's look at another example where class impacts both observations and outcomes. It is thought that Mexican drivers in Indiana demonstrate a lack of concern for others. That is, since Mexicans drive vehicles in need of mechanical work, some observers expressed, Mexicans are self-centered and don't care about Americans. Yet, after further investigation, many Mexicans would not get their cars fixed because they did not know how to

---

[9]For a closer look at corporate crime, see Schmalleger (1999) p. 396, who defines it as another form of white collar crime and a violation of a criminal statute either by a corporate entity or by its executives, employees, or agents acting on behalf of and for the benefit of the corporation, partnership, or other form of business entity. Corporate crimes come in many forms including product liability, price fixing, and inside trading. Culpability often results in civil suits along with criminal prosecutions is greatest when company officials can be shown to have had advance knowledge about product defects, dangerous conditions, or illegal behavior on the part of employees.

bargain with an American mechanic (Portes & Rumbaut, 1996). Clearly, depending on who is observing, the behavior of a group might be defined differently.

Just as the upper class needs the middle class as a buffer from the lower class, the middle class requires the maintenance of the lower class in order to survive. Consider the alternatives if there were but two classes in America. While it is true that America is a stratified society, a criticism about this perspective is expressed by John Adams:

> That all men are born to equal rights is true… but to teach that all men are born with equal power and faculties, to equal influence in society, to equal property and advantages through life is … gross fraud.

The fact of the matter is that many individuals do not have equal access to the avenues that can produce change and many of those individuals tend to be in the lower classes of American society. What does this have to do with police service? If the justice community is influenced by middle-class Western European influences, then criminal justice response is different for lower-class America than middle- and upper-class America. It is possible that some police agencies are guided into the belief that lower-class lifestyles tend to have less social order than other classes, especially if there are many "broken windows" in the neighborhood.

Criticism of Class

A criticism of social class is that it overlooks many ways in which equality in modern America has increased and it underestimates comfort levels and choices made by many people through capitalist expansion. Also, social-class thinking tends to disregard what appears to be at least a fair degree of public consensus about the nature of crime. That is, crime is undesirable and criminal activity must be controlled (Schmalleger, 1999).

Another criticism about class is that there are events that seem to be changing the definition of class and the definition of culture. While this chapter is not compelled to come to grips with this criticism, it must in all fairness be offered so that others can measure it in a suitable way. University professors (including this writer) who educate foreign students are increasingly aware that those students are individuals of a "time" rather than a "place." In other words, young educated urbanized American men and women are likely to have more in common with young Japanese educated men from Tokyo or young Turkish educated women from Istanbul than with their own grandparents.[10] Even among American foreign students where another language is spoken routinely in their homes, these individuals seem to conform to home rules while keeping their identity with global social class rules. For instance, Latino American students, now proudly asserting their once-precarious position on the borderlands, refuse to choose among identities or languages (De Coutivron, 2000). The pop culture, per se, is moving from a vertical to a horizontal experience and part of that movement is powered

---

[10]For a complete look at this perspective see De Courtivron, 2000.

through advanced education. So, whatever changes have happened in the last two millennia, there appears to be a boundary or division between those who have an abundance of material and nonmaterial amenities and those who don't. And those with it are above and those without it are still below, and it remains a force in the minds of many people.[11] Evidently class does exist, and it has worldwide implications.

Population Changes

The United States has experienced a 13 percent increase in population between 1990 to 2000: from 248,709,873 to 281,421,906 (U.S. Census, 2001). More people, yes, but culturally different people, too, since the growth of the U.S. population included birth rates (minus death rates) and new arrivals into the United States from other countries. The highest percentage of those new arrivals did not come from countries where new arrivals typically came from in the past.[12] One way to explain the primary difference in the new arrival trend is that people from countries such as Asia, South America, Africa, and Eastern Europe are arriving in the United States daily. That is, many new arrivals are from what we would typically consider to be non-white populations. In Massachusetts, for example, one estimate places the foreign-born population at every two of ten of the Commonwealth's population (as of 2000).[13] We can easily see that these different populations have an effect upon each other and upon the people that lived in Massachusetts prior to their arrival. Consequently, culture has changed too.

Immigration

One way to look at immigration is to consider that with the growing international power and prominence of the United States, the laws governing immigration became tools of foreign policy. The conflicts around the world including those the United States engaged in, such as in southeast Asia, created whole new categories of immigrants, which can be referred to as political refugees. The dynamic transformation in the economies of the United States and the rest of the world, along with the fall or instability of many nations, has dramatically increased immigration to the United States.

---

[11]See Dahrendorf (1959) p. 287 to get a closer look at this idea.

[12]The nation's resident population on Census Day, April 1, 2000 was 281,421,906, a 13 percent increase over the 248,709,873 counted in the 1990 census (U.S. Census, 2001). Hispanic or Latino population represented 12.5 percent of the American population or 35,306,818 while Blacks or African Americans represented 12.3 percent or 34,658,190. Also, Asians represented 3.6 percent of the American population with a total of 10,242,998. Source: U.S. Census Bureau (2001): http://www.census. gov/prod/2001pubs/cenbr01-1.pdf.

[13]For a closer look see the Office of Refugee and Immigrant Health, The Bureau of Family and Community Health, and the Massachusetts Department of Public Health. Refugees and Immigrants. June 2000.

As we look back to the 1920s, policymakers opened American shores to people from Western Europe more often than to people from other parts of the world. However, labor and agriculture required a new flow of workers and America welcomed Canadian and Mexican immigrants who became the two largest national immigrant groups. Some 1.4 million Canadians and almost 1 million Mexicans arrived in the United States between 1920 and 1960. The Refugee Relief Act of 1953 authorized admission of 205,000 "nonquota" refugees, but limited this to people fleeing persecution from the Communist regimes, especially the Baltic states.

The Immigration Act of 1965 had revolutionary consequences since it abolished the discriminatory quotas that had been in place for many years. But it also limited immigration from the western hemisphere (Canada and Mexico) resulting in the arrest and deportation of over 500,000 illegal aliens each year. After 1965, Asian immigrants made up the fastest growing ethnic groups with more than 1.5 million arriving during the 1970s as opposed to 800,000 from Europe. Asian immigration included many professionals and well-educated technical workers. For instance, immigrants from the Philippines and India included a high number of healthcare professionals: many Chinese and Korean immigrants found work in professional and management occupations. Low-skilled and impoverished Asians poured into the Chinatowns and Koreatowns of cities like Boston, New York City, and Los Angeles and worked in restaurants, hotels, and garment manufacturing. With the end of the war in Southeast Asia, refugees from Cambodia, Laos, and Vietnam arrived.

During the 1980s, an estimated six million legal and two million undocumented immigrants entered the United States. By 1990, one out of every five immigrants was Mexican-born and Mexican Americans accounted for more than 60 percent of all Latino Americans. Today, Latino Americans are the largest minority group in America.

In March of 1997, the U.S. Census reported that:

- Foreign-born population numbered almost 26 million persons or close to 10 percent of the total American population.
- Five states had a larger percentage of foreign-born than other states: California (25 percent), New York (20 percent) Florida (16 percent), New Jersey (15 percent), and Texas (11 percent).
- Persons born in Central America, South America, or the Caribbean accounted for 51 percent of the total foreign-born population (13 million).
- About 27 percent of the foreign-born were from Asia and 17 percent from Europe.
- Seven million persons or 27 percent of the foreign-born were born in Mexico.
- Approximately 35 percent of the foreign-born were naturalized citizens and about 65 percent were not citizens.
- About one-quarter of the both native-born and foreign-born populations aged 25 years and over had completed four or more years of college.
- Poverty rate among foreign-born naturalized citizens was 27 percent as compared to 13 percent among native-born citizens.

The United States is home to more immigrants than any other country on earth. Recent government statistics shows that the cities with the highest percentage of foreign-born residents are Miami with 34 percent, Los Angeles with 27 percent, San Francisco and New York with 20 percent. States such as the Commonwealth of Massachusetts have a large number of immigrants and refugees and Table 3-1 demonstrates that many of these individuals are from non-white non-European origins.

When we take into account racial and ethnic variation of the American population, today's cities display highly visible racial and ethnic diversity that is increasing. Why do so many people migrate to U.S. cities? Marginality and freedom were perceived as the answers by Robert Park (1928). Park portrayed the immigrant as a personality type, a hybrid on the margin of two worlds—a stranger belonging to neither world. He believed that colliding cultures met and fused, resulting in liberation of the person from the shackles of tradition and the expansion of individual initiatives. Periods of high immigration are invariably marked by a tide of "naturist resistance" that characterized the waves of newcomers as a threat to the integrity of national culture and a source of decay of the qualities of the native population" (Portes & Rumbaut, 1996, p. 269). Such pronouncements were issued by crusading journalists, insecure politicians, inexperienced academics, and uninformed police commanders who cloaked their lack of knowledge and bias in the grab of scientific knowledge.

When some of us think about immigration, there is a perception that many countries suffer from desperate poverty, squalor, and unemployment. Some of those points have merit, but in an attempt to stay focused, a brief narration about people coming to the United States would shed some light on another important point concerning this topic.

In addition to desperate poverty in the 1990s, the world witnessed severe deterioration in the general observance of the principles of international humanitarian law, which protects non-combatants from attack and abuse by those who wish to gain power. Some of these manifestations included deliberate targeting of civilian populations, the use of famine as a weapon, appropriation of relief supplies intended for non-combatants, ethnic cleansing, and genocide (Newland, 2000). While none of these tactics are new, they have intensified. In addition to attacks on civilians, they have come to include a marked erosion of the respect accorded to humanitarian actors, seen in an increasing incidence of attacks on humanitarian facilities and personnel. Humanitarian interventions aimed at reversing the refugee flow of earlier years were hardly effective. Therefore, running to the United States and elsewhere is seen as a prudent step for many individuals.[14]

[14]Lessons learned through earlier crises by NATO and others about the expense and occasional perverse consequences of militarized humanitarian efforts that delivered assistance were without effective protection for civilians. After the Bosnian experience, the international community decided not to get into the business of creating "well-fed dead" in Kosovo. Instead, the NATO powers initiated a military action against the government responsible for creating the humanitarian crisis. This action was neither preventive nor palliative, and was punitive in nature. For more information see Newland (2000).

TABLE 3-1   *Refugees and Immigrants in Massachusetts and the U.S.A*

Country	1990 Census U.S./Ancestry	1990/Census MA/Ancestry	2000/Est Boston/MA	Primary Language
Albanian	47,710	7,710	33,000	Albanian
Bosnian	N/A	N/A	9,000	Bosnian, gypsy
Brazilian	65,876	7,483	170,000	Portuguese
Cape Verdean	50,771	29,326	70,000	Crioulo
Central American				
El Salvador	499,153	7,835	N/A	Spanish (but
Guatemala	241,559	5,866	N/A	there are
Honduras	116,635	3,155	N/A	numerous
Nicaragua	177,077	591	N/A	dialects)
Total	1,034,244	17,447	85,000	
Chinese	1,505,245	47,245	N/A	Seven major
Cantonese	25,020	952	N/A	Chinese dialects,
Taiwanese	192,973	4,401	N/A	Mandarin
Total	1,723,238	52,598	75,000	
Colombian	351,717	3,869	27,500	Spanish
Congolese	N/A	N/A	2,000	Kikongo, Swahili
Dominican	505,690	29,065	35,000	Spanish
Eritrean	N/A	N/A	2,000	Tigrigna, Arabic
Ethiopian	30,581	864	11,500	Amharic, Tigrinya
Haitian	289,521	23,692	75,000	French, Creole
Indian	815,447	19,719	N/A	Hindi
Korean	836,987	12,878	25,000	Korean
Portuguese Azores, Madeira, Portugal, & Macao	1,153,351	289,424	530,000	Portuguese
Somali	N/A	N/A	5,000	Oromiffa, Arabic
Southeastern Asian				
Cambodia	134,955	11,821	38,000	Khmer
Laos	146,930	3,953	8,000	Lao
Vietnam	535,825	13,101	45,000	Vietnamese
Total	817,710	28,875	91,000	
Former Soviet Union				
Belorus	4,277	99	N/A	Belorussian
Estonia	26,718	977	N/A	Estonian
Latvia	100,331	6,479	N/A	Latvian
Lithuania	811,865	68,447	N/A	Lithuanian
Russia	2,952,987	133,080	N/A	Russian
Ukrainia	740,803	17,500	N/A	Ukrainian
Total	4,644,710	227,095	72,000	
TOTALS	11,531,106	750,045	1,318,000	

Source: The Office of Refugee and Immigrant Health, The Bureau of Family and Community Health, and the Massachusetts Department of Public Health. Refugees and Immigrants. June 2000.

The fact is that the poorest countries of the world are referred to as *developing countries*; these developing countries will stay poor for our lifetimes and for several generations to come (Portes & Rumbaut, 1996). Unfortunately, there is little that can be done to alter this fact. However, immigrants do not necessarily come to the United States to escape perennial poverty or unemployment in their homeland. Instead many come to attain the dream of a new lifestyle that is impossible to fulfill in their countries. Immigrants are likely to be highly motivated individuals who desire more opportunities in their lives and are willing to learn, work, and labor to achieve the American dream. In the university classrooms, many professors experience examples of highly motivated foreign students who tend to work as hard, if not harder, than American-born students.

The very poor and the unemployed seldom migrate to the United States either legally or illegally. Many immigrants tend to have above average levels of education and occupational skills in comparison with their homeland populations. For instance, Mexico is source of 90 percent of unauthorized aliens in the past two decades for the United States. But socioeconomic origins of most immigrants are modest by U.S. standards. They consistently meet or surpass the average for the Mexican population (Portes & Rumbaut, 1996). Additionally, during the last two decades, immigrant professionals represented around 33 percent of the total, at a time when professionals and managers ranged between 17–27 percent of the American labor force. In 1990, 20 percent of native-born Americans completed college as did 20 percent of immigrants in the U.S.. Therefore, the average individual who tends to leave his or her homeland for another country is not a typical individual. It appears that many immigrants have high life aspirations and expectations and earn the means to fulfill them.

The role of race as an obstacle to full assimilation and participation is of obvious concern since almost one-half of all legal immigrants over the past decade have been Asians: Chinese, Filipino, Indian, Korean, Vietnamese, and Kampucheans (Cambodians) and slightly more than one-third have been from Latin America. Although nine out of ten people of Latino American ethnicity are allegedly "white," there is no doubt about the discrimination they face as a result of their ancestry. Fewer than 12 percent of the new immigrants arriving in the United States are Western Europeans.

The concern is that new arrivals tend to move to places where earlier immigrants have become established. And later generations tend not to wander too far off. As we look at American cities and the countryside, cultural diversity is very much alive. In a democratic society, all of us must be equally represented and protected by government, which includes police services. One idea that keeps rearing its head is that depending on who is observing, a group is considered normal or abnormal, criminal or law-abiding. The point is that social order might mean something different to different groups, and if a group believes that certain behavioral patterns are valued more than others, then the chances of that behavior continuing is more likely. If the police believe that immigrants are lazy, stupid, and useless, they might continue to place them under surveillance and/or arrest them more often than other Americans.

Poverty

"White" America numerically represents the largest group of people in poverty and therefore, there are more whites in the lower-lower class of America than any other racial group. By some accounts, there are approximately thirty-five million people in the United States living at or below poverty levels (U.S. Census, 2000). Furthermore:

- Almost 16 million (46 percent) are white or 9 percent of the total white population.
- Nine million (26 percent) are African American or 27 percent of the total African American population.
- Eight million (22 percent) are Latinow or 27 percent of the total Latino population.[15]
- One million are Asian Americans.

As these estimates suggest, among those who are poor, African Americans and Spanish Americans represent a higher percentage when compared to their overall population than whites or Asian Americans. Combined, these groups represent approximately 27 percent of the American population, but almost one-half of all those living in poverty are African American and/or Spanish American.

Poverty is generally characterized by a lack of employment opportunities for adults and often a lack of parental (economic) care for children. Clearly, African Americans have higher unemployment rates than whites; however, in spite of a very positive economic context, "Latino workers continue to have the highest unemployment rates and the worst labor market outcomes of any group" (Bowen & Green, 2001). Language barriers, skill gaps, educational achievement, and a general misconception of Spanish American issues might account for the high unemployment rate among this group in the United States. Although poverty is an important issue, let's look at part of this idea in reverse. That is, opportunities and employment are influenced by class and "color." Therefore, it could be argued that largely, a member of white middle-class America, especially males, might have more opportunities for advancement than others. The odds increase if that white male is linked to the dominant class. Then, too, many of us are inclined to mistake poverty for social disorder and with disorder comes the criminal label. That is, through the labeling process, a group of individuals can become criminals. There exists compelling evidence that poor people regardless

---

[15] This paper uses Latino and Hispanic interchangeably. The meaning of each term differs. The U.S. Census used the term Hispanic from 1970 through 1990. In 2000 the U.S. Census utilized Latino/Hispanic suggesting a paradigm shift between the old Hispanic to the newer Latino. Generally, Hispanic is used by social scientists. Latino is the current term used by the arts, media, academia, and politics. Like other identities, Latino and Hispanic are social constructions. Hispanic has been associated by some in the literature as a colonizing term that tries to extend the influence and heritage of Spain in the Americas without a critical understanding of the contributions of the peoples of Africa and the native populations in the Americas. Most Latinos prefer their national identity and utilize Latino as a situational identity.

of their color or their culture can be dehumanized. Consequently, as history suggests, incarceration of these criminals, and/or their elimination on gallows or in death camps is meritorious. Thus, the criminalization of poverty is a rationale that promotes the control of the poor through any means necessary.

Eurocentrism

It is clear that many Americans pattern United States history with England and others of European ancestry. When most of us think about the dominant social class in America, we tend to link class with the British. Somehow, social refinement and "arriving" socially in America is linked to Anglo or English ideals. In fact, historical events and British values and goals are highly regarded, reducing the attention to the historical accounts, values, and goals of others. Herein, lies some of the puzzle.

Eurocentrism

Eurocentrism can be defined as the dominance of European, especially Anglo, cultural patterns in the criminal justice community and the United States.

It should be noted that although Eurocentric ideals might have served the United States well in the past, the future of the United States is clearly in the hands of individuals who represent other cultures and ideals, but clearly remain in middle-class hands.

Sometimes it is as though other people and their cultures including their hopes, prayers, and decisions are invisible. Molefi Kete Asante, an advocate of multiculturalism, argues that, "the fifteenth-century Europeans who could not cease believing that the earth was the center of the universe, many today find it difficult to cease viewing European culture as the center of the social universe." (1988, p.7). Defining the world from a multicultural perspective is different than the way it was defined by European immigrants (Macionis, 2000). Heavy immigration has made the United States the most multicultural of all industrial nations in the world. Yet, has police service advanced enough to care for their constituents or are they still an occupational army defending the interests of dominant Anglo elite classes of the United States? As one community member remarked, "The history books say Britain was an enemy of America at one time and lost the war with us. But, I guess they figured out how to lose but win."

Summary

We briefly discussed social influences that affect behavior of individuals and groups of people. We examined culture, described social class, and described population and immigration changes. We discussed poverty and offered a perspective, referred to as the criminalization of poverty. There was also a description of the most dominant set of values in America, referred to as Eurocentrism.

We looked at the idea that Eurocentrism impacts justice service response and American life more than any other cultural perspective. As a result, many groups of American residents are ignored or victimized by the criminal justice community. There was concern that the "melting pot" perspective linked to diversity perspectives has not necessarily taken place, but cultural pluralism is alive and well in American society.

Do You Know?

1. What is the central theme of this chapter and how has the writer made the point that these specific issues impact police strategy?
2. Why do you think the author wanted you to use your own experiences and knowledge to aid in understanding this chapter?
3. In what way do your beliefs, opportunities, limitations, and expectations shape life outcomes? And in what way do culture and class influence those outcomes? Give a couple of specific examples.
4. Define culture in your own words. Identify several material and nonmaterial cultural elements in your own culture that might be less visible or nonexistent in another culture. Why?
5. Define instincts and describe the differences between instincts and culture. In your opinion, what do you see as the primary difference between instincts and culture?
6. Describe what is meant by McDonaldization. In what way do you think McDonaldization influences world culture and in what way might it not impact it?
7. Characterize cultural pluralism in the United States and explain how this dynamic affects police-community relations. Give specific examples.

8. Characterize the dynamics of the melting pot perspective and explain why you think this perspective tends not to describe the American society.
9. Define ethnocentrism and give an example of an ethnocentric group. In what way can the police department be ethnocentric?
10. Define social class and explain how social class impacts outcomes of police-community relations especially as they apply to problem-solving strategies.
11. Identify several primary reasons why many people immigrate to the United States. Why do you agree/disagree with those reasons?
12. Identify the major shifts in the American population from the 1990 to the 2000 census. How would these population shifts impact city services?
13. Define Eurocentrism and explain its relevance to policing and American society. In what way can Eurocentrism impact police-community relations?
14. John F. Kennedy said, "If a free society cannot help the many who are poor, it cannot save the few who are rich." How does his quote relate to this chapter?

4

Cities, Neighborhoods, and Communities

"The worth of the state, in the long run, is the worth of the individuals composing it."

John Stuart Mill

Key Terms

City   Gesellschaft Lifestyles
Community   Neighborhoods
Gemeinschaft Lifestyles

Key Topics

- Environmental influences that affect behavior and police response.
- Development and changes in American cities.
- How neighborhoods and community organization affect policing.

Cities

Where you live has an impact on your behavior and your life chances. Most Americans live in cities. Some are born in cities and some move there for a variety of reasons including employment and quality of life issues. Others have relatives or friends who migrated to the city and they want to live near people they are comfortable with.

Development and Change in American Cities

In 1900, cities were home to approximately 9 percent of the world's population. A century later, one-half of the world's population live in cities. The city is the setting for all aspects of the human drama (Macionis & Parrillo, 1998).

City

An American city can be described as an incorporated urban center in the United States that has self-government, boundaries, and legal rights established by state charter.[1]

The inhabitants in cities may be characterized as the best-educated individuals colliding with the most ignorant, unimaginable wealth adjacent to degrading poverty. Recently, there has been a movement from the industrial northern and eastern American cities to Sunbelt cities. The population in Chicago and Boston, for example, has declined. There has also been a movement from large cities to small cities. However, just as affluent people moved from central cities to the suburbs, they are now moving even farther away. Business and industry also responded to the complexity of the city by relocating to avoid high taxation, city regulation, congestion, outmoded plants, high union wages, and excessive heating costs.

[1]Why is this description important? Because cities in other countries are described differently. For instance, a large town in Britain that has received the title of city from the Crown. It is usually the seat of a bishop, and so often has a cathedral. *Source:* Encarta Dictionary. http://dictionary.msn.com

Cities with declining populations and business and industry lose federal funding and political representation, resulting in city budget cuts impacting services and aid to the poor and elderly. Inner suburbs also begin to deteriorate. Additionally, because of lost revenues, city services are directly affected, which can include police protection and street repair.

American inner cities are left with residents who cannot move due to their personal resources and consequently inner cities often attract immigrants and other individuals who lack the resources to live elsewhere. Job opportunities, urban services, infrastructure, facilities, and police service are not sufficient to serve the population growth of poor people. In anthropological terms, poverty and urbanization outpace industrialization and the creation of adequate urban institutions, resulting in *over-urbanization* or *hyper-urbanization* (Perlman, 1976). Urban poverty can impact both quality and quantity of police service and more "broken windows" are visible. Some of the indicators of urban poverty include streets, sidewalks, and yards bustling with trash; abandoned vehicles and burned out buildings; graffiti, and, of course, broken windows everywhere.[2]

Many people continue to perceive the phenomenon of urban overpopulation—especially if newcomers have migrated there from other countries—as essentially a problem of crime and an attack on middle class, European values. Some people link migration with lower mortality rates. That is, in cities with rapid growth, mortality levels supposedly decline, but birth rates remain constant. However, this growth in many ways is a natural process of expansion for all cities, as suggested by Janice Perlman (1976) in her study of Rio de Janeiro, over thirty years ago. Also, overpopulation usually leads to population density and it is that density (how many people live in a square mile) that many writers connect to crime.

While many American cities might suffer from the pains of disparity, a young professional class of people is refurbishing sections of cities such as Washington, DC, Chicago, Boston, and Los Angeles. These cities are experiencing a renaissance of sorts.

Early Studies of Cities

Scholars including Maine, Morgan, Tonnies, Durkheim, Simmel, and others contrasted status-oriented, face-to-face relationships in villages with the depersonalized, formalized ones characteristic of today's cities. In earlier (smaller) communities, individuals were placed in the "same conditions of existence" (Durkheim, 1984, 1933, p.229). Although each individual was different, his or her relationship to everything in that environment was shaped similarly and therefore, that particular society or community possessed a *collective consciousness*. Each individual accepted and reinforced similar goals, values, norms, and other beliefs of their common social environment. Think of a rural small town and the interactions that can be observed there.

---

[2]One expectation of the broken-window perspective of Wilson and Kelling is that poverty leads to criminal activity. Furthermore, families in poor neighborhoods, many inaccurately believe, lack love, respect, and motivation to advance.

Gemeinschaft and Gesellschaft Lifestyles

As community feelings or "consciousness" become abstract and vague because society grows more immense and by today's standards more diverse, individuals' links to each other change. People lose the previously accepted societal belief systems, which they substitute for their own. Ferdinand Tonnies' (1855–1936) explanation of *Gemeinschaft* and *Gesellschaft* offers a perspective of the related issues.

Gemeinschaft Lifestyles

Gemeinschaft lifestyles are characterized by kinship and tradition.

Gemeinschaft societies consist of social relationships that are centered on personal ties of friendship and kinship, face-to-face experiences. Everyone knows everyone else and everyone else's business. Personal interactions are frequent and intense. People tend to be family- and community-oriented. Similar experiences and expectations include values, goals, attitudes, and behavioral patterns. People comply with public sentiment, and they respect each other. We could call this type of community *homogeneous* since culture, living experiences, and relationships are more similar than dissimilar. Accordingly, there isn't a need for anyone to formally control behavior since face-to-face intervention among family members and a concerned population is a continual experience. Think of it this way. Reliable supervision of children leaves children fewer options to be victimized, and reliable supervision also provides fewer opportunities for children to engage in deviant or criminal behavior. In a Gemeinschaft lifestyle all families are caretakers for everyone's youngsters and when immediate family members are not present, other community members accept responsibility for those children. Equally important, children accept the authority of all community members. Of course, a Gemeinschaft lifestyle might exist in some form today, but not necessarily in the modern city. It may exist informally in some communities. A Gemeinschaft lifestyle promotes face-to-face interaction and promotes community responsibility toward collective behavior.

Gesellschaft Lifestyles

Gesellschaft lifestyles can be described as self-interest.

On the other hand, Gesellschaft is a type of society in which social relationships are formal, contractual, impersonal, and specialized. Laws must be written and documents are more important than a person's word. Neighbors might not know neighbors, and life is centered on individual versus community goals. Personal interactions are limited in number and often quite impersonal. The differences between Gemeinschaft and Gesellschaft lifestyles is that generally speaking, in Gemeinschaft societies, most members know one another and interact frequently, and they accept responsibility for each other. Modern urban living, with its emphasis on privacy and individuality, typifies Gesellschaft lifestyles.

Early Perceptions of City Dwellers

Tonnies' ideas can be found in the work of Louis Wirth (1933) who held that by the very nature of segmented roles of city dwellers and their secondary relationships with others, city people act out their roles as opposed to being in a role. When individuals interact with others, they are not involved with the whole person, only the role a person is playing.

Formal mechanisms are more important in the city than informal ones. Because relationships aren't as often face-to-face, this complicates the class structure within the city, resulting in impersonal and transitory contacts between people, which leads to immunization of self against others (Perlman, 1969). Kinship ties weaken, neighborhood solidarity wanes, and mental breakdown, delinquency, and crime of all sorts results (Perlman, 1969). Wirth's overall image of city dwellers is depicted as a mass of nameless people, separated from their neighbors and relating to others primarily in superficial weak relationships. An end result can be a social condition referred to as *anomie*: people cannot agree on a common course or appropriate behavior. Agreement is lost, much like a boat without a rudder. Under these conditions, police officers must take the role of enforcers as opposed to proactive community partners, since individuals are unlikely to follow any direction unless it satisfies their own self-interest. German theorist Georg Simmel (1905, 1964) argued that many city dwellers are faced with psychotic episodes or the inability to handle all the sensory and auditory information that constantly bombards them.

As city people are characterized, they would tend to be oriented toward individual objectives rather than group goals. However, individuality in American society is the centerpiece of the American spirit. Some might say that a degree of selfishness comes into play, and therefore, it would follow that in cities, the likelihood of community unity might not be as easily developed as in a rural community. It could be argued that people with too many individual rights become selfish.

Too Many Rights

A French nobleman, who was also an astute political scientist, reinforces the thought that Americans have too many rights and look inward to fulfill their goals. Alexis de Tocqueville[3] visited the United States in 1831 and reported on democracy. His thoughts seem to continue to chime in the minds of many who wonder about selfishness and "too many rights of Americans." City life and individualism and selfishness seem to be related variables, which among other things, can lead to crime.

This implication is characterized by de Tocqueville's statement, "In democratic times.... when the duties of each individual… are much more clear, devoted service to any one man becomes more rare; the bond of human affection is extended, but it is relaxed" (Heffner, 1953, p. 193). de Tocqueville's implication is

---

[3]Richard D. Heffner (1956). *Democracy in America: Alexis de Tocqueville.* NY: Mentor Books, pp.192–195.

clear: individualism in a democratic society produced selfishness. His words were echoed by some of the individuals who were surveyed and interviewed for this textbook. For instance, a police officer in Alexandria, Virginia said that one way to control the crime in his jurisdiction, "was to stop and search people at the Virginia border. Americans have too many rights," the officer adds. Thus, the ills of city life in America have to do with too many rights, and in cities where those rights are encouraged through Gesellschaft or urban lifestyles, individual rights encourage selfishness, which can lead to crime.

Cities and Social Unity

On the other hand, many writers found more social unity and community structure in cities than suggested by Wirth's analysis. For example, a study of two Los Angeles neighborhoods reported one-half of the residents in the study visited relatives at least once a week (Greer, 1956). Herbert Gans' study, called *The Urban Villagers*, showed how rural Italians adapted to life in Boston and it implied that many of the participants maintained their former social structure in the new environment. This practice provided immigrants with a sense of identity and preserved their bonds with other Italian Americans. Other classic sociological studies have identified strong feelings of community in several lower- and working-class neighborhoods in Chicago (Hunter, 1974; Suttles, 1968). Even contemporary writers argue that cities such as Chicago are honeycombed with block clubs, civic associations, social action groups, and churches with a strong commitment toward the community (Skogan, 1991). Chicago chose a community policing program with much public involvement, in large part because city unity was already present. Also, the energy from that unity could be harnessed in a new program. One assumption Skogan operated from was more right than wrong: most cities possess various levels of unity through numerous organizations and networks, yet, police policymakers want to start their own community networks because they see community unity as competition (Ramsey, 2002). In fact, what seems to be neglected by policymakers and police commanders are democratic practices in those newly formed meetings. These findings are consistent with results from the 2010 participants surveyed.[4]

? Something to Think About

One reason for the lack of attention toward existing community groups by policymakers and police executives is that those individuals continue to use the Western European mind to define the rest of the world.

Wirth's view of urbanism developed into an alternative interpretation called the *compositional perspective* (Fischer, 1984). This view explains the special qualities of urban life as the result of the distinctive social and cultural traits of the kinds

---

[4]The 76 individuals interviewed said they never attended community meetings.

of people who live in the city. Those who accept the compositional perspective see the city as a mosaic of social worlds made up of different groups, each of which shares factors such as kinship, ethnic origins, and/or social class (Fischer, 1984). Yet, it should be stressed that a "mosaic" does not necessarily refer to a "melting pot" concept, an idea discussed in the previous chapter.

In contrast to Wirth and his followers, these opponents deny that cities weaken social solidarity. For example, when immigrants from other countries settled in large cities, they normally developed and maintained strong social ties with one another. These bonds helped to insulate them from the pressures of city life.

Subcultural Perspective

Claude Fischer (1984) proposes that an urban subculture exists. Fischer agrees with Wirth that the physical and social realities of urban life—size, density, and the mixing of people from diverse backgrounds—do affect the structure and strength of social groups. But, in contrast to Wirth, and more in accord with the compositional perspective, he argues that urban life does not destroy the unity of subgroups but rather strengthens them and increases their importance. In fact, urban life actually creates subcultures that might not exist otherwise, because it brings together people with common backgrounds and interests. In Salt Lake City or Charlotte, for example, it might be more possible to form a group of left-handed tuba players than it would be in a small town. Unfortunately, the same holds true for left-handed drug dealers and car thieves.

Urban Social Relationships

There is also some evidence that urban social relationships are more "privatized" among neighbors and that they are less frequent and less positive. Consequently urban dwellers are substantially less helpful and considerate to strangers. In this tradition, Robert Redfield (1959) defines a folk urban continuum moving from the small, isolated, homogeneous, collectively-based rural village to the large, central, heterogeneous, socially disorganized city.

What exactly is the urban way of life and why is it important in a community policing context? Understanding urbanism and the cultural and social patterns of a city, and how a city might differ from a small town environment might bring a clearer perspective about delivering quality police service in a community.

Urbanites apparently have at least as many friends and acquaintances as rural people. In the United States, people who live in more populous places tend to be less content with their environments, but most indicators of mental health and psychological stress are not very different in urban and non-urban settings.

Furthermore, we could use network analysis to re-examine some long-standing issues, such as Wirth's perspective on urbanism. If a social network consists of all the relationships, formal and informal, that one person has with others, we might come away with an understanding that communities are really social networks, and therefore we do not have to think of them as neighborhood-based. That is, groups of people can participate in strong, cohesive social networks even if their members are scattered around a city. What matters is the strength and number of the interpersonal ties and common goals among the members. Using this perspective, network analysts have argued that local urban communities are well adapted to the geographical mobility that is typical of modern life (Wellman, 1988). Therefore, communities can develop, direct, and/or provide many of the solutions necessary to enhance their individual life experiences, reduce the fear of crime, and curb criminal activities in their community.

Neighborhood

It is easy to confuse the concept of *neighborhood* with *community*. A neighborhood is an imprecise consensus on its location by those individuals who live there (Williams, 1985). Sampson and Bartusch (1999) suggest that a neighborhood is "a collective efficacy." This efficacy can be seen when neighbors develop a trust in each other and a willingness to intervene for the common good. Certainly, there are homogeneous (similar) characteristics such as race, ethnicity, and/or socio-economic status that can be part of this definition, but these characteristics can and do vary. According to Milton Kotler (1969):

> The most sensible way to locate the neighborhood is to ask people where it is, for people spend much time fixing its boundaries. Gangs mark its turf. Old people watch for its new faces. Children figure out safe routes between home and school. People walk their dogs through their neighborhood, but rarely beyond it. Above all the neighborhood has a name: Hyde Park, or Lake View in Chicago; Roxbury, Jamaica Plain, or Beacon Hill in Boston.[5]

Sure, there are physical characteristics of a neighborhood that are generally identifiable, such as rivers, bridges, flatland, hills, and expressways. There are centers such as parks, shopping malls, schools, historical sites, and entertainment attractions. Neighborhoods are usually both geographically precise and formally defined by local government for the purpose of providing public services such as levying taxes, police service, and educational benefits. Neighborhoods have boundaries that are officially recognizable. Yet, with trust in your neighbors and a collective willingness to intervene in both the troubles and the celebrations of the neighborhood, doesn't it appear that something stronger exists between those members?

Community

If neighborhoods have easily identifiable boundaries, for the most part, we can say that they are generally geographically defined. In other words, what *it is*. On the other hand, what a neighborhood should be, might be one way of under-

[5]For a closer look at this perspective, see Milton Kotler. (1969, pp. 64–65). Neighborhood government: The local foundations of political life. Indianapolis: Bobbs-Merrill.

standing the concept of community. That is, what it *ought to become*. Geography may or may not play a role in defining a community because a community is more a state of mind than a specific area. Therefore, a neighborhood is often a place where individuals can find community. One way to explain neighborhood movements or trends is to see that they are usually conscious attempts by the people living in a specific location to build and preserve a community.

? *Something to Think About*

People live in a neighborhood, but it is through community that they organize to fulfill needs.

It can be explained this way: trust in your neighbors and a collective willingness to intervene in the troubles and celebrations of the neighborhood.

For many of us, our behavior can be characterized as largely social. A continuing goal of humans is to seek and encourage other individuals to be part of our social world. Beyond other goals of food, shelter, and safety, we want and most of us need, a sense of stability and belonging in our world. What we want is community. Community can mean that we think others care what happens to us, and that we depend on people around us for personal comfort. Since human behavior is driven primarily by goals guided by our cultural influences, most of us want community life. Trusting others and having them trust us is vital to our sense of belonging. Then, too, having individuals intervene in our affairs at appropriate levels adds to that trust. For example, in a community parents keep a watchful eye and guide their children and other children who live in their neighborhood, safeguarding them against accidents and predators. This definition of community is consistent with Trojanowicz and Dixon (1974) who imply that community can be defined as a group of people who experience similar lifestyles, share similar goals, and live in a specific geographical area for the purpose of enhancing their lifestyle and the lifestyle experiences of others.

One common misunderstanding with this definition is that we might emphasize biological characteristics instead of social characteristics. Some of us find community in a city, and others find the opposite in the city—alienation—a sense of not belonging and a feeling that no one cares.

Community satisfies human functions and fulfills social goals. For the purpose of this chapter, it is relevant that we recognize several elements common to many communities:

- An aggregation of people with similar living conditions
- Shared interests, values, and goals
- Similar culture, lifestyle, language, and attitudes
- A degree of social interaction resulting from living in close proximity
- Agreement on methods of social control
- Similar leadership ideals
- A sense of belonging, a "we" identity

Ideally, a community shares many of the components that are recognizable in what can be referred to a *social group*. Productive community groups are people who share many common characteristics and who believe that what they have in common is significant. Therefore, we can have a neighborhood without it being organized but a community must be organized if it is, indeed, a community. Continuing along this line of reasoning, if a community is organized then it could be concluded that a collective consciousness exists among its members. This notion brings us back to Durkheim's (1984, 1933) notion of agreement or consensus theory, which will be discussed in a future chapter.

Depending on the community perspective and the amount of unity a community group has can determine behavioral outcome. For instance:

> The more closely knit the members of a society, the more they maintain various relationships either with one another or with the group collectively. For if they met together rarely, they would not be mutually dependent, except sporadically and somewhat weakly (Durkheim, 1984, 1933, p. 25).

The level of cohesion or the amount of unity that characterizes a group will often determine its level of accomplishment. This idea works on smaller groups, too. For instance, children growing up without caring parental intervention (that's the unity) are more likely to engage in crimes of violence than children growing up with caring parental interaction (Stevens, 1997a).

Organizing Community Groups

Even if all of these characteristics are present in a community, there is no guarantee that the community will be amenable to organizing community policing initiatives. Individuals, even individuals with similar perspectives, must be encouraged to join a group. This is the viewpoint that most community policing organizers try to impress on police managers. That is, people who could most benefit from community policing (i.e., people loosely contacted to the city power, people in the lower classes, people of color and ethnicity), must be won over by the police to participate in community-policing agendas. However, winning them over means that community policy makers can then make the best decisions for the community.

? Something to Think About

Community residents don't come to a community policing meeting because one is planned and they don't participate because they happen to be present.

The unity or togetherness of a community-policing group will determine the group's productivity. This chapter makes the assumption that it is the responsibility of the community to control crime in its own community. And, it is the responsibility of the police to point the way as facilitators to accomplish the task of community control of their neighborhoods. Preparing for community meetings, the police agency's first step is to raise public awareness and police personnel awareness. Part of awareness includes feedback from community members and police personnel. Announcing to anyone that community-policing exists has little merit unless the awareness activities are backed with programs that provide residents and officers with skills to practice community policing and problem-solving techniques. It is recommended by Washington, DC's Police Chief Charles Ramsey (2002) that all concerned parties have hands-on training and practice. Because residents and officers have new responsibilities that include terrorist identification, training is essential.

Committee members need to know how to access information, whom to call to provide municipal services or report legitimate concerns about terrorism, and how to follow through in problem-solving committees. They need to know how to evaluate their activities, and how to change their problem-solving strategies to optimize remedies. Problem-solving strategies can exist without a community-police component, but community-policing strategies cannot exist without a problem-solving component. Therefore, awareness, training, evaluation, and change can be accomplished only if the community members and police personnel know what they are doing. Further chapters will explore these ideas in more depth.

Community Meetings

As community groups accomplish the task of becoming a strong democratic influence in the community, they should expand and change themselves.[6] There are several reasons for such a system:

1. An organization's tendency to get the job done leads to an increase in its capacities.

2. Expansion is often the simplest way of dealing with problems of internal stress.

3. Expansion is also a direct method of handling problems in a changing social environment.

4. The rules and roles in a bureaucracy are quite susceptible to ever more elaboration.

5. The very ideology of organization encourages growth.

This concentration of power and resources emerging from organizational growth has other uses as a formal system. Perhaps strong community groups should consider working on resolutions of neighborhood issues that traditionally are handled by individuals, families, friendship, neighborhood groups, and other less formal structures. A step further than community-policing efforts may be recommended. The possibility that the community step up and take responsibility for community issues is clear. That is, city services such as health care, garbage collection, day care, building inspection, housing rehabilitation, property management, crime surveillance, recreation, and city employment guidance, are all areas of concern. Community involvement in all areas of community issues is recommended. It starts with shared lifestyles and responsibility and accountability.

[6]For an indepth look at this process, see Michael R. Williams (1985, pp. 206–209).

Summary

This chapter further examined environmental influences on behavior and police response. We described the development and changes in American cities, provided descriptions of a neighborhood, and defined community. We looked at the effects of neighborhood and community upon resident behavior and police response. Common characteristics of communities in general were offered; methods of advancing the organization of community groups were revealed; and tips for community groups to become a strong influence in their community were explored.

Do You Know? _____

1. Define the word "city" and explain why people live there.
2. Characterize the developmental process of the American city.
3. Describe some of the early theories and studies of cities.
4. Describe Gemeinschaft lifestyles and explain why enforcement might not be required in those societies.
5. Describe Gesellschaft lifestyles and explain why enforcement might be required in those societies.
6. Describe some of the early perceptions of city dwellers and in particular explain the "too many rights" relationship with crime.
7. Characterize urban social relationships and their impact on policing strategies.
8. Define a neighborhood and a community. In what way are they similar and in what way are they different?
9. Identify the social characteristics common among many communities and give an example of each social characteristic.
10. Discuss the pitfalls of organizing community groups into productive groups and identify how some of those pitfalls can be addressed.
11. In what way does the following statement by John Stuart Mill link to our work in this chapter? "The worth of the state, in the long run, is the worth of the individuals composing it."

5

Thinking about Behavior

"A long habit of not thinking a thing wrong, gives it a superficial appearance of being right."

Thomas Paine—*Common Sense*

Key Terms _____

Attitudes	Conflict Theory	Model or Theory
Authoritarian Personality	Consensus Theory	Reinforcement
Behavioral Conditioning	Control Theory	Social Role
Cognitive Dissonance	Interactionist Perspective	
Community-Policing Rationale	Labeling Theory	

Key Topics _____

- Why we should study human behavior.
- Psychological models of behavior, including attitude, cognitive dissonance, and authoritarian personality.
- Sociological models of behavior, including conflict, consensus, interactionist, labeling, social bond, and control.

Introduction

We've all witnessed behavior that made us ask, "Why did they do that?" One purpose of this chapter is to help answer that question. Most of the material applies to police-community relationships but these ideas can also be used to explain most behavior. The perspectives outlined are not the only models that explain the conduct of others. There are other equally valid theories; therefore, what follows should be looked upon as a working draft for understanding community-police relations.

Why We Study Behavior

We study behavior:

- To give meaning to things we do and see.
- To distinguish between cause and effect.
- To understand the influence of social change.

Police officers believe that looking at behavior theoretically isn't their job. "Social workers do that, and we ain't social workers," one officer reports. Given the new challenges officers face with community-policing strategies, they could link their experience with theory to aid them in making informed decisions.

There are different ways of looking at behavior. Often, the way a police officer understands behavior will influence the way he or she deals with an individual during an altercation, a community member during a problem-solving session, or a family member during a dispute. For instance, by law and in theory, an officer is expected to enforce all laws at all times and to arrest anyone they see committing a violation. Not only is that an absurd expectation but highly unlikely to happen (Carter & Radelet, 1999). Why? There are many reasons, but one good reason relates to how an officer (or a policy maker) views the nature of the crime. For example, in a domestic violation, if an officer thinks the justice system will not alter an abuser's conduct, the likelihood an arrest will be made, even if an arrest is mandated, is less likely than if an officer thinks the system will change the conduct of the suspect.[1] Also, some officers will overlook violations if they disagree with the sanctioned penalties linked to those violations.

Understanding behavior can give meaning to a police strategy such as community policing or a problem-solving effect or outcome. It can help clarify things we see in a particular setting by relating those observations to other ideas or conditions that we hear about. For example, explaining expectations to new police recruits might be clearer if veteran officers revealed their experiences to recruits. Veteran officers could explain how regulations, laws, and strategies changed as they were going through the ranks, and that new recruits should expect practices to change in their police careers, too. They could discuss ways that police practices might change based on community cultural differences and community influence on policing decisions.

By studying behavior you will better understand cause and effect relationships and be empowered to make recommendations and/or predictions with a higher degree of accuracy. For instance, urban population density (a cause) is associated with high crime rates (an effect or an outcome). Even crime mapping shows high urban population density closely related to high rates of crime. There is a theory that overcrowding can increase aggression and ultimately, crime. Understanding behavior can help simplify complex ideas such as urban population density and help you think in terms of images, comparisons, and behavioral patterns. It will then become clear that overcrowding and crime are not necessarily related issues.

Learning about behavior can help you link one study to others for the purpose of making reliable recommendations and/or predictions. In the early 1990s, for instance, a study on the early childhood experiences of incarcerated male felons at Attica Penitentiary in New York revealed that one of their most memorable experiences was the intense quarreling between their parents.[2] Family tension was so engrained in their childhood memories that they reported being isolated and neglected. A similar study was conducted among female incarcerated felons with the same findings. Therefore, it could be argued that an important childhood memory for many male- and female-convicted felons is parental quarreling. An informed decision could be made from this knowledge.[3] With this information, a youth officer

[1]For a closer look at this idea see David L. Carter and Louis A. Radelet (1999), pp. 403–410; and Dennis J. Stevens. (1998c). Mandatory arrest, spouse abuse, & accelerated rates of victimization: Attitudes of victims and officers. *The Criminologist.* Evidence was presented suggesting that a high percent of officers in a mandatory domestic violence arrest state, did not conduct an arrest due to the officer's perspective of the justice system. Other officers would refrain from an arrest because it "took two to tango," suggesting that both parties were responsible. In another study, see Stevens, (1999h), Interviews with women convicted of murder: Battered women syndrome revisited. Evidence showed that when officers where called to a crime scene where a women was robbed, beaten, and/or raped by her partner, officers did not make an arrest depending on how they viewed her role in the relationship. Dennis J. Stevens, (2002b). Civil liabilities and arrest decisions. In Jeffrey Walker, Policing and the Law, pp. 127–141, and Dennis J. Stevens (2001b), Civil Liability and Selective Enforcement. In this study, 658 sworn officers in 21 police agencies located in 11 states were surveyed about their experiences. Results showed most encountered more suspects, yet reported fewer arrests as compared to past experiences because paper work, training, waiting on warrants and citations, and the threat of civil liabilities were obstacles.

[2]For more detail see Dennis J. Stevens (1999h). Interviews with women convicted of murder: Battered women syndrome revisited. International Review of Victimology, 6(2).

or a DARE officer could counter or neutralize family influences if she or he knew what influences were the most harmful for youth.

Understanding behavior can help us look beyond a limited view. For instance, if you were a police manager in Columbus, Ohio, your immediate world might be limited to the police experiences of Columbus or to your general assignment area. But, a look at police performance in St. Petersburg, Florida, might add to your knowledge of policing and you could modify the Florida model to work in Columbus.

Understanding a behavioral model or theory can help a police agency and a community better deal with the forces that change a community, a police agency, and their social worlds. These influences could include community demographics, police and community resistance, and political intervention as they, the agency and the community, move toward community-policing prerogatives such as problem-solving strategies. However, many theorists believe that an idea or theory is useless if it is not practical, and that it is impractical if it is not used in real-world experiences.

The application of an uncomplicated idea takes precedence over an elegant theory because a good idea is based on outcome as opposed to elegance. The dynamics of an excellent police theory, for instance, is in its ability to help bring a police agency closer to its mission of controlling crime, reducing the fear of crime, and enhancing the quality of life experiences for its constituents.

Theory of Social Order

Scholars, police practitioners, and politicians have different ideas about social order and policing efforts. But, let's not forget that community members and individuals in private and public organizations also hold viewpoints about social order, how to maintain social order, and how the police should support it. Different individuals have different ideas about social order and policing because they start with different assumptions about the basic character of human social life. Social order as defined earlier means public safety. However, maintaining public safety might depend on who is defining social order and what maintaining public safety means to them.

Some see social order and social stability as more important than conflict and change, while others take the opposite view. Some see personality as determining behavioral outcome, and others see physical predisposition taking precedence in behavioral determinations. Some focus their attention principally on the larger institutional structures of society, while others concentrate more on human interaction in small groups. Such choices define the elements of a theoretical model. With so many competing models, which one might be closer to the truth?

Each of us has a unique way of relating to others, a unique way of behaving, and a unique set of values and attitudes. Therefore, each of us has a unique personality (Holmes & Holmes, 1996). Attitude, personality, and its impact on behavioral patterns, may be variables that are more unrelated than expected. It takes biology, society, and psychology to develop a personality. The next two sections describe psychological and sociological models that will help explain behavior.

[3]For more detail see Stevens (1997a) as compared with Stevens (1997e).

Psychological Models

Only a few psychological theories focus on an examination of communities and policing. To broaden our understanding, let's review some of the fundamental assumptions of most psychological theories as advanced by Frank Schmalleger (2000, p. 231).

Psychological Models Emphasize:
- The individual is the primary unit of examination.
- Personality is the major motivational element within individuals since it is the seat of drives and the source of motives.
- Crimes result from abnormal, dysfunctional, or inappropriate mental processes with the personality.
- Criminal behavior although condemned by the social group may be purposeful for the individual insofar as it addresses certain felt needs. Behavior can be judged inappropriate only when measured against external criteria purporting to establish normality.
- Normality is generally defined by social consensus—that is, what the majority of people in any social group agree is "real," appropriate, or typical.
- Defective, or abnormal, mental processes may have a variety of causes including:
  - A diseased mind
  - Inappropriate learning or improper conditioning
  - The emulation of inappropriate role models
  - Adjustment to inner conflicts

Psychological Models

Psychological models focus on the individual and criminal activity is linked to the personality.

There also appear to be two primary psychological perspectives. One emphasizes conditioning and the other focuses on personality disturbances and diseases of the mind.

Conditioning

In policing, a major concern is on conditioning because it relates to an observable, measurable event—things we can see. Behaviorists, however, make several assumptions:

- All behavior is caused or determined in some way.
- All behavior obeys certain laws.
- The environment molds behavior.
- Each sensory stimulus results in a response.
- Explanations of behavior based on internal causes and mental states are useless.

Conditioning was popularized through the work of Ivan Pavlov and B.F. Skinner. Pavlov experimented with dogs. He fed them in the presence of a ringing bell and learned that dogs salivated as he rang the bell. But he also rang the bell when food was not present and found that they still salivated. Therefore, salivation, Pavlov argued, was an automatic response to the presence (or expectation) of food, a behavior that could be conditioned to occur in response to some other stimulus. He called this finding *unconditioned reflexes*. Animal behavior could be predicted through association with external changes arising from the environment. How often can human behavior be altered depending on stimuli?

Although human behavior is different from animal behavior, let's consider drug tolerance to see how unconditioned reflexes might apply. Users of certain drugs experience progressively weaker effects after taking drugs daily. Drug tolerance is different from one person to the next, but in many cases drug tolerance can be a learned response (Kalat, 1993). When drug users inject themselves with morphine or heroin, the injection procedure is a stimulus that reliably predicts a second stimulus, the drug's entry into the brain. The drug alters experience but it also triggers a variety of body defenses and countermeasures against the drug's effects; for example, changes in hormone secretions, heart rate, and breathing rate.

Classical Conditioning

Whenever one stimulus (something that arouses interest) predicts another stimulus that produces a response, we have the conditions necessary for *classical conditioning*. That is, the first time someone takes a drug, there's a certain delay between the time the drug enters the brain and the time the brain mobilizes its defenses. After classical conditioning has taken place, the injection procedure, acting as a conditioned stimulus may trigger the *defense reactions*, even before the drug has entered the brain. As the defense reactions are aroused earlier and earlier, the effects of the drug grow weaker and the user can tolerate heavier and heavier dosages.

Thinking back to the "broken window" model of James Q. Wilson and George L. Kelling that helped move community policing into the forefront of policing service, is there a suggestion that broken windows per se, can elicit a response from criminals? Similar to Pavlov ringing a bell, community disorder can become a target for criminals.

Conditioning

Conditioning is defined as a psychological model implying that the frequency of any behavior can be increased or decreased through reward, punishment, and/or association with other stimuli.

Reinforcement increases the probability that the response will be repeated in the future; it "stamps in" or strengthens the likelihood of the response. Stimuli, especially when reinforced, creates a response. However, a specific response might depend on the attitude of an individual since human beings make choices.

Attitude

Some people say our attitudes determine how we will act. An *attitude* is a learned like or dislike of something or somebody that can influence our behavior toward that thing or that person. It is believed that behind every action is an attitude. The logic is that if those attitudes can be identified in advance and measured accurately, actions or behaviors can be predicted or anticipated (Champion, 1993). Most social psychologists agree that an attitude is a predisposition to respond to a focal object (attitude object), that these predispositions are learned through experience, limited by our culture and capacities, and that the existence of an attitude is inferred from consistencies in an individual's behavior.

Attitude

An attitude is a personal view about something or someone.

An attitude can be an opinion or general feeling about something. We probably hold many attitudes about all sorts of things and people. Attitudes include an emotional or affective component (the way you feel about something), a cognitive or evaluation component (what you know or believe), and a behavioral or action component (what you are likely to do). However, the attitude-action relationship is far from certain. People hold many attitudes about things, but their behavior might never demonstrate the extent of their attitude. In fact, sometimes observing someone else's conduct might produce a different set of attitudes for a person. For instance, a patrol officer wants to help residents in numerous ways, but never giving a traffic violator a pass might suggest to others that this officer believes in a zero-tolerance perspective when it comes to traffic violations. They might decide that "he's a hard-nose cop who doesn't care about anything except his track record." Surprisingly, conduct often correlates weakly with attitudes because many variables other than attitudes also influence behavior. There is always more than one cause for every effect or outcome.

The conduct of some people is more consistent with their attitudes than is the conduct of others. Hopefully this doesn't sound like a contradiction. In Van Maanen's (1978) classic paper titled "The Asshole" it appeared that police tend to focus, not on suspects, but on big-mouths, individuals who had not committed a legal violation but who in their conduct displayed resentment about the intrusion of the police into their affairs. Van Maanen captured the moral dimension of the use of coercion in that work, but of interest in our discussion of attitudes, he suggests that the police believe that they exist, in part, to protect the world from assholes. But a cop could not know who an asshole was until he or she encountered one. Consider the process of labeling someone an asshole during an encounter. When an officer determined that an individual was an asshole, the more likely the officer would deal with that individual in a specific way—maybe custody, maybe street justice.

On the other hand, some individuals are consistently inconsistent. Whenever they face an unfamiliar situation, the first thing they do is to determine what is expected of them and what everyone else is doing. Such people often behave in ways that do not match their attitudes but rather what impression they wish to present. For them, performance is the heart of social interaction as it involves presenting the self to others.[4] As expressed by one writer, there is a tendency for people everywhere to interact with others as if they were performing on the stage of a theater. In a sense, we make decisions about our behavior like actors following a script that we have learned from our parents, teachers, friends, and others. That script tells us how to behave according to our roles at the time. Therefore, we could say that criminals tend to behave differently depending on whom they are talking to. For instance, when confronted at different times by their parents, teachers, police officers, case workers, or DSS workers, their behavior is "managed" to fit the person in front of them at the time and to make a certain impression.

Cognitive Dissonance

Sometimes our behavior shapes our attitudes. The concept of *cognitive dissonance* tells another story about the link between attitude and behavior. We talked about how attitudes shape behavior; now we're going to examine how behavior shapes attitudes.

Cognitive Dissonance

> Because humans need balance, if our belief is different than our behavior, we change our attitude—not our behavior.

Cognitive dissonance tells us that when behavior changes, attitudes follow. Cognitive dissonance is a state of unpleasant tension that an individual experiences when a contradictory attitude is held or when the individual behaves in a way inconsistent with his or her attitude about that behavior. According to Leon Festinger (1957), cognitive dissonance is centered on the idea that we try to "establish internal harmony, consistency, or congruity" among our "opinions, attitudes, knowledge, and values."

The basic assumption of this model is that most of us seek stable environments, relationships, and jobs. That could mean to a community police officer when confronting community members that he or she should be approachable and nonjudgmental. Then people will feel relaxed around them since most people have "comfort zones" and making them uncomfortable or on guard, disrupts their comfort zone. People like to think they are in control of their lives and can predict outcomes from interactions. If an interaction produces an imbalance in their comfort zone, it is easier to change their attitude as opposed to their behavior. Schoolteachers see this all the time. When a student feels that a course is too demanding, the student will blame the teacher for the student's inability to develop a firm plan to successfully complete the course. The student will continue with perhaps poor study habits or demanding outside activities (including late-hour

---

[4]For a closer look, see Erving Goffman (1971). Interaction Ritual. NY: Random House.

parties) and suggest that the educator should be more mindful of the student's priorities. Imagine what some people think about the police when those individuals have difficulty controlling their criminal responses? People try to reduce tension or contradiction in their lives in several ways:

- They change their conduct to match their attitude.
- They change their attitude to match their conduct.
- They adopt a new attitude that justifies their conduct.

For example, Monica believes the community to be unsafe and buys a handgun despite her attitude that shooting people is an inappropriate response. Although Monica thinks that individuals who lack appropriate firearm training might fall victim to criminals, she carries her handgun every day to and from work. The inconsistency between her attitude and her behavior creates dissonance, an unpleasant state of arousal. To reduce this unstable state of mind, Monica can do one of the following:

- Take a firearms training course.
- Dispose of the weapon.
- Change her attitude by deciding that carrying a handgun without adequate training is not really dangerous.

She rationalizes that carrying a handgun reduces her stress and in turn, keeps her from gaining weight because she tends to overeat when stressed. Although a person might adopt any of those options or others, most findings show ways in which dissonance changes attitudes not behavior. That is, Monica could adopt an attitude more consistent with her conduct by convincing herself that carrying a weapon is not really dangerous and that the benefits far outweigh any health problems that might be linked to a lack of training. "I'd rather be dead than fat and a nervous wreck," she might proclaim. Individuals in dissonance will discount information about results produced from their conduct, alter logical information that explains those results, and rationalize their motives. They may even say it to themselves so often that eventually they believe it to be true. As Albert Einstein (1879–1955) said: "We can't solve problems by using the same kind of thinking we used when we created them." Perhaps you can see how this thought applies to Monica and probably ourselves when we think about our behavior.

Dissonance is generally connected to individuals, but, group behavior can also be explained through a dissonance model.

Dissonance

Dissonance refers to a tension between two items of knowledge, two attitudes, or two values.[5]

[5]See Carter and Radelet (1999), p. 296 for an indepth discussion on this matter.

Contracultural dissonance can be a collective form of cognitive dissonance (Festinger, 1957). There are five conditions under which collective cognitive dissonance can occur:

1. Dissonance can exist after a decision has been made between two or more alternatives, i.e., community members want police to reprioritize service calls and respond to teenager activities before business disturbances. Then they feel they made a mistake.
2. Dissonance can exist after an attempt has been made, by offering rewards or threatening punishment, to elicit overt behavior that is at odds with private opinion.
3. Forced or accidental exposure to new information may create cognitive elements that are dissonant with existing cognition.
4. The open expression of disagreement in a group leads to the existence of cognitive dissonance in the members.
5. Identical dissonance in a large number of people may be created when an event occurs that is so compelling (such as September 11, 2001) as to produce a uniform reaction in everyone.

Post-decision dissonance varies with the importance of the decision, the relative attractiveness of alternatives not chosen, and the similarity of both chosen and discarded alternatives. The degree of the dissonance or imbalance resulting from an attempt to elicit forced compliance is greatest if the promised reward or punishment is seen as barely sufficient to elicit the overt behavior. The presence of dissonance gives rise to pressures to reduce it. Reducing dissonance calls for changing one of the dissonant elements of knowledge: opinion, attitude, or value; adding new, consonant elements to support the decision taken; or decreasing the importance of the dissonant elements.

The relevance of this perspective from police-community relations might well relate to understanding better the elements of culture shock. Most of us have visited other cities and recall differences in the collective behavior of the cities we visited, especially if those cities were in different geographic sections of the country. For example, driving an automobile in Boston can be a challenging experience for an out-of-towner, even an experienced driver.[6] An officer from a different cultural background than the members of a community might experience a number of stages that relate to the culture shock syndrome.[7] Four stages were identified:

1. A "honeymoon" period during which an officer can be fascinated by the novelty of a strange culture. The officer can be overly polite and friendly.
2. An officer settles down to a long-run confrontation with the conditions of life in the community and the need to function effectively there. The officer can become hostile and aggressive toward the culture and its people. The officer might attribute his or her difficulties to troublemaking on their part.

---

[6]The writer is referring to his own personal experiences in this case.
[7]See David L. Carter and Louis A. Radelet, 1999. p. 296.

The officer can develop elaborate, stereotypic cartoons of the local people and suggest that they deserve the crime problem they have because they are lawless and rude.

3. The officer (assuming reasonable passage from Stage 2) begins to open a way into the new cultural environment. The officer might adapt an arrogant attitude toward the community members and might joke about the community members as opposed to criticizing them and their culture. This might suggest that the officer is on the way to recovery from the cultural shock.

4. An officer's adjustment to the community members is complete: the officer accepts the attitudes, values, and norms of those community members as another way of living and doing things.[8]

As officers work with community groups, they will encounter different ideas about social order and stability, police service, community norms and demands, and their own expectations might be challenged through those differences. If an officer doesn't fully comprehend the expectations and language of a group, he or she might become as uneasy with the group members as they are uneasy with him or her. Fascination with the culture begins to fade as an officer increasingly feels a cultural separation from the group. As a defense mechanism, probably spiced with some stereotyping aid, an officer's attitude can take on a hostile response. If the relationship cannot be redirected, it may become difficult to salvage the relationship.

Some additional problems that arise relate to questions of integrity. For instance, what does an officer do after working hard to be accepted by a community group only to discover that some of its prominent members abuse alcohol, and when they are drunk, often make fun of the police? Does an officer ignore those members, argue with them about the merits of policing, or arrest them? One answer is that the officer should tell the group that any illegal activity in his or her presence would end in an arrest and some form of social balance must be sought.

Authoritarian Personality

Some individuals think that many police officers seem to demonstrate authoritarian behavior. It should be noted that an authoritarian personality is linked to prejudice. Specifically, a general finding is that prejudice is directly related to rigidity of outlook, to intolerance for ambiguity, to superstition, and to suggestibility and gullibility.[9]

The *authoritarian personality* looks for hierarchy in society and in all relationships. This individual seeks power arrangements, something predictable from their perspective. Authority and discipline are a focus, and this individual tends

[8]See Gunnar Myrdal (1944). *An American Dilemma: The Negro population in the U.S.* NY: Harper & Brothers. p. 50–64.
[9]See Carter and Radelet, 1999, p. 255.

to distrust other people and see the world as a hazardous place. People who display strong prejudice toward one minority group are likely to be intolerant of all minorities. An authoritarian personality rigidly conforms to conventional cultural values, sees moral issues as clear-cut matters of right and wrong, and looks upon society as a naturally competitive arena where better people (like themselves) inevitably dominate those who are weaker. Carter and Radelet (1999) suggest that authoritarian personality types are the Archie Bunker types. Prejudice exists, according to this perspective, because a person is convinced that he or she gains something by being prejudiced.

Educated officers who were raised in caring families tend to be more accepting of others than individuals raised in hostile environments among aggressive adults. There is a tendency to be more flexible in moral judgement and to treat other individuals as equals. Therefore, one equalizer if you will, can be education. Some writers believe that the elements of danger, authority, and efficiency contribute to responding authoritatively.[10]

Sociological Perspectives

Most sociological perspectives are diverse, and centered in an analysis of influences from environmental sources. For instance, in an earlier chapter we learned that cultural influences shape decisions, which eventually shape behavior. However, when examining behavior from a sociological perspective remember that:

- Norms and values are different among groups, neighborhoods, and communities.
- Socialization affects the dynamic interaction of individuals within groups.
- Subcultures exist within communities.

Behavioral and sociological factors influence the development of community policing strategies. We will cover some macro (global) explanations, such as conflict and consensus perspectives as well as a micro (individual) explanation, such as an interactionist approach.

Conflict Theory

Conflict theory was originally advanced by Karl Marx 150 years ago when he wrote about poverty, capitalism, and revolution. This theory has been criticized and challenged, studied and modified, rejected and accepted, many times over the past one hundred years. It remains an important way of evaluating the behavior of groups of people (as opposed to individual behavior in psychological models). Overall, *conflict theory* sees society as a generalized arena of inequality that generates conflict and change. There are a few assumptions that require clarification. The first assumption is that conflict theory deals with generalizations as

---

[10]See Trojanowicz and Dixon (1974), pp. 72–75 for a closer look at their explanation of an authoritative response.

opposed to daily life experiences. Second, people in general (even those who are poor) dislike poverty and poverty lifestyles. Third, wealthy people use power to control others to enhance their own power. Fourth, there is a continual struggle in process between various groups over resources, and the assumption is that most of us will participate in this struggle.

A conflict perspective suggests that race, class, ethnicity, gender, age, and other social factors are linked to unequal distribution of resources including money, power, education, networks, and social prestige. Conflict analysis rejects the idea that social structure promotes the functioning of society as a whole, focusing instead on how every social pattern benefits some of the people while depriving others.

Conflict Theory

There are three principles that explain how conflict theory works:
- Groups always engage in a struggle over resources.
- Groups with the most resources win.
- Winners exploit losers.

How are losers exploited? Through resources. That is, middle-class America struggles with lower-class America. Middle-class America holds more resources than the lower class: wealth, income, occupation, networks, and education. Middle-class America exploits the lower class by depriving them, as a group of wealth, income, occupation, networks, and education. Exploitation includes the development of a set of "truths" about the losers. For instance, lower-class people are mostly welfare recipients and are perceived as lazy, criminal in nature, and uncaring about their children. They live off the fat of the land. These assumptions help further to exploit welfare recipients. Lower-class people's perspective on social life is considered to be the model of social disorder. Therefore, the middle class has the legal and moral right, supposedly, to detain and incarcerate lower-class individuals more than other classes in America. The lower classes can never rise up and take the middle classes' place because they are the criminal class of America. This set of beliefs is called the *criminalization of poverty*.

Therefore, groups are pitted against each other—whites versus blacks, middle class versus lower class, women versus men. This perspective seems to ignore the idea that inequality produces shared values and interdependence, thereby unifying groups of people toward greater productivity. In Marx's tradition, inequality generates conflict and change, as opposed to the consensus model where agreement and tradition take precedence.

Consensus Theory

Emile Durkheim was one of the primary advocates of the consensus perspective. This behavioral model suggests that a universal agreement exists among a citizenry about the rules of the game, norms, and/or issues. Although conflict is expected in a democracy, it cannot live long without consensus about some basic norms such as the right of residents to form political organizations. *Consensus the-*

ory argues that successful democracies devise policies that unify different groups by giving them all an interest in national political stability.[11] Therefore, these groups can be more productive through cooperation as opposed to conflict. For instance, community-policing strategies share in this concept by suggesting that community members and officers be empowered to influence police decisions when engaged in problem-solving activities.

Consensus Theory

Consensus theory sees society as a complex social structure whose parts work together to promote solidarity and stability.

Consensus theory focuses on the social structure (i.e., social institutions, social relationships, and social roles) and considers the social function or the consequences of any social pattern for the operation of society as a whole. According to this perspective, each part of society—the family, the school, the police, the economy, the state—performs certain functions for the society as a whole. All parts are interdependent or connected. The family depends on the school to educate its children, and the school in turn, depends on the family or the state to provide financial support. The state, in turn, depends on the family and the school to help children grow to become law-abiding taxpayers. These interdependent parts of society create stable social order. Crime builds unity among its members. Social consensus or agreement through cooperation enables society to achieve social order. Social order can be best obtained through traditional perspectives and no one part of society can be greater than another part.

A *social dysfunction* refers to any social pattern's undesirable consequences for the operation of society. This perspective sees society as a complex system whose parts work together to promote unity and stability. "Things are the way they are because everyone agrees that that is how it is," might be a comment heard by an individual who advocates this perspective.

The focus is on the social structure (i.e., social institutions such as the schools and police, social relationships such as parents and children, and social roles such as mother, police officer, and/or teacher). This perspective looks at the social function of the police, which is to serve and protect the public. According to consensus theory, each part of society including family, school, police, economy, and/or state performs a specific function. All parts are interdependent or connected to each other. The family depends on the police to protect their children, and the police depend on the family to provide police with support. As officers and parents, part of their job is to help children become law-abiding taxpayers who further the institution of policing. As institutions support each other, social order develops and is maintained. Thus, social agreement leads to cooperation, and a society achieves its desired goals. When the public sees themselves in the role of community members striving to aid other institutions, such as the police, in order to contribute to society as a whole, they are individually accepting

[11]For more detail, see *The Encyclopedic Dictionary of Sociology*. Third Edition. Dushkin Publishing, p.58.

the social norms and mission of their community. These community members see their community as part of a complex system whose parts must work together to promote unity and stability.

Interactionist Perspective

The *interactionist perspective* finds its roots in Max Weber's (1864–1920) notion that understanding a community is best accomplished through the point of view of the people in it. Weber saw society as a product of the everyday interactions of the individuals.

Interactionist Perspective

> Interactionist perspective focuses on social exchange and the individual in his or her daily life.

For the interactionist, conduct is explained through the interactions of individuals as they try to make sense of their social encounters. Central to this model is what an individual thinks, feels, and what motivates him or her to make decisions. Equally important, however, is how an individual interprets his or her social world. That is, each of us makes our own social reality. We see our own world from the perspective of our own experiences, capabilities, and expectations. Since human beings think as individuals, we create or construct our own social world or reality.

What W.I. Thomas (1863–1947) seemed to have in mind when he made his famous dictum: "If people define situations as real, they are real in their consequences," was that fear itself is greater than the reality. People are able to change socially constructed inner realities (their ideas, attitudes, or feelings) into a socially observable outer reality (conduct). If they are afraid of the dark, they will behave in the dark as if they are afraid, even when there is nothing to fear. Do they believe they are afraid? Yes. As Max Weber once implied, the same person who tells the lie believes it. If a police officer believes that Latinos are not to be trusted, even though the officer has little experience with this cultural group, what is the likelihood that this officer will become excessively watchful when around Latinos? The interactionist perspective is linked to a self-fulfilling prophecy—changing behavior to match the label. That is, do people who believe that a police officer thinks they are not to be trusted act differently when around that officer?

The self-definition developed by each of us concerning our social world does not necessarily come from within. These definitions often arise from social interaction with others. For example, children under the age of nine often evaluate how good or bad they are at their schoolwork based on what parents or teachers say to them. Children describe themselves in ways such as "I am a good girl in school because daddy says so." Or they might think they're stupid "because my teacher says I am." Labels certainly play a role in how community members see themselves.

Furthermore, how children develop a sense of self comes from interactions with their parents and the community at large. Children see how others treat them and their family members, and learn how to take the *social role* expected of them.

Social Role

> A social role is a part played by somebody in a given social context, with any characteristic or expected pattern of behavior that it entails.

Charles Cooley (1864–1929) viewed society as a group of individuals helping each other to develop their personality. How? In effect, we acquire a "looking-glass self" that we develop from the way others treat us. Their treatment is like a mirror reflecting our personal qualities. If we see that others treat us with respect, we enjoy a feeling of self-respect, and will return respect. We can't see our own face, but we can see another individual's face. If they smile, we smile back. This self-image emerges from the looking-glass process and often impacts our individual conduct. If community members hold a low self-image of themselves due in part to the presentation of the community-policing officers, the consequences are likely to result in poor participation.

Labeling Perspective

The heart of the matter is that labeling is a process. What that means is that a crime does not need to happen to have someone tagged with the label of a criminal. This perspective implies that deviance in a society is relative. That is, conduct can be deviant when *labeled* as such by others. In order for a label to stick, those doing the labeling have to have more power than the recipient of the label—parents, police officers, teachers, counselors, judges, or the "in-group."

There are four primary steps in the labeling process:

1. Observation of perceived misconduct or the act by authorities or people in power.
2. Labeling of the individual as a deviant.
3. Acceptance by the labeled individual that he or she is deviant.
4. Self-fulfilling prophecy: individual accepts the label and acts out the label.

For a deviant act to have social consequences, important people have to think they see it. Being publicly labeled a deviant or a juvenile delinquent, for example, by a person in authority is probably the most significant step in the career of a criminal. Think about juveniles who might be labeled juvenile delinquent because they are bored at school and cut classes. If you're wondering about the power of the label, think about the stereotypes that are attached to an ex-convict or even the label of being a "big mouth" or a "troublemaker" at a community-policing meeting. Labels that promote positive behavior from community members might be more productive for community officers.

First is the observation of the perceived misconduct or the act by the people in power, such as police, municipal agencies, and community-meeting members. For instance, suppose it is widely believed that immigrants come to the United States to get welfare. Next comes a label: immigrants want American welfare. What follows is the acceptance by those labeled; they treat me as if I were a welfare cheat. And, finally, the individual accepts the label, resulting in a self-fulfilling prophecy. Therefore, they act out the label.

If municipal personnel, including police officers, thought newcomers to America were welfare recipients and/or welfare cheaters, in what way would the services they provide, equal the level of other constituents? "They have welfare money already, they don't need to come to me for more freebies," a city employee in Alexandria was heard saying at a community meeting. Labeling is powerful. If community-meeting members thought that mentally challenged individuals deserved fewer services than others, it would seem that municipal personnel might be inclined to accept those thoughts more readily. The labeling perspective is drawn from the interactionist perspective and relates to W.I. Thomas' (1863–1947) notion of "definition of the situation." If you believe the consequences of your behavior are real, then they are real. That is, if an individual believes she's a bad student, her study habits will probably reflect her self-image and her grades will deteriorate accordingly.

Control Theory

Another perspective that stems from the interactionist perspective is control theory. Control theory assumes that human beings are self-interested and that strong desires inside most of us try to get us into trouble. For example, temptations, cravings, hostilities, and so on, urge us to make decisions about our conduct. Yet, the question isn't why we commit crime, but rather why many of us don't commit crime, since most of us ignore these desires most of the time.

Walter Reckless (1973) developed *control theory*, which stresses that two control systems work against our motivations to commit deviance. Our inner controls include our internalized morality conscience—our ideas of right and wrong—or our religious ideals. Inner controls can include fears of punishment, feelings of integrity, and a desire to be a "good" person. Our outer controls consist of people and relationships such as family, friends, and law enforcement, which can influence us not to deviate. This perspective looks beyond social class, economic status, and culture.

Control theory can build on psychology by suggesting that some individuals are less likely to control their inner impulses than others. Control theory suggests that criminals lack a positive self-concept, resulting in an inability to control their inner urges. Law-abiding individuals think through what will happen if they give in to their impulses. But criminals think they are worthless and what ever happens to them, nothing will change their uselessness.

Control theory includes Travis Hirschi's (1969) *social bond perspective*, which suggests that when our social bonds or links to society are greater, the more effective are our inner controls. Social bonds have four components:

1. Attachment—feeling affection and respect for people who conform to the norms and to the values of a particular society and/or community at large. From the perspective of a police agency, this means accepting the philosophy of community policing.

2. Beliefs—holding certain behavioral outcomes as morally appropriate, such as a belief that crime prevention is worth the effort for the good of the children in the community.
3. Commitment—having a stake in our society and/or in our community that we don't want to risk, such as a respected place among family and friends, a respected voice at community meetings, and career stability.
4. Involvement—putting time and energy into socially approved activities such as Night Watch and helping kids with activities.

Some time after Hirschi's social bond theory, Michael Gottfredson (1990) and Hirschi revised social bonds to a self-control theory rejecting biological, psychological, and sociological explanations of crime. The revised theory implies that people commit crime because they lack self-control, the ability to control impulses, and to defer gratification.

Violent Crime

A quick review of personal and property victimization reports show that crimes of violence represent approximately 26 percent of most crimes, and a review of arrest rates show an approximate 12 percent represent an arrest for a crime of violence.[12] Most crimes in the U.S. are not violent. Most crime involves the use and/or the threat of force or fraud.[13] Individuals vary in their propensity to use criminal force and fraud. Most crime is trivial and mundane, resulting in little loss and few gains. In fact, "criminal acts are events whose temporal and spatial distributions are highly predictable, require little preparation, leave few lasting consequences, and often do not produce the result intended by the offender."[14] As such, it is caused behavior, and its causes have been influenced largely by physiological, psychological, and environmental effects. The question is, what promotes crime?

What Promotes Crime?

Most crime (aside from predatory crime) is the result of living conditions, relationship expectations, pure selfishness, and a lack of self control.

If violence, for instance, is seen in relation to the situation that inspires it, then crimes of violence can be viewed as interpersonal, as a form of social conduct comparable to other forms of social conduct.

Most of us are goal driven. When pursuing goals, some of us do what's right by the standards and expectations of society and some of us use other means than those considered appropriate by society. For most of us, behavior can result from a continual process of self-interaction through individual interpretation of the

[12]See BJS 2000, Table 3.30 Estimated percent distribution of personal and property victimization and Table 4.1 Estimated number of arrests, 1999. http://www.albany.edu/aourcebook/1995/pdf/t330.pdf
[13]For a detailed examination of this thought, see Michael R. Gottfredson and Travis Hirschi (1990). *A general theory of crime*. Stanford University: Stanford University Press. pp. 3–21.
[14] bid p. 16.

social environment. Each of us chooses a response that best brings us closer to our goal (at the moment), and then we pursue it, limited by our physical capabilities, personal experiences, social values, and level of expertise.[15] Behavior changes depending on how we see or interpret a situation linked to our goals. Our goals change, of course, shaped by our changing capacity (aging, for instance, which might produce different biological advances or declines), our ability to perform, our changing values, and our experiences.

A predator possess the goal or intent to commit the crime of rape for the benefit of let's say, sexual gratification. For example, once an opportunity presents itself, the predator does not hold back an attack. Serial rapists, for instance, are self-indulgent people pursuing objectives without regard for the welfare of others or themselves. When a rapist thinks a victim could not or would not resist an attack and an opportunity presents itself by circumstance or manipulation, he attacks regardless of the time of day, whose company the victim's in, age, or circumstances. Thus, the predator has the intent and seeks only the opportunity or victim prior to the attack.[16]

To control behavior, American society relies on collective resources of the justice system. However, most of us are not criminals and comply with most of the rules and the laws. Why? One answer is that we have inner and outer controls, as discussed earlier in control theory. We make a choice not to risk our personal status, homes, jobs, family and friends, and/or our potential. Some of us turn to our religious perspectives for guidance. We see ourselves as morally and ethically good and have confidence in our decisions and our abilities. We respect ourselves and maintain control over our conduct. We exercise self-control, suggesting we have a strong self-image.

Equally important, people who tend to follow the law lack intent to commit crime. Clearly, intent and opportunity must be present, in most cases, when we talk about criminal behavior. Finally, some of us get caught up in a situation, maybe a relationship, and make a mistake. Those troubled people are far different than the predators mentioned earlier and deserve guidance and help from our public resources.

Crime Is Healthy

There is another compelling argument that might aid us in understanding crime. Borrowing lines from Kai T. Erikson:[17]

> In 1895 Emile Durkheim wrote a book called *The Rules of Sociological Method* . . . sociologists should formulate a new set of criteria for distinguishing between "normal" and "pathological" elements in the life of a society. Behavior that looks

---

[15]See Dennis J. Stevens. (2001d). *Inside the mind of a sexual offender*. See Chapter 10 for more detail.
[16]Ibid
[17]See Kai T. Erikson, (1966). Wayward Puritans. NY: John Wiley & Sons, p. 3. A criminal who wants to commit a crime of violence will—no matter where the criminal is, no matter who stands before him including a police officer with a drawn weapon, and no matter the physical, psychological, or mental condition of their target. If they perceive a target to be vulnerable, they will attack. For more detail see, Stevens (1998) Inside the Mind of a Serial Rapist. Bethesda, MD: Austin Winfield.

abnormal to the psychiatrist or the judge, he suggested, does not always look abnormal when viewed through the special lens of the sociologist . . . To illustrate his argument, Durkheim made the surprising observation that crime was really a natural kind of social activity, "an integral part of all healthy societies."[18]

Two thoughts emerge: 1) if aberrant forms of individual behavior are a matter of definition depending on whose dictionary you use, so too is social order or stability a matter of definition by the community in question. 2) If crime is a normal and a continuing condition of a healthy society, crime will always be present in American society. The reality that crime is important to our society becomes clear to police officers after they practice their profession for a period of time. They realize that they tend to apprehend the same individuals engaged in similar behavior, time and again, and they often stop wondering why crime is a natural outcome of the behavior of those whom they repeatedly apprehend. Sometimes officers share those ideas of apprehension with other officers, suggesting that officers may well form their own occupational culture. Finally, it is easy to be misled about crime, especially violent crime, in the United States. Watching television or reading news accounts often leads some of us to believe that crime is routine and commonplace in America. But a vast majority of criminal activity is "trivial and mundane affairs that result in little loss and less gain" according to Gottfredson and Hirschi (1990), a notion that congruencies corroborated in government statistics on crime (BJS, 2000). The next chapter will discuss crimes of violence in more detail.

Summary

We looked at reasons why we should study human behavior. Some of the most provocative reasons have to do with being able to give meaning to things we do, give meaning to things we see, help sort through cause and effect relationships, link one study to another study, give a broader understanding, and make clear the influences of social change. We examined psychological models of behavior, including attitude, cognitive dissonance, and authoritarian personality. We investigated sociological models relevant to policing strategies. Some of these models are conflict theory, consensus theory, interactionist perspective, labeling perspective, social bond, and control theory.

Do You Know?

1. Define crime and explain why most of us do not commit crime. Think of examples that support the reasons why most of us do not commit crime. What are some outer or inner controls that were not mentioned in this chapter?

2. Describe the importance of examining behavior and characterize in particular the advantages of examining police behavior.

3. Describe a behavior model or a set of ideas and explain how that model can help predict behavior.

[18]These quotes are from Durkheim's own work.

4. Describe a social fact and explain its relevance to police behavior and a policing organization.

5. Describe how, from one point of view, the locus of crime causation is centered in the personality and the process of personality development.

6. In what way can cognitive dissonance alter the attitude of an individual? How would cognitive dissonance relate to community-policing outcomes?

7. Define conflict perspective and show how it applies to a specific model in the real world.

8. Describe the labeling perspective. Explain how it works. How can a person's label be removed?

9. Explain how a self-fulfilling prophecy works. How can it be avoided?

10. What fuels crime? How can it be controlled other than through enforcement?

11. Explain the decision-making process leading to most explanations of behavior.

12. In what way is crime healthy to a society? What real-life example could you bring that would support or reject this perspective?

13. In what way does Thomas Paine's statement apply to this chapter? "A long habit of not thinking a thing wrong, gives it a superficial appearance of being right."

Websites

Dead Sociologists Society

http.//www.runet.edu/~Iridenener/DSS/DEADSOC.HTML/

Comprehensive overview of the lives and writings of prominent social theorists, including Karl Marx, W.E.B. DuBois, and Emile Durkheim.

Durkheim Pages

http://eddie.CSO.UIUC.edu/Durkheim/

A wealth of information about Emile Durkheim, one of the pioneers of sociology. The site includes full-text writings, a bibliography of Durkheim's work, and a glossary of terms and concepts.

Marx/Engels Archie

http://www.marx.org/

A comprehensive resource for students interested in the work of Marx and Engels. The site includes a bibliography, a photo gallery, and references to related scholarly work.

Resources for Social Researchers

http://soc.umn.edu/~edwards/soclinks.htm

A virtual laundry list of links to sites of interest to students of sociology, including publications, data archives, research organizations, news media, and much more.

6

Thinking about Police Culture and Police Management

"Justice is incidental to law and order."
J. Edgar Hoover

Key Terms _____

Community Policing Rationale	Occupational Socialization	Total Quality Management
Leadership	Police Conservatism	
Managerial Rational and Style	Police Culture	

Key Topics _____

- Police culture and occupational socialization.
- Leadership perspectives in corporate America and within justice agencies.
- Traditional and contemporary managerial styles.
- Corporate managerial style in community-policing.

Introduction

Police managers have to respond differently than, for example, a corporate manager of IBM or Ford Motor Company. Nevertheless, there are managerial styles that might aid community-policing strategies better than others, and a recommended managerial style is discussed in this chapter. While it is possible that police culture might stand in the way, managerial change is critical within the ranks of professional police agencies.

Police Culture

In an earlier chapter, we saw how groups of people who shared and transmitted a similar lifestyle achieved and preserved their own culture. Can an occupation be characterized as having its own culture, too? Individuals who share an occupation engage in similar activities, which include both material and non-material elements. They transmit and socially control the obligations, responsibilities, and expectations of their profession through both formal and informal training, values, and norms (laws). Therefore, individuals engaged in an occupation are part of an occupational culture or in this case a *police culture*.

Police Culture

> Police culture is defined as an occupational culture because it provides a shared and transmitted lifestyle consisting of material and non-material elements.

When we look at a police culture, we see a shared language, gestures, ideals, goals, and rules among police officers. We see similar initial training for new recruits and similar ongoing in-service training across the United States. Senior officers act as gatekeepers and teach appropriate activities and expectations to junior officers, a process that maintains a set of attitudes and values that are recognizable and standardized in many agencies. It could be said that those activities maintain a way of thinking shared by most sworn officers regardless of their jurisdiction. This thought process can be found among the lowest to the highest ranks of officers.

There are also material items valued and shared, such as uniforms, equipment, technology, and vehicles. When material items and attitudes and beliefs are shared and valued to a point of becoming institutionalized (setting a standard), we say that police officers share an occupational culture. These thoughts are consistent with John Crank (1998) who argues that when officers are delivering police services, their method of delivery has become institutionalized or routine. Officers conduct themselves in a certain way because it is "the right thing to do," as one officer commented. In other words, it's a standard.

The standard is introduced when an individual becomes a police cadet. The cadet actively seeks mentors and relationships with other officers to fulfill expectations and to fit in with other members of the department. The cadet seeks a sense of belonging, security, honesty, mutual understanding, and trust (Mink, Dietz, & Mink, 2000). Rookie officers strive to meet their earlier expectations about policing; yet they also take cues from their new role models about their jobs, their ideals, and their lifestyles in general. They tend to accept police practice that is communicated and rewarded by other cops in spite of an individual's previous ideals, training, and expectations. As social relationships form, the individual moves closer towards achieving a sense of personal wholeness that typically translates into optimum commitment to and performance of the job.[1] According to John Clark, "diverse aspects of organizational activity merge into a whole united by commonly held values and shared ways of thinking." (1998, p. 15).

The description of the police as an occupation fits the definition of a culture. However, culture cannot be explained merely by the existence of particular topics or examples as described here. Rather, an occupational culture (much like culture in general) is a mixture of many elements and experiences in a particular occupational setting. An occupational culture includes the way issues or examples influence and justify behavior, brings meaning to the job and the fallout from the job, and is expressed in stories told among police officers after a long shift (Strecher, 1988).

When examining police culture, the influence of peer pressure should not be overlooked. There are strong indicators that a "blue code of secrecy" or what some call the thin blue line, does apparently exist. For instance, officers are expected to back each other even when behavior might be suspect. To "rat on" another cop will more likely produce disrespect and ostracism than respect and acceptance. Most officers see this code as a fact of life. Lastly, when thinking about police culture, larger police agencies have several cultural groups: one at the line level (lower rank levels), another at the supervisory and middle-management level, and another at the upper-administrative level. Some attitudes and beliefs will be common at all levels, and some will differ and may even be in conflict with other levels.

Cynical and Authoritarian, Isolationist, and Conservative Characteristics

By breaking down police culture into specific elements, it can be "characterized as being cynical, authoritarian, isolationist, and conservative."[2] These character-

---

[1]For more details, see Carter and Radelet, 1999; Mink, Dietz, and Mink, 2000.
[2]See David L. Carter and Louis Radelet, 1999, p. 181.

istics seem to describe policing during the reform era of policing as discussed earlier, but are often visible characteristics among officers today.

Cynical and Authoritarian Police officers who exhibit cynical and authoritative behavior are acting inappropriately on the one hand; yet under certain circumstances officers must assert a great deal of cynical and authoritative behavior during a crisis or when involved in a volatile encounter. It is expected that officers take control of a situation to resolve danger (Ericson & Haggerty, 1997). At the same time, we expect authoritarianism tempered with reason and responsibility. Training, education, and professional supervision can be positive steps toward controlling authoritarian tendencies (Alpert & Moore, 1997). Yet, one of the most positive methods of tempering authoritarianism is linked to an empowerment process aimed at the community through a community-policing initiative (Stevens, 2001a). Part of an empowerment process includes a decentralization of the agency or what can be referred to as a leveling of police authority to line officers and community members with an eye towards problem-solving strategies (DuBois & Hartnett, 2002).

Isolationist During the reform era we made police officers more mobile, controlled independent corruption, enhanced professionalism, and made officers aware of the threats associated with policing, and therefore increased their isolation from mainstream American society (Carter & Radelet, 1999; Manning, 1997). Isolationism may have been more prominent during the 1960s and 1970s when the police were referred to as "pigs" and were labeled as symbols of oppression by civil rights and anti-war protesters. Community-policing strategies, especially problem-solving techniques, help remove the barrier between the police and the community—building a "we" instead of "them and us" perspective (Skogan & Hartnett, 1997).

Conservative One factor of police culture that has not changed as much as expected is police officer conservatism (Carter & Radelet, 1999).

Police Officer Conservatism

Police officer conservatism is defined as a philosophy aimed at resisting change and maintaining the established order.

By police conservative, we mean an individual who accepts status-quo responses or a traditional notion about social order, and often, that status-quo perspective of social order is centered in Eurocentric ideals.

However, conservative officers see the justice process as one that should be retributive rather than rehabilitative or preventative. Retribution implies the act of taking revenge upon an offender.[3]

The idea of "just desserts" applies: that is, when sanctions are brought against a violator, they are getting exactly what they deserve. It should be noted that retribution as a philosophy seems to prevail in the criminal justice system as evidenced by the "get tough on crime" attitudes held by many Americans, policymakers, and police officers. Whether this philosophy is appropriate or inappropriate, a conservative perspective about violators might undermine community-policing efforts in a number of ways.

Specifically, if the police view social order couched in a Western European framework, then individuals who hold a different view about social order will come under suspicion. Why do officers tend to be conservative?[4]

Police Officer Conservatism Can Be Produced Through:
- Occupational socialization suggesting that they made choices making them the "good guys" and that offenders made choices making them the "bad guys."
- Free will prevails and good choices produce righteous citizens.
- Frustration with correctional systems (early releases) and the courts (dismissals based on perceived technicalities).
- Witnessing traumatic victimization.
- Witnessing offender replication.
- Witnessing the increase in officer litigation.
- Witnessing the failure of reform methods.
- Witnessing the detrimental effects of social problems.
- Accusations by the media that officers are bigots and part of the "good ole boy system."
- Witnessing reforms produced through street violence demonstrates that violence is a valuable tool for officers to use, too, in order to further their own agendas.
- Being accused of being ignorant and undersocialized.
- Lack of community support and trust in issues promoting police officer stability.
- Mass media's inaccurate portrayal of officers as members of a covert violent society.

Police Officers Live in Two Social Worlds

Can a person belong to a world within a larger social world? A police officer works in a police culture but, at the same time, lives in the larger world with its cultural nuances (Crank, 1998). A police culture is grounded in the everyday interactions with other individuals, and those interactions take on meaning within the context of the job and/or the situation. Trying to make sense of interactions

[3]In the criminal justice community there are six primarily philosophies that prevail: retribution or just deserts (a model of criminal sentencing which holds that an offender deserves the punishment received at the hands of the law and that punishment should be appropriate to the type and severity of crime committed); incapacitation (the use of imprisonment or other means to reduce the likelihood that an offender be capable of committing future crimes); deterrence (a goal of criminal sentencing which seeks to prevent others from committing crimes similar to the one for which an offender is being sentenced); rehabilitation (an attempt to reform a criminal offender); restoration (a goal of criminal sentencing that attempts to make the victim "whole again." Restitution and community participation to aid victims as opposed to offenders).

[4]These ideas are guided by David H. Bayley, 1991; David L. Carter and Louis A. Radelet, 1999, p.181; Wesley G. Skogan and Susan M. Hartnett, 1997; and Dennis J. Stevens, 2002b, 2001b.

apart from an officer's job, doesn't necessarily help us see the entire picture. By understanding the model of the larger world's culture, maybe we can relate to a police subculture. The police subculture can be expressed as an organized sum of a police perspective relevant to the role of a police officer. Yet, the accounts presented here are only one part of the story. Police cadets undergo a process of occupational socialization through which they become identified as officers and share all the ideas and expectations relevant to the role of police officer.

Socialization

Socialization is a process whereby an individual learns and internalizes attitudes, values, and behaviors appropriate to functioning as a responsible, participating member of society. Humans possess not only instincts (biologically inherited capacities for performing relatively complex tasks), but also the capability to perform many different responses to any given stimuli (something arousing interest). Therefore, society must teach acceptable responses. This process is known as *socialization*.

Socialization

Socialization has two components: one relates to learning socially approved behavior and the other is to behave in accordance with what was learned.

Sociologists suggest that while nature puts limits on what individuals can achieve, socialization plays a large role in determining what we do achieve. Socialization is linked to learning and performing.

However, a model that might aid us in understanding the process of occupational socialization relates to children. At birth, all human beings possess four basic elements aside from their biological development:

1. Humans are dependent on caretakers for everything, including food, warmth, and protection.
2. Human responses to stimuli vary among individuals.
3. Humans are selective; they choose certain voices over other voices, certain foods over other foods.
4. Humans have a natural propensity to learn.

Each of us learns in a different way and at a different speed. How quickly we learn is not necessarily a good indicator of our performance or general capability. However, slow learners are often stereotyped as individuals with fewer skills than others.

Humans learn by watching, listening, and interacting with others. We learn to smile, for instance, in order to fulfill needs. A child might learn to smile and make small sounds to get more attention or no attention or something in between. A child might see herself through the eyes of her caretakers or parents—Cooley's looking-glass self perspective. Children develop their self-image through a socialization process. Self-image determines a person's self-respect and lays a foundation for the individual's personality. Personality is linked to behavior in a variety of ways. Therefore, the early formative years of a child are the most crucial period, since that is when he or she learns socially approved behavior.

Socialization Types

There are four types of socialization that are experienced by most of us: anticipatory, developmental, resocialization, and occupational socialization.

Anticipatory socialization is the process where we learn to assume a role in the future, such as when children play house. As the experience of a police recruit moves from the academy to field training with a training officer, and to becoming a full-fledged police officer, a recruit's ideals about the expectations of the police work might change. For example, experiencing the streets as a patrol officer might alter early idealistic expectations about saving the world from itself.

Developmental socialization is a process by which we learn to be more competent in playing a currently assumed role. Children learn, for example, their acquired roles of daughter or son, student, and friend. A police recruit learns the role of patrol officer, community-police officer, and/or criminal.

Resocialization is less common. This process is where people are forced to abandon their old self and develop a new self in circumstances such as in prison, mental health facilities, or military training, and might include specialized police work such as undercover operations.

Occupational socialization is a process of learning the appropriate values, attitudes, and conduct expected of an officer. It is a process because those expected values, attitudes, and conduct are continually reinforced (Stojkovic, Kalinich, & Klofas, 1997).

Occupational Socialization

Occupational socialization is a process whereby personnel learn the extent of their jobs, its obligations, expectations, and roles.

Occupational socialization can start long before police employment actually begins and it continues through the entire career of an officer, especially since certain perspectives may change as an officer's experience changes. That is, seniority brings prerogative. Learning "the ropes" of an occupational social system includes intentional influences, such as academy training, special seminars (critical tactical units), and training-officer directives. It also includes unintentional influences such as locker-room discussions, peer-group pressure, and specialized work-group influences. Officers, like most professionals, engage in a process of interaction with other officers, and meanings that emerge from those interactions usually are defined in a practical, commonsense way (Crank, 1998). We create meaning daily, as an ongoing process, through interaction with people and events in simple everyday life. We might add, modify, or completely change our values, attitudes, and conduct based on those new meanings. Officer interpretation of both intentional and unintentional influences acquired as a result of occupational socialization can include those regarded as appropriate and legitimate for the job as well as those that are illegitimate and even illegal (Stojkovic, Kalinich, & Klofas, 1997).

Habitual conduct of police officers, both good and bad, can persist as long as the attitudes and the values that support the conduct are reinforced and rewarded, regardless of official decisions or sanctions. That is, beliefs and perceptions, habits and expectations of organizational members can remain constant, and in some cases official intervention can be seen as "the enemy." This consistency is particularly evident in police agencies where the practice of policing is unchanged over the course of many years.

Social or informal sanctions and rewards can be more powerful than official sanctions. Formal sanctions are often abstract and stem from impersonal sources such as medals of honor for performance (Stojkovic, Kalinich, & Klofas, 1997). Receiving cheers from peers for police performance has a far greater effect on conduct than a medal. Informal sanctions are personal and are evoked by sources valued by the individual receiving sanctions. It's the informal reactions, therefore, that can shape the conduct of an officer more often than formal mandates. One assessment of legal efforts to change the behavior of police officers is that courts tend to effect procedural rather than substantive change (Stojkovic, Kalinich, & Klofas, 1997). This accounts for the high levels of officer resistance to change relative to community-policing efforts. In earlier research, it was learned that officer resistance to proactive intervention techniques was a matter of grave concern to many top commanders within the agencies that were being investigated (Stevens, 2001a). Police managers need to master professional techniques in reducing officer resistance to policy in order to move community policing from a unit program to a department-wide philosophy.

Generally, learning police work (like all jobs) is a process of occupational socialization. You may compare the process to childhood socialization. However, the socialization process does not stop at the end of the initial training period. Although adult socialization experiences differ from those of childhood in the sense that adult participation is at a different level, socialization continues with the emergence of adulthood and stops only when a person dies. Understanding the socialization process of individuals can produce great rewards for community-police investigators as they evaluate the viewpoint of constituents while engaged in problem-solving strategies. How top managers receive these evaluations might depend on their philosophical leadership perspectives.

Leadership

Leadership

Leadership can be defined as the process of directing and influencing the actions of others.

Leadership skills are typical of efficient management regardless of the service or product produced by an organization.[5] Police agencies can have two types of leaders. The first type is easy to recognize. This person can be called an *instrumental leader* or *task-oriented leader*. This leader keeps police personnel, community members, and other groups of individuals from getting sidetracked, reminding them of the mission and goals of the agency. The second type of leader, the *expressive leader*, might not be recognized for his or her leadership skills since his or her primary mission is to increase harmony and minimize conflict among everyone. Instrumental leaders focus on the mission of an agency and expressive leaders focus on morale. Striking a balance between the two leadership styles is difficult because instrumental leaders sometimes create friction as they push everyone to move toward the mission and goals of community policing. Expressive leaders tend to be peacemakers who stimulate personal bonds and reduce friction. They tend to be popular leaders because of their concern for the individual rather than the agency.

There are three basic styles of leadership:

1. Authoritarian leader—a police manager who gives orders to community members.
2. Democratic leader—an officer who works toward agreement and harmony within the group.
3. Laissez-faire leader—a police manager who is highly liberal among group members, allowing them to control the group's progress.

Originally, it was assumed that a leader was born with leadership characteristics or traits but research has demonstrated that personal characteristics of leadership patterns can be viewed separately from an individual's personality or situational context (Tosi, Rizzo, & Carroll, 1986). Another approach explaining leadership skills are behavioral approaches, which emphasize distribution of influence and the tasks and social behaviors of leaders. A third approach, the contingency approach, tends to emphasize multiple variables, particularly situational variables that constrain leadership. These situational variables, argue Stojkovic, Kalinich, and Klofas (1997), include characteristics of subordinates, the organization, context, and style of leadership. Keeping in mind the complexity of community-policing strategies, it appears that the contingency approach might apply more often than a behavioral perspective, largely because police management operates in an adversarial environment that tends to constrain police leadership rather than advance it. Therefore, police leadership can be seen as a process that effectively accomplishes organizational objectives but depends on how a commander interacts with other domains of leadership outside the police agency and subordinates of the agency.[6]

Managerial characteristics among police leaders are seen as crucial for commanders because they must work closely with individuals who provide police

[5]For more details, see Cox, 1990; Hatten, 1997.
[6]See Klockars, 1985; Stojkovic, Kalinich, and Klofas, 1997; Tosi, Rizzo, and Carroll, 1986.

service (i.e., their own subordinates), and officers over whom they have little control (i.e., local, state, and federal personnel from other law enforcement agencies) (Trojanowicz & Dixon, 1974). But unlike their police sergeants, commanders have little direct influence over the daily lives of any of those officers (Klockars, 1985). They must also work closely with community members, business and social agency executives, and civic officials who can vigorously influence police service, yet these commanders seldom possess decision-making power in most of the enterprises they represent (Alpert & Piquero, 1998).[7] Finally, police managers are held accountable through courts and disciplinary committees with individuals whom police service affects, and again it appears that commanders have little influence in directing courts or committees to action (Carter & Radelet, 1999).

Taking a clue from manager trainers, Jim Kouzes, president of Tom Peters Group/Learning Systems, suggests, "If people don't believe in the messenger, they won't believe in the message." How does a police commander build credibility? Kouzes offers the acronym: DWWSWWD (Do What We Say We Will Do).

Leadership Changes in Management

There are changes in the philosophical mandates of police agencies across the country, and many of those changes challenge the way police agencies are managed.[8] One of the primary changes is the community-policing initiative. Police managers can no longer take comfort in the traditional response of a punishment-centered organizational bureaucracy accentuated through a reactive policy because of the due process revolution. The people in a democracy demand to be heard, one way or another. Are police leaders prepared to professionally manage community-policing initiatives?

Many police leaders have decisions to make about their managerial style because one assumption is that many police leaders tend to reflect managerial characteristics typical of a traditional police strategy as opposed to a community-policing philosophy (Stevens, 2001c; 2000d). Fewer police leaders than expected graded their own agency's community-policing initiatives as excellent. These same managers reported high scores in delegating work, trust in subordinates and in the general public, saw organizational change as inherent in police service, and solicited the aid of community members in making decisions about deployment and police practices. One implication of this study is that police managers tend to operate more from an antiquated control, arrest, and command hierarchy with top-down dictates about deployment, tactical and use-of-force limits, and constituent conduct.

A brief review of the literature shows that police officers have a high burn-out rate, due in part to a lack of coping adequately with family problems, occupational stress, little status, low public trust, and are likely to be involved in a civil liability

---

[7]In fact, the political leadership in St. Petersburg, Florida recently invited Chimurenga Waller, president of the St. Petersburg chapter of the National People's Democratic Uhuru Movement, to the Citizen Review Committee, which examines decisions of the St. Petersburg Police Department. Mr. Waller and his organization are bitter critics of the St. Petersburg Police Department. See Landry, 1998, for more detail.

[8]See Bayley, 1998; Carter and Radelet, 1999.

suit more than any other occupation. Also, many officers often deal with violators and people who generally have a different opinion about social order and compliance than most law-abiding individuals.

Why aren't police managers advancing with the times? One answer comes from the idea that there should be a balance police managers work toward, which often is unnoticed and unlikely in other organizations. That is, while police agencies need to address the root causes of crime through community partnerships, if real crime is ignored, it will escalate both in frequency and in intensity. Specifically, many officers at all levels hold on to their individual integrity to keep the public safe during their watch. Furthermore, since street crime is a response in most cases to living conditions, relationship expectations, and pure selfishness, most of those issues are not the business of the police. Therefore, finding the balance between professional intervention for the purposes of prevention, crime escalation, and police responsibility is a complex task of police officers, advisers, and policymakers. Yet officers, virtually at every rank, cannot follow through with community problem-solving decisions if policy, regulations, and employment expectations dictate otherwise. The traditional, incident-driven police organization (and policing as an institution) must alter policy, regulations, and expectations to fit within a contemporary framework of policing strategies for the twenty-first century. Just as community-policing models are different in different jurisdictions and within those jurisdictions, so are the community groups.

Another consideration in this discussion are the obstacles faced by police middle managers and top managers from political leaders who have little knowledge of policing strategies but have a great deal of input concerning the employment of any officer (including chiefs) who might oppose a political mandate. One example comes from Camden, NJ, where the department failed at community-policing initiatives due to both unstable political and police leadership, incisive police history, pervasive officer resistance, ramped crime, and devastating poverty (Stevens, 2001b). The Camden police department remains a paramilitary operation with the politicians dictating police policy and the police following those policies for arrest, calls, and stops as indicators of their success. What it came down to for Camden was "too many chiefs of police, too many involved officials, too much poverty, too much crime, too much officer resistance, and too little professional leadership."[9]

Community Policing Rationale and Importance of Managerial Style

Observers of community-policing strategies realize that community policing requires an outreach by the police to the community. Its purpose is to promote a partnership with the community to enhance public safety, reduce the fear of crime, and improve the quality of life.[10] At the core of this relationship lie problem-solving strategies linked to social problems that might lend themselves to eventual crime (Goldstein, 1977, 1990).

[9]For a closer look at this finding, see Dennis J. Stevens (2001b) Case studies in community policing. pp. 228–250.
[10]See Skogan, Hartnett, Dubois, Comey, Kaiser, and Lovig, 1999.

Priorities of Community Policing

The priorities of community policing include a preventive response to public order through a level of delegation of authority with community members and line officers as a response to future crime as opposed to a response after crimes have occurred.[11]

Police executives must demonstrate facilitative skills as opposed to enforcer skills in order to move their agencies into a twenty-first century police model (DuBois & Hartnett, 2001). Community-policing initiatives expand the responsibility of crime control and public safety to the community at large. Through this association problems relating to social disorder are identified, prioritized, and attempts are made to resolve problems to the mutual satisfaction of the partnership without compromising Constitutional guarantees. To accomplish this objective, a community-policing philosophy becomes a department-wide philosophy, making community policing the standard way the agency will do business and, of course, the way police executives manage the business of police service. However, there is not, and probably never will be, one best way to lead, manage, and assist any organization, including a police agency in the areas of strategy, policy, performance, productivity, human relations, or implementation. According to Police Chief Ramsey of the Metropolitan Police in Washington DC: "In a very short period of time, community policing has fundamentally changed how American police officers and executives view themselves and their respective roles in the community. Community policing has also significantly changed—and raised—public expectations of what the police can, and should, do when it comes to the old concepts of serving and protecting" (personal communication, 2000).

The success of community-policing strategies will depend on the methods used by police executives. Police leaders must possess proficient managerial characteristics in order to deliver contemporary quality police service. It could be argued that leadership characteristics aid in bringing about appropriate police strategies. Cox (1990) makes a suggestion that the quality of police leadership will automatically improve, not because of managerial training, professionalism, or public demand but because the gap between private enterprise and public service will narrow in terms of administrative skills, technology, and fiscal responsibility. Cox believes that police leadership will see the value of managerial styles represented in corporate America and will emulate those styles. However, there are universal characteristics that can be utilized by police leaders in a systematic way to move the agency to a community-policing philosophy.[12]

Managerial Rationale

Managerial characteristics can lend themselves well to a greater level of compliance among the individuals located inside and outside a police agency. These

[11]See Carter and Radelet, 1999; Kelling and Coles, 1996.
[12]See Carter and Radelet, 1999; Harrison, 1998; Houston, 1999; Keiger, 1997; Klockars, 1985; Manning, 1997; Nowicki, 1998; Skogan, 1990; Stojkovic, Kalinich, and Klofas, 1997.

characteristics relate to a style of motivating others toward the mission or objectives of the agency. Once appropriate police leaders are in place, they need to select a managerial style that best furthers the philosophy of community policing (Hatten, 1997).

Management

Management can be defined as the process of planning, organizing, and controlling resources in order to achieve public safety through community-police initiatives.

Part of a managerial style includes police leaders developing a mindset to recognize creative opportunities and different ways to deliver police services. It may require toughness and decisiveness in making difficult choices or changes that must be made for the health of the department and the well-being of the community. Appropriately empowering rank-and-file officers and community members, enabling them to mutually solve community problems, might be a laborious task within a paramilitary hierarchy-of-command organization. Yet, it is a task that must be accomplished if community-policing strategies are to bring the partnership closer to social order expectations. Decentralization might be one of the few options available to move the organization closer to its mission through quality police service. Also, decisions about patrol deployment, technical and use-of-force limits, and police disciplinary prerogatives might be decisions that require input from many sources, contrary to traditional methods of control.

While there is a prescribed process of resolving violator challenges, including due process remedies, the philosophy of the twenty-first century for police service emphasizes that action be taken by police leaders as that of a facilitator rather than an enforcer, as in traditional police organizations. Discovering what is being experienced by rank-and-file officers and by community members is vital, and those experiences must be articulated to everyone concerned in order to improve the quality of police service. Regardless of rallying by public servants to this contemporary philosophy, evolutionary methods of sharing command is a method of doing business that is both inevitable in a democratic society and required to accommodate the changing demographics and expectations of American society.

The primary concern seems to relate to police service models that depend on the managerial skill level of police leaders, regardless of rank.

A number of managerial characteristics were selected, consistent with the *Management Review's* study and characteristics observable of successful police managers engaged in community-policing activities, to understand the managerial attributes professional police leaders will need for the twenty-first century.[13]

[13]For an evaluation of police leaders in many police agencies and their managerial skills to meet the challenge of community police leadership, see Dennis J. Stevens, (2001c). Community policing and managerial techniques: Total Quality Management Techniques. *The Police Journal*, 74(1), pp. 26–41. See also Dennis J. Stevens, (2000d, October). Improving community policing: Using managerial style and Total Quality Management. *Law and Order*, pp. 197–204.

These characteristics when professionally employed would tend to motivate others, and bring the department closer to its intended objectives. This is accomplished in concert with an empowered community that emphasizes problem-solving prerogatives. Those managerial characteristics are as follows:

- **Organizational Change** Police leaders must encourage organizational change and treat change as a continuum in order to fulfill community-policing initiatives.
- **Creative Ability** A leader must develop a mindset to see creative opportunities and different ways to deliver police services in keeping with Constitutional guarantees and community-policing initiatives.
- **Toughness** Leaders must be willing and able to make difficult choices and institute changes for the well-being of the department and the community.
- **Subordinate Trust** Leaders must empower line officers with enough authority to enable them to solve community problems. Helping officers make good decisions is one mark of an excellent leader.
- **Public Trust** Leaders must empower community members to aid officers in solving community problems. Helping the public make informed decisions is crucial for twenty-first century leadership.
- **Delegation of Responsibility** Leaders must delegate responsibility to others in order to build rapport and to ultimately meet the mission of community policing. Controlling crime is everyone's responsibility. Delegating responsibility to others would be an impossible task within a paramilitary hierarchy-of-command organization. For that reason, decentralization of command, along with its responsibilities, is one of the few options available to move the agency and the community closer to their mission.
- **Police Decisions** Leaders must incorporate community member and rank-and-file officer input in decision-making processes about police services such as patrol deployment, technical and use-of-force response limits, and police disciplinary prerogatives. Guiding those individuals to make informed decisions is what being a facilitator is all about.
- **Taking Action** Leaders must take initiative in solving community problems if those leaders wish to develop and keep the support of community members and police personnel.
- **Communication** Discovering the experiences of rank and file officers and community members is vital to a leader involved in community-policing initiatives. Once those experiences are learned, they must be articulated to everyone in order to improve the quality of police service.
- **Sharing Command** Evolutionary methods of sharing command is a method of doing police business that is both inevitable and expected in a democratic and a pluralistic society. Largely, the future role of policing is that of guiding the public to police themselves.
- **Visionary** Leaders must be able to develop a mental picture of where the department is heading and must be able to describe their vision to others so everyone is headed in the same direction.

- **Integrity** The conduct of police managers must reflect an inner strength and integrity to win the trust of personnel and other community members.
- **Commitment** Leaders must solve the difficult as well as the easy problems to demonstrate a commitment to the individuals whom they serve and the public who depend on their commitment to public safety.

Are police commanders professionally prepared to meet the organizational changes expected of them to better serve constituents? Some observers have described police departments as if they were little countries, clans, or tribes rather than rational units, mechanistic entities, or a service centered on professional management processes. Clearly, police leaders must be visionary and have a mental picture of where the department is going. They must be able to describe their vision to others in order for everyone to be headed in the same direction. Finally, police leaders should be morally, ethically, and legally guided by an inner strength that speaks of their integrity.

Total Quality Management

One managerial philosophy that advances foremost quality police service and customer satisfaction is *Total Quality Management* (TQM), which has served private enterprises such as Ford Motor Company as well as some criminal justice agencies.

Total Quality Management

Total Quality Management can be defined as a managerial style where its rank-and-file are empowered to participate in goal attainment of the organization through problem-solving strategies.

Like community-policing practices, much has been written about TQM recently, blurring some of its meanings and value. TQM is consistent with community-policing principles as a philosophy that focuses on problem-solving and control. TQM, like community policing, was never intended as a panacea or cure-all. TQM is based on the writings of W. Edward Deming, who helped teach the concept of quality to Japanese manufacturing at the invitation of General Douglas MacArthur after the Second World War. Using David L. Carter and Louis A. Radelet (1999) as a guide, police agencies might adapt TQM's core principles:

- The organization must address both internal and external customers (police personnel and community residents).
- Most individual performance measures are counter-productive because they invite conflict and competition rather than cooperation. Moreover, individual performance measures do not measure customer needs; instead they focus on organizational expectations (arrest, service calls, and dollar amounts of confiscated property and contraband).

- The organization should have a constancy of purpose subscribed to by all employees and the desire to constantly improve service rather than be satisfied with what has been accomplished so far.
- Evaluations should be done on the basis of team accomplishments and comparisons.
- Emphasis should be placed on providing the best possible service the first time and not rely on inspections and reparations.

Organizational members are goal-driven and participate in goal attainment by the team, as opposed to personal achievements. It is ironic that TQM appears to be a managerial tool that has strong parallels with community-police initiatives.

Summary

We investigated the parameters of occupational culture and learned that a police culture does exist. We explored cynical and authoritarian, isolationist, and conservatism characteristics of police culture. Various types of socialization processes were discussed, including occupational socialization among officers. Leadership perspectives were described and leadership changes in police management were suggested. Community policing rationale and the importance of managerial style were explained. Managerial characteristics or traits that fit well with community police managers were reviewed and finally, a managerial style that best fits the community-police model was recommended.

Do You Know?

1. Define culture. In what way does the author suggest that a police culture exists? Why do you agree or disagree with the existence of a police culture?
2. Describe the issues raised concerning an authoritarian and isolationist position linked to policing. How can these issues be resolved?
3. Describe conservatism. In your observations of police officers in general, what experiences do you have that might support the conservative nature of officers?
4. In what way do officers live in two different social worlds? What are the consequences, if any, for this dual existence?
5. Define socialization and explain why socialization is necessary among human beings.
6. Identify the types of socialization that most of us experience and indicate the outcome of each type.

7. Define leadership and explain the ideal types of leadership.
8. In what way is managerial style important to community-police strategies? Describe its rationale.
9. Identify the managerial characteristics of a successful manager and explain how these characteristics apply to police managers.
10. Describe Total Quality Management and explain in what way it relates to community-police strategies. In what way do you agree or disagree that TQM is the best fit for community-police philosophy.
11. In what way does J. Edgar Hoover's statement fit this chapter: "Justice is incidental to law and order"?

7

Testing Police Strategies

"We can't solve problems by using the same kind of thinking we used when we created them."
Albert Einstein (1879–1955)

Key Terms

Applied Tests	Explicit Tests	Reliability
Cause and Outcome	Fixed Measurements	Replicatible
Relationships	Mutually Exclusive Lists	Sample
Documentation	Objective Thoughts	Subjective Thoughts
Exhaustive Lists	Pure Tests	Validity

Key Topics

- Measuring or testing the performance of police strategies.
- How ethnocentrism impacts testing.
- Exhaustive and mutually exclusive categories.
- Five stages when developing, conducting, and finalizing a test about attitudes.

Introduction

Although fixed measurements about police strategies are important, the focus of this chapter is on explicit measures: how to develop and conduct them, especially using website resources. Each explicit test is different because it is conducted by a different investigator. Each investigator uses a different method or design to conduct a test, with different objectives or goals. Each test relates to a different group of people or what is called the *sample*. Tests are unique because investigators have their own ideas, experiences, skill levels, and issues. However, there are specific procedures and objectives that are recommended and appropriate when producing a professional test. This is a practical guide provided to aid investigators as they develop and conduct tests. However, there are variations that might appear to be more credible and in keeping with traditional research methodology, but we are not limited to past research methods. You might consider this chapter a working draft to help you understand the investigative process.

Fixed Measurements

There are many ways to measure such things as trends, practices, and performance, including the use of fixed or conventional measurements. We measure everything from the productivity of factory workers, to rates of infectious illness, to the endurance of shortstops. When it comes to public safety, the measurement familiar to most of us is the Federal Bureau of Investigation's (FBI) Uniform Crime Report. These reports are one of the best examples of nationwide standardization of categorizing crime.[1] This type of measurement is called a fixed or conventional measurement and it might include a day-to-day monitoring by a public or private agency or organization. *Fixed measurements* are routinely conducted and used by organizations including human services, corporations, and private and public agencies such as the police.

[1]Available online at: http://www.fbi.gov/ucr.htm

Fixed Measurements

Fixed measurements can be defined as specific items numerically counted and placed into number sets.

Police typically measure the following:

- Arrests
- Patrol stops and citations
- Calls for service
- Response time (to the scene of a reported crime)
- Complaints against officers, and/or
- Dollar amounts of confiscated contraband and property (drugs, weapons, and cash)

By making comparisons between different sets of numbers, we could get an idea about the effectiveness of a policy. The principal mechanism for determining police effectiveness has historically been fixed measurements because most data (always plural) are easy to collect, and it is easy to understand the results of these measurements and to compare them with other number sets or variables.

Police agencies today are discovering the impact of new ways to test a number of variables. Agencies are recognizing that what they do and how well they do it is essentially subjective (from the eyes of an individual) and personal to those who receive their services. Police agencies have used (and appropriately so) fixed data to help them obtain resources to further their mission of controlling crime. For instance, Chief Carolyn M. Kusler, Broken Arrow, Oklahoma Police Department reported in the year 2000 that:

> Lack of manpower was a major concern...an aggressive recruitment campaign to bring the department from 74 sworn officers to its authorized strength of 81. One area of concern was the number of calls for service the department received which in 1998 totaled 25,067 and another 41,812 which were initiated by the department for a total of 66,879 calls for one year. Additionally there were 665 domestic violence reports, 9,807 citations, 1,470 arrests, 555 arrest warrants served, and 36 problem-solving projects completed. ...budget process, increasing the number of authorized positions to 87. Further manpower increases were approved in the 1999–2000 budget moving the authorized strength of sworn personnel to 94 (Stevens, 2001a, p. 32).

Fixed data serve a valuable purpose; yet resident perceptions about quality-of-life issues, such as fear of crime, is genuinely as important as arrest numbers. Therefore, agencies might want to consider fear-of-crime perceptions if they are concerned with quality police service. Finally, with the concern moving toward police service and police accountability, police executives are discovering that fixed measures fall short in helping to guide community-policing and problem-oriented initiatives and they seek other methods to discover what residents are thinking.

Why Study the Explicit Test Process?

There is no "best way" to discover what residents think. Yet, an explicit test helps. This chapter is a guide to develop, conduct, and analyze the performance of others at a skilled level, yielding professional results. Possessing skills others don't have at the workplace can help an individual become highly competitive. Personally, it can enhance an individual's level of confidence because you'll know something others don't know. Equally important, testing performance during problem-solving tasks can provide reliable options for decision-makers. That is, it aids in an informed decision-making process, which is where most community policing strategies start. Wouldn't you rather know many of the options before you tell the world your plans?

? Something to Think About

Evidence is far greater than expertise or opinion:
Strength in Numbers

Explicit Tests

Understanding police performance through fixed measures might prove less efficient in revealing how well a police agency has preserved the democratic process and enhanced quality-of-life issues. The need to develop efficient ways of testing performance, attitudes, and perceptions in the twenty-first century is a big issue among public agencies, especially police departments (Eck & LaVigne, 1994). For instance:

> The amount of research on law enforcement matters continues to grow, as does the number of police agencies that volunteer to participate in research efforts. However, law enforcement agencies cannot afford to wait for someone else to publish studies or to wait to be asked to participate in research. They must assume the initiative and conduct studies that directly address pressing concerns. Certainly, in the area of police problem-solving efforts, it is the agency's obligation to research and analyze the effectiveness of these efforts (p. 64).

Explicit Tests

Explicit tests refer to observing behavior (directly and indirectly) and testing a claim about a causal relationship (cause and outcome).[2]

One goal of explicit testing techniques is to enhance predictive abilities about programs, policies, and/or organizational outcomes. Here's how it works.

[2]For an in-depth discussion on cause-and-effect relationships, see Dean Champion (1993).

Applied Tests versus Pure Tests

Before you spend a great deal of time developing an investigation, make sure it can be used in a practical sense. Measuring performance should generally have a specific use or application. There are tests that have a limited use and are referred to as *pure tests*. Often pure tests are conducted for the sake of undertaking an investigation. For instance, measuring the extent of a police culture would seem to offer few rewards once the work was conducted, unless we had a good reason to examine police culture. The most challenging test for organizations is called an *Applied Test*. That is, an explicit method of testing performance, designed and conducted with a practical use in mind.

Applied Tests

Applied tests work toward some practical goal and generally can apply to police practice.

There is an applied test and a pure test of explicit measurement, but most of the time, an applied test is more valuable to a public agency. As you develop your own test, think in terms of application, and think in terms of objective, as opposed to subjective or personal opinion.

Writing Style

It should go without saying that professional writing skills (such as those practiced by the American Psychological Association) should be adhered to (more about this later in the chapter). Additionally, writers must understand they are not writing for themselves. They are writing for organizations, institutions, and policy makers. They are writing for readers. Therefore, an efficient investigator addresses issues that influence readers. And objectivity is key.

Personal Opinion

One of the rules often violated by investigators relates to personal opinion or what can be called *subjective* as opposed to professional or *objective* responses. This happens because policy makers, police managers, and for that matter, you and me, view the world through our own experiences, values, and knowledge.

Sometimes we all rely on stereotypes or our cultural understanding to help us shape our thoughts when we're investigating a question, even a non-police question. When an investigator is subjective (there is a tendency to prove his or her belief is right), a personal bias can alter the evidence, producing suspect conclusions. This might ultimately have an effect on public safety issues. For instance, whose idea will be used as a model of social order in a community? If police have a different viewpoint than the community, whose notion will be accepted, and consequently determine police deployment practices? Police service calls might also be subject to a different set of priorities, depending on whose view is considered realistic.

Subjectivity supports an unprofessional approach to policing through ethnocentric perspectives. Although it has been mentioned earlier, it is worthwhile to review this concept because of its impact on test results. There are two detrimental effects of *ethnocentrism*: first, judging others and other events on our own set of beliefs.

Ethnocentrism

Ethnocentrism is a belief in the superiority of your own social or cultural group.

The second impact of ethnocentrism is reinforces the idea that our own belief system and/or judgments are right. Hopefully, you can see that this is a bigger problem than you thought when testing the attitudes of others. For instance, if a police officer believes that frightening a status offender (i.e., curfew violator, runaway, and/or truant) with jail will teach the juvenile a lesson, how often will the officer confine and/or deny due process rights to a status offender as opposed to assisting that offender with his or her homework? Sound strange? Maybe. But the point is well taken since some officers use different means to accomplish goals (most with good intentions).

Personal opinion, or what can be called ethnocentric beliefs, can easily bias an investigator's vision. As a result, bias can alter the predictive value of a study because an investigator believes more in the need to convince others that the premise of the study is right than in allowing the evidence to speak for itself. Objective or professional behavior is difficult because many of us have difficulty leaving our cultural and personal baggage behind. Objectivity means that an investigator must remain nonjudgmental throughout the evaluation process.

Thinking about Causal Conditions

When thinking about performance, you might link together ideas that help shape a body of knowledge about the subject. That is, you could talk about the results of certain activities: "If this happens, then we can expect this as an outcome." For instance, if we think drinkers comply less with alcohol laws when there is a full moon, we must ask, "Why is that? Because light from the full moon lets drinkers see better, so they drink more?"

Test the causal condition (a full moon) against the expected effect or outcome (drink more) to see if there is any predictive value present. See what happens when the moon is full. Is there an increase in arrest rates among alcohol abusers? Ask questions of known drinkers. Observe activities of drinkers at clubs and at sporting events on those nights when the moon is full. Compare your results with results from nights when the moon isn't full. If your evidence supports the idea that on a full moon night, people drink more, then we need to create a way to keep the moon full less often. Let's review what we've covered so far:

- Causal Condition: Full moon
- Effect or Outcome: Drink more

- Predictive Value: When moon is full, people drink more
- Recommendation: Make the moon full less often

This fun research idea is not worth your time, of course, since you can't do anything about the moon. However, we see that a complete lunar idea or theory about alcohol consumption would contain specific propositions or ideas about the causal nature of the event. In other words, a good question to examine provides a complete understanding (all sides) of an issue.[3] If your idea is logical and realistic, it will stand even with continued scrutiny. Of course your idea can provide a degree of understanding, but it must still be tested to determine how strongly related it is to the causal condition. It is good practice to measure a well-connected group of assumptions, propositions, and definitions linked in such a way as to explain and predict outcomes based on the causal condition, that is, the relationship between two or more variables (Champion, 1993).

Causal Facts and Outcomes

Let's turn to a real example. At a community meeting, we learn that juvenile crime is on the rise and something should be done about it. If behavior is anything like we expect, we might argue there is always more than one cause for every effect. In other words, there are many reasons why juveniles engage in crime. To help build a rationale, let's try a small quiz. Identify five reasons why juveniles commit crime, especially violent crime:

1. _____
2. _____
3. _____
4. _____
5. _____

Now, which idea of yours is most on target?

1. _____

Your choice might be a good one. One purpose of a study is to discover which of your five reasons contributes most to juvenile crime. Ask in what way is your idea logical and reasonable? For the sake of argument, let's say you decide that neglect is a causal factor leading to juvenile crime. That is, leaving a juvenile alone or unsupervised provides the opportunity to engage in a crime of violence. Reasonable, isn't it?

Exhaustive and Mutually Exclusive Categories

Conceptually, however, neglect can be seen in a number of ways since it can mean different things to different people. When you define the concept of neglect, you are specifying its attributes or what is called operationalizing it. In other words,

---

[3]This is like gathering evidence at a crime scene and linking it together to understand who, what, where, and when.

neglect is a conceptual variable that can possess the attributes of "leaving a juvenile alone." Does this attribute of neglect tell the whole story? Every variable has two important qualities:

- Exhaustive
- Mutually exclusive

Exhaustive suggests that if the variable is to have any utility at measuring performance, we should be able to classify every observation (neglect) in terms of one of the attributes composing the variable. We would be in trouble if we conceptualized neglect strictly in terms of the physical attributes of abandonment. Isn't it true that neglect could include an emotional side, too?[4] And attributes such as rejection, denial of love, and a lack of a sense of belonging could lead to some pretty strange behavior? You can make your list exhaustive by adding other attributes to it. That is, neglect through child abandonment might produce an opportunity for a youth to engage in criminal activity; yet abandonment might produce other factors leading a juvenile to commit a crime of violence.

At the same time, attributes composing a variable must be *mutually exclusive*. Neglect can mean more than abandonment. Even when a juvenile is in the company of her parent/s every day except for school, in what way could she be neglected? If parent/s drank too much or fought all the time with each other (even if the parents lived apart), couldn't those continued patterns of behavior give rise to neglect, too? Therefore, we should develop attributes of neglect in such a way that it is a product of parental behavior, including abandonment and continued inappropriate behavior such as parental drunkenness and quarreling. In this case, attributes should be defined more precisely by specifying "neglect" as meaning more than juvenile abandonment because neglect can be both physical and emotional.

Now let's test our idea about neglect leading youths to crimes of violence. First, develop a question to investigate: Does neglect lead to juvenile crimes of violence? Next, test your idea.

Test It

Start your testing process with a question, leading to a causal statement. For example, the question developed for this textbook is: Does police practice enhance neighborhood safety issues and provide social order? The causal statement developed for this work is: Community-policing strategies give rise to crime control, reduction in the fear of crime, and enhancements in resident quality-of-life experiences. It will be suggested that the more that community members, especially culturally diverse members, influence the decisions of the police, the greater the likelihood that public safety and lifestyle experiences will be enhanced.[5]

[4]For a closer look at a study similar to the one under discussion, see Dennis J. Stevens, (1997a). Influences of early childhood experiences on subsequent criminology violent behaviour. *Studies on Crime and Crime Prevention*, 6(1), pp. 34–50.
[5]Note that in a causal relationship, the cause must be antecedent in time (prior) to the outcome.

Once you have developed an applied test question and causal statement, define or operationalize your principal variables. Now you're ready to prepare a well-documented description of the causal statement under investigation through a media search, develop a design to test your case, report findings, and offer ideas linked to those findings. Naturally, at the end of the road, an evaluator disseminates the information to others to ultimately change behavior. Therein lies the mission of evaluation: to change behavior. Here's how to go about it.

The Stages of Testing Police Strategies

First a suitable question is developed, leading to a cause and an expectation (which should be answered in the conclusion of a study). Testing performance in an explicit format consists of all the activities that pertain to five stages: Media Review and Problem Formulation; Test Design and Sample; Gather and Process Information; Results; and an Analysis of Results.[6]

Stage One: Develop the Question to Examine Media Search and Problem Formulation

State the question you will investigate followed by the causal relationship, which should include both your causal factors and its expected outcome. It is expected that in Stage One the problem under investigation will be framed in a coherent and documented (cite your references) narrative. Your job is to search the media. Searching the media for *documentation* helps describe cause-and-effect expectations. It is time consuming, but it is during this process that a student learns a great deal more about the subject.

Documentation

Documentation can be defined as collected evidence that can be referred to when describing key issues about your investigation.

What have others said about the key issues? To be an efficient investigator, try to anticipate obvious questions that readers might raise and address those questions in the narrative. A critical discussion needs to be presented about influences that affect your causal explanation, such as historical accounts, public policy, and maybe even current attitudes from the perspective of the public, the police, and the policy makers.

An investigator should address various ways in which the causal component can alter the value of the expected outcome. Stage One includes a review of other experiences to aid a reader to better understand the problem. What have other police agencies, consultants, and organizations reported about bringing an agency toward a community-policing philosophy?[7] This search can be conducted

---

[6]Stages were inspired by Popenoe (2000). Many of the definitions were borrowed from Champion (1993) and Thio (2000).

[7]Community-policing philosophy includes among other things community member participation in police decisions.

at libraries (usually academic libraries are best), and/or justice academy archives. But the most accessible source is the web.

Searching on the Web   Let's review our knowledge about searching websites. Appendix A offers a list of Website Tutorials that help. Online narratives can help you learn how to search the web.[8] There are likely to be hundreds of hits on any item you search, and sorting through all of them to find a useful page about the issues in your investigation might be harder than you think. (Examine Appendix B for evaluating hits, references to search tools, and definitions of search functions.) Also, keep in mind, everything written about a subject is not available online because:

> The dream behind the creation of the Internet [is] the possibility of universal access in a digital age—where any author's work could be available to anyone, anywhere, anytime. The experience of most people, however, is not that the Net contains great works and crucial research information. Instead most of what is there is perceived to be of low value. The root of the problem is that authors and publishers cannot make a living giving away their work."[9]

Search Engines   The *Internet Library* tells us search engines are software tools that allow you to ask for a list of Web pages containing certain words or phrases from an automated search index.[10] (See Appendix C for Internet Tools.) An automated search index is a database containing some or all of the words appearing on the Web pages that have been indexed. Search engines send out a software program known as a spider, crawler, or robot. The spider follows hyperlinks from page to page around the Web, gathering and bringing information back to the search engine to be indexed. A search engine lets you seek specific words and phrases.

Most search engines index all the text found on a Web page, except for words too common to index, such as "a," "and," "in," "to," "the" and so on.[11] When you submit a query, the search engine looks for Web pages containing words, combinations, or phrases you requested. Engines may be programmed to look for an exact match or a close match. They might rank hits as to how close the match is to the words you submitted. However, once the engine and the spider are programmed, the process is totally automated. No individual examines the information returned by the spider to see what subject it might be about or whether the words on the Web page adequately reflect the actual main point of the page.

---

[8]For a closer look, see The Criminal Justice Distance Learning Consortium, (1999). *The definitive guide to criminal justice and criminology on the worldwide web.* Upper Saddle River, NJ: Prentice Hall. [On-Line], Available: http://talkjustice.com And, A+ Research and Writing for High School and College. The Internet Public Library. Available online at: http://www.ipl.org/teen/aplus/search And, Dennis J. Stevens, (2001). *Measuring Performance: An easy guide to master the skills of a researcher.* NY: Authors Choice.

[9]See Mark Stefik, (1997). Trusted systems. *Scientific American*, 276(3), pp. 297–301.

[10]All of this information is through the Internet Public Library, which can easily guide you through each and every aspect of searching online. For an in-depth look, visit: http://www.ipl.org/teen/aplus/internet.htm

[11]Ibid.

All search engines are not equal. They index differently and treat users' queries differently. The burden is on the searcher to know how to use the features of each search engine.[12] Table 7-1 is a list of search engines that will help you find your way around.

The ones you elect to use will depend on the way you're searching. Some are search engines, directory/search engines, and some are multi-engines (for details, see Search Tools in Appendix B).

Stage Two: Design Your Test and Identify Your Sample

Knowledge is built on experience and observation. Hence, the crux of a valid applied test is centered on getting information or data. Data-collection techniques or test design occurs through a variety of ways (e.g., observation, experiment, content analysis, and direct inquiry in the form of interviews, surveys, and sample identification; see Table 7-2). The design explains how you will perform your direct or indirect observations to obtain data and how you will process it. Develop a design to investigate it. However, your test must be *replicable*.

TABLE 7-1 *Search Engines*

Search Engine	URL
All in One	www.all4one.com
AltaVista	www.altavista.com
Excite	www.excite.com
Galaxy	www.einet.net
Google	www.google.com
HotBot	www.hotbot.lycos.com/?query
Highway 61	www.highway61.com*
InfoSeek	www.go.com
LookSmart	www.looksmart.com
Lycos	www.lycos.com
Mamma	www.mamma.com
Meta-Crawler	ww.metacrawler.com
Monster Facts	www.monsterfacts.com
OneKey	www.onekey.com
Overture	www.overture.com
Web Crawler	www.webcrawler.com
Yahoo	www.yahoo.com

*Your search is submitted to Yahoo, AltaVista, Lycos, WebCrawler, InfoSeek, Excite, and more. Insert http:// before www.

[12]See Jack Solock, (1996, September). Searching the Internet Part I: Some basic considerations and automated search indexes in InterNIC News. Available online at: http://www.ipl.org/teen/aplus/bibliography.htm#Kuhlthau%201993

Replicable

> Replicable means that other investigators who test your causal statement and use a similar design, should produce similar findings.

Whatever design you choose, a narrative should be offered about your selection and how it will function.

Observation   Observation is a design used by many investigators because it is relatively easy to accomplish. While attending community-policing meetings, I was able to observe the "give and take" between police officers and community members. I can write that it thereby helped my readers with a picture of that relationship.[13] For some tests, observation might be the best method available. For example, cultural anthropologists might use this technique to study rural civilizations, and sociologists might use it to study motorcycle gangs. Observation means just that: to observe people in action. Sometimes, investigators might go further and actually participate in the group. For example, when sociologists investigate gang members they might join the gang and report on the gang's activities. Of course, there are many problems with this method but advantages, too, from participant observations. This method produces first-hand experience with real-life experience, but applicable to only the case being observed. And results are only as professional as the observer.

Sometimes observer biases occurs. That is, observers follow an initial tendency to rate certain objects or subjects in a biased manner. When this phenomena occurs it is called the *halo effect*. Also, when subjects know they are being studied, their conduct changes. This is called the *Hawthorne effect*. Both are common effects that might influence study results.

Experiment   An *experiment* is a process of manipulating variables to ascertain their outcome on the sample in the field or in the laboratory. One concern is that an investigator's presence will influence outcomes in the field. In the laboratory, individuals might act differently than when outside. The experimental method is often used by psychologists and biologists. It probably isn't as efficient when studying community policing for a variety of reasons. Can you identify some problems that can surface when testing police performance using an experiment design?

Content Analysis   *Content analysis* is another method of testing performance. In this design, primarily other studies would be used to make decisions about the causal question; for example, converting statistical explanations to verbal explanations from other studies. Content analysis is best when used to investigate historical information. Interpretation of other studies would more likely be subjective than objective.

Direct Inquiry: Interviews, Surveys, and Samples   Lastly, interviews and surveys are what can be referred to as *direct inquiry designs*. Usually, these designs

[13]See *Case Studies in Applied Community Policing.*

include large samples that have input through surveys and/or interviews. Often, the two techniques are merged. For instance, The Madison Wisconsin Police Department surveyed residents through their own officers.[14]

A word of caution: often when human subjects are included in a study, it is advisable to obtain their consent, and in many cases consent may be required. One way of protecting the identity of participants, organizations, or communities is the use of pseudonyms (false names) in your work.

Interviews Interviews can produce rich responses, if conducted in an appropriate manner. An interview should not be confused with a survey. A survey has a set number of specific questions, and the responses of the participant are generally consistent with the questions. In an interview, short abstract questions are asked so that the person being interviewed can offer a variety of responses that are linked with the participant. Also, interviews tend to the face-to-face while often times, investigators might never see a survey participant.

A face-to-face inquiry can produce excellent information. For instance, ten students in Boston interviewed 76 individuals as part of this textbook's investigation of the performance of the Boston Police Department. Most of the students were Latinos—many whom were not U.S. citizens, as were the individuals interviewed. Therefore, it is more likely that the information tends to be more accurate than if the interviewers were from different cultural groups. One approach to interviewing is to develop a short list of general topic questions for the respondents, such as: "Tell me about your job." As the respondent reveals information, and the interviewer is trying to build rapport (trust) with the respondent, the interviewer should follow a few commonsense rules:

- Listen attentively.
- Refrain from judgmental comments.
- Use nonverbal cues to ask the respondent to continue.

When investigators are talking, they tend to learn less than when they are listening. The mission of the interviewer is to gain as much information as possible from the participant, not the other way around. As a respondent gives general information, specific questions should be asked by the interviewer to gain concrete examples of those experiences. For example, an experienced investigator asks, "Can you give me an idea about how that works?", even when the interviewer has expertise in the subject area.

One successful method of investigation is to interview one sample, and survey a different but similar set of individuals to see how closely their responses are related. Differences and/or similarities between survey results and interview results should be explained. Another method is a phone interview which can be conducted easily and inexpensively, but it tends to produce questionable results.

[14]For a closer look at this process see both versions: Masterson, M., & Stevens, D.J. (2001, December). The value of measuring community policing performance in Madison, Wisconsin. *Law and Order*. 49(10), 98–100. And Masterson, M., & Stevens, D.J. (2002). The value of measuring community policing performance in Madison, Wisconsin. In Dennis J. Stevens (Ed.). *Policing and community partnerships*. (pp. 77–92). Upper Saddle River, NJ: Prentice Hall.

Overall, if a respondent takes issue with an investigator during the survey or the interview, what those participants tend to report might be different among different investigators. For instance, if an older Irish American were interviewing or distributing a survey to African American females, the participants might respond differently than to a young African American female handing out surveys. In general, interviews are time-consuming and can be costly, but a wealth of information can be produced through this method.

Surveys   I developed a survey used at community meetings (see Appendix D) and had students who were from the countries represented by the sample, distribute the surveys and conduct the interviews. There were 2010 completed surveys from eight jurisdictions across the United States as part of the investigation for this textbook. Those jurisdictions included Alexandria, Virginia; Boston, Massachusetts; Columbia, South Carolina; Columbus, Ohio; Palm Beach County, Florida; Miami-Dade County, Florida; Midland, Texas; and Sacramento, California.[15]

Developing the survey itself is a difficult process and often requires a great deal of time, patience, and input from many sources. Even when it is completed to your satisfaction, it should be tested and revised to get the bugs out. Surveys generally consist of several components:

- Confidentiality statement: use of survey (see Appendix D).
- Qualifier question, such as "What district of Boston do you live in?"
- Demographics, for example, length of time in the community, age, renter/owner, gender, ethnic identity/race.
- Questions relating to your causal question.

Never use your causal question in surveys. For instance, if studying corruption or alcohol abuse among narcotic officers, don't bother asking if they are corrupt or an alcoholic. In those surveys, the outcome should never be in the survey question.

Students are encouraged to develop a survey consisting of 25 questions since those questions generally fit on two pages (brevity aids survey performance and survey management). Of 25 questions, 18 should relate to causal issues, 2 should relate to outcome issues, and 5 to demographic issues (age, gender, job, and so forth). One of the demographic questions should be a qualifier. If you're testing community performance, ask participants where they live. Surveys should have ample space between each question with ample margins (but not justified) around the page. It goes without saying that the survey shouldn't contain spelling errors or words that your sample might not understand or appreciate. (KISS: Keep it Simple and Short!) Don't ask questions to fill space. Each question must have a purpose and surveys with a large number of questions (fifty or more) are probably too long.

The wording of questions and answers (if closed-ended) must relate to the people being surveyed. That is, the words selected must be in the vocabulary of

[15]See *Case Studies in Applied Community Policing.*

the respondents (barring profanity and nasty language). Each question should probably contain a set of answers (give answers that make sense) that a respondent can check or circle. The survey in Appendix D contains answers for the convenience of the respondents. Surveys with closed-ended answers are faster to complete, easier to record and to tabulate. Give "way out" answers. That is, if a respondent doesn't want to answer a particular question, there is a way out for them, such as "don't know," or "not sure," or "other" type responses. That includes answers that are "Yes" or "No" (should include a "don't know" response).

How do you develop questions and answers? For best results, don't use your outcome expectation in any question. For instance, when examining my idea that the more that community members influence police decisions, the more public order would be enhanced, any part of public order cannot be used in the questions, but it can be used in a closed-ended response. In order to enhance validity (accuracy),[16] participants must report to the investigator the answer as opposed to the other way around.[17] By putting your outcome in a question, a participant could easily guess what's on your mind and might try to win your approval or the approval of their friends as they conduct the survey by offering an inaccurate response. For instance (see survey Appendix D, Question 12):

1. All things considered, do you think the neighborhood a year from now will
   Be a better place to live _____
   Stay about the same _____
   Become a worse place to live _____
   Not sure _____

There are a variety of reasons why a participant might respond inappropriately, including incriminating themselves in unacceptable or illegal activity. Be mindful that when developing interview questions for your survey many of us have been programmed to respond to certain questions with specific "socially approved responses" or "socially approved rhetoric." For instance, if you ask an offender if he committed the crime of child molestation, most often what answer might he give? How often would you guess that he would say that he was molested when a child? Ask a cop if she ever arrested anyone based primarily on gender or race; what answer could you expect?

There are many ways to discover truth and some of those ways have to do with finding social indicators. A *social indicator* might include asking criminals about their early life experiences. Ask police officers about their arrest experiences and ask community-police supervisors about their notions about crime and justice. Are you getting the idea? When quizzing alcoholics, ask about punctuality and work experiences. You're looking for indicators and patterns. Therefore, from the media search you conducted, you would confirm information you know already about certain indicators that are suggestive of certain behavioral patterns or conditions. When I investigated corruption among narcotics officers, obviously I

---

[16]Are you measuring what you think you're measuring?
[17]Try to follow this advice in interviews for more valid results.

couldn't ask if a respondent were corrupt. I had to uncover social indicators of what corrupt behavior looks like and ask the officers about those indicators.[18] However you develop your survey, discuss the primary points of its process so that your readers have an idea about that process. For instance, the survey used in my study (as shown in Appendix D) was developed over a period of time by the principal researcher in collaboration with police practitioners.

In reviewing surveys they used at their departments, certain ideas came to mind. For instance, a Madison, Wisconsin survey had some relevant questions that, in part, were developed for my survey. Also, in reading the Bureau of Justice Assistance's (1992) *Helping Communities Mobilize against Crime, Drugs, and Other Problems*, the researcher learned much about what makes communities work. Lastly, Skogan et al.'s (1999) compelling work in Chicago helped the writer frame questions, too. The finished product was reviewed by many colleagues, including Jill DuBois in Chicago, Captain Michael Masterson in Madison, and Professor Kurt Kerley at the University of Mississippi. The survey was tested on several groups prior to being distributed nationally. Adjustments were made accordingly. (It is expected that a narrative similar to the one offered here is in your methods section or Stage Two of your work.)

Some of the disadvantages of surveys are that the questions developed cannot easily be changed once the study is underway because it's hard to go back and ask respondents to retake a survey. Results from surveys are reduced to statistical explanations including averages (e.g., the average age of your respondents).

The design for your investigation could be similar to those illustrated in Table 7-2.

Samples   Stage Two consists of articulating the design you will use to test your idea. It includes a plan for sample selection, collection, recording results, and statistical methods (averages, percents, cross tabulations, chi square, and others) to be used. A study population must be selected (for me that meant residents in several cities across the United States, including Boston). The total survey participants numbered 2,010 in that study and the results can be seen throughout *Applied Community Policing in the Twenty-First Century* and in its accompanying book, *Case Studies in Applied Community Policing*.

A sample of at least twenty-five participants can produce results that provide a window of information. It goes without saying that the individuals in the sample should not be family or personal friends of the investigator. Of course, the number of participants can go as high as several thousand individuals depending on the resources of the investigator(s) and the size of the population group in question. Whichever sample is selected, a narrative is expected that reports the decisions made by the investigator.

All of the participants of a test should have something in common, and should be relevant to the causal question. My sample, for example, was all residents in the jurisdiction where community-policing programs were underway and

[18]See Stevens (2001c).

TABLE 7-2   *Investigation Designs*

Method	Characteristics	Advantages	Disadvantages
Observation	Watching individuals at community meetings. Participating in community meetings and/or concealing oneself watching gang activity from a van.	Firsthand experiences with real-life activities.	Observations might apply to only the case being observed. And results are only as professionally drawn as the observer.
Experiment	Manipulating variables to ascertain their outcome on the sample in the field or in the laboratory.	Ease of testing theories and ease of controlling conditions of the experiment.	Investigator's presence will influence outcomes in the field. In the laboratory, individuals might act differently than when outside.
Content Analysis	Evaluating other studies. Converting statistical explanations to verbal explanations.	Time. Also, may be best way to evaluate historical information.	The interpretation of other studies would more likely be subjective than objective explanations.
Direct Inquiry	Surveys. Interviews.	Large samples can have input through questionnaires. Interviews produce richer responses. Phone interviews can be conducted easily and inexpensively.	Questions developed can't easily be changed once study is underway. Results from surveys are reduced to statistical explanations. Interviews are time-consuming, costly, but allow more flexibility. Phone interviews lack face-to-face advantages.

most of the respondents reported that they participated in community-policing meetings. How you select your sample is relevant too, and it affects the credibility of the findings. That is, if you are studying crime, ask criminals; if you are investigating schools, ask students; if you are examining arrest rates, ask police. Whenever possible, always go to the source. An efficient investigator knows that almost every member of a targeted population must have an equal chance of being in the study.

In my study, my assistants and I attended community-policing meetings and had permission from the leaders of those organizations to distribute a survey to the members. There was only one version of the survey used in all cases (more about survey development in the next section). The survey had been translated from English into Chinese, and Spanish (and translated back into English when evaluating the results). Once participants completed the survey, it was collected; surveys were brought to my office; each survey was numbered; and graduate students and/or myself (depending on who was available) recorded answers to each question in a computer grid.

Which members of the community did not have an equal chance to complete my survey? Answer: Those who didn't go to meetings. Maybe they were on vacation, or ill, or sitting in a classroom. How many people in a community might not join a community meeting? Why? What about their ideas on police performance? One of the tasks of a good investigator is to try to get as many members in a targeted population to be heard. In other words, in what way can an unscrupulous and/or an ignorant investigator bias results?

Some police agencies have a survey online. If a survey is available only online, residents without a computer might not be able to respond to questions. If Wal-Mart is the only place in a city where an investigator asks shoppers about policing, what members of the community are not likely to be represented? If the survey is conducted in the evening, shoppers who work at night won't be represented. If the survey is conducted at the local community college, depending on the time and the building (biology or natural sciences, or behavioral science, or the athletic building) can the survey results be biased? Officers in Madison, Wisconsin, who walked their beat and knocked on doors asked questions of residents they encountered. Which individuals were probably under-represented in their test? How about individuals who might not speak the same language as the test-takers?

Finally, much of the time, permission needs to be obtained from an appropriate individual to conduct a survey—at Wal-Mart (the manager) or at the community college (the president). An investigator should establish access to a survey population in advance. It isn't automatic that specific populations (prisoners, parents, counselors, community members) are available because you're a surveyor or a cop. Allow time to get approval and it is best to get it in writing for your files so that there are no misunderstandings. In the agreement letter, indicate among other things who will conduct the survey, which days/nights, and at what times. But never discuss the central idea of your study, since that might alter the validity of the test.

Stage Three: Gather and Process Information

Gather and process data using guidelines explained in Stage Two. Data are assembled, classified, and organized to help an investigator test the question. This might include codes for each question and answer on the survey, spreadsheets to help organize and interpret the data, and/or transcribing interviews that were conducted (using recorders or notes written by the investigator). The supporting components used in this stage depend on the size of the sample and the instruments used to develop data. For example, large-scale survey results might be best interpreted by computerized statistical packages that validate or compute data using a number of statistical tests, such as chi square, or *t*-tests. However, it is recommended that you learn statistical formulas only if you're comfortable with them. Otherwise, let computer software assist you. However you develop this stage, a narrative is expected and should be part of the narrative developed in Stage Three. Some researchers call Stage Three the methodology or method section.

Stage Four: Results

 Describe the results produced from the test design in a clear and logical manner (i.e., without your opinion). How often do some of your findings parallel some of the experiences of the media discussions, which are in your narrative in Stage One? If this is the case, write something like "this finding is consistent with what the Madison Police Department (Masterson & Stevens, 2002) found when they surveyed residents in their community." Be sure to cite it appropriately.

Accuracy and significance of findings are assessed in terms of their *validity* and *reliability*.

Validity

Validity refers to the degree to which a study or the social instrument such as a survey actually measured what it was intended to measure.[19]

Reliability

Reliability refers to the degree to which a study or social instrument provides consistently accurate results.

If the study were conducted by another police agency using similar methods and designs, they should be able to produce similar results. In other words, the findings can be repeated or replicated. Again, a narrative is expected and perhaps a table highlighting your findings. It is often helpful to develop a table first to help you stay organized.

Stage Five: Analysis of the Results (Conclusion)

With all the data available, what are your thoughts or your conclusions? Answer the question you originally asked: Do culturally diverse community members engage in police decision-making processes? In Stage Five, it is that question that will take center stage. In what way has the causal question been supported? Link major points of

[19]For more detail, see Dean Champion (1993). There are four types of validity. Content validity refers to the logical conclusions of a sampling of items taken from the universe of items that measure the trait in question. Predictive validity is based on the measured association between what an instrument predicts behavior will be and the subsequent behavior exhibited by an individual. Concurrent validity is closely connected to predictive validity but differs in that the scores are obtained simultaneously with the exhibited behavior. And lastly, construct validity is both a logical and a statistical validating method.

the conclusion to the media (experiences of others as reported in Stage One). Make the leap from specifics to generalizations (inductive reasoning). What are your recommendations based on the findings? Link sample to population, or larger population, if feasible. A narrative is a critical component of Stage Five.

Format   The professional writing format of your study is very important, and should match the professional level of your audience. One strong recommendation is that the American Psychological Association (APA) citation style be followed throughout your work. An inexpensive manual can be purchased online.[20] The following recommendations should be considered when writing your study:

- paper size and color: white paper 8½ x 11 and black ink
- font selections and point size: New Times Roman, point size 12
- margins: one inch around the page
- double-spaced, except single-spaced in indented quotes
- justified margins throughout work, except tables, references (only on reference page), and the survey itself
- appropriate citations
- citations must match references in regard to spelling and publication dates
- reference page
- references should match the citations and vice versa and should match the source of those references
- endnotes at end of chapter
- spelling and grammar should be as accurate as possible
- third person is more appropriate than first person
- verb tense agreement is required
- avoid quotes; interpret what others say and cite accordingly
- be consistent

Two last points. Once you have completed a final draft, develop a short executive summary or what is referred to as an *abstract*. That is, in one sentence or so, tell your reader about each stage of development. Be sure to mention your sample, and how closely the findings meet your idea. Include a recommendation based on your findings. Generally, an abstract should not exceed 150 words.

Finally, it is strongly advised that you have someone look over your work to ensure accuracy. For instance, the community-policing study was reviewed by Professors Nina Silverstein, CPCS; Xiaogang Deng, Department of Sociology; and Melissa Driscol, University of Massachusetts, Boston.

? *Something to Think About*

If people don't believe the messenger because of a poor presentation, how much of the message will they believe?

---

[20]See *Publication Manual of the American Psychological Association*, 4th ed. (Spanish Edition Available). Also *Mastering APA Style: Student Workbook and Training Guide*. www.apa.org

In writing, style reflects our abilities. Sometimes, people are effective at persuading others and sometimes they are not. The effectiveness of persuasion depends on who says what, how, and to whom. Recently at a police psychologist conference, Professor Oscar Mink (2000) described what he called a *parasite ecology* about this idea. That is, the method of communication is more important than the knowledge it contains. Communicating a message in a professional way can effectively persuade someone regardless of the content. As an example, think of discreditable newspaper and television show accounts of an incident and how the presentation might have this effect on unsuspecting viewers. Because of the polished method of delivery, the public might believe almost anything they say to be true.

The Five Stages of Investigation
- **Stage One: What question are you going to investigate?**
  Explain it
  Media search
  Problem formulation
  Anticipate questions of readers
  Relevance of investigation
- **Stage Two: How will you test your question and who is your sample?**
  Sample
  Design
- **Stage Three: Gather and Process Data.**
  Collect it
  Code it
  Spreadsheets
  Statistics
- **Stage Four: What were the results produced from your design?**
  Link some of your findings to your references.
- **Stage Five: What do you think about what you found?**
  Your opinion is valid here based on the evidence.
  Answer the investigated question.
  Link your opinion to some of your references.
- Tables, Endnotes, Copy of Survey, and References at end of work

Summary

In this chapter we examined different ways to measure or test the performance of police strategies. We discussed measurement models, including a description of fixed measurements. We suggested that traditional methods of counting trends and incidents plays a role in police operations. However, we saw that the fixed measurement model falls short in getting a picture of constituent attitudes; therefore, an explicit measurement test was recommended. Information came to light about the differences between applied explicit tests and pure explicit tests, suggesting that an applied test is more beneficial in police evaluations because it can be used to enhance police services. The impact of ethnocentrism was characterized relative to professionalism of investigators. Exhaustive and mutually exclusive categories were explained, suggesting that items have more than one meaning. We discussed in detail the five explicit measurement stages when developing, conducting, and finalizing a test about the attitudes of others. We mentioned website searches and how to work with search engines. Various measurement designs were revealed, and information was presented about the construction of a survey and interviewing techniques. A writing format was reviewed, prompting a discussion about believing the messenger of an investigation. We concluded with a chart presenting the five stages of an investigation.

Do You Know?

1. Define fixed measures and identify their importance in police operations.
2. Below are fixed methods of evaluating police activities. In what way can these activities aid the police to better deliver their services?

   arrests _____

   patrol stops & citations _____

   calls for service _____

   response time_____

   complaints against officers _____

   dollar amounts _____
3. Identify the limitations of a fixed measure and an explicit test. What are the advantages of both techniques?
4. When you're at work or in school and you're thinking about a program and/or policy that you think is inappropriate, how would you test it in order to make a good recommendation to whoever could alter it?
5. Identify a good idea that you want to understand better.
6. Break down your idea. Identify:

   Cause _____

   Outcome_____

   If this, then that (predictive value) _____

   Why do you want to investigate it?_____
7. Identify a few reasons why an applied test (as compared to a pure test) might be more useful to a non-policing business?
8. Identify specific groups that hold suspect perspectives about other groups.
9. Describe the outcomes produced through ethnocentric perspectives of the groups you mentioned in Question 8.
10. Identify the five stages of developing an investigation. Describe the purpose of each stage.
11. In what way does Albert Einstein's message apply to this chapter? "We can't solve problems by using the same kind of thinking we used when we created them."

Appendix A

Web Search Tutorials

Principles of Web Searching (Cornell University)
http://www.mannlib.cornell.edu/reference/tutorials/search/index.html
> Comprehensive introduction to how the Web is constructed and how the search tools work. Sections on Robot-Assembled Databases, Human-Assembled Databases, Subject-Based Databases, Multiple Search Engine Interfaces and more. Links to the search engines described in the article, along with their strengths and weaknesses.

Introduction to Literature Searching (Cornell University)
http://www.mannlib.cornell.edu
> Cornell University's Mann Library tutorial intended to help students learn to search the online periodical indexes, has a very helpful example of Identifying Your Search Topic, followed by examples of how to use Boolean Logical Operators (AND, OR and NOT).

The Spider's Apprentice
http://www.monash.com/spidap.html
> A service from Monash Information Services, this site has Search Engine FAQ, How to Plan the Best Search Strategy, How Search Engines Work, and analyzes and rates the major search engines in different categories. Also provides a Web Search Wizard page from which you can conduct your search.

Search Engines: What they are, how they work and practical suggestions for getting the most out of them
http://webreference.com/content/search/
> A service of webreference.com, this article explains how to take advantage of knowing the way search engines work, how to choose which engine to use and explains some of their useful features.

Appendix B

Evaluating Hits, Search Tools and References, and Definitions of Search Functions

Evaluating Hits

This is usually the hardest and most time-consuming part of a search. The number of hits you obtain can range from none to hundreds of thousands, and their relevance or usefulness can vary from considerable to negligible. There are some things you can do to help produce more relevant hits for the fewest total number:

- An excessive number of hits is caused by queries that are too general. Use specific terms.
- Too few hits are usually caused by too restrictive a query, misspelled words, and inappropriate terms.
- Start with a subject search and continue down the path to the last relevant title.
- Narrow the scope of your search by choosing a specific field of search offered by the search engine, such as a time period or geographical area.

Success in any particular search query is usually more a question of which search tool has the best database for the subject and how the information is organized for retrieval. This is why it is often necessary to try a number of different search tools when searching for obscure information.

Some search engines list the hits by titles, some by brief text, and some give you a choice. When available choose the brief text, as it is easier to evaluate. Even so, it is often necessary to click the link to see the entire document before you can assess its content. Some sites may not be of apparent interest, but will contain links that have great relevancy.

Some searches yield the desired information quickly, and some you may just have to plod through.

As you gain experience, you will find the search tools to use that are most appropriate for your particular interests and how best to evaluate the hits.

Search Tools

Various websites will make finding information on the Web possible. From among the many Web search tools, twelve were chosen as the most useful. Table 1 lists preferred search tools by the search method each employs. As can be seen in its headings, the search methods are: Directory, Search Engine, combined Directory/Search Engine, and Multi-Engine.

TABLE 1 *Preferred Search Tools by Search Method*

Directory	Search Engine	Directory/Search Engine	Multi-Engine
LookSmart*	AltaVista	Excite	All in One
–	OneKey**	InfoSeek	
–	Hotbot	Google	Mamma
–	–	Yahoo	MetaCrawler

* Provides a keyword option independent of the subject search.
** Provides a subject option independent of the keyword search.

Search Methods

The following briefly describes each of the search methods employed and suggests exercises for achieving a familiarity with their use:

1. A directory search tool searches databases by subject matter. It is a hierarchical search that starts with a general subject heading and follows with a succession of increasingly more specific subheadings. It is also called a "subject search."
2. A search engine search tool accesses databases by using keywords. It responds to a specific item, or query, of interest with a list of references or hits. It is also called a "keyword search."
3. A combined directory/search engine is a search tool that uses two allied search methods in concert. As a directory search, it follows a directory path through increasingly more specific subtopics. At each stop along the path, a search engine option is provided to enable the searcher to convert to a keyword search. The subject search and keyword search are allied, because the keyword search can pose a query on a subject or topic along the directory's path. The further down the path the keyword search is made, the narrower the search field.

4. A multi-engine, also called a meta-search engine, searches databases by employing several search engines in parallel. It then lists the hits either by search engine or by integrating the results into a single listing. The search is conducted via keyword using commonly-used operators or plain language. All-in-one searches operate differently than the others in the multi-engine category. It provides a convenient way to search a large number of search tools one at a time.

Most directory search tools today supply search capabilities by both directory, i.e., subject search, and by search engine, i.e., keyword search. Because of their greater complexity, keyword searches receive far greater coverage here than subject searches.

Operators Used in Keyword Searches

Operators are the rules or specific instructions used in a keyword search for composing the question or query. You begin a keyword search by placing your query in the search box of the search engine's home page. To construct the query, use the appropriate operators for the selected search engine. While each search engine has its own operators, some are common to a number of search engines. The following describes the more frequently used operators, each of which is shown as a numbered heading:

1. Boolean employs AND, OR, NEAR and NOT to connect words and phrases, i.e., term, in the query wherein: AND requires that both terms are present somewhere within the document being sought. NEAR requires that one term must be found within a specified number of words. OR requires that at least one term is present. NOT excludes term from query. This one is excellent for cause-and-outcome relationships.
2. Plus and minus signs employ [+] before a term with no space in between to retrieve only the documents containing that term. It is similar to the boolean "AND." Employ [-] before a term with no space in between to exclude that term from the search. It is similar to the boolean NOT.
3. Quote marks indicate that the words within the quote marks are to be treated as an exact phrase, or reasonably close to it. It is similar to the boolean NEAR.
4. Brackets are used much like quote marks but with the additional constraint that the words within the brackets will be considered and searched as a single entity.
5. "As per example" is a technique that directs a search to that of the example by requesting "more like this."
6. Case-sensitive adjacent capitalized words are treated as a single proper name. Commas separate proper names.

For more detailed information on the use of operators go to Help Sections of the search tools. **AltaVista** provides the most detailed operator help section; **Excite** and **Hotbot** provide the most concise.

Keyword Searching

You will find that keyword searches are easy to use, but not easy to use well. Unfortunately, most search engines developed their systems of search independently. Therefore, there are no standards in nomenclature, database organization or retrieval systems. Thus for each search engine, you get the best results by composing the query for that particular engine.

Table 2 is organized to help you to select the frequently used operators for the preferred keyword search tools. More specialized operators can normally be found in the search tool's help section. [See "Search Tool Reference" in the Appendix.] As can be seen, the table contents above are somewhat incomplete. The authors have contacted the search tools' webmasters both to verify and supplement the information provided, and now await responses for future inclusion in this table.

TABLE 2   *Keyword Searching by Search Operators*

Search Tool	Boolean	Plus/Minus	Quote Marks	Brackets	Case Sensitive
All in One	–	–	–	–	–
AltaVista	yes	yes	yes	yes	–
Excite	yes	yes	–	yes	yes
HotBot	yes	yes	yes	–	yes
Infoseek	excludes	yes	yes	–	yes
LookSmart	–	–	–	–	–
Magellan	–	–	–	–	–
Mamma	yes	yes	yes	–	yes
MetaCrawler	–	yes	yes	–	–
OneKey	–	–	–	–	–
SavvySearch	excludes	yes	yes	–	excludes
Yahoo	yes	yes	yes	–	yes

In addition to the search operators in the table, most search tools also have unique operators. The more complex searches benefit from broader and stricter adherence to the use of operators.

Search Tools References

The following explains terms used and provides some helpful hints:

Address: is the Web address or URL. You can access an address by clicking it.
Automatic Document Scanning: This is the means of identifying, indexing and cataloging websites. It employs robots or spiders for scanning virtually all websites to augment and update the databases of search engines.
Bookmark: To access Home and Help Pages conveniently, create an address folder for each under Bookmarks. This is done by going to the Home or Help Pages

via the links provided in this guide and adding them to the appropriate book-mark folder.

Common Operators: We use this term to describe a set of most-used operators of the popular search engines. Common operators are generally compatible with multi-engine search tools use as well.

Default: The operating mode when no other is specified.

Frame-based Information: That which resides in a box within a Web page. Some search engines will not search within frames and therefore the information there is not indexed and retrievable.

Full Text: Indicates every word in the text is scanned. The information recorded is therefore potentially accessible via keyword use.

Relevance Ranking: Each search engine has its own way of assigning relevance. Higher relevance is normally given to query terms in the title and first few words in the document. For some search engines, proximity and frequency of use are also factors. It is unusual that the best source ranks first, unless the query terms are optimally located in the document.

Appendix C

Internet Tools

Evaluation of selected Internet tools (part of Northwestern University Library)
http://www.library.nwu.edu/resources/internet/search/evaluate.html

Getting the most out of your search engine (part of webreference.com's "Search Engines" articles)
http://webreference.com/content/search/features.html

In-depth analysis of popular search engines (part of The Spider's Apprentice)
http://www.monash.com/spidap3.html
     Analysis of AltaVista, Excite, Open Text, InfoSeek, Lycos, WebCrawler, HotBot, and Yahoo.

List of search engines (part of Cornell University's Principles of Web Searching)
http://www.mannlib.cornell.edu/reference/workshops/WebSearching/list.html
     Comparison and brief list of strengths and weaknesses of about 20 search engines and Web directories, including multiple-database search engines and subject-based search engines.

Search Engine Comparison (part of Sink or Swim: Internet Search Tools & Techniques)
http://oksw01.okanagan.bc.ca/libr/connect96/search.htm#compare
     Compares AltaVista, Excite, HotBot, InfoSeek, Lycos and Yahoo.

Web Searching (part of the Internet Public Library)
http://www.ipl.org/ref/websearching.html
     Description of the features of AltaVista, Argus Clearinghouse, Excite, InfoSeek, Lycos, NLightN, Open Text, Yahoo.

Appendix D

Survey

Do not write your name on this survey. It's confidential. Your survey will be seen only by the researcher: Dennis J. Stevens, University of Massachusetts, Boston who is evaluating the promises of the police through their community-policing efforts. Your input will be compared with other residents to better understand your experiences and your needs. Feel free to mail this survey to me, or if you have any questions, I can be reached at:

University of Massachusetts, Boston
100 Morrissey Blvd.
Boston, MA 02125-3393
Email: dennis.stevens@umb.edu

1. What is the name of the neighborhood and the city you live?
   (neighborhood)_____

   (city) _____
2. How long have you lived in this neighborhood? _____
3. Would you briefly describe your occupation? _____

   _____

4. In the past year, has your neighborhood become: (Check one only)

   _____ A much safer place to live

   _____ A safe place to live

   _____ About the same

   _____ An unsafe place to live

   _____ A very unsafe place

5. If you've had contact with the police in the last year, what was the nature of some of those contacts?

_____ I reported an accident

_____ or a crime

_____ I was issued a citation

_____ I was the victim of a crime

_____ I was arrested

_____ I was a witness to a crime

_____ I was in a motor vehicle accident

_____ I was contacted about a problem or disturbance

_____ I requested information

_____ I attended community policing meetings (where) _____

_____ I was involved in another way with the department (please specify)

6. Overall, how would you rate the performance of the officers involved?

_____ Professional

_____ Fair

_____ Frightening

_____ Intimidating

If you've remembered their names, please list:

_____

7. Based on your contact with police at a crime scene, rate the following:

Item	Excellent	Good	Fair	Poor	Very Poor
Response Time					
Solved the Problem					
Made Me Feel Comfortable					
Helpfulness					
Dress/Appearance					

8. How often do community members help the department make decisions about: (Circle one choice for each item)

Item	Always	Very Often	Often	Seldom	Never
Routine Police Auto Patrol	5	4	3	2	1
Routine Bike/Boat Patrol	5	4	3	2	1

continued

Item	Always	Very Often	Often	Seldom	Never
Decisions at Mini Stations	5	4	3	2	1
Building Owner Notification	5	4	3	2	1
Use of Police Force	5	4	3	2	1
Priorities of Calls for Service	5	4	3	2	1
Police Officer Disciplinary Actions	5	4	3	2	1
Police Training Courses	5	4	3	2	1
Officer Promotion Committees	5	4	3	2	1

9. How willing are the residents in your community to work with police addressing problems in the neighborhood?

_____ Very willing

_____ Somewhat willing

_____ Somewhat unwilling

_____ Very unwilling

_____ Don't know

_____ Community members have their own agenda

10. In general, how effective has the department been in responding to problems in your neighborhood?

_____ Very effective

_____ Somewhat effective

_____ Somewhat ineffective

_____ Very ineffective

_____ Don't know

_____ The police have their own agenda

11. Please indicate how strongly you agree or disagree with the following statements:

	Strongly Agree	Somewhat Agree	Somewhat Disagree	Strongly Disagree	Not Sure
Police officers should spend more time making personal contacts with neighborhood residents and businesses.	5	4	3	2	1
Police officers should be assigned to a neighborhood on a long-term basis.	5	4	3	2	1

continued

	Strongly Agree	Somewhat Agree	Somewhat Disagree	Strongly Disagree	Not Sure
I would like to see officers more involved in community programs such as school activities.	5	4	3	2	1
At community meetings, police talk down to us.	5	4	3	2	1
The police listen to our non-criminal concerns and act upon them.	5	4	3	2	1
I feel comfortable contacting the Police Department to make suggestions or complaints against their personnel.	5	4	3	2	1
Making communities safer is a responsibility that should be shared by police, community residents, and business operators.	5	4	3	2	1

12. All things considered, do you think the neighborhood a year from now will:

_____ Be a better place to live

_____ Stay about the same

_____ Become a worst place to live

_____ Not sure

13. I would like to ask a few general questions about you and your ideas.

_____ How old are you?

_____ Do you own your residence?

_____ Rent your residence?

_____ Live with someone in their residence?

15. How would you describe your race?

_____

16. Which country do you consider to be your homeland?

_____

17. Your Gender:

_____ Male

_____ Female

18. What language is usually spoken at home?

   _____

19. Identify the 3 biggest problems that need to be addressed in your community?

   _____

   _____

   _____

20. In your opinion, what actions should be taken to curb the 3 biggest problems in your community?

   _____

   _____

   _____

21. At community meetings, do folks usually work together?
Most of the time _____ Some of the time _____ Seldom _____ Never _____

22. Would you say that everybody (e.g., elderly, youth, former offenders) in the community is encouraged to attend community meetings?
Most of the time _____ Some of the time _____ Seldom _____ Never _____

23. How often do community members leave meetings with mental "to do" lists?
Always_____ Very Often_____ Sometimes_____ Seldom_____ Never_____

24. How often are the actions to resolve community problems actually developed by the community members?
Always_____ Very Often_____ Sometimes_____ Seldom_____ Never_____

25. How often are police actions talked about at meetings?
Always_____ Very Often_____ Sometimes_____ Seldom_____ Never_____

26. How often are those actions changed to fit the results?
Always_____ Very Often_____ Sometimes_____ Seldom_____ Never_____

27. Would you say the plans made at community meetings concerning crime control is generally:
Practical_____ Impractical_____ Not Sure_____

28. In what way is the community safer since the community started meeting?

   _____

29. In what way have the police contributed to a safer community?

   _____

30. What would you like to add?

   _____

   _____

   _____

8

Testing Police Strategies in Eight Jurisdictions

"I think that people want peace so much that one of these days government had better get out of their way and let them have it."

Dwight D. Eisenhower

Key Terms

Oversight Committee	Quality Municipal Services
Participants	Quality Police Services

Key Topics

- Distribution, collection, and analysis of police-strategy survey in eight jurisdictions.
- Demographics of survey, including respondents' collective characteristics.
- How survey respondents rated police behavior and neighborhood safety.
- Implications of survey results on problem-solving community problems.

Introduction

In early 2001, the survey described in the previous chapter was completed by 2,010 residents in eight jurisdictions across America.[1] These jurisdictions included Alexandria, Virginia; Boston, Massachusetts; Columbia, South Carolina; Columbus, Ohio; Miami-Dade County, Florida; Midland, Texas; Palm Beach County, Florida; and Sacramento, California.

This chapter offers a guide to look at individual attitudes without the use of abstract and/or complicated statistical equations. In fact, complex analysis can easily move a reader away from the integrity of a thought, in part, due to a failure to communicate.

The primary question asked at the beginning of the investigation was: Does police practice enhance neighborhood safety issues and provide social order or stability? It was believed that community-police strategies gave rise to crime control, reduction in the fear of crime, and enhancements in residents' quality of life. It was advanced throughout the investigation that the more community members, especially culturally diverse members, influence police decisions, the greater the likelihood that public safety and lifestyle experiences will be enhanced. Based on the evidence provided by residents and public records,[2] community-police practices were suspect in most of the jurisdictions investigated. The expectation was that community-police practices furthered community safety and lifestyle experiences, but this premise was not supported by data.

---

[1]Although this chapter will provide data collective findings on all jurisdictions, the supplemental work contains a breakdown of each of the eight jurisdictions surveyed: Dennis J. Stevens, (2003). *Case Studies in Applied Community Policing*. Boston: Allyn Bacon.

[2]Public records included official website pages, newspapers, and other public documents many of which were archived in city and county governmental agencies.

Design

Most of the *participants* surveyed attended meetings at neighborhood associations, chambers of commerce, community policing, general public gatherings, and university events.[3]

Participant

> A participant in this work refers to 2,010 surveytakers in eight jurisdictions.

In many cases, the assistant investigators who helped distribute, collect, and return surveys were police officers and deputies who worked for the agencies under investigation and/or university students.[4] Many others were neighborhood association officials. The survey was created in English, Spanish, and Chinese. An effort was made to survey minorities, people of color, people at both ends of the socio-economic earning scale, people who don't speak English, and newcomers to the United States.

Characteristics of Survey Respondents

Table 8-1 shows the number of survey respondents in each jurisdiction and their collective characteristics.[5] Highlighting some of the important data: the surveytakers averaged 44 years of age; 859 were female and 1,124 were male; 987 were white; 294 were African American; 355 were Latino; 160 were Asian American.[6] Over one-half spoke English at home; 2 of every 10 spoke English and another language; and 284 spoke only Spanish or Portuguese at home.

---

[3]The individuals who distributed and collected the surveys were police officers, university professors, university students, neighborhood association leaders, and concerned community members. The internet was probably used to communicate with those individuals more than any other device other than personal visits by the primary investigator. Often the principal investigator was engaged in ongoing discussions with individuals in most of the jurisdictions studied. In fact, many of those individuals became more than information providers or associates, those discussions continue.

[4]Also, investigative assistants in Boston conducted 76 interviews primarily of immigrants and non-English speaking minorities. Teaching officers how to become "researchers" is not an unusual. See Captain Michael Masterson, and Dennis J. Stevens, (2002). The value of measuring community policing performance in Madison, Wisconsin. In Dennis J. Stevens (Ed.) *Policing and community partnerships*. (pp. 77-92). Upper Saddle River, NJ: Prentice Hall. And, Michel Masterson and Dennis J. Stevens, (2001, December). Madison Speaks Up: Measuring community policing performance. *Law and Order*, 49(10), 98-100. Officers were trained to conduct interviews with residents of Madison. Also, the principal investigator trained inmates in a high custody penitentiary to interview other inmates. See Dennis J. Stevens (2001). *Inside the Mind of Sexual Predators*. NY: Author's Choice.

[5]For a detailed discussion on each item, see *Case Studies in Applied Community Policing*.

[6]When the categories might not make a total you think is an appropriate, remember that missing cases are not shown. Participants do not always answer every question and sometimes their answers might be hard to read.

TABLE 1-8 *Characteristics of Sample N=2010*

	Numbers	Percentage*/Range
Locales		
Alexandria	101	5
Boston	897	45
Columbia	146	7
Columbus	181	9
Miami	212	11
Midland	213	11
Palm Beach	155	8
Sacramento	105	5
Length of Time	14	0–71 years
Occupation		
Other/Missing	335	17
Blue Collar	384	19
White Collar	416	21
Retired	183	9
Students	160	8
Retail	217	11
Business Owners	315	16
Age	44	15–78
Gender		
Females	859	43
Males	1124	56
Race		
White	987	49
Black	294	15
Latino	355	18
Asian	160	8
Missing	214	11
Homeland		
West Europe	343	17
East Europe	54	3
Haiti/Dom/Caribbean	139	7
Central/South America/Mexico	197	10
Cape Verde/Cuba	57	3
China/Asia	69	3
United States	1098	55
Missing	53	3
Language spoken at home		
English	1131	56
English & Another	430	21
Only Spanish or Portuguese	284	14
Other	165	8
Residence		
Renting	1233	61
Own	662	33
Missing/Others	115	6

*All percents rounded. Missing cases not included in all categories.

Survey Summary

Most of the participants attended community meetings, but few reported that they engaged in any police or municipal decision-making processes.

Rating Police Behavior

Over one-half of the participants rated police behavior as professional. Of course, as with all responses, this varied from jurisdiction to jurisdiction. Almost one in five characterized police performance as intimidating and/or frightening. They reported that their respective police agency was largely ineffective in dealing with neighborhood issues. Grading individual officers in solving problems arising from police calls, neighborhood problems, and police problems, resulted in high grades and in some areas, excellent grades. Despite reports that most of the participants wanted to participate in police decision-making processes,[7] especially concerning disposition of abandoned buildings, use of police force, officer discipline, training, and promotions, most said they were rarely invited to do so and the few who were, had little authority in those meetings.

Safety

One-third of the participants felt unsafe in their neighborhoods and only a very few, depending on their race, felt safer than they had a year ago. When participants were asked about their future safety, they reported the neighborhood a year from now would be:

- A better place to live—400 (20 percent).
- About the same—704 (35 percent).
- A worse place to live—652 (32 percent).
- A worse place to live—652 (32 percent).
- Not sure about its future—254 (13 percent).

Serious Neighborhood Problems

The most serious community problems were identified as street drug activity, home invasion and car-breaks, conditions of the neighborhood, and fear and/or lack of trust of police. A neighborhood's serious problem list varied depending on the jurisdiction surveyed. In five of the jurisdictions, fear and/or lack of trust of police was at the top of the list, and in other jurisdictions it was at the bottom of the list.

Solutions to Neighborhood Problems

The respondents overwhelming response to fixing neighborhood problems was the need for quality police service and quality municipal/state services.

[7]Those areas included deployment of routine auto, bike, and boat patrol, decisions on mini stations, building owner notification, use of police force, priorities of calls for service, police officer disciplinary actions, training, and promotions.

Quality Police Service

Quality police service can be defined, in part, as visible patrols, increased arrests, a decreased response time to 911 calls, and professional behavior.

To resolve community problems, about one-half of the participants reported police should increase patrols, increase arrests, and the courts should administer severe sanctions against offenders. They also said that youths should be supervised, but the youths they were referring to were those offenders who lived outside of the community. By no means were they referring to themselves or their youths; in other words, they were advocating *selective enforcement*.

Also, there was a consensus that more residents should have an opportunity to become homeowners and new businesses should be persuaded to build in the neighborhood. There was a strong correlation between resident status (renters versus owners) and the fear and/or lack of trust of the police and a willingness to aid in solving neighborhood problems. Respondents also recommended that officers should be residents of the neighborhoods they patrolled, which inferred that the officers should have a cultural perspective similar to the neighborhoods where they worked. Quality policing, as explained, refers to strict but selective enforcement.

However, almost one-half of the participants reported that they believed quality municipal/state services were better solutions than police services.

Quality Municipal Services

Quality municipal services included most public services, regardless of authority (county, city, and/or state), provided to residents of a community.

Quality municipal services appeared to be of greater importance in solving neighborhood problems than police services. The consensus was that police have no business in neighborhood problems—that is, the best way to stabilize a community is through the people who live there and through municipal public agencies. In a sense, participants saw little difference between municipal services and police services, but assumed police had some form of control over municipal services such as highway repair and maintenance, quality schools, and business licenses, including apartment building controls.

It was also argued that businesses catering to criminal activity such as bars, massage parlors, and poorly run businesses that tolerated pubic disorder such as convenience stores who allow youths to hang around, should be closed after a second warning; that the business owners' licenses should be revoked, and slum building owners' should be evicted, especially when it concerns abandoned buildings. Abandoned buildings should be leveled and/or rebuilt into livable dwellings or business properties for local residents. The police were seen as a major influence over each of these situations. In fact, when problems arose in licensing, for instance, it was believed that "the cops were involved."

As part of this response, about one-fourth of the respondents reported home-ownership as another way of controlling neighborhood problems. However, this conceptual solution meant something different in each jurisdiction surveyed. For example, some of the participants wanted police and/or city management to help gain possession of their communities through private and public investment opportunities. They wanted police leadership to show them how to attract investment dollars, especially home mortgage lenders, in order to purchase their own homes. Homeownership was seen as a method of curbing crime.

In some jurisdictions, homeowners wanted authorities to step in and curb the huge influx of new homebuyers who brought to the community "big city ideas about sex and drugs and crime." Other participants wanted their property values to increase as other property values of their city in order to borrow the funds to upgrade their homes. Yet, they weren't able to get an equity loan because their homes were in need of repair. Others looked to the police as community leaders and as enforcers of all laws, including civil laws where the police have little jurisdiction. The catch-22 was that while many participants view the police as their government representatives, they also possessed a fear or a lack of trust in police but a larger fear or lack of confidence in municipal management. In a final analysis, community members blame police agencies when other public agencies don't do their job.

Oversight Committees and Information

Many participants said they want input into police decisions and municipal decisions through *oversight committees* dealing with issues such as hiring, training, discipline, practice which included use of force and critical incident limitations, priorities, and promotional boards.

Oversight Committee

For the purpose of this work, an oversight committee can be defined as an empowered group overseeing police practices and policy.

They wanted an empowered position on those committees to an extent that their influence was relevant in most cases and unchallenged in other cases.

Participants wanted more information about their neighborhoods. They wanted to know the city workers and police officers who provided services. They particularly articulated the hiring of their "own kind" as municipal workers and police officers or at least individuals who could speak their language and understood and respected their heritage. Women municipal workers, including police officers, were not as welcomed as males. Respondents wanted to know about official procedures, and one of their greatest concerns was the discipline of abusive workers, especially among police officers. Their greatest fear was the use or threat of excessive force during a traffic stop or a rude city worker. Their fear of "out of control cops" was equaled by their fear of "out of control municipal workers."

Community Municipal Services

Some participants responded that police and other municipal and/or governmental agencies such as welfare, housing, corrections, streets, including city, county, and state agencies must work through community committees to resolve neighborhood problems as an empowered team. However,in one jurisdiction, participants overwhelmingly wanted the police to take control of municipal agencies because they trusted the police more than their elected officials and had more trust in the police than city agencies.

Overall, survey-takers relied on police help because residents had little contact with, for example, housing authority personnel. Redirecting traffic and preserving open spaces would be a state-task that might involve a number of "unknown" agencies. They wanted to take their case to the police and the police could lobby towards communicating their wishes. There appeared to be the thought that police could do anything, including the elimination of slum-building owners or the boarding-up of abandoned buildings.

Conclusions

Some police advocates argue that lower crime rates are direct results of police policy in concert with community opinions such as "getting tough on crime." If we listen to the 2,010 participants in this investigation, few were involved in a "get tough on crime" discussion with police agencies, let alone influencing any process linked to deployment, mini-stations, building and vehicle notification, use of force, priorities of calls of service, officer hiring and disciplinary actions, training, and/or promotional decisions. When residents sat on advisory boards, they made no mention of any power relative to those committees. Thus, there appears to be strong opportunity for police as an institution to stabilize community-police relationships through community-police strategies. One reality that becomes clear is that many police advocates confused the difference between community attendance and influencing police decision-making processes. The police saw community meetings as an event where constituents could talk about their problems and learn what the department was doing. Many participants saw community meetings as an activity to socialize and an opportunity to "be seen." They saw police officer presentations as "a necessary evil."

A larger question emerged beyond the scope of this work: If those community members who came forward and interacted with police and completed a survey about police efforts don't participate in a police decision-making process, what about those who don't interact with police at any level? Who speaks for them? Are their views about social order or even their serious problems considered? How does the saying go: squeaky wheels get the grease? But, who speaks for the uninvolved such as the disadvantaged, the aged, the young, or those incarcerated? It reasonably follows that public order or a feeling of safety does not exist at the level claimed by official rhetoric. Additionally, due in part to the differences between official claims of police and justice agencies and actual practice, there are reservations about the intention of police intervention.

One explanation of the findings about official claims versus actual practice is that police practice hasn't changed—official rhetoric has. Since police practice is founded on Western European notions of law and order, which could be characterized as a cuff'em and stack'em practices, some writers would argue that the real mission of law enforcement is to maintain dominant class interests. Keep in mind, there is little wrong with that idea, and police have served the American public well, all things considered. However, policing in a changing democratic society means that changes must also take place in the practices of the institutions that safeguard and serve a free lifestyle. The purpose of this investigation was to achieve a broader understanding of those concerns. However, since September 11, 2001, the responsibilities have increased among the police and it goes without saying that the police and the community—all residents in the community—must move forward to protect the greater public good.

Summary

Conceptual community-policing strategies exist. However, municipal services have more to do with social order and stability than law enforcement, and it isn't enforcement that's an issue; rather it is how police service is delivered. The catch is that how well a police agency is doing depends on how efficient other public agencies are since community members view officers as their window to government. The public sees the authority of the police as legal and moral as long as potholes are filled and schools provide quality education, and officers behave themselves in a professional manner (no favorites). Although reported crime is on the decline, fear of crime and fear and/or the lack of trust in police are on the rise. Also, since most community members do not influence police decision-making processes, it follows that those who don't or can't attend community meetings are rarely represented in neighborhood matters. What is reflected in the voice of these participants is that community government—an empowered community involved in all public services—is necessary to reduce the fear of crime and to enhance lifestyle experiences.

Do You Know? _____

1. Identify the eight jurisdictions in this study. In what ways are they similar and in what ways might they be different?

2. Take another look at the characteristics of the participants in this investigation and if major things about them were different such as age or race, in what way might their responses be different?

3. Describe the safety issues of the participants. In what way do you agree or disagree with their responses?

4. Identify the serious neighborhood problems of the participants. In what way might your own neighborhood agree or disagree with those responses?

5. Identify the remedies suggested by the participants. How might they solve their most serious neighborhood problems?

6. In what way do municipal services, in general, impact community members?

7. Since the socio-economic level of many of the participants is probably different from residents in an affluent neighborhood, in what way might responses from an affluent resident be different concerning neighborhood problems and remedies?

8. If you were a police commander in one of the jurisdictions tested, in what way(s) would you change your method of delivering police services?

9. If you were a typical community member living in one of the jurisdictions tested, in what way would you respond to the police during a community meeting once you knew the results of this test?

10. In what way does Dwight D. Eisenhower's statement connect to this chapter? "I think that people want peace so much that one of these days government had better get out of their way and let them have it."

9

Testing Police Performance in Boston and Columbus

"I never give them hell. I just tell the truth and they think it's hell."

Harry S. Truman

Key Terms _____

Neighborhood Policing
Same Cop/
  Same Neighborhood

The Neutral Zone
The Strategic Response Bureau

Key Topics _____

- Discussion of police agency, refugee and immigrant trends in two target cities: Boston, MA and Columbus, OH.
- Survey results and analysis of both cities.
- Implementing problem solving strategy.
- Six steps to survive the neutral zone.

Introduction

Although there were eight jurisdictions investigated, two will be discussed and compared in this chapter: Boston, Massachusetts and Columbus, Ohio. The methods used in this explicit test were developed in a previous chapter. A survey was developed, distributed, and collected in a similar fashion in both cities, and numerical findings were established for each answer on the survey. A copy of the survey can be found at the end of Chapter 7.

Boston and Columbus were compared because these two cities, although they both consist of a large urban population, they are remarkably different from each other. For instance, one city has received numerous awards for its outstanding accomplishments in police strategies and the other is under investigation by the Department of Justice. One boosts huge reductions in crime over a ten-year period through its community-police programs, while the other shows little difference in crime rates from year to year despite efforts to enhance police outreach.

Boston, Massachusetts

Founded in 1630, Boston is an historic city of contrasts.[1] Its red brick sidewalks twist past handsome Federalist houses on the way to soaring glass towers housing state-of-the-art technology. In the harbors of Boston lie both the majestic *USS Constitution*, still commissioned to fight America's battles, and scores of sleek white fiberglass pleasure boats. Boston is a diverse city of neighborhoods: Immigrants from every corner of the globe live in Boston and they have become Americans whose memories and customs enrich the community. Boston is home to freedom, and when history books talk about young America, they talk about this city. Historically, this is the city where people who wanted freedom and choice and a better life came. They still do.

[1]Source: Massachusetts Historical Commission.

Population of Boston

> Boston has 589,141 people; among that population, approximately 55 percent are white, 25 percent are African American, 15 percent are Spanish American (of any race), and 8 percent are Asian American, living within approximately 49 square miles.

Refugees and Immigrants in Massachusetts, 2000

Footsteps of the earliest Western European settlers in the New World echo through Boston and the Commonwealth. In the last century, more settlers arrived but those individuals came from other parts of the world. That is, Irish, Italian, and African Americans used to be the predominate groups who laid claim to Boston and the Commonwealth's public services, including public safety. All indicators suggested that an exodus was in progress in Massachusetts—a changing population. For instance, in a single year, 146,000 more white residents left Massachusetts than moved there. And a net influx of 25,000 new people arrived who were nonwhite and Latinos.[2]

One conclusion that can be drawn from estimates produced by the U.S. Census[3] and other sources is that there are approximately 11.5 million (5 percent of total U.S. population) refugees and immigrants residing in the United States in the year 2000. There are 1.3 million (21 percent of total Massachusetts population) refugees and immigrants residing in Boston and the Commonwealth of Massachusetts. Albanians, Brazilians, Cape Verdeans, Haitians, and Portuguese have more than doubled their immigration numbers in the Commonwealth.

Boston Police Department

As one of the oldest police department in the country, the Boston Police Department (BPD)[4] has a rich history and a well-established presence in the Boston community. The BPD was one of the first paid, professional public safety department in the country. It was patterned after the model developed by Sir Robert Peele for the London police force. As of September, 2001, the city of Boston had 2,220 sworn officers[5] and 826 paid civilians who serve approximately 574,283 residents[6] of which 63,300 are public-school aged children. The police officer/population ratio is one officer for every 259 residents.

[2]Sege, I. (1991, July 23). All signs point to Massachusetts exodus. *The Boston Globe*, p. 1. For a closer look at the population changes in Boston and the Commonwealth see The Office of Refugee and Immigrant Health, The Bureau of Family and Community Health, and the Massachusetts Department of Public Health. Refugees and Immigrants, June 2000.

[3]See U.S. Census Bureau at http://www.census.gov/

[4]The Boston Police Department's homepage is http://www.ci.boston.ma.us/police/
In addition, they have 471 Marked Patrol Vehicles, 438 Unmarked Vehicles, 94 Specialty Vehicles, 68 Motorcycles, 43 Bicycles, 5 Boats, 14 Horses, 13 Canines, 2 Bomb Disposal Vehicles, and they received 593, 139 Total Calls for Service in 1999. BPD budget in FYE 2000, 204 million dollars.

[5]Sworn officer median age is 41, with an average of 17 years on the job.

[6]Living in 48.8 square miles with a density of 11,814 residents per square mile.

Boston Police Department Mission Statement

We dedicate ourselves to work in partnership with the community to *fight crime, reduce fear,* and *improve the quality of life in our neighborhoods.*

Our Mission is Neighborhood Policing

Crime Statistics

- Violent crime fell in 2000 for the ninth consecutive year.
- Since 1990, serious crime dropped 48 percent (2000).
- Serious crime remains at a level the city had not seen in three decades.[7] However, it should be acknowledged that as of August 2001, there were 43 (YTD) homicides reported in Boston, and there were 39 for the year 2000.[8] In 2000, yearly crime reported was: 39 homicides, 325 rapes, 2,451 robberies, 4,507 aggravated assaults, 4,051 burglaries, 17,228 larcenies, and 7,269 vehicle thefts.

Neighborhood Policing

The primary community-policing strategy used by the Boston Police Department is called *neighborhood policing.* The following letter can be found in departmental brochures available to the general public.

Fall, 1999

Dear Neighbor:

The strategic plan outlined in this brochure is the product of many hours of hard work by both members of the Boston Police Department and community partners like you. During the past several months, this team and 16 others like it all across the city have been meeting to set new strategic priorities for the future of our Department. Nearly 500 people have actively participated in this process, which has one goal: to realize our mission of working together with the community to reduce crime and fear, and improve the quality of life in our neighborhoods.

We have undertaken this work because we believe that partnerships between police and the community are essential to effective Neighborhood Policing. Our goal in carrying out the Strategic Planning and Community Mobilization Process in 1999 is to build on, and reinvigorate the partnerships we developed in the first round of planning during 1995–96.

The participants set out to deepen the collaborative efforts that have been at the heart of the dramatic crime reductions that have taken place in our city.

---

[7]These figures are tabulated according to the national reporting criteria established by the Federal Bureau of Investigations' Uniform Crime Reporting Program.
http://www.ci.boston.ma.us/police/1999%20Annual/23.htm
[8]Ibid.

We've learned that the best solutions to crime and disorder issues often originate from those who are the closest to the problem. As a result, the people who have created this plan, and are now embarked on its implementation, feel a deep sense of ownership of the ideas and programs that are expressed below. Together they have assumed accountability for this plan and the measures they feel will be necessary to make it a success.

To the team members who developed this plan, we say thanks for the hard work. To everyone who reads this plan we invite you to contribute to its successful implementation by contacting the team leader whose name and telephone number appear on the front of this brochure to see how you can become involved. Working together, we can continue to make our city the safest it can be in the years to come.

Signed

Thomas M. Menino   Paul F. Evans
Mayor of Boston   *Police Commissioner*

Implementation of Neighborhood Policing

The implementation of neighborhood policing in Boston required an improved capacity to identify problems and evaluate services. The BPD, having shifted from reactive to proactive policing, could no longer rely exclusively on reported crime to assess agency effectiveness. Rather, the BPD needed a tool to include citizens' perspectives in its day-to-day policy decisions. To that end, the BPD conducted its first bi-annual public safety survey.

In 1999, 2,000 randomly selected Boston residents participated in the Boston Public Safety Survey. Those residents responded to 70 questions relating to neighborhood concerns, quality of life, fear of crime, and police services. Some of the highlights from that survey included:

- More than one-half of Boston residents rate their quality of life as "high."
- Three-quarters of Boston residents (76 percent) were willing to volunteer their time to work on public safety issues in their neighborhoods.
- During 1999, education replaced crime as the top concern of Boston residents.
- On a scale of one to ten (with one meaning "not at all satisfied" and ten meaning "very satisfied"), Bostonians rated police services an "eight."
- Bostonians noted "car breaks" as the most serious crime-related problem in their neighborhoods.
- Since 1995, fear of crime has dropped 51 percent, with nearly eight out of ten residents reporting they felt safe walking alone at night.

With these results it's no wonder that the National Crime Prevention Council suggested that Boston was one of the six leading cities with the largest crime reduction over the past ten years.

In early November of 1999, nearly 500 community leaders from neighborhoods across Boston gathered to celebrate the first phase of "Strategic Planning

1999." Composed of a broad spectrum of both citizens and BPD personnel, this gathering capped thousands of hours of planning sessions that had been held citywide during the previous six months. This important initiative also built on many of the key elements from the BPD's prior community mobilization and planning process during 1995–1996.

Some promising early results were highlighted at the event, as each of the 17 planning teams unveiled their newly customized strategic plans for the coming years. The teams represented each of Boston's 11 police districts, as well as BPD's Bureaus of Administrative Services, Investigative Services, Internal Investigations, and Professional Development, and it's Operations and Special Operations Divisions.

Mayor Thomas Menino congratulated team participants for their willingness "to work together to drive down crime and fear." Commissioner Evans also praised and thanked each team and noted that the celebration marked "not an end, but a beginning of the tasks of implementing the goals of each team."

By bringing people together in this manner, the Department's Strategic Planning process acknowledged the effectiveness of police and community partnerships and provided an important catalyst for many of the dramatic crime reductions that have taken place since that time. These partnerships were expected to continue to be one of the most effective tools in increasing the effectiveness of neighborhood policing.

Same Cop/Same Neighborhood (SC/SN), an outgrowth of the neighborhood policing concept, is one of the cornerstones of Commissioner Evans' commitment to the effective delivery of public safety services to every neighborhood in Boston. More detail about how SC/SN works can be found in his comments to a community meeting later in this chapter.

Several important techniques have been identified as particularly effective in promoting the success of SC/SN thus far, including:

- Reconfiguring boundaries for police districts and sectors.
- Training and education sessions with supervisory personnel.
- Identification of potential roadblocks and suggestions on how to avoid them by middle managers.
- An ongoing dialogue about implementation issues with assistance from Boston Management Consortium.

As a result of this new management approach, the official website for the BPD reports that beat officers developed their own partnerships with members of their neighborhoods through attendance at community meetings and participation in a growing variety of neighborhood activities and events. This new approach won the 1997 Boston City Excellence Managing for Safer Neighborhoods Award and has been a useful tool in helping to bring the City of Boston to its lowest level of overall crime in 29 years. Perhaps most importantly, it is also helping officers to gain a greater familiarity with the areas they work in, and gives officers a renewed sense of ownership and participation in the positive outcomes they help to generate for the citizens they serve.

Columbus, Ohio

Columbus[9] has a larger population than Boston, but The Columbus Division of Police (CDP) has fewer officers.

Population of Columbus

Columbus' population was 711,470 individuals living in 212 square miles.[10] Of that population, 68 percent are white, 25 percent are African American, 3 percent are Asian American, and 3 percent are Latino.

There are approximately 1,800 sworn officers, which is an equivalent of 2.6 sworn officers per 1,000 residents.[11] Columbus is one of the fastest growing cities in the Midwest, and its downtown is evidence of its energy and distinguished character. It is the home of Ohio State University, and it is the state capital of Ohio. Boston, on the other hand, with more than twenty institutions of higher learning, has the second largest university population in the United States.

Chief James G. Jackson said (in early 2001) that community policing and problem-oriented policing "are often described as solutions to traditional policing strategies, and have become buzzwords and/or icons in many police and academic circles. The ideals of policing in collaboration with the community and policing to solve problems are sound principles that can hold promise for increasing the effectiveness of police agencies like the CDP."[12] Although the CDP was successful in meeting many of their goals, it was not without fault and the threat of federal litigation against the CDP has yet to be resolved.[13]

Early Experiences of the CDP

One spokesperson for the CDP explained that what the CDP experienced in the last decade was that most efforts by police agencies to become community oriented were programs or "smoke screens" (walking patrols, bicycle patrols, police cars, police stations, and websites decorated with community-policing emblems) intended to improve relations or resolve hostility between residents and the police.[14] While those practices are helpful to their understanding of community

[9]The Columbus Division of Police can be found on their website at http://www.police.ci.columbus.oh.us/

[10]Source: U.S. Census, 2000. http://www.census.gov

[11]For a complete report see Dennis J. Stevens (2001). *Case Studies in Community Policing*. Upper Saddle River, NJ: Prentice Hall. Pages 91-120.

[12]Found on CDP's website: http://www.police.ci.columbus.oh.us/

[13]As of July 2001.

[14]Commander Kent Shafer, Strategic Response Bureau, CDP. Also, in some respects, what the officials at CDP could have added was that some agencies' federal funds were also a large incentive to develop and maintain a community policing program. For more information, see Kent R. Kerley (2002). Perceptions of community policing across community sectors: results from a regional study. In Dennis J. Stevens, (2002). *Policing and community partnerships* (pp. 93–110). Upper Saddle River, NJ: Prentice Hall.

policing, they do not result in a long-term philosophical change in the way a police organization conducts business. In the early twenty-first century, the CDP realized that when a police agency attempts to reduce the fear of crime and crime itself and enhance the quality of life for its constituents, creating a piecemeal community-policing program is neither efficient nor effective. During their early period of transformation from an agency centered in a reactive response to a proactive response, the CDP learned that:

1. Community-oriented policing initiatives are generally characterized by unclear objectives and lack of shared vision among police personnel (including command officers), community members, and civic leaders.
2. Community policing as a department-wide philosophy is rarely practiced by any police agency.
3. Many police agencies practice a form of community policing but few understand its major concepts.

Some experiences that brought the CDP to these conclusions included a survey conducted in 1994 with Columbus residents. The CDP wanted to know residents' ideas about police services. In general, residents reported they wanted police services tailored to individual community needs, a better resolution of crime and safety problems, more police presence, greater input to and communication with the police department, increased enforcement of quality-of-life violations, and closer relationships with the officers working in the neighborhoods. To meet these aims, police leadership developed the Mission Aligned Policing Philosophy and the Strategic Response Bureau to conduct strategy.

The Strategic Response Bureau (SRB), with a staff of nearly one hundred officers and supervisors, was created to better identify problems related to the police mission and to develop creative solutions to impact them. The difficulty came in getting officers to break the mold of reactive responses and learn to solve problems creatively and collaboratively. The bureau's primary function was problem solving.

Implementing Problem Solving

To accomplish a transition from a crime-fighting agency to a problem-solving one, the CDP focused on four activities:

1. Taught problem-solving skills to officers.
2. Collected, analyzed, and disseminated crime statistics.
3. Held group discussions with officers about "best solutions."
4. Monitored officers' results.

Through skill development, application, and feedback, community officers learned to be proficient problem solvers.

Resistance to Change

The change to a community-policing program was publicized and poised to be an immediate success story. The first two years that followed the notoriety were characterized by struggles, frustrations, and unexpected circumstances. Bridges (1991) described what he called "the neutral zone," a "very difficult time" when command becomes impatient and asks, "How long is it going to take you to implement those changes?" In retrospect, "the neutral zone" seemed to be one of the experiences of men and women of the CDP, too. Top command wanted quantifiable results and put pressure on the SRB to demonstrate success. Meanwhile, members of the new operation felt the pressure to produce, yet found they were unable to follow their own plans of operation. The principal planners at the SRB were unable to successfully implement the program. Many questioned the plan itself and the ability of those involved to conduct it. Little did they know that what they were experiencing was a normal part of a process of change. What the CDP was experiencing was the unpleasant period of transition known as the neutral zone. Bridges lists six steps to take to survive the neutral zone:

1. Protecting people from further changes.
2. Reviewing policies and procedures.
3. Examining relationships and organizational structure.
4. Setting short-range goals.
5. Promising obtainable goals.
6. Helping supervisors and managers learn what they need in order to function successfully.

The time in the neutral zone can actually be a creative period if proper actions are taken. Without the benefit of Bridges' advice, members of SRB eventually discovered these steps for themselves. Policies and procedures were evaluated and changed with input of workers, supervisors, and community members. Unproductive reporting relationships were changed and the organizational structure modified to make communications easier and maximize the ability of the various components to accomplish their tasks and collaborate with other units. It should be noted that almost from the beginning of the new initiative at the CDP, independent evaluation was conducted by the Ohio State University Criminal Justice Research Center, under the direction of Professor C. Ronald Huff.[15]

Department of Justice Investigation

In addition to some police personnel resistance to a change in the method of police service through community-policing efforts, the CDP experienced other situations that seemed to complicate police efforts. That is, the U.S. Department of Justice (DOJ) initiated an investigation of the department for alleged misconduct of police officers.

Specifically, a former and apparently disgruntled police officer, who quit the department to avoid being fired, went to the DOJ alleging violations of citizens' rights regarding use of force in Columbus. He provided a few names of potential victims. The DOJ conducted a preliminary investigation. They came to Columbus to meet with officials and the information provided indicated that they informed

---

[15]Professor Huff was president of the American Society of Criminologists in 2000–2001.

Columbus officials that they did not see a major investigation but wanted to follow up on the information they had been presented by the former officer.

Coincidentally, this investigation occurred during the same time period when the Columbus city administration attempted to redirect police services since they were unhappy with the results from community-policing efforts. There are indicators that some city officials may have encouraged the DOJ to conduct a full investigation as they felt it might lead to the chief's dismissal. The DOJ was given additional names, mostly of people who had filed complaints alleging excessive or unnecessary use of force. It appears that DOJ investigators did not interview any of the police personnel involved in those situations, only the alleged victims. They did, however, review official police documentation. The DOJ eventually asked the city to enter into a consent decree that would require intervention and oversight of CPD.

The Fraternal Order of Police (FOP) intervened and was named a party to the case. The DOJ, the City, and the FOP tried to negotiate but talks broke down and the DOJ filed suit in Federal District Court. The judge in the case reviewed it and told the parties to go back into negotiations. Not much has happened since that time, but DOJ lead investigators in the Columbus case spoke at a conference in Chicago. They gave the impression (according to a CPD/FOP person in the audience) that they would like to find a way to get out of the case.

The long and short of it is there may be a few cases of improper conduct but nothing close to the "pattern and practice" of abuse alleged by the DOJ. There may have been some motivation on the part of some former city administration officials to use the DOJ investigation to accomplish their goal of getting rid of the chief. The case was still pending in the summer of 2001, and there is no indication at this point of when and how it will be resolved.

Crime Report

In reviewing a nine-year crime report (see Table 9-1, and 9-2), there appears to be no marked improvement in crime prevention in Columbus, Ohio. Despite minor changes in the population base, the crime rate per 1,000 population has been consistently around 90 for the past four years and at 88 for the two preceding years. Therefore, it could be argued that the crime rate has not necessarily reflected a significant change in the past six years. However, as we review crimes in 2000–2001, it becomes clear that the number of violent crimes is significantly less.

Chief James G. Jackson Talks about Community Policing

It is my pleasure to share with you some of the benefits I believe the Columbus, Ohio Division of Police has enjoyed regarding our commitment to Community Policing. The process for developing the Division's commitment to the COP philosophy, and the corresponding process for implementing the mechanics is both time consuming, and often problematic. Changing attitudes and responses in the policing business requires patience and persistence. However, it seems this is the direction we in law enforcement should be going, and more importantly, it appears this approach will prove to be (long-term) effective and efficient.

TABLE 9-1   *Uniform Crime Index Offenses**
Nine Year Comparison

Crime	1990	1991	1992	1993	1994	1995	1996	1997	1998
Murder	92	139	113	105	100	78	90	83	79
Rape	647	651	685	658	679	636	571	696	668
Robbery	3541	3747	3595	3887	3599	3330	3318	3104	2615
Aggravated Assault	2735	2686	2859	2496	2383	2582	2238	2103	2040
Burglary	14982	16398	15064	13055	13088	13146	13013	13453	13526
Theft/Larceny	32387	32989	31051	29051	29776	31905	34244	35882	36338
Vehicle Theft	8466	8874	7136	7070	6720	7038	7610	7118	7343
Arson	926	875	995	1029	1035	915	808	778	813
Total	63622	66359	60503	57351	57378	59630	61892	63217	63422
Population	632910	638533	643028	646933	647860	657487	657045	696849	696849
Rate per 1,000 Population	100.7	103.9	94.1	88.7	88.6	90.7	91.7	90.7	91.0

Source: The Columbus Division of Police

TABLE 9-2   *Crime Report 1999*

Offense	Year 1999 Totals
Murder/Manslaughter	113
Rape	650
Robbery	3026
Aggravated Assault	2046
Burglary	14070
Larceny over $500	8919
Larceny under $500	25740
Vehicle Theft	7277
Other Assaults	19306
Forgery	2268
Fraud/Embezzlement	1906
Indecent Exposure	150
Molestations	249
Other Sex Crimes	193
All Other	19585

Source: The Columbus Division of Police, http://www.columbuspolice.org/precinctstats/

Community Policing with the Columbus Division of Police probably began, as it did with most agencies, with our old Crime Prevention Unit. While very popular with the community groups it trained and interacted with, and effective as far as it could be within its limited scope and range, most community members were not dramatically impacted by its efforts.

Our fairly recent commitment to the COP process via the creation of the Strategic Response Bureau has provided our Division and the community with a fresh approach to addressing community problems and concerns. With the inclusion of a number of service units under one umbrella bureau, our goal is to permit a comprehensive approach to dealing with often endemic and long-standing challenges. Additionally, other Division resources including traditional patrol officers, community resource officers, bike patrol officers, and walking officers supported by other Division (and outside resources) all help to round out our ability to assist our community members.

Not surprisingly, in-house responses to non-traditional, proactive and problem-solving oriented strategies have been mixed, however, it is my belief that with both officers and community members alike seeing improving results from community responsive policing, there will ultimately be greater general support for our efforts. In conclusion, there is little question that COP is the philosophy for law enforcement agencies of the future. The challenges are many and sometimes difficult to overcome, however, with persistence and commitment, the challenges facing COP will prove to be the stepping stones to success. You have my best wishes for your continued and future success.

James G. Jackson, Chief of Police, 12/6/99

An Evaluation of CDP's COP/POP Efforts

Surveys were utilized, inside the CDP and with the public, to assess the impact of COP.[16] For instance, research was conducted between September 1998 and August 1999 to evaluate community-policing efforts. CDP personnel measured the COP/POP attitudes of three groups of individuals: 40 CDP uniformed patrol officers who had little direct contact with COP/POP initiatives, 70 community members in Columbus who had direct contact with these initiatives, and 36 commanders and related personnel in major departments in Ohio and similar departments in the United States. The test was conducted two years after CDP established its COP/POP initiatives in Columbus.

Survey 1: CDP Patrol Officers   When the patrol officers were polled, distinctive patterns arose. For example, the following typical response from a patrol officer typified the reports of the patrol officers concerning the Community Liaison Officers (CLO). They "have the hardest job (on the CDP) dealing with the public and police." Furthermore, "liaison officers (have) access to people and (patrol) officers to answers to questions." Liaison officers "help explain what patrol is really all about."

Statistical evidence supported these comments. More than one-half of the patrol officers reported that they felt confident about the SRB and the bureau's

---

[16]This study was conducted by Commander Kent Shafer of the SRB.

liaison officers specifically assigned to interact with community members, community organizations, and CDP personnel such as the patrol officers themselves. Evidently, patrol officers saw the SRB and CLOs as assets to both the community and the department.

Survey 2: Community Members   Specifically, there were several remarks that seemed to typify the primary issues addressed by the community-member respondents. For instance, the efforts of the community-policing liaison officers were typified by the respondent who stated that "The liaison officer in our community has been very effective and supportive of our concerns." Another respondent added, "He comes to all the meetings and is well respected for his response to our needs." Accordingly, the statistical results were no surprise when 95 percent (67) of the respondents reported that COP was a change for the better for Columbus, yet only 48 percent (34) felt that CDP was doing all it should be regarding COP. Seventy-two percent (50) of the community members polled reported the CDP was effective in solving crime in their neighborhood and 76 percent (53) felt that police effectiveness had improved since the inception of COP. When asked specifically about the SRB and the COP program, most of the respondents were aware of the program and 87 percent (61) felt the program improved police service. Regarding the CLOs almost all of the participants reported that liaison officers provided assistance in problem solving, that better information was available due to those officers, and 91 percent (64) felt that the officers were an improvement in providing police services.

Survey 3: Other Police Agencies   Of 36 similar-sized police agencies, 88 percent (32) of their commanders endorsed COP and most reported similar experiences as CDP.

Survey Conclusion   The survey reported that the CDP had strengthened its relationship with the community, involved citizens in efforts to address crime and safety problems, and enhanced its ability to effectively police the City of Columbus. The Division has become a high-performance police organization, focused on not only increasing effectiveness in dealing with crime and safety problems, but also on fostering on-going learning, encouraging innovation, and maximizing the use of information technology to improve law enforcement.

Section Summary

CDP's community-policing initiative began with community forums from every neighborhood soliciting input into what type of police services were desired. After program concepts were developed, information sessions with community members were conducted. Surveys were used regularly to gather input and resident perceptions. It was recognized early that residents stayed initially involved with community groups as long as they felt they were threatened and needed the police to solve a particular problem. After immediate crime or safety concerns were solved, the community meetings experienced a decrease in resident participation.

Testing Police Performance

In the fall of 2000 and spring of 2001, 897 Boston residents and 181 Columbus residents were surveyed. The participants in the survey were largely people who attended community-policing meetings.[17] There are many similarities between the characteristics of the samples from both cities despite the differences in sample size. For instance, typical participants lived in their cities for 14 to 15 years and were 44 to 46 years old. Almost two-thirds of both samples were females, and approximately 70 percent of both samples rented rather than owned their residences. Furthermore, almost two-thirds of both groups spoke English at home, and one-fourth spoke English and another language at home, such as Spanish, French Crio, or Cantonese. There were similarities between the samples in the race the respondents characterized as best describing themselves, and about the homeland they felt they belonged to.[18]

Similarities between Boston and Columbus Samples
- Length of Time Living in the City
- Age
- Gender
- Property renters/owners
- Language
- Race
- Homeland

One area of difference between the samples was occupations as Table 9-3 demonstrates.[19] It is hard to assess the impact respondents' occupations played in the final analysis, but it might lend itself to a better understanding of the samples.

Professionalism

Over sixty-two percent of the survey-takers in both cities reported police officers' behavior was generally professional. However, approximately one-fourth of the participants said their officers were intimidating or frightening. These findings far surpass a recent national survey conducted by the Harris Poll.[20]

[17]In that investigation, there were 2010 individuals surveyed in eight jurisdictions across the United States.
[18]Approximately 70% reported they were white, the balance were black, Latino and Asian. 9% of each sample did not respond to the question. There were more blacks in the Boston study, but those blacks had not described themselves as African Americans but rather from countries such as Haiti, Cape Verde, Dominican Republic. The respondents also reported that the country which best describes their homeland was largely the U.S. and Western Europe.
[19]Self-reported blue collar work was truck drivers, laborers, trade persons, and mechanics. White collar work was work that was administrative or professional such as nurses, accountants, manufacturing sales, clerical, teachers and professors, and office workers. Retired selections included clergy; students included vocational training, on the job training, leave of absence to enhance job skills, and home-workers such as caretakers and parents. Retail work included jobs in small shops, and large supermarkets; business owners were those who owned hair salons, realtors, and retail businesses. Also, there were missing data included in those who were unemployed, worked part time, or were between jobs.
[20]See BJS. (2001). Respondents' rating of performance of police in own community. p. 109, Table 2.28.

TABLE 9-3   *Occupations of Samples*

Self Reported Jobs	Percent of Boston Participants N=897	Percent of Columbus Participants N=181
Blue Collar	23	14
White Collar	19	13
Retired	18	8
Students	15	8
Retail	6	20
Business Owners	5	18
Other/Missing	14	18

Safety

Forty-eight percent of the Boston sample as compared to 58 percent of the Columbus sample reported that there had been little change in their community concerning safety over the past year. An almost equal percentage of the sample in both cities reported that it was less safe as compared to last year, but 9 percent more of the Boston sample reported it seemed much safer in the spring of 2001 as compared to last year.

Finally, approximately 30 percent of both samples revealed that their future looked brighter; yet more Bostonians thought the future would be about the same, and a similar percentage of both samples reported that the future would be worse than today.

In summary, professionalism among police officers was rated high in both cities despite the reports that little had changed over the year, and next year, things would probably remain the same. However, Bostonians were more optimistic about the future than the Columbus sample. Fear of crime was high in both cities despite the professionalism of the officers.

Neighborhood Problems

Table 9-4 shows the five most serious neighborhood problems reported by participants in Boston[21] and Columbus.

Reported neighborhood problems between the two samples were different. For example, criminal activities in Boston was reported in the top three, and in Columbus, criminal activities were in the top two. In Boston, 30 percent (streets, fear, and parking) reported non-criminal items as compared to 38 percent in Columbus (fear, streets, and parking). Since Boston is an older city, it was expected that environmental conditions (parking, streets) would be of more concern

---

[21]Since no one was interviewed in Columbus, the data from those interviews in Boston can be found in *Case Studies in Applied Community Policing*. Boston: Allyn & Bacon..

TABLE 9-4 *Five Most Serious Neighborhood Problems in Boston and Columbus*

Boston N=897 Problem	Percent*	Columbus N=181 Problem	Percent*
Street Drug Activity	29	Home	33
Home/Car BE**	20	Street Drug Activity	18
Gangs and Juveniles	14	Fear or Lack of Trust of Police	15
Streets, Lights, Empty Buildings & Graffiti	12	Streets, Lights, Empty Buildings & Graffiti	15
Fear or Lack of Trust of Police	11	Parking, Traffic, and Speeders	8
Parking, Traffic, and Speeders	7	Gangs and Juveniles	8
No Problem or Other	7	No Problem or Other	3

*All percents rounded
**BE = breaking and entering. Carbreaks was limited to the Boston sample.

than in Columbus. This information is inconsistent with a national survey suggesting that education, crime, and drugs/alcohol were the top three serious problems facing local communities.[22]

Remedies

Also, when reviewing the remedies to these neighborhood problems, quality police service and quality city service were at the top of the list along with home ownership and business reinvestment. Yet it should be clarified that city services took precedence over police services. However, what was meant by quality police service and quality municipal service in Columbus and Boston was vastly different.

Columbus

In Columbus, quality police service referred to honest communication by the police with the neighborhood and consistent enforcement of laws. Solutions for home invasions could be controlled through more auto, biking, and walking police patrols. Yet, the Columbus participants wanted to know what crime and related events happened in their neighborhood (as opposed to knowing what was happening in the police agency and the rest of the city) and they wanted everyone treated "fairly," which should not be construed as "equally."

The participants made an effort to describe differences between their terms of fairly and equally. "Fairly" meant that since they felt they were law-abiding

---

[22]See BJS (2001). Respondents' attitudes toward the most important problem facing their local community, Table 2.0015. http://albany.edu/sourcebook. As a point of interest, another survey showed that ethics, moral, family decline followed by quality of education, and dissatisfaction with the government were the top three categories concerning problems facing the nation. See BJS (2001). Attitudes toward the most important problem facing the county, Table 2.1. http://albany.edu/sourcebook

residents, they should receive more respect from police and as a result more quality city services. That is, they should receive the bulk of public services, "especially," one respondent typified, "more than those lazy welfare people who get everything for free." The survey-takers clarified that they should receive more of everything from city services including holiday parades in their neighborhoods, more control over social services (they saw state and U.S. Government agencies as city services), and more control over building, street, and park departments in Columbus. Several mentioned that it was unfair to have community correctional facilities and halfway houses in their neighborhoods. They wanted those facilities placed in the "bad parts of town where other animals [residents] like them lived, not here," one survey-taker wrote.

They wanted empowerment on police and municipal oversight committees. They saw little distinction between law enforcement services and city amenities including street repairs, street light replacement (they wanted taller and brighter street lights), tree removal, demolition of abandoned buildings, unused schools and city buildings converted into affordable housing (not welfare housing), fire department concerns, and greater cooperation between the police and the city services. Finally, they wanted police service and city service to work under a similar directive in the sense of a resident oversight (but when they said "resident" they meant from their neighborhoods).

Boston

When the Boston participants were asked what action should be taken to curb their most serious neighborhood problems, they reported quality police service and quality municipal service. They added home ownership and business reinvestment. Like the Columbus sample, they reported the best way to curb neighborhood problems was strict enforcement and punitive action for violators especially youths and gangs, and strict enforcement among property owners and business owners who contributed to disorder and crime. But police service came in second to municipal services.

The participants said that city agencies such as the Boston Housing Authority, street department, and business licensing agencies should aid police in solving community problems that lead to poor life experiences, which the participants saw as public disorder. Many focused on the Boston Redevelopment Authority and wrote that that agency supported large construction companies and the wealthy, rarely reaching out to the "common person." Abandoned buildings should be leveled and/or rebuilt into livable dwellings or business properties for local residents. One clear message was that the residents wanted the Boston PD to enforce laws and to direct (not lead or influence) other city agencies to aid in enhancing neighborhood lifestyles. Most of the participants perceived crime as criminal intent to harm others and put slum and business owners into the classification of "criminal." Therefore, the Boston police had the responsibility of dealing with these issues.

They wanted more people to own their homes. Keep in mind that Boston's housing market is one of the highest priced home markets in the country.[23] They wanted help getting a loan through public investment opportunities, but they also wanted big businesses in their communities.

The key difference between the samples was that Columbus participants wanted influence through committee meetings and they wanted authority linked to their oversight positions. They were willing to invest time and wanted to work on enhancing their community. Boston participants, however, were less willing to enhance their community and trusted political leaders far less than the police. They wanted the Boston Police to assume authority over city agencies. Optimally, community members would provide input about neighborhood requirements to the police and the police would get the job done. The Boston participants wanted little responsibility or work in committee activities or any activity for that matter. Their concerns were more personal than community-wide. In part, making a living in Boston probably took precedence over community matters.

Part of Boston's thinking was that city and/or state agencies such as welfare, housing, corrections, streets, including city, county, and state agencies must work together to resolve neighborhood problems. The participants reported that cooperation by city agencies was necessary because community members could not reach housing authority personnel. Redirecting traffic and preserving open spaces would be a state task that might involve a number of "unknown" agencies, the respondents reported.

Summary

It is ironic that Boston has received much praise from federal authorities for its community-policing concepts and Columbus is under threat of a federal lawsuit for police indiscretions. Boston's (reported) crime rate is down and Columbus' rate has not changed significantly. Nonetheless, Boston and Columbus survey-takers produced some similar responses. However, huge distinctions arose when they talked about ways to solve community problems. Boston's sample wanted police to take control of city services and distribute city services to the residents. Home ownership concepts as opposed to police enforcement were seen as a better answer to solving crime than in Columbus, where enforcement was vital but selective. Boston's sample trusted police more than their political leaders. Columbus' sample trusted the police less than the politicians. But Boston wanted little responsibility in gaining police and city services. Columbus' sample, although they ranked police behavior as professional as that of the Boston sample, feared police more than trusted them and wanted to guide police practice through oversight committees. They also felt that they were more deserving than others in the jurisdiction and consequently should receive more of what the city had to offer.

[23]At the time of this writing, March 2002.

Do You Know? _____

1. In what way is Boston a city of many contrasts? In the city you live in, how many contrasts can you describe? In what way might those differences impact the decisions made by the police department to provide quality police service?

2. What might attract such large percentages of refugees and immigrants to Boston and the Commonwealth of Massachusetts? In what way might these different populations affect government services including schools, religious, police, and health-care agencies? What advantages might Boston look forward to from diverse populations?

3. Describe the early police department in Boston and its development to present day. In what way might its history be similar and dissimilar to police agencies in similar-sized cities? In your opinion, what are some of the reasons why Boston employs more police officers than Columbus?

4. Describe neighborhood-policing concepts in Boston. What are its advantages and disadvantages?

5. Outline the implementation process of the Boston PD's neighborhood policing initiative. How different might it be from another city? Why?

6. Identify the most serious neighborhood problems in both cities.

7. Identify the remedies to the serious problems in both cities.

8. Describe the primary differences between the responses of the Boston sample and the Columbus sample. What accounts for these differences?

9. In what way does Harry Truman's statement fit this chapter? "I never give them hell. I just tell the truth and they think it's hell."

10

Problem-Oriented Policing

"A behaviorist is someone who pulls habits out of rats."
Anonymous

Key Terms

CAPS	Nuisance Properties	SARA
Medical Model	Problem-Oriented Policing	SARAM

Key Topics

- Community policing in the twenty-first century.
- Experiences and expectations of community policing.
- Ramifications of using the SARA design.
- Common themes among agencies winning the POP award.

Introduction

The most popular twenty-first century policing strategy is based on the community-police strategies, which has brought about new and creative approaches to crime control. However, it has also raised many issues about public order, including the very essence of policing itself. Traditional policing relied almost exclusively on reactive practices, such as the enforcement of laws supported by western European ideals. In this new millennium, police managers are experimenting with a broader range of tools and tactics, including preventive practices, to address policing issues and redefine the function of policing. However, despite these experiments and definitions, reactive practices remain crucial to crime control, fear of crime issues, and the community's quality of life.

One purpose of this chapter is to examine some of the strategies used by different police agencies in the United States as they create a partnership with the community and collaborate on problem-oriented policing techniques to control crime. One assumption is the need for accountability of police agencies and a greater public share in the decision-making processes, which should ultimately control crime, but at the same time protect individual civil rights and personal liberties.

In Chapter 1, we saw that the "best fit" model of community policing exists in part due to the many nuances and resources of a department and the community it serves. Because the social climate is different in every community, even within the same police district, it is likely that strategies also vary. In any police district, for instance, there are several distinctive neighborhoods, each with its own culture and ethnicity including language, customs, and ideals. Community-policing initiatives that work well in one community don't necessarily work well in another. Therefore, it is likely that there are as many different police strategies as there are communities throughout the United States.

According to Charles H. Ramsey, police chief of Washington, DC, after two decades of experimentation with and implementation of community policing, two concepts—partnerships and problem solving—have become firmly ingrained in the vernacular of almost every police department in the country.[1] Specifically,

[1]See Charles Ramsey, (2002). *Preparing the Community for Community Policing: The Next Step in Advancing Community Policing.* In Dennis J. Stevens (Ed.), *Communities and Community Policing,* (pp.29–44). Upper Saddle River, NJ: Prentice Hall.

"The federal government supported the new policing philosophy," the chief clarifies, "and community leaders have embraced community policing as a viable and progressive way to give residents a voice in determining the policing priorities in their neighborhoods and a structure for channeling their energy and resources" (p. 30). Police agencies have demonstrated their commitment to this new strategy through eloquent mission statements backed by new programs, catchy slogans, and sophisticated websites. However, as the following statements indicate, this is not the whole picture:

- Uniformed police officers, especially those in larger jurisdictions with significant demands for service, are still largely "slaves of 9-1-1"—rushing from emergency call to emergency call (and many nonemergencies in between), without the time or opportunity to develop partnerships or engage in sustained problem solving.[2]
- Many residents and other community stakeholders view their role as being little more than another set of "eyes and ears" of the police—looking out for trouble and then stepping back and calling in the law enforcement professionals when they see it.
- The concepts of partnerships and problem solving have been reduced to monthly meetings, attended by the same small core group of activists, hashing over many of the same problems.

Despite the shortcomings of community policing, the new philosophy represents a vast improvement over policing practices of fifteen or twenty years ago, the chief maintains. What follows is a discussion of some unique strategies that have resulted from community-policing initiatives. This discussion is not comprehensive, nor is it implied that these are the best strategies (this topic will continue for the next five chapters). Should some strategies or practices be missing, do not assume that they are less than meritorious, but simply escaped the grasp of the investigator or were beyond the space allocated to this discussion.

Medical Model Analogy

There are some lessons we can learn from the field of medicine that relate to quality-of-life experiences and crime. Historically, medicine moved from a time when people expected medical experts to save lives, to a time when patients played a large role in their own well-being. Medical science once held the promise of a cure-all: the hope that things like cancer and heart disease would be controlled by a new drug or an operation. While this idea continues to persist, some people feel that another component of physical soundness relates to preventive practices such as healthy diet, regular exercise, competent hygiene, and an elimination of unhealthy decisions that include smoking, drinking, and bad relationships. Conceptually, the "broken windows" of aging or unhealthy conditions can be revitalized through

[2]See Charles Ramsey, (2002). *Preparing the Community for Community Policing: The Next Step in Advancing Community Policing.* In Dennis J. Stevens (Ed.), *Communities and Community Policing,* (p. 31). Upper Saddle River, NJ: Prentice Hall.

prevention. Similarly, police cannot ignore violators; otherwise violent crime will increase. Then, too, the police recognize the contribution of both prevention and intervention. With medical problems, a patient needs to take medication and exercise—similarly, crime in the community means arresting violators and preventing future violators through solving underlying problems such as domestic violence, substance abuse, illiteracy, and even to boredom on the part of young people. Since all police agencies are as different as the communities they serve, policing strategies are different, too. The strategies to facilitate cooperation between the police and the community to prevent crime is the focus of this chapter. However, it must be clarified that like the medical model, people must participate in appropriate ways to control crime, reduce the fear of crime, and enhance quality-of-life experiences. This latter thought seems in some sense to be as great a problem as getting agencies to accept the challenge of preventive strategies.

Problem-Oriented Policing

The most common community-policing strategy used by police agencies across the nation can be described as problem-oriented policing (POP).

Herman Goldstein, the architect of POP, has urged police to expand their response beyond arrest-oriented practices to encompass a variety of possible responses to problems. One of those responses includes police problem-solving efforts that focus on the underlying conditions that give rise to crime and disorder. This method means the police will address the problem rather than simply ameliorate the symptoms. The results of such a problem-solving focus should be more effective and long-lasting. Indeed, improving police effectiveness is at the center of POP. Community-policing initiatives tend to use POP within their strategy to solve problems. Community policing cannot operate without a problem-solving component, but POP can stand without a community-policing philosophy to support it.

The concept of POP can be illustrated in the following example. Suppose police find themselves responding several times a day to calls from one particular apartment complex to disperse disorderly youths and stop acts of vandalism. Dispatching an officer to the scene rarely does anything to resolve the long-term problems of disorder and vandalism. If, instead, police were to incorporate POP with their approach, they would examine the conditions underlying the problem and go after the root of the problem, ultimately bringing it under control. One way to accomplish this task is through collaboration with community members, school districts, and possibly even local churches.

As POP has evolved over the last two decades, researchers and practitioners have focused on the evaluation of problems, the importance of solid analysis, the need for pragmatism in developing responses, and the need to tap other resources, including members of the community. Indeed, the role of the community continues to be a subject of discussion in POP, and problem solving is a key element in many community-policing strategies. This conceptual model of problem solving is known as *SARA (Scanning, Analysis, Response, Assessment).*

SARA

SARA is one of the best models utilized by police agencies to aid in problem-solving efforts. Each step in the process is summarized.

Scanning
- Identify recurring problems of concern to the public and the police.
- Prioritize problems.
- Develop broad goals.
- Confirm that the problems exist.
- Select one problem for examination.

Analysis
- Identify and understand events and conditions that precede and accompany the problem.
- Identify consequences of the problem for the community.
- Determine how frequently the problem occurs, why it occurs, and how long it has been occurring.
- Identify conditions that give rise to the problem.
- Narrow the scope of the problem as specifically as possible.
- Identify resources that can aid in the development of a deeper understanding of the problem.

Response
- Search for what others with similar problems have done.
- Brainstorm interventions.
- Choose among the alternative solutions.
- Outline a response plan and identify responsible parties.
- State specific goals for the response plan.
- Identify relevant data to be collected.
- Carry out planned activities.

Assessment
- Determine whether the plan was implemented.
- Determine whether the goals were attained, and collect qualitative and quantitative data (pre- and post-response).
- Identify any new strategies needed to augment original plan.
- Conduct an ongoing assessment to ensure continued effectiveness.

Problem-oriented policing (POP) or problem solving is a cornerstone of community policing in Savannah, for instance. Although structured as separate approaches to policing, community policing and POP are terms used interchangeably by many officers, police managers, and citizens. Some view the efforts as a single approach, while others see distinct differences.

POP is so closely related to community policing that in order for it to be successful, the two must be considered effectively inseparable. POP strategies employ law enforcement as well as community resources to attack the problems that not only breed crime, but contribute to other common annoyances that generate dissatisfaction in the community. This proactive police strategy eliminates, or at least mitigates, these conditions before they develop into incidents requiring a traditional police response.

Community policing removes the barriers that have traditionally existed between the police and the public. By acquainting the police with the people they serve and, as a result, acquainting the public with individual officers, citizens no longer view police as nameless blue uniforms. One police manager sums it up this way, "community policing is the philosophy; POP is the strategy. This strategy is used throughout the department and starts with the initiation of a POP project."[3]

Problem-Oriented Policing in Savannah, Georgia

At the Savannah Police Department anyone (sworn or otherwise) can initiate a POP project.[4] The problem need not be a specific crime. For example, several projects have involved neighborhood conditions that affect residents' quality of life. Other problems have involved procedures that need improvement, such as the development of a medical protocol for handling child abuse victims. Officers who initiate projects are encouraged to make the contacts with other agencies or resources necessary to complete the project. The role of the supervisor is to facilitate the process through SARA.

The most significant organizational change the Savannah Police Department made when implementing community policing was the establishment of the precinct system. Each precinct has a substation. Any type of fixed beat or service area system would probably have addressed the geographical accountability problem the crime control study highlighted. The precinct system was developed to put the police and community together and to give the captains "ownership" of their part of the city. There is a great deal of responsibility along with this freedom. Captains report that the precinct system truly made them police managers. They have to be more actively involved in long-range planning and in developing support systems in the community.

San Antonio, Texas Police Department

The San Antonio Police Department[5] (SAPD) uses POP to produce long-term solutions to problems of crime or decay in communities. That is, SAPD feels that problem solving is successful only if it produces a long-term solution. This police department believes that many POP responses tend to produce short-term positive results that rarely last longer than months without constant intervention by police. In other words, "Has the problem been solved?"

---

[3]This comment was made by police Major Lyght, the Patrol Commander of the Savannah Georgia Police Department.
[4]See Jeff Young, (1996). Community Policing in Savannah, Georgia. In *Police Executive Research Forum Themes and Variations in Community Policing*. (pp. 69–80). Washington, DC: PERF.
[5]San Antonio, Texas Police Department. http://www.ci.sat.tx.us/sapd/saffe.htm

POP projects are documented problem-solving efforts. A formal process for addressing a problem is set forth in a standard operating procedure. A project starts with the submission of a project proposal, through the chain of command, by an officer or other employee who has identified a problem. Personnel follow the chain of command to eliminate duplication of effort, facilitate cooperation between involved units, and ensure that projects are not started for minor matters that can be resolved by other means. SARA is utilized but SARAM is preferred. That is, S is for scanning to identify and describe the problem, A is to analyze, R for response, A is for assess, and M is for maintenance. An example of a department ignoring long-term objectives can be found in the line-solution problems practiced by the Las Vegas Police Department.

Line-Solution Problems in Las Vegas

In early 1989, Las Vegas Metro Police Department focused on a serious problem facing many of their most challenging neighborhoods. Several apartment complexes were riddled with gang-related crime. A disparate number of 911 emergency calls to those locations proved ineffective in restoring security and produced a heavy burden on police resources (Bulter, 1996). Metro's response was to operate from police substations and line-solution policing (LSP) was initiated at each substation.

LSP officers were expected to identify crime-related problems, develop plans to minimize or resolve those problems, and ensure that the solutions were implemented. LSP was driven by two objectives in concert with community leaders: reduce nonpolice related 911 calls for service, and assist field and investigative personnel in targeting criminals and known crime locations. LSP officers were not responsible for 911 calls or patrol assignments.

However, long-term goals were never developed and little was communicated to officers or the community, producing confusion about the exact definitions and dimensions of LSP, especially among patrol officers. Metro did not develop a set of strategies to implement or maintain many of their programs, including LSP. And although Metro had a planning bureau, development of their LSP program was handed over to a patrol division lieutenant, giving him several weeks to complete it.

Needless to say, due to staffing shortages and service demands, LSP developed primarily into several special enforcement units concerned more with apprehending criminals than with identifying the root causes of neighborhood problems. It became a general enforcement unit in some areas of the city and a narcotics unit in other sections of the city. While Metro experienced a reduction in call volume, Metro's commanders believed officers had minimal amounts of uncommitted patrol time to conduct LSP duties. In fact, one deputy chief estimated that 11 percent of the officers' time was uncommitted, and at another substation, a commander estimated that 20 to 40 percent of their shift was uncommitted. Metro's failure to provide long-term goals and communicate program priorities led, in part, to LSP's demise.

Barriers to Neighborhood Policing in Newport News, Virginia

Several internal and external barriers seemed to inhibit progress in implementing neighborhood policing in Newport News.[6] For example, one manager said, "If POP is done right, you don't need neighborhood policing." Line officers throughout the department believed supervisors' level of interest in, and support of, POP greatly determined how much problem solving officers did. If the sergeant or lieutenant supported the problem-solving process and mentored the patrol officers, officers would identify and work on problems. Sargents had also seen few changes resulting from the implementation of neighborhood policing. An additional factor that inhibited neighborhood policing was the frequency of "cross dispatching." The level of trust between citizens and the police department was not high, which may have also inhibited the implementation of neighborhood policing. It seemed that the local newspaper did little to promote the department's neighborhood-policing efforts. The reporter and editor who covered the police beat were alternately bored with, or suspicious of, the department's problem-oriented and neighborhood policing efforts and their opinions were reflected in the newspaper.

Excellence in Problem-Oriented Policing (POP)

When examining the success of POP, the seven finalists for the Herman Goldstein Award for excellence in problem-oriented policing[7] provide interesting information. The following are the winner for excellence in POP and the five runner-up agencies for the award:

> **Green Bay, Wisconsin Police Department**
> Baltimore Police Department
> Fresno, California Police Department
> Minneapolis Police Department
> Racine, Wisconsin Police Department
> San Diego Police Department
> Vancouver Police Department

This award recognizes outstanding police officers and police agencies in the U.S. and around the world that engage in innovative and effective problem-solving efforts and achieve measurable success in reducing specific crime, disorder, and public safety problems.[8] The depth of problem analysis, the development of clear and realistic response goals, the use of relevant measures of effectiveness, and the involvement of citizens and other community resources in problem resolution were the primary criterion utilized by the judges to make their decision.

[6]See Lynn Babcock, (1996). The Evolution of Community Policing in Newport News, VA. In *Police Executive Research Forum Themes and Variations in Community Policing*, (pp. 37–68). Washington, DC: PERF.

[7]For more details, see *Excellence in Problem-Oriented Policing*, (2000).

[8]The agencies that sponsored the awards represented the Police Executive Research Forum, the National Institute of Justice, and the Office of Community-Oriented Policing Services.

The 1999 Winner: Green Bay Police Department

Officers Bill Bongle and Steve Scully of the Green Bay Police Department initiated a strategy to revive the Broadway business district in Green Bay, a high-crime area of the city, characterized by people who were often intoxicated and disorderly and living on the street, and by litter and broken bottles. The officers gave taverns a "no-serve list" of people who were habitually drunk and disorderly or in trouble, motivated community members to pressure city liquor license regulators to increase their oversight and enforcement, modified the environment, targeted enforcement to specific locations, and worked with the community and the media to educate the public about the initiative. The result was a reduction in calls-for-service and an improved quality of life in the neighborhood.

Runners-up for the award include six police agencies:

- **Baltimore Police Department,** which reduced chronic truancy by working closely with school department officials and the courts. By engaging parents in the effort, the department reduced truancy without resorting to traditional legal remedies.
- **Fresno Police Department,** which faced a large number of child-custody violation calls. The agency focused its problem-solving efforts on increasing awareness and utilization of an existing family court-ordered program that provides a safe place for parents to exchange custody of their children. In addition, the department led a countywide effort to coordinate and improve prosecution of child custody violations.
- **Minneapolis Police Department,** which partnered with the community to revitalize the Hawthorne neighborhood. Hawthorne was affected by narcotics trafficking and quality-of-life offenses. The "Hawthorne Huddle" began as a series of community meetings and evolved into a key problem-solving forum for both the police department and the Hawthorne community. The department combined a traditional response of increased enforcement with the POP approach of cultivating community involvement. The department's participation in the community meetings ensured that the department was actively involved in facilitating communication and assisting residents.
- **Racine Police Department,** which revitalized neighborhoods by partnering with the community, other government agencies, and nonprofit organizations. One of the agency's key strategies was to purchase and restore rundown, single-family homes in troubled neighborhoods for use as temporary community-police substations. The police presence served as a catalyst for positive change. When order was restored to the neighborhoods, the homes were sold to low-income homebuyers.
- **San Diego Police Department,** which dramatically reduced school absenteeism among the most chronic truants. Police officers conducted an innovative needs assessment with truants and arranged for needed services. To ensure long-term success, the officers helped to create a mentoring program for at-risk youth.

- **Vancouver Police Department,** which addressed a decline in the quality of life in its community by restoring order at a busy urban intersection. The department relied on the community to assist in both problem identification and resolution. The project achieved lasting success by altering the physical environment, making it less conducive for criminal activity such as panhandling, and squeegeeing (washing) car windows.

Each of these agencies applied SARA and other lessons learned from policing research to address substantial problems in their communities. By working closely with other government agencies, nonprofit groups, and residents, these agencies were able to develop effective solutions to long-standing problems. Each site included enforcement in its POP strategies. Each project also clearly demonstrated an important principle articulated by Goldstein: rank-and-file officers have a lot of information, and given the freedom and support to create solutions, they can be very successful problem solvers.

Common Themes among Agencies

These agencies faced similar problems in their communities and developed similar strategies in their problem-solving approach to solve those problems. Some of the similarities, or recurring themes, are that habitual offenders created disorder, reliance on the community, value of the line officer's experience, identification of the underlying causes of problems, and leveraging resources.

Habitual Offenders Create Disorder   Green Bay, Minneapolis, Racine, and Vancouver all tackled complex problems that involved habitual offenders performing the same illegal or troubling behaviors in the same places over and over again. Over time, disorder and fear permeated the affected neighborhoods. Police officers in each site developed solutions that took advantage of the unique strengths and resources in their communities. Minneapolis and Racine, struggling with these issues in residential communities, accessed much-needed social services for neighborhood residents. Green Bay and Vancouver worked closely with the businesses in their commercial neighborhoods to make physical changes to the environment.

Reliance on the Community   The key role of the community in identifying and solving problems is well illustrated by the seven projects. Although the departments were independently able to identify many of the problems, it was the input of community members that helped them understand many of the underlying causes and citizens' priorities for intervention. Officers who led these projects spent many fruitful hours gathering information and opinions from members of the community. Along the way, the officers formed relationships that contributed to lasting community involvement and empowerment.

Value of the Line Officer's Experience   All of the sites demonstrated the importance of using the knowledge and skills of rank-and-file officers. In each site, the impetus to begin the POP project came from line officers. The officers recognized offense and disorder patterns during the course of their regular duties. The officers then conducted research, analyzed crime and social indicator data, reached out to the community and mobilized its members, and crafted creative, lasting solutions to complex problems.

Identification of the Underlying Causes of Problems   Through their analysis, the officers were able to identify and focus on the underlying causes of crime, disorder, and fear. Both Baltimore and San Diego, which addressed truancy, examined the causes of students' school avoidance, not just its consequences. Officers in each site worked closely with school district officials to address the needs of truant students and their families. The Green Bay officers identified tax liquor licensing and enforcement as an underlying cause of problems in the Broadway area of their city. Officers in Vancouver gained important insights into the underlying causes of their problems when they considered "ownership" of public space in their target intersection. In that context, solutions to the aggressive "squeegee" person problem became much easier to identify.

Leveraging Resources   In each site, the ultimate success of the project depended on the officers' ability to leverage the resources of other government agencies and private-sector resources. The Racine community-policing houses became vital to the community when public services were offered in the houses. The houses offered neighborhood-based services in previously underserved locations. The provision of services increased the community's acceptance of a police presence in the neighborhood.

Weaknesses of POP in St. Petersburg

Clearly, while each of the seven agencies are deserving of applause, there are approximately 18,000 agencies across the United States. POP operates under the assumption that officers have a great insight into the problems plaguing a community, and while giving officers the discretion to design and implement solutions is extremely valuable to the problem-solving approach, the likelihood is that community members would have liked to have been included in the decision-making process and implementation of resolutions. POP also assumes that the police can use a variety of methods to redress recurrent problems, and that their involvement in non-criminal problems will end in success. POP used by itself might create more problems than it resolves, depending on the officers involved and the response and the agenda of policymakers and community members. One response Goldstein considered meritorious includes police problem-solving efforts that focus on the underlying conditions that give rise to crime and disorder. Should the "real" roots of disorder be ignored, perhaps the success of delivering a community from the hands of some drunkards through POP might be minimized.

St. Petersburg, Florida is one of the cities that evidently ignored the roots of social order. These "real" problems of crime control continue to plague the St. Petersburg Police Department. It started long ago, but the incident that allowed the roots of social order to surface, despite POP advances, was the tragic death of TyRon Lewis (age 18) at the hands of Officer James Knight during a traffic stop at

16th Street and 18th Avenue on October 23, 1996. Two nights of civil unrest resulted and the prominence of the National People's Democratic Uhuru Movement (NPDUM) engulfed the city.[9] The NPDUM's website suggests that they are a chapter of The African People's Socialist Party. Omali Yeshitela, the NPDUM's founder, said the killing led to the emergence of the Uhuru movement, which in turn helped to unify the working-class community with portions of the middle-class community.[10] "As a consequence of [Lewis' death], the white power structure discovered the Uhuru movement," Yeshitela said. "I think that the most important thing that has come out is the development of a new social contract between the members of the progressive (black) middle class and the (black) working class," he added. While the St. Petersburg Police Department continues to provide what appears to be quality police service to its constituents, the Uhuru organization appears to meet each police outreach with reservation.

Chicago's CAPS Program

A partnership developed by the Chicago Police Department is known as CAPS (Chicago Alternative Policing Strategy).[11]

CAPS is a unique philosophy that borrows from the experiences of other cities, but breaks new ground in meeting the needs of the Chicago Police Department and the Chicago community. What makes CAPS innovative is that it brings police, community, and other city agencies together to identify and solve neighborhood crime problems as a preventive measure. Problem solving at the neighborhood level is supported by a variety of strategies, including neighborhood-based beat officers, regular beat community meetings involving police and residents, extensive training for both police and community, more efficient use of city services that impact crime, and new technology to help police and residents target crime hot spots.

With CAPS, police officers continue to enforce laws and respond rapidly to serious crimes and life-threatening emergencies. But CAPS recognizes that the police alone cannot solve the city's crime problems. It takes a combined effort of police, community, and city government working together.

Implementation of CAPS began in April 1993 with the official rollout in 5 of the city's 25 police districts. These five districts are diverse in terms of their demographics, economics, crime problems, and levels of community organization. They provided a valuable laboratory for testing and improving the CAPS model before it was expanded citywide.

[9] For a closer look at this situation see Dennis J. Stevens, (2001). *Case Studies in Community Policing*, pp. 205–206.

[10] In a 1966 protest, Joe Waller, now known as Omali Yeshitela, marched down the street with the mural (depicting black minstrels playing music for white people on Pass-a-Grille beach) that hung in St. Petersburg City Hall. Yeshitela served two and one-half years in various jails and prisons for tearing down the mural. "When I tore that mural down, I was castigated in a lot of quarters as a criminal and I in fact served time in prison for it," Yeshitela said.

[11] For more information, see Chicago Police's website: http://www.ci.chi.il.us/CommunityPolicing/. See also Skogan, W.G., & Hartnett, S.M. (1997). *Community policing: Chicago style*. NY: Oxford University Press.

Implementation of CAPS in the other 20 police districts began in 1994, and the strategy is now operational in all of Chicago's neighborhoods. The five original prototype districts continue to serve as a laboratory for testing new ideas and new technology.

By opening up the dialogue between police and community, CAPS is producing a number of important success stories at the neighborhood level. Across the city, the CAPS partnership is tackling serious crime problems, as well as those neighborhood conditions that breed crime—conditions such as abandoned buildings and vehicles, vacant lots, drug houses, and graffiti.

On a special episode of Chicago CrimeWatch, entitled "Block by Block," viewers are taken on a guided tour through the CAPS five-step, problem-solving process. This episode explains the five steps of problem solving, and shows how effective problem solving can be when police and residents tackle the process together. The success of problem solving is told through the story of Gill Park, and how residents and police on Beat 2324 used the five-step process to reclaim the park from gangbangers and drug dealers and, thus, bring back the families and children.

Step 1: Identify and Prioritize the Problem   The first step in the problem-solving process is to identify and prioritize the problem. On Beat 2324, Gill Park was identified as the top priority during beat community meetings and community training sessions. Everyone, it seemed, knew Gill Park was a problem.

Step 2: Analyze the Problem   Using a device called the Crime Triangle, police and residents then analyzed the Gill Park problem from three perspectives: offenders, victims, and location. They developed specific information on gang members in the park and on those who were buying and selling drugs. The victims were identified as the families who could no longer use the park, plus nearby property owners whose buildings were devalued by the criminal presence at the park. Regarding the location, residents analyzed several problems with the park—from poor lighting and overgrown shrubbery to an overall design that provided ideal hiding places for illegal activity. "As soon as you saw the back of the park, you could see it looked like it was designed for drug dealing," says Jackie McKay of the Friends of the Parks organization.

Step 3: Design Strategies   Based on their analysis of the problem, police and community developed a number of strategies to address the offender and location issues of the Crime Triangle. To target offenders, foot patrols would be instituted at strategic times; curfew and loitering laws would be energetically enforced; and neighbors adjacent to the park would keep a watchful eye and report suspicious activity. On the location issue, residents and city crews decided to get together to totally redesign the park—to make it less conducive to criminal activity and more conducive to recreation.

Step 4: Implement Strategies   This is the "just do it" aspect of problem solving. With Gill Park, police, community, and city agencies all did their parts. The community, in particular, stepped forward to provide architectural services and raise money for the park redesign. "They were looking for a new way to redo the park so it was safer, and basically we came up with a theme to put in a new sports field, a baseball diamond," says local architect Mike Eichorn.

Step 5: Evaluate and Acknowledge Success   During this step, all of those involved review their success. Which strategies worked? What challenges remain? In Gill Park, the signs of success were everywhere. "A lot of people over here are using the park now," says resident Hakeem Durojaiye. "It just didn't seem possible last year."

The department maintains that the five-step problem-solving process enables ordinary people to do extraordinary things.

Chicago Beat Meetings   Beat community meetings are held on a regular basis on each of the 279 police beats in the city. Beat community meetings are hosted by the police department and are chaired by a police officer who is a member of the beat team. A member of the community, often called a beat facilitator, might co-chair the meeting and assist in establishing the agenda.

Beat community meetings are an important first step in the CAPS problem-solving process. The meetings provide the opportunity to help set the crime-fighting priorities in the community—to let community members work with beat officers in identifying and prioritizing crime and disorder problems, in analyzing those problems, and in developing strategies to address them. Information from the beat community meeting is used by the beat team to develop the beat plan, a tool that helps police officers and the community keep track of priority problems and the progress made in addressing those problems.

Success Stories   Of course, in a city the size of Chicago there are always success stories but a few are being offered to give you an idea how CAPS works. Austin District police personnel became aware of numerous citizen complaints around the 700 block of North Waller, regarding rampant narcotics activity. At the direction of District Commander LeRoy O'Shield, 15th District tactical teams, neighborhood relations staff and beat personnel conducted a survey of area residents to determine the scope and parameters of the problem.

Using the survey results, police were then able to identify six area homes around which the illegal narcotics traffic seemed to be concentrated. Additionally, one of the neighborhood residents allowed police to use his home to conduct a surveillance of suspected narcotics traffickers. When they were ready, police teams saturated the area, making more than fifty arrests within a two-week period.

The District's Court Advocacy Committee was closely monitoring these criminal cases, as the various defendants made their way through the court system. Following this resounding success, other Austin residents, particularly those in and around the 5900 block of West Rice, were working with 15th District police to incorporate the same coordinated anti-drug tactics in their neighborhood. Major drug arrests have also been made in the Rice Street operation.

Another success story comes from Beat 1512. It began with a close-knit group of neighbors who formed the 3M Block Club, so named because the club included

Mason, Menard, and Mayfield Streets in its service area. The club undertook a number of activities to improve the neighborhood, such as prayer vigils, cookouts, and cleanups. In the process, residents drew closer together. As local resident Hassan Muhammad described it, "[Those efforts] formed a relationship with some neighbors who hadn't spoken to each other in some time, who began to communicate with each other not only to say, 'This is who I am,' but, 'This is something I can bring to uplift my community'." However, neighborhood improvement and solidarity could only go so far as long as a significant drug-dealing problem remained. This is where the Chicago Police Department came in. "What we had to do is put a squad car over here to patrol strictly this area, all day long," says Commander Lorenzo Davis of the district. With drug dealing almost eliminated as a result of the police presence, "the kids started coming out, people were on their porches again, and that is really telling of the success we had," as Rev. Dr. Michelle Bentley of the 3rd Unitarian Church observes. The Church has been a cornerstone of the revitalization efforts, and a key provider of social services in the community. It is currently working with 30 young people to improve their job skills and teach them "they can get what they want in life without standing on the corner and doing illegal activities," in the words of 3M Member Dorethea Stafford.

Another notable project was the renovation of a home set for demolition, to provide housing for homeless women and children. CAPS has been an important part of the success. "At one point, many people felt CAPS and beat meetings were irrelevant, but they learned. . . . it really became a vehicle to bring the kind of services to the community that make a difference" says Hassan Muhammad.

Chicago's extensive public education and outreach strategy for CAPS has relied on both the mass media and grass-roots organizing, and everything in between. A coordinated mass media campaign included both paid and public service advertising for radio, television, and newspapers; transit advertising; billboards; information kiosks; and other outlets. The police department also began producing a biweekly television program that airs on both the municipal cable channel as well as a local network affiliate. At the grass-roots level, outreach was made to churches, block clubs, community organizations, and other entities with a strong presence and history in the city.

These types of comprehensive marketing initiatives are not inexpensive, especially when agencies are competing with thousands of other commercial advertising messages during critical time periods. But the return on investment can be tremendous. In Chicago, public recognition of community policing rose from 53 percent to 79 percent in the two years that coincided with the public education strategy. The largest percentage of residents reported hearing about CAPS through television—both news reports, advertisements, and the department's cable program.

However, while things sound good for CAPS, unfortunately for everything we examine (including this text) there is always a down side that deserves attention. Clearly, when measuring performance, there is a risk of discovering the other side of things. In a reasonable way of measuring community outcomes, it becomes clear that there is unequal participation in community-policing strategies. Middle-class homeowners who already get along with the police and share many of the same views jump on programs quickly, and historically they have gotten most of the benefits from these strategies, according to Jill DuBois and Susan M. Hartnett (2001).[12] These groups are also more likely to be well organized already, with lots of effective block clubs, high voter turnout, and downtown clout. As a result, better-off neighborhoods are the ones that improve. African-Americans and Spanish Americans, as well as poor people of all denominations, fall behind. It is very important to watch out for this, as well as to figure out what to do about it.

In Chicago, according to DuBois and Hartnett (2001), CAPS has been a real success in the African American community. But it is most successful in the large middle-income part of that community. However, many of the shortcomings of the program seem to fall most heavily on immigrant communities, which represent the fastest growing part of the city. By immigrants, these writers are referring to Chicago's Latino communities. There are perhaps 500,000 Latinos in Chicago, mostly originating from Mexico and Puerto Rico. "To put it in a nutshell, compared to the city's largest communities, Latinos have been left out" (p. 9). They are less likely to know about community policing, less likely to know that beat meetings are being held nearby, less likely to attend beat meetings, less likely to turn out for training, and less likely to get involved in problem solving. For all of Chicago's success, it appears that the culturally diverse groups are left out of police outreach.

Many Chicagoans have received benefits from CAPS. However, as compared to other neighborhoods, CAPS hasn't made things much better in culturally diverse neighborhoods. It's not that they do not need help; their problems are as complex as any in the city. Latinos consistently identify gang and drugs as their neighborhoods' biggest problems, and those are tough problems.

DuBois and Hartnett (2001) indicate that compared to others, Latinos in Chicago have even more problems with the physical decay of their communities. Among these problems are graffiti, vandalism, abandoned buildings, abandoned cars, loose garbage and rats in the alleys, and a collapsing infrastructure. Another issue is that beat meetings underrepresent Latinos who live in the beat by "30 to 50 percent" (p. 11). Even when they know about beat meetings, they are less likely to attend. Unfortunately, this is consistent with what we will find when we look at other police agencies across the United States.

The Chicago Challenge   So why is engaging Latinos in a partnership with the police such a challenge? Well, above all, they do not have a history of getting along with the police. Especially in poor and disenfranchised neighborhoods, residents often have a history of antagonistic relationships with the police, write DuBois and Hartnett (2001). The police may be perceived as arrogant, brutal, and uncaring—not as potential partners. Residents may fear that more intensive policing could generate new problems with harassment, indiscriminate searches,

---

[12]DuBois and Hartnett (2001) researched and worked diligently on the CAPS program in Chicago and have intimate insight into its operation.

and conflicts between them and the police. These findings sound similar to the implications of St. Petersburg.

DuBois and Hartnett (2001) surveyed Chicagoans in the months before CAPS was instituted. They found Latinos and African Americans to be almost three times more likely than whites to think that police serving their neighborhoods were impolite, and more than twice as likely to think the police treated people unfairly. About 35 percent of Latinos felt police weren't concerned about the problems facing people in their neighborhoods, as did 25 percent of African Americans, but only 15 percent of whites felt that way.

Other findings by the writers included the implication that poor and high-crime areas are often not well endowed with an infrastructure of organizations ready to be involved with the police. Since their constituents often fear the police, groups representing poor and minority areas can be more interested in monitoring police misconduct and pressing for greater police accountability than being involved in coordinated action with them.

DuBois and Hartnett explain that measuring participation in organized crime-prevention programs also reveals that those participants are not easily initiated nor sustained in poorer neighborhoods. Crime and the fear of crime stimulate their individual withdrawal from community life rather than involvement in community meetings. In crime-ridden neighborhoods, mutual distrust and hostility are often pervasive. Residents view each other with suspicion rather than neighborliness, and that in itself undermines a capacity to forge collective responses to local problems. These individuals fear retaliation by drug dealers and neighborhood toughs; thus, programs requiring social contact, neighborly cooperation, or public involvement are less often successful in areas with high levels of fear.

The problem is consistent with program boundaries imposed by a police department in diverse communities. Suspicion and fear divides the area along race, class, and lifestyle lines, leaving residents and the organizations that represent them at odds with one another. It's part of a "divided we fall" perspective, if initiated intentionally. They will almost inevitably point fingers at one another over who causes what problems, and the police will be forced to choose sides or look like they are choosing sides, regardless of what decisions they make. Groups contending over access to housing, municipal services, infrastructure maintenance, and public sector jobs and contracts may also find themselves battling one another over policing priorities and the fear of the district commander.

As previously discussed, the St. Petersburg Police Department continues to try to provide quality police service to its constituents, many of whom are poor and apparently many of them, including the Uhuru organization who appear to meet every police outreach with suspicion. Accordingly, Uhuru engages in block-by-block organizing of the city of St. Petersburg. Specifically, "Currently, the crucial work of the Uhuru is block organizing," said the Uhuru organization's official website.[13] "We've got a map of the city and we're dividing the city up into sections. We've created 30 sections now, but they're larger than I want them to be. For every section we want to have a section leader right out of that community. For this we're trying to win people who are Uhuru supporters. We want to commit them to just doing Uhuru work in the neighborhood where they stay. The solidarity forces are currently dividing up the white community into sections as well."

"In every section we want to have a section leader, and in every block we want to put a block captain. We will organize the entire city in that fashion so that no matter where the government attempts to go, no matter what kind of thing they want to do down the road, we will have put down Uhuru houses throughout the city. Every house becomes an Uhuru house. That way, we'll be able to maintain the high ground that we have now." A good model for community policing advocates to follow.

Summary

A medical model is used as an analogy for community-police strategies. At one time, people expected medical experts to save lives through simple operations. Contemporary thinking is that patients play a large role in their own well-being. Medical science once held the promise of a cure-all through medicines and operations, but it takes preventive techniques to stay healthy. A prominent police chief reveals that partnerships and problem solving are part of a philosophy in most police agencies in the U.S., producing new programs, catchy slogans, and sophisticated websites. Yet, it takes more to police a twenty-first century community. Problem-oriented policing (POP) has evolved to a conceptual model of problem solving known as SARA, and this chapter discusses many variations and barriers of SARA and POP within a variety of agencies. Several award-winning agencies are reviewed. A large Midwestern police agency and its ideals of problem solving are explored, including some of its success stories, and failures, which include exclusion of Latinos and other culturally diverse groups in community police matters.

Do You Know?

1. With so many different policing strategies, how does a police agency know which one will best serve their constituents? How might you develop a community-police strategy if you were in charge?

2. In what way does the medical model discussed in the chapter resemble community-police models?

3. What does SARA stand for, and how would you operationalize each step in your community if you were in charge?

4. A few police agencies added a twist to SARA. Describe those twists and discuss their relevance to problem-solving solutions. In what way do you agree with those twists? Disagree?

5. Excellence in problem-oriented policing seemed to be based on what standards? In what way do you agree or disagree with those standards? Outline some of your own standards.

6. Identify and describe the CAPS five-step program and its relevance to a city where it is currently operationalized. In what way do you agree or disagree with the overall model?

7. In what way is the quote at the beginning of the chapter relevant? "A behaviorist is someone who pulls habits out of rats." Anonymous.

---

[13] For more detail, see The African People's Socialist Party (1999).

11

Saturation Patrol, Zero Tolerance, Refugees, and the Elderly

"Action speaks louder than words."
Proverb

Key Terms

COMPSTAT
Community Prosecution
Conflict Intervention Unit

National Night Out
Nuisance Properties
Saturation Patrol

TRIAD
Zero Tolerance

Key Topics

- Community policing on a university campus and the roadways.
- Community prosecution.
- Programs for the elderly.
- Policing refugees and immigrants.
- No margin police policy to make arrests.
- Technological advances in policing.

Saturation Patrol

Charlotte, North Carolina

One component of community-oriented policing is strategic policing or *saturation patrol*.

Saturation Patrol

> Saturation patrol is an increase in police enforcement bearing on a specific strategy such as roadblocks.[1]

There are three methods in strategic policing of a targeted area or problem: directed patrol, aggressive patrol, and saturation patrol. Of the three, saturation patrol involves the largest drain on police resources and greatest show of force.[2] More specifically, saturation patrol generally uses a collection of officers, often from various agencies, shifts, or tactical units, who, in uniform, saturate a designated area for days or even weeks. After an initial period in which police establish their presence in an area with multiple arrests, investigative stops, or traffic stops, they then remain in the area, in force, for an additional period. The goal of a saturation operation is to temporarily displace or eliminate a problem from a designated area.

Saturation patrol is most closely associated with drug crackdowns (Sherman, 1990; Zimmer, 1990), but is effective for both criminal and order-maintenance issues. The effects of saturation patrol upon crime and order-maintenance problems, however, have not been well researched.

[1]Oliver, W. (1998). *Community-Oriented Policing*. Upper Saddle River, NJ: Prentice Hall.
[2]See Thomas B. Priest and Deborah Brown Carter. (2002). Community-Oriented Policing: Assessing A Police Saturation Operation. In Dennis J. Stevens (Ed.) *Community and Community Policing*. (pp. 187–195). Upper Saddle River, NJ: Prentice Hall.

Charlotte Mecklenburg Police Department (CMPD) conducted a saturation operation for several weeks in a predominantly African American residential area, located about one mile southwest of the central business district.[3] Some of the results of that research project are described as follows: Residents, business owners, and managers complained about speeding and other traffic problems in the area selected for the operation. Traffic fatalities and hit-and-run accidents were common. Residents and businesspeople were concerned with crime, disorder, and the physical deterioration of the area. Local neighborhood associations relayed these complaints and concerns to the CMPD via a community police officer (CPO). Largely in response to neighborhood complaints and concerns, the CMPD decided to initiate a saturation operation in the area.

The saturation operation involved the coordinated action of officers from a number of law enforcement agencies and units. These included the Highway Interdiction and Traffic Safety (H.I.T.S.) Unit of the CMPD, the Adam Service Area Street Crimes Unit of the CMPD, the Alcohol Law Enforcement Division of the North Carolina Department of Alcohol and Public Safety, and the Mecklenburg County Sheriff's Department. Approximately 30 officers, agents, and deputies were involved. The operation largely occurred during the second, or 4–11 P.M. workshift because of concern with speeding during evening rush hour.

The number of traffic arrests was more than ten times the usual number. When officers or agents apprehended offenders, the offender was brought to the shopping-center parking lot and formally arrested. Formal arrests were highly visible in all directions. Note, however, that formal arrests probably were more visible to business owners and managers than to most residents of the area.

After the operation, a survey was distributed to residents and businesspeople. Residents generally were aware of quality-of-life problems in the area. Prior to the saturation operation, a high percentile of the participants reported that they knew that young people hung out on the corner, people drank on the streets, prostitutes walked the streets, and drug dealers sold drugs on the streets in the neighborhood.

After the saturation strategy, substantial proportions of both residents and businesspeople in the area perceived decreases in quality-of-life problems, in the number of people speeding through the neighborhood, and in crime in the area. The saturation operation appeared to have at least a modest effect upon crime in the area.

Yet, survey data and reported incident statistics were contradictory. While many residents and businesspeople stated, for example, that prostitution decreased in the area in the period after the saturation operation, incident statistics indicated that sex offenses increased after the operation. Similarly, while residents and businesspeople stated that speeding decreased in the area in the period after the operation, hit-and-run accidents increased and a traffic fatality occurred after the operation. The perceptions of residents and businesspeople were not completely congru-

[3]See Thomas B. Priest and Deborah Brown Carter. (2002). Community-Oriented Policing: Assessing A Police Saturation Operation. In Dennis J. Stevens (Ed.) *Community and Community Policing.* (pp. 187–195). Upper Saddle River, NJ: Prentice Hall.

ent with official statistics. Yet, statistics were down from previous reports, suggesting that the show of force represented by a saturation operation has a modest deterrent or displacement effect upon crime in an area. Some potential offenders apparently react to the unusual number of police officers in the area either by thinking twice before committing crime or by leaving the area.

University of Illinois, Chicago

Chief Bruce Lewis advises that community policing at the university police level "builds a basis of trust when our community sees themselves reflected in their police department."[4] The says out that that isn't an easy task, especially when the community is one of the most diverse university populations in America. Additionally, residents around the campus represent large groups of Latino, African American, Italian, Greek, Jewish, Arab, and Asian populations. One goal of the chief was to develop a department that mirrors that diversity. In terms of geography, the officers divided the campus based on shared interests and backgrounds. For instance, Officer Kirk Roberts was assigned to the west campus that included the School of Public Health and the College of Nursing where his wife was a student. Officer Zyad Hasan volunteered to work with the Muslim student associations, and Officer Luis Arboleda chose to work with the Latino Cultural Center due to the similar cultural backgrounds between officers and groups. One of the first tests occurred when one of the officers was accused of abuse during an arrest. In the past, that accusation would have been met with campus unrest. Instead there were comments of support for the police from many groups and individuals within the cultural group associated with the offender. Overall, the feeling of commonality of interests served as a foundation for a number of police-community endeavors such as a bike safety rodeo, a blood drive, a clothing drive, and a bike donation project. To capitalize on success, the chief has made plans to expand the liaison approach department-wide. Many departments are not in a similar position as the university police, but the example of promoting similar cultural interests between officers and the community served has some meritorious considerations for other departments. Constituents support officers who understand their culture.

Zero Tolerance

New York City Police Department

Zero Tolerance

Zero tolerance is a no-margin police policy to make an arrest.

[4] See Mike Cherry, (2000, January). Cultural Diversity: Reaching out to the communities with the community. Washington, DC: Community-Policing Exchange, (p. 8).

Prevention of criminally violent behavior can include *zero tolerance* strategy. Zero tolerance is a policy of taking into custody individuals who commit lower-level offenses such as a weapons charge since those individuals might be the same individuals who commit violent crimes, the New York Police Department (NYPD) theorizes. By targeting and detaining offenders for less serious infractions, the NYPD is preventing a more tragic incident from occurring (Albrecht, 2001). Since zero tolerance's inception in 1994, it apparently has been highly effective and contributed to an enormous decrease in violent crime.

Here's how it works. Officers aggressively enforce lower-level offenses including panhandling, public intoxication, excessive noise, and disorderly conduct. All NYPD patrol personnel are supplied with pocket-sized cards outlining legal references and procedural guidelines. Part of this aggressive strategy includes stop-and-frisk and pretext-stop tactics (Ismaili, 2001). The police department's own records indicate that in 1997 and 1998 the Street Crimes Unit frisked more that 45,000 people thought to be carrying guns, but arrested fewer than 10,000. Many cities, such as Nashville, Tennessee, are using zero tolerance. Nashville has used zero tolerance as a strategy for the several years and the chief has implied that one of the reasons crime is down is largely due to zero tolerance policing (Stevens, 2001a).

Downside of Zero Tolerance Policing

Aggressive stop-and-frisk strategies do not enhance quality lifestyle experiences of individuals who were not engaged in criminal activity. On the contrary, it might mean that innocent individuals are subject to stop and frisk. Minorities, especially poor minorities, are stereotyped as dangerous, subjected to intensive surveillance, and inevitably find themselves disproportionately arrested, convicted, and imprisoned. Therefore, since the police are selective about their targets, it is much more likely that in urban centers this contact will be felt by the poor and by minorities (Ismaili, 2001).

The police, indeed the entire crime-control industry, is not focused equally. Allegations of racial profiling and harassment have plagued the NYPD at the same time as crime rates across almost all major crime categories have fallen. Separate investigations by the New York State Attorney General and by federal prosecutors in Manhattan have concluded that many officers unfairly single out African American and Latino residents for stop-and-frisk encounters.

Operation Condor, a year-long zero tolerance program implemented in January 2000, typifies the NYPD's difficulty in achieving both crime reduction and general community satisfaction. Originally designed to crack down on drug dealing, the program quickly expanded to become an aggressive quality-of-life campaign focused on a wide range of low-level offenses in African American and Latino neighborhoods. The NYPD asserted that the focus on such communities was justified by drug arrest patterns. Yet the nature of deployment—aggressive, unrelenting, and brash—generated resentment, even from those law-abiding citizens who would seem to be natural allies to the police, and thus supportive of their efforts. The death of an unarmed black man during a buy-and-bust encounter with an undercover police officer fanned the flame of resentment. The mayor's subsequent decision to unseal the victim's juvenile record was viewed by many as an effort to divert attention away from the police action, and to impugn the character of the victim. Bottom line, advise Ismaili (2001) and Albrecht (2001), if it becomes routine to be subjected to forcible stops and intrusive frisks, the practice will engender hostility, promote distrust, and exacerbate tensions by fueling a greater sense of resentment and mistrust over police tactics. If it can be shown that zero tolerance contributes to a lower crime rate, but can it also be shown it's worth the cost? Elliot Currie recently addressed this issue when he stated: ". . . nobody has . . . ever shown that nasty policing is responsible for declining rates of violent crime in our cities—even less that you have to have nasty police to have decline in crimes" (Currie, 1999, p. 4). There is compelling evidence suggesting that zero tolerance tactics can produce negative consequences.

Zero tolerance tactics can produce
- aggressive tactics ultimately seen as police agency norms, goals, and agendas.
- negative effects on police morals, recruitment, attribution, and stress.
- opens doors to abuse by some officers and potential corruption.
- unconstitutional searches that undermine social organization of a community.
- erosion of public confidence.
- racial profiling.
- class bias.
- selective enforcement.
- violation of legal constitutional guarantees.

With so many negative outcomes from zero tolerance practices, it is curious that police policy encourages this strategy. One issue raised through this practice is linked to the function of policing in America. If the function of policing is to heighten public disorder, then clearly zero tolerance might be the fastest way to accomplish that objective.

National Night Out

A *National Night Out* provides information, educational materials, and technical assistance for the development of effective year-long community-police partnerships that can reduce crime, violence, and substance abuse at the community level.[5] The program is administered by the National Association of Town Watch (NATW), a nationwide organization dedicated to the development, maintenance, and promotion of community-based, law enforcement-affiliated crime prevention activities. Coordinated by local law enforcement and trained volunteers, National Night Out events are designed to engage neighborhoods in local anti-crime and anti-drug abuse activities.

---

[5]See Bureau of Justice Assistance, (1995, November). National Night Out: A community-police partnership program. http://www.communitypolicing.org/eleclib/txtfiles/natw.txt

National Night Out

National Night Out is a crime prevention awareness program in the community
that operates through a multitude of local events, such as block parties, cookouts,
parades, contests, youth events, and seminars.

NATW annually distributes more than 10,000 National Night Out organizational kits that guide residents and law enforcement leaders through the planning
and implementation of a community's National Night Out activities. In addition,
National Night Out local and national media campaigns generate extensive print
and broadcast coverage. National Night Out generates community support for
anti-crime and anti-drug abuse activities, as well as a high level of community
participation. The presence of local law enforcement in the community under the
positive circumstances of a National Night Out allows many residents to meet
their officers on a one-to-one basis—in many cases for the first time. This opportunity helps to establish a much-needed relationship among neighborhood residents and local law enforcement personnel. National Night Out demonstrates
that partnerships and coalitions can be built and nurtured at the community level
for the purpose of establishing cost-effective crime control strategies. As a result
of National Night Out activities and events, neighborhoods also become involved
in related programs, such as Neighborhood Watch, Safe Haven, and Crime
Prevention Through Environmental Design (CPTED).

When first launched by NATW in 1984, the National Night Out program's
community-building and crime-watch activities involved 2.5 million people in
400 communities in 23 states. Since then, with continued BJA funding, the campaign has vastly expanded. The twelfth annual National Night Out, held in 1995,
included a record 28 million people representing 8,800 communities in all 50
states, the District of Columbia, the 5 U.S. Territories, numerous Canadian cities,
and U.S. military bases worldwide. Project 365, introduced in 1994, is a targeting
component of the National Night Out program that helps communities identify
specific problem areas and then work to resolve these problems over the next 365
days. The project begins on the annual National Night Out celebration day (the
first Tuesday in August) and ends 365 days later. Project 365's first year was
extremely successful and it continues to generate an outstanding response from
hundreds of communities. Activity highlights include the cleanup of local parks,
the removal and prevention of graffiti, the establishment of domestic violence and
homeless prevention initiatives, and an increase in the number of Neighborhood
Watch groups, and in crime prevention programming in multifamily housing
areas. Program Objectives National Night Out's objectives include the following:

- Refining the nationwide crime prevention campaign.
- Identifying and documenting successful crime prevention strategies.
- Expanding Project 365.
- Disseminating information about successful community-based strategies.
- Providing telephone technical assistance.

National Night Out meets these objectives by providing information to as many communities as possible. In 1996 alone, more than 10,000 communities were contacted for program participation. Program Services NATW offers a number of no-cost services to communities participating in National Night Out. It provides community leaders with how-to materials, including program guidelines, questions and answers, camera-ready artwork, tips, suggestions, sample press releases, and a sample National Night Out proclamation. In addition, NATW's trained staff provide telephone technical assistance directly to the community. Also, local law enforcement personnel provide onsite technical assistance for Neighborhood or Block Watches. Finally, NATW assists in preparing post-project reports detailing the National Night Out events and activities. These reports are reviewed and evaluated by NATW for use in national, state, and local presentations; future National Night Out materials; and technical assistance.

Marketing Community Policing: Cincinnati Police Department

The Cincinnati Police Department (CPD) consistently markets its community-policing ideas on a daily basis through the efforts of its members. Formal and informal meetings with the public, as well as everyday contacts emphasize community policing. Additionally, the CPD received a grant for public education of community-policing initiatives. A professional marketing firm decided the best vehicle to market community policing in Cincinnati was the radio. A series of infomercials concerning CPD's initiatives and the neighborhood-officer concept were developed and aired on three radio stations. Private-sector radio stations assisted these efforts by providing additional time slots for the infomercials at no cost to the CPD.

It should be noted that since the shooting by Officer Stephen Roach on April 7, 2001, which resulted in the tragic death of Timothy Thomas, an African American Cincinnati resident, many residents throughout the city feel racial conflict is at the core of many of the neighborhood problems in the city. During the many riots that followed, the mayor proclaimed a citywide curfew on April 12, 2001. The only individuals who could leave their homes between 8:00 P.M. and 6:00 A.M. were people going to work or on an emergency. Months later, it was determined that the white police officer had conducted a "righteous shoot."[6] But the tension lingers, and on October 25, 2001, the Cincinnati Police Department received the preliminary recommendations from the U.S. Department of Justice Civil Rights Division regarding use-of-force policy, reporting, public accountability, monitoring and auditing, and training. Thus, community-policing concepts in Cincinnati will probably play a major role in returning social stability to many residents.

Policing Refugees and Immigrants
Roanoke City, Virginia Police Department

Roanoke, Virginia has a population of approximately 97,000. The city has become a major middle-size city for refugee placement. Refugees from Vietnam, Bosnia,

[6]See Cincinnati Police Department website at: http://www.cincinnatipolice.org

Croatia, Iraq, and Kosovo have formed significant immigrant groups in Roanoke. The rapid and considerable influx of refugee populations has contributed to a sense of community instability that requires responsive changes in the way the police agency provides police service. Some of these issues were addressed successfully under the Roanoke City Police Department's (RCPD) Vietnamese Community Outreach Program.

In May 1997, RCPD initiated a dialogue with several community and local government agencies, including Refugee Immigration Services, a civic group known as the Vietnamese Association, legal offices, housing authorities, local schools, and health and social services.

This dialogue revealed significant cultural, ethnic, and language challenges in the interaction between the police department and the Vietnamese community. Many refugees did not understand or trust the American criminal justice system, and local police officers did not understand the Vietnamese language or the community's cultural mores. The FBI's Uniform Crime Reports indicated that the level of crime in Roanoke was not a significant problem, but there was growing concern that disaffected Vietnamese youth were being recruited into organized gangs by transient Vietnamese refugees from other communities. Specific programs were designed to create positive activities for youth and to foster police-community involvement that went beyond traditional law enforcement activities.

RCPD created a position for a community resource specialist and filled it with a member of the Vietnamese community. Through daily interaction with the police officers, the resource specialist, in tandem with supportive training for police staff, acts as a liaison between the police and the local community, providing a channel for improved communication among police officers, court personnel, and Vietnamese residents:

- Outreach and education for Vietnamese adults.
- Cultural training for police department staff.
- Assistance to Vietnamese businesses.

Education is at the core of each component, including the cultural program and tutoring of Vietnamese youth, outreach citizenship training of Vietnamese adults, and cultural diversity training for police officers. An important resource for the outreach project is the Vietnamese Youth Group, organized through the Catholic Church. Adult community leaders conduct Vietnamese language and history classes and provide recreational and cultural activities. The resource specialist also convenes regular after-school tutorial sessions with a small number of Vietnamese youth. To expand Vietnamese adults' understanding of the justice system, the resource specialist has translated criminal justice system terminology into Vietnamese. A local Vietnamese restaurant received a contract to provide catering services to police-sponsored community events. The community resource specialist is critical to the success of this program. Proactive community policing within refugee communities presents new challenges for police departments. To initiate this contact, police departments must overcome stereotypes and entrenched perspectives on police and community relations.

Chelsea, Massachusetts Police Department and Conflict Intervention Unit

Sammy Mojica's job is to make angry people happy. Mojica operates Chelsea's Conflict Intervention Unit (CIU), and he and the other 36,000 people who live in the city face some big-city problems. Chelsea is the poorest city in Massachusetts. That the people here argue and fight, call the police, and take one another to court is no surprise; people everywhere do. The city of Chelsea created CIU as an experiment. Of the 111 disputes CIU mediated from May 1998 through August 1999, only 5 have gone to court. The program has saved the Chelsea Police Department thousands of dollars and hundreds of patrol hours. Officers who were initially skeptical of the program now refer cases to CIU nearly every day. Students now speak 39 languages in Chelsea's public school system, and 75 percent of its student population are minority students. The Chelsea Police Department was slow to respond to this demographic shift, and officers' relationships with the city's minority communities deteriorated to the point that a riot broke out against the police in 1983.

From the outset, CIU was designed to address noncriminal disputes. The Chelsea Housing Authority offered office and mediation space at each public housing site, and the Health and Human Services Department made staff available from the city's refugee program to provide translation services in Spanish, Vietnamese, and Cambodian.

The first important test for CIU was whether it would be embraced by officers in the Chelsea Police Department and the Chelsea Housing Authority. Mojica and CIU's first director, Ginny Burnham, introduced the program to Chelsea's police officers at roll call in spring 1998, and the officers were skeptical. Chelsea police officers assigned to elementary, middle, and high schools were very supportive of the program, as are the department's officers assigned to domestic violence and child abuse cases.

But, the Chelsea Police Department reports that having an officer respond to CIU situations costs an average of $150 per visit. One reward is that these visits do reduce other justice system costs by providing an inexpensive alternative to lawsuits. All indicators are that the program, despite its initial cost, is successful. Chelsea's city manager, chief of police, and director of administration were all asked the same question: Is there something special about Chelsea that made this program succeed? Their answers included the comments that Chelsea's CIU staff work and live in the community they serve. Recruiting the right people to serve as mediators was crucial to its success. When police officers respond to noncriminal disputes, their options are limited. A typical police officer has little time to devote to a nuisance call.

Although CIU works out of an office at the Chelsea Police Department, the unit is an independent group. This independence has been critical to gaining people's trust in Chelsea's poorest neighborhoods. "If you don't follow up with people," Mojica said, "conflict intervention won't work."

In fiscal year (FY) 2000, BJA will supplement the city of Chelsea's award to expand training in conflict resolution to more community agencies and residents.

In FY 2000, building on CIU's successful collaboration with the Chelsea Housing Authority, CIU staff will begin an effort to teach all new housing residents how to manage conflict within their homes and with their neighbors. It has reduced calls for police service in civil disputes. But the program is making a bigger impact on people's lives than on the police department's budget. Among the residents of Chelsea's neighborhoods, CIU is confirming a growing feeling that the Chelsea city government is working to improve the quality of life.

Technology Activities

The National Institute of Justice's Advanced Generation Interoperability for Law Enforcement (AGILE) program is using the Alexandria, Virginia Police Department as its first operational test bed. Two technologies are being tested now. First is a crossband communication switch that has the capability to cross-connect the department's radio system with the Metropolitan Police, United States Park Police, as well as other federal, state, and local agencies. The second is a portable scanner and software package developed by the AGILE team that will allow an officer on the scene of a missing child to scan a photograph and transmit it to circulating officers and other agencies from the field in a matter of minutes. This same software can be used to transmit photographs of missing adults and wanted suspects. More information about the AGILE program is available at their website: www.agileprogram.org.

The Alexandria Police Department has acquired 50 new mobile computers, bringing the total number of units in the Tactical Computer System to 131. These new Panasonic touch-screen computers have increased functionality to allow the officers and supervisors on the street greater access to electronic data collection and retrieval. All state accident reports are completed on the computer. These reports are more accurate and orderly than the handwritten reports. Many jurisdictions are moving toward tactical computer systems.

COMPSTAT: New York City Police Department

Since his appointment in 1994, former NYPD Chief Anemone advocated holding police executives completely accountable for the operation of their commands. Police commanders have now been granted the discretion to assign their personnel as they deem necessary, and no longer as per staffing percentage guidelines.[7] This idea is consistent with community-policing concepts of decentralization and a leveling of authority, thereby empowering others to make decisions that generally would have been made by top command. Also, in order to be best informed and to appropriately deploy manpower, it is clear that police commanders must have readily available information regarding current crime trends and productivity indicators. Due to the archaic handwritten fashion in which criminal incidents were

[7]See James Albrecht (2001). The police state in New York City: The impact of the zero tolerance initiative on racism, police brutality and corruption in the NYPD. Paper presented at the annual conference of the Academy of Criminal Justice Sciences, March, Washington, DC.

recorded in the past, statistical information regarding index crimes, arrests, and summary activity was often available only 30 to 90 days or later after the fact. To remedy this situation, the NYPD undertook the task of inputting all crime incident reports and arrest information into a computerized database. Precinct commanders and police executives now receive a weekly report that outlines summary statistics involving command demographics, precinct/unit staffing levels, civilian complaints, overtime, summons activity, sick rate, radio runs, and response time with comparisons to prior year and city-wide data.

Of equal importance is the weekly comparison report that documents criminal incident, arrest, and summons activity on a weekly, monthly, and year-to-date basis. Each commander must prepare a weekly response delineating efforts being made by their respective units to further improve the statistics and reduce serious crime. In order to ensure that police commanders are continually analyzing this information and addressing necessary concerns, they are summoned to COMPSTAT meetings at police headquarters at least once each month. These commanders are subjected to direct questioning by the Police Commissioner, the Chief of Department, and other higher-ranking executives regarding the efforts being conducted to address recent violent crimes in their respective jurisdictions and to ensure that crime reduction strategies, as instituted, are effective.

Nuisance Properties: DC, Chicago, and Fayetteville

Some of these new tools and strategies that police agencies have experimented with have taken the form of new laws targeting such things as nuisance properties, illegal dumping and other environmental crimes, aggressive panhandling, problem liquor license establishments, and other quality-of-life concerns. In many cases, police departments have formed new alliances with other government regulatory agencies or private concerns to enforce these laws. In the District of Columbia, for instance, Operation Crackdown is a program created by the Young Lawyers Section of the DC Bar Association. Using volunteer attorneys who work with police, community prosecutors, and residents, the program targets the owners and managers of nuisance properties. While the ultimate sanction is the potential filing of criminal and/or civil charges, the program usually accomplishes its goals—elimination of the nuisance and a commitment to make long-term improvements to the property—through voluntary compliance that is generated by the threat of legal action. Chicago and Fayetteville, North Carolina combine similar legal and quasi-legal approaches with extensive training programs for landlords on how to screen tenants, improve building safety, and evict problem tenants. While these practices sound elaborate, what follows are many other strategies used by police agencies to meet their goals that includes quality-of-life issues.

Community Prosecution, Chicago Style

Community-oriented lawyering or community prosecution is a response to the success of the police working with the community and to increased pressure for attorneys to collaborate with the community (Chicago Community Policing Evaluation Consortium ([CCPEC] 2000). While success is traditionally measured by winning cases, community prosecution measures success by reducing the severity of the problem and improving the quality of community life. The role of the community in traditional prosecution changes from complainants, clients, and witnesses to partners who influence priorities in community prosecution. The community is active in community prosecution and the tools are not necessarily investigation, negotiation, and litigation, but include community mobilization, training, and civil remedies.

What Is Community Prosecution?

In a West Side neighborhood, an apartment building with a grocery store on the ground floor was considered an open-air drug market by the police, and a danger to its residents. In the previous six months police had made nearly 90 arrests, 50 of which were the result of reverse stings (when police pose as drug sellers and arrest the buyers). Heroin sales were observed near the grocery store's entrance. The case was presented to the assistant corporation counsel (ACC) handling the district where it was located. The attorney went to see the building and found it was a disaster. Outdoor locks were broken, allowing anyone entry. The building was falling apart, and it was infested with rodents and roaches. "The residents had cats to deal with the rats," he explained. In one apartment, a board running above the floor was described as a way for the rats to get to the other side of the apartment without coming near the children. The ACC and Strategic Inspection Task Force inspectors found more than 80 building-code violations. The ACC filed for an administrative hearing immediately. The building owner kept an office in the building, so it was obvious that he saw what was happening but chose to do nothing.

> At the hearing, the owner agreed to settle the matter rather than go to trial. The ACC met with community members a number of times to determine what outcome they wanted. He then negotiated with the owner over a settlement: the owner agreed to hire two security guards for the courtyard, fix the building violations and pay a $40,000 fine that could be reduced by the amount put into fixing the building. He was also required to evict the grocery store. The police also increased patrols around the building to discourage renewed drug traffic. Since the settlement, the situation has improved. The owner has done substantial work on the building; most likely he will put more than $40,000 into repairs and will not have to pay the fine. The owner is currently trying to sell the property, but the ACC and his community partners will continue to monitor the building's progress and engage the new owner, if it is sold (CCPEC, 2000, p, 129).

Chicago has two programs: Drug and Gang Housing Enforcement Section (DGHES) and the Community Prosecutions Division of the Cook County State's Attorney's Office. DGHES focus on eliminating crime in and around gang and drug houses, vacant lots, and abandoned buildings. Primarily, these lawyers attack drug and gang activities. When going after property, they cite municipal

code violations and target the property's owner rather than the persons committing the crime.

The Community Prosecutions Division goes further than the DGHES in that
they prosecute the property owners. The goal of the unit is to partner with the
police/CAPS, businesses, religious institutions, elected officials, schools, government entities, social service agencies, and community groups to identify public
safety issues in the community. Aside from being accessible to the public, and to
act as a liaison between the community and other parts of the State's Attorney's
Office, they prosecute quality-of-life crimes affecting the community. The goal is
primarily met in three ways: prosecution, problem solving, and prevention. At
last writing (2000), while the Community Prosecutor Program works, resources
are key and as the funding dries up, so does the effectiveness of the program.

TRIAD, a Program for the Elderly

TRIAD

> TRIAD is a three-way commitment between senior citizens, law enforcement
> agencies, and support and protective services to address the fear of crime and to
> prevent crime among the elderly.

TRIAD's goals are to reduce the criminal victimization and fear of crime of
older citizens, enhance delivery of police services to that population, and to
improve their quality-of-life experiences.[8]

Although TRIAD focuses on the individual needs of the senior community, it
is unique in each police agency due to resources, experiences, and commitments of
both the police and the seniors in the community. In most cases, a protective service organization such as SALT (Seniors and Lawmen Together) governs TRIAD.

Historical Information

The TRIAD concept was developed in 1988 by the National Sheriff's Association,
the International Chiefs of Police, and the AARP in an effort to aid police service
to the elderly. As community-policing concepts grew, it became clear that the
crime-related needs of the elderly could be best met by a partnership through
cooperation and collaboration. It was recognized that the senior population of the
United States was fast becoming the largest growing segment of the population.

Why TRIAD?

There are new issues and problems for the criminal justice system as most communities experience a growth in the senior population. This calls for a change in

---

[8]Much of this information was supplied by Deputy Chris Bell, Director of TRIAD, Norfolk County
Sheriff's Office.

the services that are provided to the community. One way to alleviate this problem and understand the needs of the senior community is to partner with them. Together, a safety and educational plan specific to their needs can be developed. Also, since each community has its own individual problems, there are no best-fit models for this program. Therefore, each community must further its own efforts to empower seniors to enjoy similar lifestyles as younger people do without the threat of criminal activity that seems to be present against many seniors.

TRIAD Programs

There are many programs, depending on the resources and experience of the community and the agency, yet most share the following agenda:

- Alert the community about scams and fraud.
- Prevent physical abuse.
- Personal and home safety tips.
- Neighborhood watch.
- Telephone reassurance programs (Are you O.K.?).
- Adopt-a-senior visits for shut-ins.
- Emergency preparedness plans for seniors by seniors (911 flashlight).
- Safe-shopping days.
- Emergency medical cards (file of life, key chains).
- House numbering (Is your number up?).
- Community-police academy.
- Fire safety and prevention.
- Travel safety for seniors.

Norfolk County, Massachusetts's TRIAD Program

The Norfolk County Sheriff's Office budgeted $28,000 as startup money for municipalities within the county that signed a TRIAD agreement with the Sheriff's Office. Each municipality received $1,000 from the sheriff to aid them in developing TRIAD. Many local businesses also donated supplies and money when solicited by TRIAD's members. Programs such as Neighborhood Watch, House Numbering, Senior Survey, and Mail Fraud alerts, are generally inexpensive to operate. Equally important, the personal time that deputies and seniors volunteered proved beneficial. Currently, the Norfolk Sheriff's Office employs two full time deputies..

Many senior citizens fear crime because they feel vulnerable to it. Government statistics show that the rate of crime against senior citizens is relatively small; however, their fear of crime is very real. The Bureau of Justice Statistics reports that people who are 65 and older are substantially less likely to be victims of a violent crime than younger people. In an explicit test conducted between 1992 and 1997 there were only 5 violent crimes per 1,000 U.S. residents aged 65 and older as opposed to 56 violent crimes per 1,000 residents aged 12–64. This information was gathered as part of the Bureau's National Crime

Victimization Survey. However, it was noted that personal theft, purse snatching, and pocket picking were more frequent crimes committed against the elderly than with other groups surveyed. There were also some disturbing findings relating to crime against the elderly:

- A weapon was more likely to be used against the elderly in a violent crime.
- Twenty-two percent of elderly victims were injured when victimized.
- Twenty percent of all crimes against the elderly were committed by relatives, friends, or acquaintances.
- Crimes against the elderly were more likely to occur in their homes or nearby and during the day.

In addition, 22 percent of the elderly responding to the survey related that they never went out at night for entertainment, shopping, or other activities, due to their fear of crime. This is the type of fear that TRIAD is focusing on and trying to alleviate by working together with seniors and law enforcement agencies.

However, many senior citizens demonstrate that they have a fear of police officers, too. TRIAD seeks to alleviate this fear by working together with seniors on their issues and concerns instead of unilaterally deciding what is best for them.

The Director of the Norfolk County Sheriff's Office TRIAD Program, Deputy Chris Bell states that it is his responsibility to see that the TRIAD Program is established throughout Norfolk County, and to ensure that the enhanced police services of the program are delivered in keeping with the mission of the Sheriff's Office. Since becoming director, Chris Bell has been successful in establishing TRIAD in twenty of the twenty-eight cities served by the county.

Palm Beach County, Florida's TRIAD Program

The Palm Beach County TRIAD Program was formed in 1998. TRIAD's membership includes the Palm Beach County Sheriff's Office and other local police departments, senior citizen representatives; individuals with government and/or law enforcement experience; community service providers; local municipal, county, and state government agencies and organizations; and citizens/organizations having an interest in reducing crime and victimization of senior citizens.

Since the first half of calendar year 1998, Palm Beach County TRIAD's Council members have engaged in various activities, such as:

- Regular monthly, periodic, and special meetings are held on the first Tuesday of each month at the Sheriff's Office.
- Ongoing meetings and communication with the National TRIAD and representatives from other local TRIADS throughout the United States.
- Formation of local citizen groups.
- Arranging for the training of such local citizen groups.
- Meeting and communicating with sources of funding and support.

TRIAD provides an opportunity for an exchange of information between officers and senior citizens, provides training for members and SALT participants, and seeks financial aid and support.

The engine that drives TRIAD is in the SALT Council (Seniors and Lawmen Together). The SALT Council plans activities and programs to involve and benefit both law enforcement and seniors. TRIAD-sponsored activities include information for older persons on the following:

- How to avoid criminal victimization.
- Increased involvement in Neighborhood Watch.
- Home security information and inspections.
- Knowledge of current frauds and scams.
- Coping with telephone solicitations and door -to-door sales people.
- Elder abuse prevention, recognition, and reporting.
- Training for deputies and officers in communicating with and assisting older persons.
- Telephone reassurance programs for older citizens.
- Adopt-a-Senior visits for shut-ins.
- Emergency preparedness plans by and for seniors.
- Victim assistance by and for seniors.
- Courtwatch activities.
- Refrigerators cards with emergency medical information.
- Citizen Police Academy to educate the community.
- Information tables at senior centers and malls.
- Intergenerational projects beneficial to seniors and youth.

Effectiveness of TRIAD Programs

Examples of TRIAD effectiveness follow:

- When a seventy-year-old man is the victim of a vicious attack after refusing to give up his wallet, TRIAD's victim assistance program helps him through the ordeal, from emergency room to courtroom.
- Before sending a large advance fee to a company selling timeshare vacation condos by phone, a sixty-five-year-old retiree hesitates. She refers to information distributed during a TRIAD crime prevention presentation warning against just such a venture.
- A frail and crippled widow will no longer be mistreated by her nephew because her newly assigned TRIAD buddy notices the bruises and reports the abuse.
- A fiercely independent ninety-year-old man who lives alone won't lie helpless for hours after a fall. Failing to get a call from him at the usual time, the telephone reassurance volunteer contacts his neighbor. A deputy is sent to investigate and finds the man immobilized by a broken hip.

Summary

Our discussion included programs that link prevention to policing strategies. We described saturation patrols, zero tolerance, National Night Out, marketing community policing, policing refugees and immigrants, technology activities, and COMPSTAT. The chapter reviewed nuisance property strategies, community prosecution, and programs for the elderly. What becomes clear is that every police agency has its own particular style of police strategies; sometimes that style works for them and other times it is less effective.

Do You Know?

1. Describe the key points of a saturation patrol strategy. In what way do you agree with this strategy as prevention and in what way do you feel prevention is not the primary goal?
2. Describe why zero tolerance seems to be working and explain the social cost of this strategy. In what ways do you agree or disagree with its results and this method of crime control?
3. Describe the unique situations relative to policing refugees and immigrants as discussed in Roanoke and Chelsea. Can you think of other ways to deliver quality police service to these groups of individuals?
4. Describe COMPSTAT. In what way could this technique make a difference to police decisions?
5. Describe community prosecution. In what way does this technique differ from typical prosecution? Why is it expected that it will succeed and what situations might cause its failure?
6. Describe a TRIAD program and its importance to the group it serves.
7. In what way do these strategies differ from the strategies of the previous chapter?
8. In what way do you think the Proverb, "Action speaks louder than words," applies to this chapter?

12

Family and Domestic Violence and Sexual Assault

"Injustice anywhere is a threat to justice everywhere."
Dr. Martin Luther King, Jr. (1929–1968)

Key Terms

Community Notification Act
    of 1997
Cost of Crime
Family and Domestic Violence

Homicide
Megan's Law
Repeat Offenders Programs
Sexual Assault

Street Justice
Victimization

Key Topics

- Further discussion of police strategies.
- Victimization in the United States.
- Crimes of violence, including domestic violence and sexual assault.
- Notification of sexual offenders living in the community.

Introduction

There is a need for greater accountability of police and a greater public share in the decision-making process in order to curb crime. Research supports the fact that many residents want input into the decision-making process of policing, but not everyone wants to help, let alone be responsible. However, one estimate is that the annual *cost of crime* in the United States is well over $110 billion in medical expenses, lost earnings, and public victim assistance programs.

Cost of Crime

Cost of crime can be described as an estimated loss of money, services, productivity, and/or a nonmonetary emotional loss.

For victims, crime costs can include the following:

- Out-of-pocket expenses for medical bills, property losses, replacement costs, and insurance.
- Reduced productivity at work, home, and/or school.
- Enhanced fear of victimization.
- Purchase of security systems, equipment, and other devices and services, including personalized training to protect yourself and your family.
- Nonmonetary experiences such as fear, pain, suffering, and reduced quality of life.

One estimate puts the annual cost of crime in the United States at $450 billion: $87 billion relates to other tangible costs such as property damage and loss, and lost productivity; $18 billion for tangible costs including medical and mental health care; and intangible costs for pain, suffering, and reduced quality of life.[1] Also, these estimates should include the following expenses:

[1]See Ted R. Miller, Mark A. Cohen, and Brian Wiersema, (1996, February) Victim Costs and Consequences: A new look. U.S. Department of Justice, National Institute of Justice Research Report. Washington, DC: GPO. p. 17.

- Expenditure by the criminal justice system to find, prosecute, and supervise offenders.
- Social costs associated with the fear of crime.
- Mental health costs associated with healing from victimization.
- Funds spent by companies to train employees.
- Costs of lost productivity of employers.
- Workers' compensation and disability payments.
- Legal expenses in recovering losses.

Crimes of violence, in particular, reduce a person's quality-of-life experiences. Family violence is particularly costly, especially domestic violence, sexual assault, and homicide.

Family and Domestic Violence

General Information about Family Violence

If ever a problem demanded a community-police approach, it is the complex and serious challenge of *family violence*.

Family Violence

Family violence is any act or omission by persons who are cohabitating that results in serious injury to other members of the family.[2]

As our understanding of the dynamics of human behavior grows, it becomes ever clear that family violence is a key to the expanding cycle of violence that puts many of us at risk. This cycle of violence asserts that violent behavior is learned within the family and bequeathed from one generation to the next.[3] Those crying children, many of whom are victimized themselves, are more likely to become the next generation who act out on the street and at home in ways that make many of us need to defend ourselves. Even with the new emphasis on mandatory arrest, no one is naive enough to suggest that arrest alone provides a simple fix.[4] In what way do partnerships between the police and the community deal with violence in our homes?

Pleas of Family Violence Workers

Interpersonal domestic violence is as dangerous and serious a crime as any random attack on the street, yet our instinct in the past was to pull back and dismiss it as a "family matter." As the late Robert Trojanowicz, a pioneer in the community-policing movement would have said, "Until we are all safe, no one is truly safe."

---

[2]See Harvey Wallace, (1999). *Family violence: Legal, medical and social perspectives*. Boston: Allyn & Bacon. p. 23.
[3]Ibid. (p. 23).

For decades, family violence workers pleaded with the public and policy makers to take family violence seriously. These workers have pointed to inadequacies in state and federal laws; to systematic neglect by police, prosecutors, and judges; to meager funding for overburdened hot lines and shelters; and to the absence of protection for at-risk victims, especially spouses and children.[5] For instance, while there are an estimated two million incidents of female battering each year, one national study shows that only 14 percent of women who were beaten, choked, or subjected to other forms of severe violence reported the incident to the police.[6] Furthermore, government reports show chronic spousal abuse often ends in *criminal homicide*. In fact, up to 42 percent of all female homicide victims are killed at the hands of their partners (BJS, 2000).

Criminal Homicide

The Uniform Crime Report (UCR) category that includes and is limited to all offenses that cause the death of another person without justification or excuse.

Battered Woman's Syndrome

Lenore Walker identified a cluster of behavioral and emotional features that are often shared by women who have been physically and psychologically abused over a period of time by the dominant male figure in their life, a phenomenon Walker referred to as *battered woman's syndrome* (BWS).[7]

Battered Woman's Syndrome

Battered woman's syndrome (BWS) can be defined as a pattern of responses and perceptions presumed to be characteristic of women who have been subjected to continuous physical abuse by their mates.

[4]For an indepth look at this situation, see Dennis J. Stevens, (1999j). Interviews with women convicted of murder: Battered women syndrome revisited. *International Review of Victimology*, 6(2). Stevens, (1998). Mandatory arrest, spouse abuse, and accelerated rates of victimization: Attitudes of victims and officers. *The Criminologist.*

[5]For the purpose of this article, spouse abuse includes all chronic physical abuse, psychological abuse, progressive social isolation, economic control, and sexual assault. Partners include married, separated, divorced, cohabiting and formerly cohabiting couples.

[6]Two million men reported assaults by their female partners. A 1985 National Family Violence Survey showed that men and women were abusing one another in roughly equal numbers. About 24 percent of spouse abuse is initiated by women, 27 percent by men. One group of experts asked: Could spouse abuse be a product of both males and females who are bound in their dance of mutual destructiveness, their incapacity for intimacy and appreciation of differences?

[7]Feelings of low self-esteem, depression, and helplessness are among the important components that frequently accompany continual domestic violence. BWS is considered to be a subtype of post traumatic stress syndrome. For a closer look see Eaststeal, P.W. (1993). *Killing the beloved: Homicide between adult sexual intimates.* Australia: Australian Institute of Criminology.

Spousal abuse affects both perpetrators and victims (no matter their gender or their part in violence), threatening the integrity of the entire family unit, which in turn demoralizes community and societal norms (Straus, 1994). Many writers see an escalation of violence on American streets as a product of family violence.[8]

Mandatory Arrest for Spousal Abuse

Some states regard spousal abuse as a serious criminal matter. For example, statutes have been enacted by the North Carolina State Legislature to try and decrease the spousal abuse rates throughout the state. This is defined by General Statute 50-B, which provides for mandatory arrest in domestic violence encounters when evidence suggests a crime has been committed. Such statutes allow the officer to arrest the partner without the victim's cooperation. Another law is the Domestic Violence Protective Order, which grants the spouse the residence or which prohibits one party from harassing or interfering with the other and mandates a warrantless arrest. An attempt by President Clinton to aid police in the fight against domestic violence is the *Violence Against Women Act,* which allows police to arrest anyone who crosses state lines to assault a spouse or partner. These tough new laws are intended to lower the incidence rates of these cases. Individual police officers are also taking action to aid the abused in seeking help from other sources and agencies, such as shelters.

Twenty-seven states have mandatory domestic violence arrest laws similar to North Carolina. The language varies, but the way it works on the street is that the investigating officer looks for a visible injury, no matter how minor. "We teach, if you see an injury, you have reasonable cause to believe a felony has occurred," says Sgt. Bob Medkeff of the LAPD.

Lt. Michael Moyes of the Michigan State Police Special Operations Division Prevention Service Program argues that spousal abuse is not a spontaneous response but rather a "premeditated crime of power." It is a "horrible imprisoning action that is learned in society." Moyes thinks that mandatory arrest is sending a loud and clear message to abusers that they will do the time if they commit the crime. "It is important that people are made aware of other means of working out their problems than resorting to violence," Moyes adds.

Mandatory arrest forces action by local authorities and increases an investigating officer's importance and discretion by allowing him or her to size up a situation and make an arrest without agreement from the victim and without being required to witness the violence, the *Los Angeles Times* asserts. Policing involves investigation, and along with mandatory arrest more emphasis must be placed on training that helps officers recognize the defensive wounds a victim might suffer in trying to protect herself, and training that helps an officer determine the primary aggressor. A 1981 study funded by the Minneapolis Police Foundation found mandatory arrest to be the most effective police response for reducing further violence. This places the arrest requirements on the police, making the abuser account-

---

[8]Domestic or partner violence, battering or spouse abuse is defined as intentional violence or controlling behavior in the context of an intimate relationship.

able. This thought is consistent with most law enforcement training, which suggests that apprehension and punishment can decrease criminal activity. That is, mandatory arrest reduces domestic violence.

There is another side to the issue. Some police officers who oppose mandatory arrest say their discretion has been stripped away from them since they have to arrest someone even if it might be the wrong person. Alana Bowman, the Los Angeles City Attorney's Special Assistant adds that there is an attitude in law enforcement that implies if the legal authorities treat officers like children by requiring an arrest, officers will follow the letter of the law regardless of whom it hurts. As a result many violators can and often do successfully manipulate the system.[9]

Many enforcement officers feel they have to "deal" with domestic violence instead of playing an active role to prevent it. For example, the presence, attitude, and demeanor of the abuser at the time an officer reaches the domestic violence scene can guide the behavior of the officer. In addition, the attitude and family situation of an individual officer have been shown to influence police response to spousal abuse.

Popular writers who advocate the traditional cuff'em-and-stack'em perspective about violent offenders in general, politicized domestic violence producing further myths of male perpetrators and female victims.

Neither the technique nor the philosophy works, says the police chief of Broken Arrow, Oklahoma. Also, compelling evidence reveals that an officer's view of human nature appears to be related to his or her conception of the police officer's role (Carter & Radelet, 2000; Stevens, 1998). This worldview tells an officer what is and what is not police business. Also, many officers are aware that the chance of assault and/or their own liability during domestic violence cases is great. When liability comes into question for an officer, some may back away from performing their job, at least from a regulation standpoint.

Results show that an officer who fails to make a domestic violence arrest sees the justice system as an ineffective tool against family abuse; he or she believes that both victim and abuser are equally instrumental in the violence.[10] Sometimes, officers might intimidate an alleged aggressor, and part of that intimidation relates to *street justice.*

Street Justice

Street justice occurs when a police officer uses discretionary powers to respond to an individual in an arbitrary fashion, suggesting denial of due process guarantees.

An officer who does make an arrest is likely to think that an officer's responsibility is to conduct an arrest and might not concern him or herself with the eventual outcomes of the individual arrested since officer satisfaction derives from the

[9]Some believe BWS is not a legitimate defense; the majority of the killings are premeditated, and many women have previously committed violent crimes. Therefore, women who kill are not acting in self-defense; they are the victors of domestic fights. See Mann, C.R. (1996). *When women kill.* NY: SUNY Press.
[10]For more details, see Dennis J. Stevens, (1998). Mandatory arrest, spouse abuse, and accelerated rates of victimization: Attitudes of victims and officers.

arrest itself. Another reason to arrest or not to arrest comes from an idea that an officer may feel that he or she has to deal with domestic violence instead of playing an active role to prevent it. For example, presence, attitude, and demeanor of the abuser at the time an officer reaches the domestic violence scene can guide the behavior of the officer. In addition, attitude and family situation of an individual officer has been shown to influence police response to spousal abuse. Other officers prefer to let the chips fall where they may, and many might even think that a chronic offender is not afraid of the threat of jail or for that matter capital punishment.[11] Then, too, arrest and confinement produce angry offenders.[12]

How about the victims?[13] Frankly, mandatory arrest and prosecution is too threatening and too unresponsive to battered women. For example, prosecutors unintentionally act in ways that are frighteningly similar to batterers since they do as they please, when they please, without consulting the victim. The law mistakenly attempts to eradicate violence by completely removing the batterer from a woman's life, never attempting to grasp how he may be a necessary part of her cultural, emotional, or financial life. Finally, the law involves two people who have in some ways become one, and state-imposed efforts to separate them may be ineffective or inappropriate.

Does it "take two to tango" in spousal abuse? It might! In those few cases, what variables might push spousal abuse victims toward another offender to replace the one left behind? Why would someone want to be a victim? Could it be that the male and the female in a spousal abuse relationship are bonded in mutual destructiveness? According to one expert, they need each other to perpetuate personal and collective dramas of victimization and lovelessness, and so, regrettably, neither can leave.[14]

Family Violence Is the Leading Offense

Family violence is the leading offense in the city of Broken Arrow, Oklahoma, according to the police chief.[15] A federal grant to fund domestic violence counselors during the evening hours was sought and eventually awarded. The counselor recruited volunteers to be a part of the Divert Team—someone who could be called if services were needed on scene at a domestic dispute for assistance such as child care, transportation, and procurement of a protective order. At first,

---

[11]See Stevens, D.J., (1992a). Research Note: The death sentence and inmate attitudes. *Crime and Delinquency 38*, 272–79, (1992b). Examining inmate attitudes: Do prisons deter crime? *The State of Corrections—ACA: 1991.* pp. 272–279.

[12]See Stevens, D.J. (1994b). The depth of imprisonment and prisonisation: Levels of security and prisoners' anticipation of future violence. *The Howard Journal of Criminal Justice, 33* (2), pp. 137–157.

[13]Battered Woman's Syndrome is an ineffective self-defense argument for women who kill their abusers. If she had tried to flee prior to the homicide, she would have been killed by him.

[14]For a closer look at this perspective see Sherven, J., & Sniechowski, J. (1996). Men and women both cause domestic violence. In Karin L. Swisher (ED.) *Domestic Violence.* San Diego, CA: Greenhaven Press. pp. 83-85.

[15]See Dennis J. Stevens (2001a). Case Studies in Community Policing. p. 26–56.

the officers were reluctant to call on the counselors but eventually they developed problem-solving activities that included a domestic violence response unit during problem-solving discussions. Counselors were commonplace ride-alongs after a while. Although the BAPD knows they will never stop domestic violence, their chief sees the association between the police and individuals trained to interact with violent families as successful in reducing the number of crimes committed in homes. The focus is on prevention through family problem-solving strategies, rather than utilizing traditional methods to deal specifically with offenders.

Many people think domestic or family violence is confined to adult couples. It isn't—young people experience it too. "More and more case reports I see, it's not just a husband-and-wife situation. It's a boyfriend-and-girlfriend situation, and the victims are getting younger," observes Officer Elizabeth Gass of the Chicago Police Department, an active participant in Chicago's CAPS program. This thought is consistent with survey results from Chicago's public schools. That is, 30 percent of the female public school students said they had experienced some sort of violence in a dating relationship. That's why the Tenth District sponsored a domestic violence prevention seminar for students in their district. Speakers talked about date rape drugs. They talked about developing healthy relationship habits. "We want to highlight the fact that violence, abuse, and control are not an inherent part of a dating relationship, so [victims] recognize that this isn't normal, shouldn't be tolerated, and [they should] reach out for help," explained Leslie Landis, City of Chicago Domestic Violence Coordinator.

In each Chicago district, domestic liaison officers work with a network of service providers to get help for victims, young and old. "I review all case reports on a day-to-day basis . . . We send out flyers to the victims. If they need court advocacy, I go to court with them," says Officer Gass. Chicago police officers respond to over 200,00 calls for service each year related to domestic violence. This translates into 75,000 verified offenses.

All Chicago police officers undergo specialized training to respond to domestic violence situations. Residents work with the police to develop prevention programs and public awareness campaigns. So far, 19 of the 25 districts have set up a domestic violence subcommittee to give residents an ongoing opportunity to work with police on this issue.

Unfortunately, there is another side to the domestic violence and community-policing prerogative, say community policing and domestic violence sources.[16] The temptation is to seek special funding and form a task force. But task forces can deal with only a fraction of the cases, and the danger is that the commitment lasts only as long as the money holds out. Of even greater concern is that this can be perceived as making domestic violence a specialty assignment, rather than something that everyone in the department must address. It is usually wiser to integrate efforts to deal with this pervasive and corrosive problem throughout the department as part of an overall community-policing approach.

---

[16]See Community policing & domestic violence. (200). http://policing.com/articl/cpanddv.html

Quincy, Massachusetts Police Department

In examining the domestic violence program of the Quincy, Massachusetts Police Department, which advocates an integrated systemwide approach to domestic violence, investigators found that despite aggressive enforcement, recidivism rates remained high, especially within the first month after arrest.[17] The study tracked 353 defendants in male-to-female domestic violence cases for up to one year after arraignment. Victims interviewed for the study indicated a 50 percent revictimization rate during the follow-up period. Findings did not support the model of passive female victims; almost 3 of 4 victims had prior complaints on the same offender. Other major findings indicated that 71 percent of domestic violence incidents involved violence; only 36 percent of the offenders were influenced by alcohol or drugs, and almost 85 percent of the offenders had prior juvenile or adult criminal records.

One implication of this study relates to another investigation that shows that spousal abuse arrest gives rise to more, not fewer, spousal abuse incidents, a finding supported by the data from victims and police officers.[18] That is, spousal abusers who were arrested intensified their victimization after an arrest. Some of the methods chronic abusers used included night attacks, destroying victims' possessions such as cars, telephones, and clothes; victims were isolated from friends, parents, and bank/credit accounts; and victims met with sexual assault from foreign objects, friends, and in some cases the children of the abusers. Most of the officers who interacted with victims and offenders were reluctant to intervene; they were apprehensive to make an arrest despite evidence suggesting they should; surprisingly enough, their behavior during the intervention appeared hostile to victims. Also, arrest had not protected victims from abuse and when victims fled from their homes, many of them sought out other individuals who abused them.

Sexual Assault

Alexandria, Virginia Police Department

Sexual assault is strongly related to domestic violence. The Alexandria Police Department (APD) describes *sexual assault* as an act of sexual violence and aggression that occurs when a person is forced, threatened, or coerced into sexual contact without his/her consent.[19]

One perspective taken by the APD is that sexual assault is committed primarily out of anger and/or a need to feel powerful by controlling, dominating, or

[17]See Buzawa, Hotaling, Klein, and Byrne (2000). Buzawa, E., Hotaling, G.T., Klein, A., & Byrne J. (2000). Response to domestic violence in a pro-active court setting—Final Report. NIJ Research Review. NCJ 181427. http://www.ncjrs.org/rr/vol1_3/18.html

[18]See Dennis J. Stevens (1998b). Mandatory arrest, spouse abuse, & accelerated rates of victimization: Attitudes of victims and officers. *The Criminologist.*

[19]See the Alexandria Police Department's website for more detail at:
http://ci.alexandria.va.us/city/officeonwomen/sara/aboutassault.html

humiliating the victim.[20] Examples of sexual assault include rape, sodomy, fondling, indecent exposure, peeping Toms, obscene phone calls, childhood sexual abuse, and sexual harassment.

- People of any age can be victims of a sexual assault.
- Sexual assault happens to women, men, and children.
- More than 70 percent of all sexual assaults are committed by someone the victim knows, such as a friend, spouse, family member, date, coworker, or neighbor.
- One in four females, and one in six males, will be sexually assaulted before the age of 18.

The Alexandria Police Department offers a number of services that relate to domestic violence and sexual assaults. The program is called The Sexual Assault Response and Awareness (SARA). They offer the following services to victims of sexual assault/abuse, and their families and friends:

- 24-hour hotline: 703-683-7273.
- Professional staff and trained volunteers, including Spanish-speaking interpreters, are available 24 hours a day. Staff and volunteers provide confidential emotional support, crisis intervention, medical and legal options, and referrals.
- 24-hour staff and trained volunteers are available to accompany an assault survivor to the hospital or other medical facility, police station, or health department.
- Short-term individual counseling is available for women, men, and children who have been the victims of sexual violence. This service is free of charge to residents of Alexandria, or to anyone sexually assaulted in Alexandria. A variety of support groups are also offered, with a minimal fee charged to non-Alexandria residents.
- Court advocacy staff or volunteer advocates provide information about legal options, and accompany victims through the court process.
- Community education presentations and workshops on sexual assault and related topics can be provided for Alexandria schools, recreation centers, after-school programs, housing communities, and other community groups. This includes presentations for children, adolescents, and Spanish-speaking audiences.
- Rape, aggression, defense (RAD) system classes are available to women and adolescents. RAD is a self-defense course that combines physical techniques, awareness, and prevention strategies to assist women in making educated decisions about defending themselves.
- A variety of support groups are offered throughout the year.

[20]There are many other perspectives relating to sexual abuse including lust, righteousness, blaming the victim, and peer pressure. Also, there are many varieties of rapists including predatory or stranger, pedophiles, date rapists, and incest to name a few. For more detail see Dennis J. Stevens (2000) *Inside the Mind of a Serial Rapist*, and Frank Schmalleger, (1999) *Criminology Today*. Upper Saddle River, NJ: Prentice Hall. pp. 36–67.

About Alexandria's SARA

Since its inception in 1974, the Alexandria Office on Women, with the support of the Commission for Women, has served as an advocate for the women of Alexandria. Services provided by the Office on Women include employment support services; 24-hour domestic violence and sexual assault response programs; mentoring for young teens; and educational programs on women's health and a variety of issues that affect women and children.

In August of 1975, the Commission on the Status of Women, in Alexandria, Virginia, established the Rape Victim Companion Program, which was later to become the Sexual Assault Response and Awareness (SARA) Program. The SARA Program offers support to victims of sexual assault, and to their families and friends. Trained volunteers and staff are available 24 hours a day to provide the following:

- crisis intervention and emotional support
- advocacy with medical, police, and court systems
- short-term individual and group counseling
- information and referrals

Volunteers are an integral part of the SARA Program.

Community Notification Act

One goal of community policing is to reduce fear among community members. One controversial way to accomplish this goal is to inform residents when convicted sex offenders relocate to their neighborhood, in order to prevent sexual victimization. There was a great concern in this country for crime victims in the 1980s and 1990s as evidenced by the Victim and Witness Protection Act of 1982 (VWPA) and the Final Report by the President's Task Force on Victims of Crime in the same year.[21] Congressional concern for crime victims was to

1. Enhance and protect the necessary role of crime victims and witnesses in the criminal justice process.
2. Ensure that the federal government does all that is possible to assist victims and witnesses of crime, within the limits of available resources, without infringing on the constitutional rights of the defendant.
3. Provide model legislation for state and local governments.

These items were catalysts of significant advances in victims' rights. As a result, many states enacted laws that legislate victims' rights and as of January 2001, there were approximately 27,000 victim-related state statutes on the books.

Few movements in American history achieved as much success in prompting legislative response as did victims' rights activists' campaigns.[22] For instance,

[21]For more detail, see Frank Schmalleger and John Ortiz Smykla, (2000). Corrections in the 21 Century. NY: Glencoe McGraw Hill. pp. 430–434.
[22]Ibid.

in 1996, the federal Community Notification Act, known as Megan's Law was enacted to ensure community notification of the locations of convicted offenders. In response to widespread public concern about the release of sexual offenders from prison, the federal government and eventually most state governments passed laws referred to as "community notification statutes," which authorized or required communities where sexual offenders would live to be notified of their arrival in those communities.[23]

Furthermore, in the Victims' Rights Clarification Act of 1997, Congress asserted victims' rights to attend proceedings and deliver victim-impact statements with the federal system. The common goal of victims' rights is to prevent additional victims by notifying potential victims that a threat exists in their neighborhood. Thus, the broken-windows perspective or preventative options might well apply to victims' rights legislation and thereby reduce anxiety and the fear of crime.

However, in many states such as Massachusetts, Megan's Law has come under litigation due to the unconstitutional nature of notification for sexual offenders and a lack of resources in the Commonwealth, which made the program, at best, faltering. For a time, sexual offenders in the Commonwealth were not encouraged to register. The dilemma associated with community notification is balancing resources, public opinion, and constitutional issues for police agencies and other public agencies connected to notification issues.

The statutes vary widely in complexity and the level of state and local interaction. In some states, for example, the public can request information about convicted sexual offenders living in their communities. Private citizens can access registration information at the local police department.[24] Sometimes websites are available to the public such as in the states of California, Illinois, and Florida. Another type of notification system, in Louisiana for example, requires paroled child molesters to identify themselves as sexual offenders to residents in the neighborhoods where they live. Other states, for example Wisconsin, authorize local and county police agencies to decide whether to release information about convicted sex offenders. Those police agencies decide the method and extent of notification, including the amount of information to provide the public.

In a study conducted in Wisconsin, 704 neighborhood residents at 22 community notification meetings were polled in the early spring and fall of 1998.[25] The study included a statewide survey of 312 police and sheriffs' agencies, 128 probation and parole agents and supervisors from units with sex offender caseloads, and 30 interviews. Results of the study indicated that community notification was used the way legislative policymakers intended it to be used; that is, to further community protection. But, the "decision to notify and involve the public in an informal network of neighborhood surveillance comes at the cost of

[23]For an indepth look at this discussion, see Richard G. Zevitz and Mary Ann Farkas, (2000, December). Sex offender community notification: Assessing the impact in Wisconsin. *National Institute of Justice: Research in Brief.* NCJ 179992.
[24]Ibid.
[25]Ibid.

increased community anxiety, impeded offender reintegration, and drained agency resources," argued Zevitz and Farkas (2000, p. 2). In fact, nearly an equal percentage of notification-meeting attendees left meetings feeling more concerned about the sex offender as those who felt less concerned about the offender. One frequently heard concern from those individuals who attended the meetings was their fear of being victimized by the offender. Might this finding suggest that the fear of crime was heightened among community members? Should that be the case, then this method of delivering sex offender information is inconsistent with the mission of community policing and the process should be re-evaluated.

Summary

Crimes of violence cost a victim more than trauma and physical harm. The cost must also be measured in out-of-pocket expense for medical bills, replacement costs, and security services. Crime affects fear levels, which shape personal decisions about where to shop, work, and play. Crime frightens so many of us that we stay home at night. Some of us purchase a weapon to defend ourselves or accept the physical abuse of our intimate others, youth gangs, and thugs. That is, crime and the fear of crime shapes lifestyles.

One of the most complex challenges for police agencies is domestic violence. Crimes such as sexual assault are hidden in homes across the nation. Some states have enacted mandatory arrest protocols. When officers make arrests, even when those agencies rely on an integrated aggressive enforcement strategy, investigators found that recidivism rates remained high, especially within the first month after arrest. Officers who see the criminal justice system as offering little for a victim of domestic violence tend not to make arrests, despite mandatory protocols. For example, mandatory arrest and prosecution are too threatening and too unresponsive to battered women because often prosecutors unintentionally act in ways that are frighteningly similar to batterers. On the other hand, officers think it might take "two to tango," suggesting that a few individuals want conflict in their lives.

In some cities, a domestic violence counselor rides along with an officer to domestic violence calls and in others cities, domestic violence is not seen as monopolized by adult couples. It is also seen in dating relationships. This finding has promoted domestic violence prevention seminars in area public schools.

Sexual assault is strongly related to domestic violence. A sophisticated program was initiated in Alexandria, Virginia that offers hotlines, counseling, court advocacy, education, self-defense training, and support groups. This discussion provided an opportunity to examine community notification, since many sexual offenders are required to register with local police agencies when they relocate to a community. However, the implication from one study indicated that the method used by a police agency to notify the community of a sexual offender's presence can add to their fear of crime, even to the point of concerning community members with their own victimization. Obviously, the fear of crime was enhanced by police action.

Do You Know?

1. If you have ever been a victim of a criminal act or know someone who has, what did it take for that individual to return to a normal life? Could you describe the monetary and the psychological expense of getting back to normal if your car were stolen along with all of your identification on your way home?

2. In what way does the fear of crime affect an average person's lifestyle?

3. How would you characterize a domestic violent offender? A domestic violence victim? In what way would chronic domestic violence go undetected in a neighborhood? Among some of your closest friends?

4. Under what conditions might a police officer in mandatory arrest jurisdictions not take an offender into custody?

5. Why would a partner in an intimate relationship misrepresent a domestic violent episode if s/he were the victim? The offender?

6. How would you characterize a sexual assault? How would an individual regain his or her former mental picture of themselves after being a victim of a sexual assault?

7. Describe Alexandria's SARA Program and its goals. What do you think are its strengths? Its weaknesses?

8. What do you think Dr. Martin Luther King, Jr. meant when he said, "Injustice anywhere is a threat to justice everywhere"?

Youth, Drugs, and Alcohol

"You cannot shake hands with a clenched fist."
Gandhi

Key Words _____

CAPS	National Drug Control Policy	Societal Symptoms
Driving Under the Influence	Office of National Drug	Southeastern Michigan
Hillbilly Heroin	Control Policy	Spinal Cord
Interdiction	RAND Corporation	Substance Abuse
Medical Model	Seizure of Illegal Drugs	

Key Topics _____

- Police practice as it relates to youth, drugs, and alcohol.
- Relationship between drug and alcohol abuse and performance in school.
- Preventive programs, school violence, and youth crime watch.

Introduction

Drug and alcohol abuse are referred to as *substance abuse* or *substance dependence* by many agencies, including the American Psychiatric Association.[1] Drug and alcohol abuse are pervasive in American society and are available to juveniles regardless of where they reside. For that reason, these substances are discussed together in this chapter. Police agencies cannot refrain from reactive, incident-driven strategies that include detainment to control drug and alcohol violators. In this new millennium, police executives are experimenting with a broader range of tools and tactics—such as preventive practices—to address issues including a strategy to redefine the function of policing. However, despite these experiments and definitions, reactive practices remain crucial to crime control. An accepted notion held by many, including the police, is that drug abuse leads to criminal activity. As one scholar asks, "Are drug users, and particularly cocaine, crack, heroin, and other narcotics users—driven to crime, driven by their enslavement to expensive drugs that can be afforded only through continual predatory activities?"[2]

Overview of Drug and Alcohol Abuse

Drug and alcohol abuse are linked to crime in several ways.[3] Concerning substance abuse, it can be a crime to use, possess, manufacture, or distribute drugs classified as illegal or legal prescription drugs used for purposes other than intended. This includes distributing prescription drugs such as valium and other tranquilizers from parents to their children; or the sale of the drug OxyContin (known as "Hillbilly heroin") by cancer patients to drug abusers.

---

[1]*Diagnostic and Statistical Manual of Mental Disorders,* Fourth Edition (DSM IV). Washington DC: American Psychiatric Association, (1994).
[2]See, James A Inciardi (2002*). The war on drugs III.* Boston: Allyn & Bacon. p. 195.
[3]For more detail, see: www.whitehousedrugpolicy.gov/drugfact/treatfact/treat1.html

Substance Abuse

> Substance abuse can be defined as any use of an illegal or legal drug that can cause problems for the user.[4]

The evidence shows that drug and alcohol abuse are not entirely causal factors leading to crimes of violence. That is, drugs and alcohol do not, in and by themselves, produce crimes of violence. Drug and alcohol abuse are significantly linked to symptoms of societal dysfunction among youngsters who lack appropriate tools to deal with their own behavior. There are exceptions, but most youngsters (and probably adults too) who engage in drug and alcohol abuse have few social safeguards against societal dysfunction and peer pressure if they possess low self-esteem, have little self control, and are self-centered.[5]

? Something to Think About

> Early drug use can start as a voluntary action. Continued use becomes an involuntary disease.

Continued use by an individual with low self-esteem, accompanied by a lack of self-control, impulsiveness, and self-gratification, means that the individual might never be able to overcome these personality challenges alone. More than likely, a youngster possessing most of these characteristics will eventually engage in crimes of violence, particularly if they have uninformed or uncaring parents or guardians who ignore the signs of abuse and often might not even be concerned.[6] Make no mistake, some youngsters at early ages (even as young as ten) are forced, coerced, or pressured into drug and alcohol use by parents, siblings, or family friends, and often these children become targets for sexual and physical victimization.[7] Subsequent substance dependence or what is often called an *addiction* indicates a propensity for a criminal lifestyle.

[4]More specifically, "The essential feature of substance abuse is a maladaptive pattern of substance use manifested by recurrent and significant adverse consequences related to the repeated use of substances." DSM IV, p. 182.

[5]For more information on this perspective see Michel R. Gottfredson and Travis Hirschi. (1990). *A general theory of crime.* Stanford University Press: Stanford, CA. pp. 89–93.

[6]See Dennis J. Stevens, (1997a). Influences of early childhood experiences on subsequent criminology violent behavior. *Studies on Crime and Crime Prevention*, 6(1), 34–50.

[7]For an indepth discussion on this matter, see Dennis J. Stevens, (1998g). Incarcerated women, crime, and drug addiction. *The Criminologist*, 22(1), 3–14. This exploratory study examined the relationship between drug addiction and criminal activity among 68 incarcerated women who were in a prison drug rehabilitation program. It was believed that drug addiction gave rise to criminality among females, but this was largely unsupported by the data. One implication of those finding was that drug addiction in itself is not necessarily a causal factor producing crimes of violence especially among females. These female offenders lived lifestyles comparable to that of career criminals prior to drug addiction experiences and their first arrest followed by prosecution. That is, a criminal career leads to drug addiction. Yet for all but two of those participants, marijuana, heroin, cocaine, and other drugs were part of their early childhood experiences as well as indicators of childhood sexual and physical abuse.

Substance Dependence

Substance dependence indicates continued use of a substance that plays a central role in an individual's life despite evidence of its physical and psychological impairment to the individual.[8]

In the year 2000 policing agencies nationwide made an estimated 14 million arrests for all criminal infractions other than traffic violations.[9] Among the specific categories, the highest arrest count was for drug abuse violations, 1.5 million arrests. As Table 1.13 and 2.13 show, the problem is getting worse not better. Drug abuse violations in 1999 accounted for an estimated 11 percent of all arrests. Of that total, 81 percent of the drug arrests were for possession. Heroin or cocaine was found among 25 percent of those arrested, 41 percent marijuana, and almost 16 percent consisted of other drugs. When we trace the rise in arrest rates for drug law violations in the U.S. from 1980 to 1999, clearly the patterns indicate that more and more individuals are being apprehended for drug violations.

However, when we review alcohol-related arrests, we find there were more alcohol-related arrests than drug arrests when categories are combined. For instance, there were 1,511,300 (11 percent) arrests made for offenders driving under the influence of alcohol, 656,100 for public drunkenness (5 percent), and 657,900 (5 percent) arrests for liquor laws. Also, 21 percent of all arrests were directly related to alcohol.

One source reveals that in a sample of 25,500 individuals in 1998, 9,180 (36 percent) reported that they used illicit drugs sometime during their lifetime as compared with 20,655 (81 percent) who used alcohol.[10]

Drug-Related Crime

Some clear indicators that come along with a rise in drug arrests show that overall, 16 percent of convicted jail inmates said they had committed their offense to get money for drugs. Of convicted property and drug offenders, about one in four had committed their crimes to get money for drugs. A higher percentage of drug

---

[8]Substance dependence can be defined in clinical terms as a maladaptive pattern of substance use, leading to clinically significant impairment or distress, as manifested by three or more of the following, occurring at any time in the same 12-month period (DSM IV, 1994, p. 181):

1. tolerance—a need for markedly increased amounts of the substance to achieve intoxication or desired effect
2. withdrawal, characterized by withdrawal syndrome
3. substance is often taken in larger amounts or over a longer period of time
4. unsuccessful efforts to cut down or control substance use
5. a great deal of time is spent in activities necessary to obtain the substance
6. important social, occupational, or recreational activities are given up or reduced due to substance use
7. substance use is continued despite knowledge of having persistent or recurrent physical or psychological problems caused by the substance

[9]For more detailed information: BJS: http:\\www.ojp.usdodj.gov

[10]BJS, Estimated prevalence of drug and alcohol use during lifetime. Table 3.87, p. 247.

TABLE 1-13   *Total Estimated Drug Law Violation*
             Arrests in the US, 1980-99*

1980	580,900
1981	559,900
1982	676,000
1983	661,400
1984	708,400
1985	811,400
1986	824,100
1987	937,400
1988	1,155,200
1989	1,361,700
1990	1,089,500
1991	1,010,000
1992	1,066,400
1993	1,126,300
1994	1,351,400
1995	1,476,100
1996	1,506,200
1997	1,583,600
1998	1,559,100
1999	1,532,200

*Source: Crime in the United States, Annual, Uniform Crime Reports 10/13/2000.

offenders in 1996 (24 percent) than in 1989 (14 percent) were in jail for a crime committed to raise money for drugs.[11] In 1997, 19 percent of state prisoners and 16 percent of federal inmates said they committed their current offense to obtain money for drugs.[12] Additionally, the Uniform Crime Reporting Program (UCR) of the Federal Bureau of Investigation (FBI) reported in 1997, 5.1 percent of the 15,289 homicides in which circumstances were known were narcotics related. Those murders that occurred specifically during a narcotics felony, such as drug trafficking or manufacturing, are considered drug related.[13]

Juveniles

Drug test positive rates for juveniles were essentially stable in 1998 compared to 1997 across all sites. Juvenile arrestees who are in school are less likely to test positive for drugs than juveniles not in school.[14] In Los Angeles, for example, 23 percent of the boys not currently attending school tested positive for cocaine, com-

[11]BJS, Profile of Inmates, 1996. NCJ 164620, April 1998.
[12]BJS, Substance Abuse and Treatment, State and Federal Prisoners. NCJ 172871, January 1999.
[13]ONDCP Drug Policy Information Clearinghouse staff from FBI, Uniform Crime Reports, Crime in the United States, annually.
[14]Bureau of Justice Statistics: Drug use and crime. http://www.ojp.udodj.gov/bjs/dcf/duc.htm

TABLE 2-13 *Estimated Totals of Top 7 Arrest Offenses US*

Type of Arrest	Number of Arrests*
Total Arrests	14,031,000
Drug Abuse Violations	1,532,000
Driving Under the Influence	1,511,300
Simple Assaults	1,294,400
Larceny / Theft	1,189,400
Drunkenness	656,100
Disorderly Conduct	633,100
Liquor Laws	657,900

*Source: FBI, Uniform Crime Reports.

pared to 13 percent of the boys currently attending school; nearly 10 percent of the boys not in school tested positive for methamphetamine, compared to 3 percent of the boys in school.

In 1998 among juveniles, marijuana was the most frequently detected drug in sites collecting juvenile data. Ranging from a low of 47 percent in Indianapolis to a high of 64 percent in Phoenix, on average more than half of the juvenile males tested positive for marijuana. By contrast, anywhere from 4 percent (Portland) to 15 percent (Los Angeles) tested positive for cocaine.

Additionally, 108,746 juveniles were incarcerated in public or private juvenile facilities. Drug offenders accounted for 23 percent of the state prison population in 1995, up from 6 percent in 1980, and 60 percent of the federal prison population in 1997, up from 25 percent in 1980. This increase in the drug offender prison population mirrors the steady increase in arrests for drug offenses. Also, one study conducted by the RAND Corporation to weigh the benefits of treatment, drug enforcement, and *interdiction* (Bender, 1994) is telling.

Interdiction

Interdiction is a strategy of interception of drug traffic at the nation's borders.

The findings concluded that it would be more cost effective to spend $34 million on treatment than the $1.43 billion spent on enforcement and border interdiction (1994 dollars). This finding results in a 1 percent reduction in the consumption of cocaine. The crime related to drugs would also be reduced.

Seizure of Illegal Drugs

Between 1982 and 1992, the seizure of illegal drugs by police and customs rose 237 percent, while an increase in the arrest of dealers rose 179 percent; yet drug use increased (Office of National Drug Control Policy (ONDCP), 1997). In the year ending 1998, 2,031,544 pounds of illegal substances were seized, and from 1975–1998, the federal government seized 10,916 laboratories.[15] Maritime seizures of cocaine reached a record volume of 125,904 pounds in the year 2000 compared to 111,689 pounds in 1999. Peru and Bolivia, formerly the top two suppliers of cocaine to the United States, have reduced coca cultivation 66 percent and 55 percent respectively, since 1995 (McCaffrey, 2001). Through Plan Colombia, the United States provides $1.3 billion in training, technical assistance, interdiction, and support for counter-drug initiatives.

Despite these statistics, yearly sales of cocaine were nearly $38 billion, heroin $10 billion, marijuana $7 billion, and other illicit drugs $3 billion. Considering that $500 worth of cocaine can produce up to $400,000 in profits, it is possible that narcotic officers are inclined to cut into some of that wealth (Dippold, 1998; ONDCP, 1997). With all of the above said, it appears that the control of narcotics is below the expectations of the American people (Dippold, 1998).

Overview: Drugs and School

When some students in the United States leave behind the relative sanctuary of elementary school, and make the leap to middle school or junior high, they also make another, potentially dangerous leap into an environment of new pressures, greater risk, and dramatically increased drug use.[16] Studies show that drug use jumps significantly in the critical year between sixth and seventh grade. According to the 1998 Partnership Attitude Tracking Study by the Partnership for a Drug-Free America, while one in thirteen sixth-graders have smoked marijuana, that number jumps to one in five in seventh grade. The average age of first use of marijuana is thirteen.

"Kids who are transitioning from elementary to middle school are extremely vulnerable to drug exposure and use, which makes talking to your child at this time especially important," Barry McCaffrey (2000), the former drug czar said.[17] Most likely, children will be in a situation where they will have to make a conscious decision about using drugs and, by seventh grade, will need to arm themselves with skills to reject drugs. Several factors contribute to the increased risk of using drugs during this transition. Starting middle school can be a scary time for adolescents, many desperately wish to fit in with their peers. They are also exposed to older kids who use drugs. Teens might feel pressured to experiment in order to be "cool" and to be independent.

Barry McCaffrey, who stepped down January 15, 2001, made it clear that the national drug strategy should continue to approach anti-drug efforts not like a

---

[15]Office of National Drug Control Policy, as reported in Fact Sheet: Drug Data Summary, NCJ 172873, April 1999.

[16]See drug czar Barry R. Mc Caffrey

http://www.apbnews.com/newscenter/breakingnews/2000/12/22/mccaffrey1222_01.html

[17]Perhaps the most controversial aspect of McCaffrey's tenure has been his support for a significant increase in U.S. help for the counter-drug effort in Colombia, the world's No. 1 producer and distributor of cocaine. The bulk of the $1.3 billion package is earmarked for the Colombian military.

war, but like a cancer, requiring American communities to implement comprehensive and aggressive prevention and treatment programs.

Moreover, the Monitoring the Future (MTF) study sponsored by National Drug Control in 2000, surveyed 45,000, eighth-, tenth-, and twelfth-graders and found that

- heroin use is down among eighth-graders.
- cocaine use is down among twelfth-graders.
- LSD use is down among tenth- and twelfth-graders.
- hallucinogen use is down among all three grades.
- steroid use is up among tenth-graders.
- there is a significant increase in Ecstasy usage among all three grades, the largest percentage increase among twelfth-graders for any drug in the 26-year history of the MTF study.

Another source reveals that from grades six to eight, 14 percent of a 58,619 individual sample reported they used alcohol monthly, and almost 9 percent used illicit drugs during the same time period. Also, from grades nine to twelve, 37 percent of almost 80,000 individuals reported that they used alcohol monthly as compared to 22 percent who reported illicit drug use during the same period. Finally, in a group compromised of over 16,000 individuals, 45 percent used alcohol, and 25 percent used illicit drugs monthly.[18] As a means of breaking the connection between drugs and crime, policy makers want to accelerate the expansion of programs offering alternatives to imprisonment for non-violent drug offenders.

America's "war on drugs" needs to be refocused to increase resources for prevention and addiction treatment, the United States Customs Service Chief told APBnews.com (Meek, 2000). Commissioner Ray Kelly said national policies that rely instead on interdiction and incarceration as a means to stem the flow of drugs into this country or punish those involved in the buying and selling of narcotics have not worked as effectively as hoped. Kelly (Meek, 2000) added: "I don't know of any thinking person in law enforcement who doesn't say we need more prevention and treatment."

Of the billions of dollars spent each year by the government to fight the drug problem, not enough goes to drug rehabilitation and education, Kelly argues. The national drug strategy is rooted in politics, which historically has stoked the public desire to be tough on drugs.

"I've been in this game a long time, and the emphasis has always been on interdiction," Kelly said. "It sells politically." Intercepting drug shipments by air, land, and sea will always be necessary, he predicted, but reducing the demand is also an effective way to counter the drug problem. Yet clearly it would seem that another method to reduce drug abuse is to reduce the demand, since there are approximately five million hard-core addicts in the United States in 2001, and at least another 10 million individuals who use narcotics socially. Which police strategies are being used by local agencies to combat drugs? Are they primarily preventive in nature or do they rely on the traditional perspective of detection and arrest?

[18]BJS (2000), Table 3.68, p. 234.

Police Strategies to Control Drugs and Alcohol

Earlier in this book, we learned that the Green Bay Police Department in Wisconsin initiated a strategy to rid the business district of people who were often intoxicated and disorderly. That strategy included in part a tavern "no-serve list" of people who were habitually drunk and disorderly. The result was a reduction in calls-for-service and an improved quality of life in the neighborhood. However, it is yet to be seen how helpful this strategy is in aiding individual recovery or preventing others from becoming drunk and disorderly. Curiously, this strategy won an award related to a community-policing strategy.

Strategies Used by the Chicago Police

What follows are several accounts of strategies employed by different districts of the Chicago Police Department in an effort to control drug and alcohol abuse in the city.[19] To improve lines of communication with one community, Chicago's 7th District Neighborhood Relations Office set up a complaint line and began advertising it at beat meetings.[20] When a concerned resident called about drug dealing and loitering on the 7100 block of South Perry Avenue, police responded. Neighborhood Relations passed the information on to the Tactical Unit, which assigned the complaint to two tactical teams: Officers Ronald Condreva and E.J. May, and Officers James O'Donnell and Richard Ferenzi. The tactical teams set up surveillance. When they observed the dealer removing crack cocaine from a corner fence post and making sales to several people who were congregating at the location, officers placed him under arrest. Since the arrest, loitering on the block has stopped, and no new narcotics complaints have been received by Neighborhood Relations.

In another typical account, residents on Beat 331 in the O'Keefe community on the southeast side of Chicago worked successfully to solve neighborhood problems that were related to illegal drug dealing and liquor sales at local stores. Beat 331 Co-Facilitator Yvonne Tuck explains, "Dominick's (a supermarket) at this stage of the game has discontinued selling the big bottles of beer, and Walgreens has discontinued its liquor service completely." The quality of life improved for residents on Beat 331 when three outdoor payphones were removed and gang members no longer loitered in the neighborhood. Parking problems were also eliminated after Beat 331 Officer Sandra Yancey negotiated a solution with the O'Keefe Elementary School. Says Yancey, "The school opened the gates and allowed residents to use the parking lot for parking on the weekends or when school is out." This strategy might be considered preventive in nature; although reducing the demand for drugs might still be of concern.

Beat 331 Facilitator Loretta Moore and Co-Facilitator Yvonne Tuck have a calm and cordial approach to solving problems on their beat. Moore explained, "We do a lot of walking around telling people about the Chicago Alternative

[19] All of these accounts publis record and are available at Chicago PD's website: http:\\www.ci.chi.il.us
[20] The Chicago Police seem to demonstrate traditional perspectives of arrest: for more details see http://www.ci.chi.il.us/CommunityPolicing/AboutCAPS/SuccessStories/Dist07.html

Policing Strategy (CAPS),[21] what CAPS can do, and what we can do together." The two leaders have met with many of the neighborhood's building owners and encouraged them to participate in CAPS and to attend the City's Landlord Training Program. Residents say they owe much of the credit for the success on their beat to their beat officers. Says Moore, "We really feel fortunate to have them because they see the beauty of the community and they are committed to change and to positive feedback."

When residents in the Washington Heights community, near 95th Street and Peoria Avenue, realized criminals had developed an enterprising drug business in their neighborhood, they immediately took action to shut it down. Lieutenant Patrick Kellam explains, "In a one square block area, cocaine addicts could break into a garage and steal a lawnmower, sell it to the man fencing stolen property, go to 95th and Peoria and buy a bag of crack cocaine, then go to 96th Street and Sangamon and use it in the smokehouse." Residents communicating through their block club presidents identified the burglars to the police. They also pointed out three locations: the house where suspect drug-addict-burglars fenced stolen property, the apartment building where drug dealers sold drugs, and the house used by drug addicts. Police set up surveillance and captured two burglars. At the same time, they contacted building inspectors and attorneys from the City's Corporation Counsel to investigate the three locations.

Criminal charges along with building-code violations and fines convinced one homeowner to stop fencing stolen property. The owner of the apartment building where illegal drugs were sold faces nearly $10,000 in fines for building-code violations. More than two dozen building-code violations and drug charges forced the owner of the third house to sell the property. Says Beat 2223 Co-Facilitator Sharon Snelling, "I think residents in this community let it be known they would not stand by idly and watch criminal activity take over their neighborhood. We took an active role in saving our community."

Broken Arrow, Oklahoma

The Broken Arrow Police Department (BAPD) abandoned the Drug Abuse Resistance Education (DARE) program, but maintained their presence in the schools through a School Resource Officer Program, which became a mentoring program for students.[22] Additionally, when a new chief was hired in the early 1990s, the department had many programs but they operated under the efforts of volunteers or specific officers, none of whom reported to police supervisors. For instance, the BAPD was represented on the SALT Council (Seniors and Lawmen Together) by an officer who worked with the Senior Center director on issues of

[21]CAPS was first announced in the spring of 1993 and during the next two years the program's operational details were developed based on the experiences of five prototype districts. The program was instituted citywide by the spring of 1995. Chicago's initiative shares many of the features of community policing program around the country, while adding a few distinctive elements. For a review of CAPS, see Chicago Community Policing Evaluation Consortium (2001). Community policing in Chicago, Year Seven: An interim report. Illinois Criminal Justice Information Authority. November 2000.
[22]For more detail see Dennis J. Stevens, (2001a). Case studies of community policing. pp. 26–59.

mutual concern. Most of the programs were successful; however, they were primarily identified with one individual and were not considered a department-wide commitment to community policing. Making the programs citywide in scope was one of the first priorities for Chief Carolyn M. Kusler who recognized that community policing was a departmental philosophy as opposed to several independent programs. Before decentralizing the department, she first had to centralize it under her command. This task, as can be expected, took some time. Through the individualized programs scattered throughout the city of Broken Arrow, it was clear that a concentrated consistency might serve the department and the community more advantageously at the time. However, the new administration felt the pull-and-tug of individual leaders who might have been threatened by a citywide effort to incorporate those individual programs into departmental leadership. The administration followed the principle: if you want to get people to support your priorities, you must first address theirs. Thus, Chief Kusler's administration sought to correct the perceptions of favoritism produced by individual leaders through a revamping of the promotional process to include an assessment center by outside evaluators and through the establishment of a participatory decision-making process. As expected, professional perspectives met more resistance than expected from several leaders who then felt under personal attack and responded accordingly. Going into 2002, the BAPD decentralized its authority after reorganizing their programs and is now moving into a non-program department.

Youth Programs

Policing managers are widening the net of cooperation among themselves and community members and other institutions such as schools, parent groups, neighborhood associations, professional groups, and service organizations. Their attempt is to curb some of the root causes of youth violence, such as economic instability, weak parental and community controls, lack of recognition and stake in the community, and disconnection from support systems.[23] These partnerships focus on youth violence and are complemented through community-policing initiatives. However, no single model or program will work best to prevent youth violence since department, community members, and other institutions are unique; each has its own history, resources, and experiences. To develop educational, recreational, and anti-crime programs and activities that will help youth understand and resist violence, those partnerships work best when they focus their efforts on two related goals:

1. Keep young people from becoming perpetrators of violence.
2. Keep young people from becoming victims of violence.

To reach the first goal, partnerships focus on strategies that deflect young people from violence, teach them peaceful means of resolving conflict, and heighten their awareness of the effects and consequences of violent behavior. The

[23]For more discussion on this matter, see BJA, August 1994.

second objective can be reached by showing young people ways to avoid conflict and dangerous places or situations. Some partnerships are formed after a violent event has traumatized the community, enabling young people and their parents and teachers to form supportive bonds and work with police to prevent future recurrences of violence.

The police can be an integral part of youth programs by teaching in the schools topics such as conflict resolution, peacemaking, and anger-management skills. They can emphasize positive alternatives to illegal behavior; peer-pressure resistance skills, and a young persons' importance can help bring change to their environment. School and community policies that declare school campuses and public places (e.g., parks, recreation centers) where youth tend to congregate as "drug-free, gun-free, violence-free zones" send clear messages about expected and tolerated behavior. Police personnel and teachers, as well as others who care for youth, can also become effective educators on gun safety and violence prevention, as programs such as the STAR (Straight Talk About Risks) curriculum have shown. Other examples include a chapter of Young Marines and a shooting range as proposed in Palm Beach County, Florida, by Deputy Steven Dickinson.

The Las Vegas Metropolitan Police Department   The Las Vegas Metropolitan Police Department developed a program called Cops Racing Against Violence through Education (CRAVE). Off-duty police officers spend their time helping school kids overcome problems related to violence and substance abuse. In 1995 the group awarded four scholarships to deserving high school graduates who demonstrated a positive community involvement. CRAVE is a non-profit organization with the goal of helping educate elementary school kids as well as teenagers about the dangers of violence and substance abuse. The program is funded entirely by sponsorship and donations by community members and local businesses. The CRAVE team visits local schools in the community (as well as others upon special request) to promote the idea that kids can do what is right and still win. The mission of CRAVE is to provide the members of the community with the best educational, non-profit organization by increasing their awareness of the dangers of substance abuse and gang violence. They promote cultural diversity by touching the lives of citizens and establishing honest lines of communication. The intent is to show young adults that their successes in life are limited only by their desire to achieve the goals they set for themselves. Violence and substance abuse will only impair their ability to attain these goals.

GREAT Cooking Class in Boston   The creation of the GREAT (Gang Resistance Education and Training) Cooking Class program began as the result of a new partnership between the Boston Police Department and a retailer called Bread & Circus Markets. Representatives of Bread & Circus initially approached a youth service officer (Officer Bill Baxter) to learn what they could do to help address the needs of young people throughout Boston. In searching for new ways to work together, Officer Baxter and Bread & Circus representatives developed an innovative series of cooking classes that were integrated with existing youth-oriented programs in the city.

For eight weeks, while students receive GREAT programming in their schools, Officer Baxter brings various groups of young people to a Bread & Circus Market for their weekly cooking session in an onsite cooking demonstration classroom stocked with all of the appropriate utensils, supplies, and ingredients necessary for that week's activity.

Students receive a lesson plan that details the recipes to be prepared and a short history of the particular meal they will prepare together. The meals they learn to cook are changed each week to provide an opportunity to discover a variety of unusual foods, as well as the countries where they originated. For example, one week the meal could be a Mexican fiesta, while the following week it might be a Chinese New Year celebration. The students and cooking instructor review the directions together and then take some time to discuss the particular national customs that are unique to the meal being prepared. Then the fun begins! The students prepare all of the food from the recipes, and reap their reward by sitting down to eat and enjoy the foods they have created.

Success comes from learning about tastes, interests, and histories. These cooking classes pull people together, and teach the cooks that learning can be fun. The program also allows Youth Service Officers to reach young people that they might not be able to reach in any other way. Finally, GREAT demonstrates to youths how they can work together toward common goals, and how important their own partnerships can be in providing them with positive alternatives to crime.

Peoria, Arizona: Police and School Violence   School violence is clearly an issue. However, it is not the sole responsibility of the school district or the police department. Partnerships help address issues that promote violence on school grounds. For instance, the Peoria, Arizona Police Department and the Peoria Unified School District began a partnership in April 2000 with a Memorandum of Understanding to violent crimes on school grounds (Ashley, 2001). Some of the responsibilities shared between the department and school include a representative to address issues on school-based offenses. The school district's media representative fields questions about the school district, and the police representative provides information about criminal investigations. The district's counselors and intervention teams assist with victim and witness counseling and the police provide chaplains and victims' assistance personnel. Hotlines are maintained.

Elsewhere, police officer experience and bravery averts school tragedies such as in the case of Officer Webb of the Springfield Township Police Department and the Mount Healthy School District in Springfield, Ohio. Officer Webb is a School Resource Officer. A student fired a weapon in school and announced he would shoot anyone, but wanted to talk only to Officer Webb to discuss the matter. Officer Webb met with the student and brought the situation to a safe conclusion. Nonetheless, school violence is an explosive problem across America that usually involves guns and there is a shortage of experienced officers like Officer Webb.

Southeastern Michigan Spinal Cord Injury Center   The Southeastern Michigan Spinal Cord Injury Center has developed a highly effective program in which youthful victims of gun violence, now paraplegic or quadriplegic, go before groups of students to show them the consequences of using guns. Their testimonials touch students as no classroom text or lecture can. The schools can work with police, victims' groups, and the victims themselves to make such presentations possible.

In Miami-Dade County, Florida, several groups came together to cosponsor a Gun Safety Program following a report of 137 handgun incidents in the public school system during the school year. The K–12 program features a comprehensive curriculum, teacher training, youth crime watch, parent education, and media involvement. The partners include the National Center to Prevent Handgun Violence, the Dade County School Board, Youth Crime Watch of Dade County, local agencies, and the police department.

In San Francisco, youngsters who have been trained as mediators use their skills to help classmates peacefully resolve playground disputes. The mediation training, conducted by Community Boards of San Francisco, involves youth as young as fourth-graders in learning how to help keep playground disputes from escalating into physical confrontations. Teachers and administrators credit the program with substantially improving the climate of the whole school, not just the playground area.

Another example of partnerships is the Untouchables in Alexandria, Virginia. This club helps young men develop pride and self-esteem by employing a holistic approach to empower the participants with knowledge and skills to increase their physical, emotional, intellectual, and spiritual levels of functioning in order that the members will live, work, play, and socialize in a productive and healthy manner. This club is sponsored by the Alexandria Police Department, but solely operates through the Friends of the Untouchables.[24] Adult role models serve as mentors.

? *Something to Think About*

Partnerships between police, youth, and other agencies and organizations should increase because today's children are tomorrow's parents.

DARE Programs   Project DARE (Drug Abuse Resistance Education) has been implemented in communities around the country, using police officers to teach elementary school students in classrooms how to resist peer pressure to use drugs. DARE programs can include antiviolence and positive self-esteem training along with assertiveness, stress management, and resistance to negative peer pressure.

In some cities such as Fayetteville, North Carolina the resources supporting DARE were redirected to a more effective Family Intervention Program. This new program is used to identify youthful offenders when they are very young. This way, community interests are better served as well as those of education and the family, the Fayetteville Police reports.[25] Family Intervention Teams have a long-

[24]For information, contact Friends of the Untouchables, PO Box 26292 Alexandria, VA 22314.
[25]For more details, see Dennis J. Stevens, (2001a). Case studies in community policing. p. 182–203.

lasting impact on offenders and their communities. One overall philosophy of an efficient community partnership is to reexamine programs on a regular basis. If those programs don't work, despite what other agencies are doing "across the nation, get rid of them or repackage them," argues Carl Milazzo, police attorney for the Fayetteville Police Department.[26]

Schools, recreation centers, and other places that attract young people can provide opportunities to teach youth about the personal and community consequences of violence, about alternative ways to settle disputes, and about legal and safety restrictions on handguns. Police agencies, in partnership with parents, teachers, students, and school administrators, can promote similar programs in their own communities.

Metropolitan Nashville Police Department and Child Development Program

The Metropolitan Nashville Police Department (METRO)[27] in Tennessee initiated the Child Development Community Policing Program (CDCPP).[28] This program was designed to intervene in the lives of children and families traumatized by family and community violence. METRO was one of four law enforcement agencies chosen by Yale University to replicate the highly successful CDCPP begun by Yale and the New Haven, Connecticut Police Department.

METRO teamed up with clinical social workers at Family & Children's Service, a not-for-profit family counseling agency, to provide trauma debriefing, follow-up counseling, and support groups for children who have been victims of or witnesses to community violence. Moreover, the clinicians provide 24-hour consultation to the police officers responding to violent scenes where children are present.

Why is a partnership so critical? First and foremost, the tragic consequences to children of chronic exposure to violence are devastating.[29] These experiences can produce depression, anxiety, stress, and anger. Alcohol abuse, academic failure, and the increased likelihood of acting out in an aggressive manner are examples of how the cycle of violence seems to hopelessly trap children. Police officers are all too familiar with this cycle of violence and how some families perpetuate it from one generation to the next. As first responders to scenes of violence and tragedy, police officers have frequent contact with the children and families most at risk. However, officers usually do not have training, practical support, or time to deal with the psychological aftermath of a child's exposure to violence. Mental health professionals, on the other hand, are trained to intervene so that the burden of trauma is significantly lessened. Unfortunately, clinicians often do not have access to these children and therefore critical time is lost after a violent event. Forging a partnership between the two professions provides an opportunity to develop new collaborative approaches to problems that are beyond the reach of either profession when working in isolation.

[26]D.J. Stevens. (2001a). Case studies in community policing. p. 187.
[27]See their website at www.nashville.net/~police./
[28]See Family and Children's Service website at http://info.med.yale.edu/ chldstdy/CDCP/index.html
[29]Lt. Ben Dickie, of the Metropolitan Nashville Police Department supplied some of the information for his section. He can be reached at nashcop1@aol.com.

Dr. Steven Marans at the Yale Child Study Center explains additional benefits when police, mental health workers, and neighborhood residents partner together on behalf of their communities. "At best, police can provide children and families with a sense of security and safety through rapid, authoritative, and effective responses at times of danger." The experience children have generally had with police officers prior to CDCPP aroused negative feelings. For example, the arrival of officers after a violent event can reinforce their uncertainty and helplessness. Through CDCPP they learn a new perspective about police officers.

Nashville's program began in the Enterprise Community (Napier-Tony Sudekum, Vine Hill, and Edgehill neighborhoods) during the fall of 1996. During 1999, the program expanded to the Briley Parkway loop and eventually all of Davidson County. Currently, clinicians respond to cases out-of-zone whenever a child is a victim of or witness to violence and an officer believes METRO's presence is needed. The most critical components of this program include the following:

- 24-hour consultation service staffed by clinicians responding to police.
- Officers' need for guidance in crisis interventions.
- Crisis response by clinicians for children experiencing or witnessing violence.
- Trauma debriefing for children and families experiencing violent events.
- Ongoing groups for children/families dealing with the impact of violence in their lives.
- Training seminars for police officers on topics such as childhood development, psychological and family response to trauma, indicators of child abuse, and cultural competence.
- Follow-up family/individual counseling by this staff or through referral.
- Weekly consultation team meetings with police officers and clinicians to discuss referrals and strategies for more complex cases.

METRO's collaborative effort is also greatly enhanced by the participation of the clinicians from the Victim Intervention Program and the Domestic Violence Unit. These clinicians attend weekly meetings, provide training for the officers, and share valuable insights with the Family & Children's Service clinicians involved in this program.

Overall, CDCPP provides opportunities for officers to minimize the negative experiences of victimized children and become their potential heroes. As CDCPP places officers on long-term assignments in specific neighborhoods, they are encouraged to work with community residents to analyze and solve problems. These strategies allow officers to develop relationships and assume roles in the lives of children that would not necessarily be possible in a more impersonal, incident-driven policing delivery system. Similarly, regular, non-confrontational contact with a neighborhood officer may help some previously adjudicated juveniles to abide by court-imposed restrictions. Perhaps Chief Emmett Turner best summarizes the importance of the CDCPP in Nashville when he stated, "This program will allow us to better meet the needs of children exposed to violence for it is the goal of this program to intervene with youngsters quickly so that the violence they have witnessed, whether it be in the home or on the street, will not haunt them for the rest of their lives."[30]

Miami-Dade Police Department and Youth Crime Watch   One national program that attempts to apply the principles of risk-focused prevention is the Youth Crime Watch of America, Inc. (YCWA).[31] YCWA is a non-profit organization that establishes youth crime watch programs throughout the United States and in other countries. YCWA originated in Miami, Florida in 1986 and has three primary goals:

1. To provide crime-free, drug-free, and violence-free environments for healthy learning and living.
2. To instill positive values, foster good citizenship, and build self-confidence in youth while instilling a sense of personal responsibility and accountability.
3. To enable youth to become a resource for preventing drug use and other crimes in their schools and neighborhoods.

YCWA was first developed as an attempt to replicate nationally the activities and effectiveness of a local program, the Youth Crime Watch of Miami-Dade County, which formally began in 1979. Miami-Dade County's Youth Crime Watch program began as an outgrowth of the adult Neighborhood Crime Watch. Adults involved in neighborhood crime watch programs began to realize that the youth living in the neighborhood frequently knew more about what was going on in the community and in the schools than did the adults. But, at that time, a mentality on the part of both police and residents did not strongly encourage community participation in crime prevention activities, combined with the complexities involved in merging adult and juvenile participation in the neighborhood watch, made a joint adult-juvenile neighborhood watch program difficult to organize and administer.

During this period, Lt. Jerry Rudoff of the Miami-Dade Police Department was involved with the Miami-Dade County Public School System on an anti-vandalism project. Through this project, Rudoff found that long-term success in crime prevention within the schools could occur only with the involvement of the students themselves. As a part of the anti-vandalism initiative—and as an attempt to harness the energy and knowledge of the students and apply it to the school environment—Rudoff and his team created a school-based version of the adult neighborhood watch program. This was the beginning of the Youth Crime Watch of Miami-Dade County.

Not unexpectedly, the idea of a school-based crime watch program was not uniformly welcomed. According to Good (personal communication), Director of the Citizens' Crime Watch of Dade County, the biggest barrier to the development of the program came from school principals, who had a number of objections to

---

[30]See Dennis J. Stevens, (2001a). Case studies in community policing. p. 82.
[31]See Gerald A. Rudoff and Ellen G. Cohn (2002). Youth crime watch of America: A youth-led movement. In Dennis J. Stevens (Ed.) *Community and Community Policing.* (pp. 132–156). Upper Saddle River, NJ: Prentice Hall.

the formation of a youth crime watch. While there was little objection to the vandalism-prevention program Rudoff had developed, this was a formalized youth crime prevention program that did not focus merely on one specific issue (e.g., vandalism) but on the problems of crime and disorder throughout the school system and that emphasized the concept of youth-led programs to solve these problems. First of all, many school principals felt that the students would be unwilling to participate in the program, because they could be labeled as a snitch or narc (narcotic officer). The principals were also concerned that students would be required to participate in crime watch activities and meetings during the school day, thereby taking time away from their educational activities. Finally, many principals did not want to admit even tacitly that there was a crime problem in the schools; they felt that if they even considered implementing the program, parents would become concerned or even fearful about crime in the schools.

At the same time, the greatest support for a youth-based crime watch program came from the police. Under then Director E. Wilson Purdy's leadership, the Miami-Dade Police Department eventually provided the necessary initiative and support to ensure the survival of the youth crime watch program. Rudoff, along with Betty Ann Good, the director of the Citizens' Crime Watch of Dade County (the adult neighborhood watch), persuaded the Dade County Superintendent of Schools to test the program in one school. The principal of North Miami Beach (NMB) Senior High School was reasonably receptive to the concept and the Law Enforcement Assistance Administration provided the funds to develop a handbook for student participants. Participation in the program was voluntary; this applied not only to the students involved in the program but also to the teachers and police officers who served as adult advisors. According to Rudoff (personal communication), students found the program especially attractive because they realized that they could organize their own crime watch groups and plan their own events and activities. In other words, while the adults acted in an advisory capacity, the students ran the program.

Beginning in the early 1980s, the Youth Crime Watch of Miami-Dade County sponsored an annual countywide conference focusing on youth-related crime prevention issues. Eventually, participation was expanded to include representatives from around the state of Florida. In 1985, the National Crime Prevention Council (NCPC) was invited to send a speaker to address the conference. As a result of the visit, a proposal was made that the NCPC and the Youth Crime Watch of Miami-Dade County jointly sponsor the first National Youth Crime Prevention Conference. In 1986, the Youth Crime Watch of America, a national organization, was formally incorporated and has held a national conference every year since 1987. The founding director of YCWA was Betty Ann Good.

YCWA 2001   YCWA has been recognized by Presidents Reagan, Bush, and Clinton, and has received a large number of national honors and awards, including being named a U.S. Department of Education Exemplary Program of Excellence. In 2002, YCWA has programs in over 500 sites in sixteen states and in Guam, with many more currently under development. YCWA relies primarily on government grants and private donations from individuals and corporate sponsors to continue providing programming. As the necessary funding becomes available, YCWA plans to expand into additional states within the United States and abroad. Despite the benefits that YCWA brings to schools, the only school district that currently provides a significant amount of funding to support YCWA programming is Miami-Dade County, in Florida. No other school district participating in YCWA provides a comparable level of funds to support these program activities. However, in late 1999, Congress and President Clinton endorsed a request to provide $1 million of funding to YCWA and the Department of Education earmarked an additional $500,000. YCWA is proposing to use the funds to facilitate national expansion.

In 2002, YCWA emphasizes a "watch out, help out" commitment, which encourages youth to look for problems within their school and community, and to become actively involved in solving those problems. A youth crime watch program, motivated by the principle of good citizenship, enables students to take an active role in addressing the violence, drug, and crime problems that exist in their communities and neighborhoods. Youth and youth advisors trained in YCWA methods currently run youth crime watch programs in elementary, middle, and high schools; neighborhoods; public housing sites; recreational centers; and parks. The program is able to function in diverse locations due to its flexibility and its age-appropriate programming. YCWA has enabled participants to greatly reduce crime, violence, and drug use in their environments. For example, after the formation of a youth crime watch program in 1994, Leto High School in Tampa reported a 72 percent drop in crime. In 1995, Carol City High School in Miami, reported a 45 percent decrease in student crime after beginning its youth crime watch.

Through local youth crime watch programs, YCWA sponsors and encourages a wide variety of activities. Every youth crime watch program includes at least some of the following components:

- Providing drug, crime, gun, and violence awareness and prevention education.
- Facilitating communication between police and youth.
- Creating anonymous crime-reporting systems.
- Establishing youth patrols.
- Creating a mentoring program and teaching mediation skills.
- Teaching school bus safety.
- Co-sponsoring training programs at the National Youth Crime Prevention Conference.
- Providing conflict resolution training.
- Creating action plans.
- Organizing leadership retreats for youth and youth advisors.
- Providing onsite training of youth and youth advisors, as well as regional training for youth advisors.
- Cultivating positive youth/police relations.

- Establishing community networks and partnerships all over the world.
- Planning events and activities throughout the year.

University of Florida Colleges and universities, too, have a stake in partnership with police agencies. After a rash of five murders near the University of Florida, the Alachua County Sheriff's Department and the Gainesville Police Department established a partnership with the university to address students' fears about the murders and to raise awareness about crime prevention and personal safety. The student government spearheaded a "Think Smart: Together for a Safe Community" campaign, displaying "Think Smart" posters and distributing brochures with a do-it-yourself personal security checklist. In the months following the murders, students made dramatic changes in their conduct. They increased their requests for student escorts, stopped jogging alone at night, and were more careful about securing their residences. Violent crime on campus plunged 26 percent in five months.

Knoxville PD, Metropolitan Drug Commission, and University of Tennessee SCOPE[32] is a partnership among the City of Knoxville Police Department, the Metropolitan Drug Commission, and the University of Tennessee's Institute for Public Service. SCOPE is a Regional Community Policing Institute (RCPI) funded by a grant from the COPS Office, U.S. Department of Justice.

SCOPE, one of more than thirty national RCPIs, works toward these objectives:

- Integration of community-policing principles into forms of police training.
- Application principles of adult learning to training activities.
- Development of participants' capacity for critical thinking and their ability to apply critical thinking in responding to complex enforcement, community, and organizational problems.
- Use of innovative training methods to prepare officers to work with community members to:
  - Identify persistent community problems.
  - Learn more about why those problems occur.
  - Address underlying conditions that precipitate these problems.
  - Involve police agencies, academic institutions, and local governments to utilize community organizations in training efforts.
  - Involve trainers from a variety of disciplines.
  - Incorporate train-the-trainers components.
  - Research current training curriculum.
  - Expansion training beyond the walls of the traditional police academies.

SCOPE is the only RCPI that is focused on building organizational infrastructure to sustain a community-policing strategy. Other police agencies can learn from this model.

[32]See their website at http://www.ips.utk.edu/scope/HTML/abSCP/prtnr.html

Office of National Drug Control Policy The Office of National Drug Control Policy (ONDCP) is an organization that focuses on support and understand for youths during their transition to adulthood in order to resist substance abuse.[33] In an earlier chapter, it was revealed that drug and alcohol abuse were factors significantly linked to symptoms of societal uncertainty, societal dysfunction, and peer pressure particularly among youthful offenders who lack appropriate tools to deal with their own behavior.[34] Most youngsters who engage in drug and alcohol abuse have few safeguards against societal dysfunction and peer pressure as they possess low self-esteem, a lack of self-control, and are excessively self-centered. One way to prepare parents for the critical juncture in the life of their children is offered by the ONDCP that suggests the following, especially to parents of middle school children:

- Build a positive atmosphere with your teens.
- Talk early and talk often.
- Make sure teens know that you are against drugs.
- Let your kids know that drugs will not be tolerated in your family.
- Keep close tabs on their activities.
- Know their friends, especially the ones they have recently made.
- Keep them involved in after-school activities.

The National Youth Anti-Drug Media Campaign is committed to providing parents with the tools needed to help keep their kids drug-free. The Campaign has developed free and readily available resources. The site encourages parents to help their children with difficult issues by focusing on four major concepts: love, trust, honesty, and communication. Police agencies connecting to youth and/or parenting partnerships might aid their journey by linking with such agencies.

Summary

Drug and alcohol abuse are symptoms of a much larger societal problem that are beyond the control of most youths. Clearly, early childhood prevention of drug and alcohol abuse can be curbed by enhancing self-esteem, strengthening self-control, and extending gratification beyond immediate fulfillment. Parents, police agencies, and other interested parties must deal with those issues before a child reaches the seventh grade since that is the grade when a child is most likely to be introduced to drugs and alcohol. Interdiction, apprehension, and justice sanctions are not as great a deterrent to drug and alcohol use as expected.

Police strategies that deal with apprehension are mere band-aides and might relate more to a specific street corner than a community at large. Apprehending traffickers is a temporary solution since anyone who knows the

[33]Parents are encouraged to call 1-800-788-2800 and ask for the *21 Parenting Skills* brochure, or visit their multilingual website, www.theantidrug.com. The site is designed to provide parents with strategies and tips on raising healthy, drug-free children.
[34]See Chapter 8.

streets knows that with every drug pusher arrested, there are ten to take his place. Therefore, demand has more to do with user demand than any arrest. These thoughts were congruent with preventive measures concerning gun control as well, especially among youths.

Thus, an emphasis should be placed on prevention and rehabilitation for youths concerning drugs, alcohol, and violence. As noted by James A. Inciardi (2002), criminal lifestyles drive and intensify pre-existing criminal activity more often than the other way around.

Do You Know?

1. Identify the purpose of this chapter and explain why the subject matter is of concern, and how conceptual strategies in community policing come into play.

2. In what way are drug and alcohol abuse linked to crime? Explain why drug and alcohol abuse may not cause crimes of violence.

3. Discuss the societal symptoms linked to drug and alcohol abuse.

4. Identify the drug and alcohol arrest rates as presented in the chapter and explain why you think they are so high. What are the best ways to control drunk drivers within Constitutional boundaries?

5. Describe American activity toward interdiction seizures of illegal drugs in the United States and explain the consequences of those actions on the drug user.

6. Describe the relationship between grades in school and drugs. In what way do you agree with the information provided about drug use by grade-school children?

7. Describe one of the strategies used by the Chicago Police Department and explain its preventative characteristics. In what way can you improve on that strategy?

8. Describe the major contributions of Southeastern Michigan Spinal Cord organization and explain in what way their presentations are likely to get the attention of youths.

9. Describe the YCWA's major features and explain how it provides preventative measures for youths.

10. What do you think Gandhi meant when he said, "You cannot shake hands with a clenched fist?" And how does the quotation apply to this chapter?

14

The Fear of Crime and Homicide

"A single death is a tragedy, a million deaths is a statistic."
Joseph Stalin

Key Terms _____

Criminalization of Poverty	Multifaceted Strategy	Targeting Criteria
Family Violence	Non-enforcement Strategies	
Fear of Crime	Repeat Offenders Programs	

Key Topics _____

- Consequences of the fear of crime.
- Police-community partnerships to prevent homicide.
- Paths that lead to homicide.

Introduction

Thomas Hobbes wrote in 1651 that the "fundamental purpose of civil government is to establish order," protecting residents from a fear of criminal attack that can make life "nasty, brutish, and short."[1] Hobbes might argue if he were living today that it appears that social stability and fear of crime are highly related variables. For the past thirty or forty years, police have exclusively utilized motorized patrol, rapid response time, and interrogational methods. However, none of these strategies goes to the core of community problems.[2]

One central problem for most Americans has been the fear of becoming a victim of violent crime. Due in part to fear, some individuals made choices about their way of life that actually enhanced their own chances of becoming a victim of a violent crime such as murder, and/or have victimized others. That is, people often react to an imagined level of victimization. But police practice seems to ignore the fear of crime and/or responds to it through more aggressive enforcement efforts. On the other hand, in an attempt to establish social stability, some police agencies have experimented and succeeded with strategies that have curbed crime of homicide. This chapter is largely about those police agencies that saw homicide as a serious threat to social order. Consequently, they pursued numerous strategies to bring offenders to justice.

Fear of Crime

Police must deal with the way people fear crime. The difficulty lies with the fact that it is an intangible quality. This thought was confirmed when the results of the investigation for this text were presented to a Boston police commander in November, 2001. While violent crime was at a ten-year low in Boston, results from 897 participants showed that the fear of crime was extremely high in the city.[3] The response of the commander can only be described as one of amazement, especially since his district worked very hard with the community. The *fear of crime* is

[1]Thomas Hobbes, (1968), *Leviathan* in C.B. Macpherson (Ed.). Baltimore: Pelican.
[2]See Kenneth J. Peak and Ronald W. Glensor. (1999). *Community policing and problem solving: Strategies and practices.* Upper Saddle River, NJ: Prentice Hall, p. 40.
[3]This finding demonstrates the power of explicit type investigations.

based on the perceptions of safety, perceptions of the frequency of crime in their neighborhood, feelings of vulnerability, and the general quality of life experienced.[4] Another perception is that violence in America works, a person with a gun has more authority than a person without a gun.

It is easy to be misled about crime and the role police play in controlling crime, especially violent crime. Watching television or reading academic materials often reinforces the notion that crime is routine in America, but only routine among poor inner-city youths. In fact, many compelling resources unintentionally imply violent crime happens only in poor urban communities.

For instance, in an excellent study as part of a long-range project on human development in Chicago, the "broken windows" perspective was evaluated along with its implications for crime control policy and practice.[5] It was proposed that crime stems from the same sources as disorder—structural characteristics of certain neighborhoods, most notably concentrated poverty.[6] Furthermore, there is *collective efficacy*, which was defined as cohesion among neighborhood residents combined with shared expectations for informal social control of public space, and it is therefore proposed as a major social process inhibiting both crime and disorder. Thus, disorder flows down the mean streets of America and consequently, the fear of crime is intensified. One implication from this finding is that poverty and crime are related variables, justifying aggressive enforcement in poor neighborhoods while validating affluent neighborhoods as crime-free communities.

Living in fear produces many by-products. Many of these by-products influence the way we live. When people live in fear of becoming victims, or are victims, sometimes by both criminals and police, they make different choices about the way they live. To understand this concept better, recall what you were thinking when you first heard about the terrorist attack on September 11, 2001 in New York City. Were you considering ways to defend yourself and the persons close to you should those attacks come closer to your home? Sometimes choices made by fearful people make little sense to observers. Other times, those choices are clear, assuming the person living in fear has the money—guns are bought, alarm systems are installed, private police agencies and protection are hired, and respect for police officers has changed. How will a police agency turn things around? Many agencies are moving in that direction and others are in the process.

Most criminal activity is mundane, characterized as single events producing few losses and fewer gains. These events tend to be fleeting, poorly planned, highly predictable, and cause few lasting consequences. Rarely do they come close

---

[4]See David L. Carter and Louis A. Radelet, (2001). *The police and the community.* Upper Saddle River, NJ: Prentice Hall. p. 230.

[5]To take a closer look at this study see Sampson and Raudenbush (2000). Although the writers go to great length to clarify their position as relating to a specific urban environment, an uniformed reader might sense that urbanized locations and crimes of violence are strongly related. The fact of the matter is urban areas vary as to the intensity of crime and rural areas can be equally as deadly (Bureau of Justice Statistics, 2001).

[6]Poverty also seems to be largely thought of as an inner city problem.

to producing the intended result of the offender.[7] Yet, officers make well over 14 million annual arrests and it is unclear how many police stops they make without issuing a citation or taking a violator into custody. Knowing the limitation of a police officer and his or her agency is another matter (sometimes an officer is unclear about those limits, too and other times he or she doesn't care any longer).[8] Recall the headlines when Timothy McVeigh was executed: "Justice Has Been Served." There might appear to be a suggestion that the government sees ultimate justice as violence or that of retribution better known as "just desserts." People engage in rigorous debate about capital punishment (a reactive activity) as opposed to discussions (and practice) about building self-esteem (preventive activity) among children in their formative years.

Many victims live in comfortable, middle-class neighborhoods. Some are victims of family violence, without resources, isolated from friends, family members, and/or agencies that can help. Protecting themselves could mean the loss of their home, children, or siblings; and maybe a job or school; and the few life comforts they do enjoy. They might be manipulated into becoming an accomplice in victimizing other family members or engage in behavior that violates their own self-respect or is counter to their ideals or spiritual views. Family violence is pervasive in our society and runs through apartment complexes, housing developments, and gated communities as well as urban ghettos.[9] The point is that most crime is a response to living conditions, relationship expectations, and/or pure selfishness.

Therefore, most issues pertaining to crime are not police business. It could be argued that police have less to do with controlling crime and more to do with shaping social order or stability.[10] On the other hand, a criminal is going to do what a criminal wants to do regardless of the threat of law enforcement apprehension, incarceration, and/or capital punishment sanctions.[11] And law-abiding people, when threatened, make reckless decisions about their lifestyle.[12]

The Fear of Crime and Homicide

In a study among 1,777 public housing residents in Charleston, South Carolina, participants responded favorably to questions on fear of crime, perceptions of crime, expectations of police service, and resident participation in crime prevention and

[7]In part, this is a perspective argued by Gottfredson and Hirschi (1990, p 37), and a position supported by the government statistics, BJS (2000).

[8]See Victor E. Kappeler (Ed.), (1999). *The police and society.* Prospect Heights, Illinois: Waveland Press. There are several articles written by observers of the police that lend themselves to a boarder perspective about this perspective. Also, Dennis J. Stevens, (1999a). Do college educated officers provide quality police service? *Law and Order.* December, 47(12), 37–41. And Stevens, (1999d). Stress and the American police officer. *Police Journal*, LXXII(3), 247–259.

[9]For more detail on the cycle of family violence see, Straus, M.A. (1994). *Beating the devil out of them.* New York: Lexington Books.

[10]For more detail, see Robert J. Sampson and Stephen W. Raudenbush. (2000). Disorder in urban neighborhoods. Does it lead to crime? http://www.ncjrs.org/ txtfiles1/nij/186049.txt

[11]See Dennis J. Stevens, (2002e; 1992a; 1992b).

[12]See Dennis J. Stevens, (1999j; 1998b)

education programs (Berhie & Hailu, 2000). About 30 percent (533)[13] of the participants were aware of community policing and believed it made a difference in crime
prevention, and about 45 percent (800) were reasonably optimistic about community policing in Charleston. They ranked important crime threats as child involvement in drugs, random shootings, crimes against children, and robbery. About 81
percent (1,440) reported that they felt safe during the day and 35 percent (622) said
they felt safe at night. There were many answers about what they had done to protect themselves, which included one-fourth (442) who reported that they stayed in
their homes at night, 17 percent (301) joined a neighborhood watch or installed new
locks, 11 percent (195) requested better lighting, 6 percent (106) carried mace. Also,
5 percent (88) obtained a gun. Almost 42 percent said that the courts were too
lenient in sentencing criminals and, therefore, those participants reported that they
had not reported crime due to a fear of retaliation. Approximately 64 percent said
police officers were responsive to crime, and 17 percent said police officers were
somewhat unresponsive.

One way to think about these findings is that traditional policing is not as
meaningful a deterrent to homicide as it might be to other crimes of violence. For
instance, 88 participants reported that they obtained a gun. One thought is that the
percentage of individuals who admitted obtaining a weapon is probably much
lower than the number who actually obtained a weapon. A compelling study
shows a strong relationship exists between race and homicide.[14] In the study, the
homicide rate in 63 of the largest cities in the United States was examined. It was
concluded from evidence that homicide was seen as an appropriate response in at-
risk environments even among law-abiding community members. In part, the evidence was based on the inequities of police protection in certain communities as
compared with other communities. When the police don't or can't do their job,
homicide rates are greater among certain populations as compared to other populations. If we require further evidence of this thought, think in terms of battered
women (of course, men and children are battered, too). When someone feels helpless and lives under constant fear from an attacker who cannot be stopped by the
courts, police, or social agencies, sometimes those individuals living in fear will, as
a last resort, commit murder to end the relationship (Stevens, 1999j).

Strategies for Reducing Homicide: Richmond, California

Traditional policing efforts viewed homicide as a crime relatively immune from
police influence.[15] While most crimes tend to be on the decline, violent crime, especially homicide as committed by youngsters, is not declining. This reality and the
movement toward community-policing efforts encouraged the Richmond Police
Department (RPD) to take a different course of action. They initiated a coordinated
effort with their communities and other city agencies, including the school system,

---

[13]Percents rounded.
[14]See Dennis J. Stevens (1998b).
[15]For more detail, see Bureau of Justice Assistance (1997). Strategies for reducing homicide: The comprehensive homicide initiative in Richmond, California. NCJ 168100.

designed to address homicide in 1995.[16] Of concern, their strategy represents an important departure from the traditional police definition of homicide as a unique offense limited to an after-the-fact investigation. The RPD defines homicide prevention as a critical police responsibility that can best be accomplished by identifying the paths that frequently lead to homicide and closing them through early intervention.

The initiative of the RPD is an acknowledgment that there are opportunities to prevent violent crimes, including homicide, through partnership with community institutions and the community itself. The RPD's plan emphasizes both a prevention focus and a strengthening of local law enforcement investigation—clearly a strategy that would save lives. The RPD's strategy grouped partnership activities supported by Bureau of Justice Assistance (BJA) funding into community based non-enforcement strategies and investigative and enforcement strategies.

Community Based Non-Enforcement Strategies

The Richmond Police Department identified the following non-enforcement strategies, which focus on youth and prevention:

- Collaborating with the community, the Richmond Public Works Department, and the Housing Authority in a crime reduction planning process emphasizing aesthetics and community pride.
- Using the Richmond Police Athletic League Computer Center to provide job skills training to Richmond youth and adults.
- Collaborating with the Richmond public schools to enlist officers in an adopt-an-elementary-school program and to develop a middle-school mentoring program involving Drug Abuse Resistance Education (DARE) officers and high-school students.
- Collaborating with the Contra Costa County Probation Department to develop a probation-officer-on-campus program for high schools.
- Collaborating with the juvenile justice system to develop a youth court program.
- Collaborating with the Battered Women's Alternatives (BWA) and the Rape Crisis Coalition to support programs and practices to reduce domestic violence.

Through partnerships, the RPD intervenes in the path of a potential violent offender and turn that person around before he or she actually commits a serious felony.

The Importance of Employing a Multifaceted Strategy

The RPD recognizes that although methods and motives of murderers often differed from those of other violent offenders, their criminal acts were not a breed apart from other nonfatal forms of crime and misconduct that often serve as pre-

[16]See Bureau of Justice Assistance, (1997). Strategies for reducing homicide: The comprehensive homicide initiative in Richmond, California. Washington, DC: U.S. Department of Justice. NCJ 168100.

cursors to homicide. The types of criminal behavior RPD believes were most likely to lead to homicide include the following:

- Domestic abuse, which accounts for the majority of violent crimes against women and children. Witnessing or suffering from domestic abuse often leads young people to believe that intimidation and brute force are acceptable means of resolving disputes.
- Trafficking in and possession of guns, the most common instruments of death in Richmond.
- Truancy, which short-circuits opportunities to learn and may expose kids to or further enmesh them in a delinquent subculture characterized by the avoidance of responsibility and disdain for legitimate achievement.
- Schoolyard thuggery and shakedowns, in which the lessons learned in abusive homes are applied to peers.
- Rape and other sexual violence, which define relations between the sexes in terms of exploitation and which often precipitate fatal violence.
- Drug abuse and involvement in drug traffic, which are associated with increases in Richmond's homicide rate.

Measuring the Impact of the Comprehensive Homicide Initiative in Richmond

The RPD established eleven measurable goals for their initiative in two broad categories. The first set of goals assesses the initiative's process in each program or plan of action by determining, for example, the number of persons contacted, the number of class hours, or the number of documents obtained or disseminated. The second set looks at outcomes for each activity, including the following:

1. Measuring the frequency of crime and violence.
2. Evaluating actual street conditions through onsite assessments of the presence, number, and nature of street users.
3. Measuring the presence, persistence, number, and nature of deleterious conditions and nuisances on streets and public places (for example, abandoned buildings and vehicles, graffiti, and broken glass).
4. Through the use of explicit tests in the community, identify the conditions that generate violent crime, and the efforts of police and other institutions to address homicide and other violent criminal acts.

Some of their strategies include an attempt to take guns away from violent environments by operating two closely related programs: gun buybacks and gun rewards.

The RPD pursued a police-operated gun buyback program in which citizens receive "no-questions-asked" cash payments for guns. Also, the agency initiated a program encouraging citizens to provide information anonymously about illegal guns. If this information results in an arrest and seizure of weapons, the citizens providing the information are eligible for a $100 reward. The program was inaugurated with assistance from the local media, which prominently covered the first citizens providing information. One citizen's call led police to several automatic weapons hidden by young people on the roof of a local school.

Another strategy pursued by the RPD is a model lease agreement in cooperation with the city attorney and the local housing authority, which facilitated code enforcement, renovation of buildings, temporary relocation of residents, removal of abandoned autos, and a variety of measures to address the "broken windows" syndrome of public housing and the crime-related behaviors associated with them. The model lease requires tenants to avoid involvement with drugs and crime on penalty of eviction and has been adapted for use in private rentals as well. The agreement allows police officers to seek restraining orders, based on convincing evidence, against residents involved in drug-related criminal activity. Violation of a restraining order results in eviction.

Preventing drug dealers and gang members from frequenting public housing developments and sensitive street and neighborhood locations is a priority for the RPD. Officers work directly with the city attorney to obtain restraining orders against individuals, but the agency may have overestimated its ability to obtain and use such orders. The police prefer to seek restraining orders on the basis of evidence, with or without conviction, that subjects are drug dealers or gang members. The city attorney, however, wants to require a documented history of crime problems, including arrests, before seeking a restraining order. In response, the RPD has established criteria for determining gang affiliation, and the courts recently upheld the constitutionality of both the restraining order process and the gang affiliation criteria.

In July 1996, the RPD distributed a citizen's guide to fighting drug trafficking and drug houses. The guide, "How to Eliminate Drug Dealing, Drug Sales, and Public Nuisances," is an extensive resource manual on neighborhood drug and crime prevention that gave community groups a resource to link their efforts to police strategies. The manual's topics include a discussion about the business/public nuisance of drugs, how to know if a drug house is active, whose responsibility it is to get rid of a drug house, and how to get rid of a drug house.

Additionally, the RPD uses their police athletic center to provide skills training, summer employment, and a youth academy for Richmond youth and adults. Many people think that athletics involves a gymnasium, sweat, and lots of noisy youth engaged in boxing or basketball under the guiding hand of volunteer police officers. The RPD transformed that traditional model by focusing services on preparing young people for meaningful employment and extending job training to Richmond's adult community. Also, in a small strip mall across the street from one middle school is an innovative computer training center used by at least 500 youths a month under the guidance of the police. The center, funded with both public and private money (including a major contribution from baseball player Willie McGee, whose roots are in Richmond), has fifty computers, an extensive software library, a network, a Web page, Internet access, and the tools necessary to teach computer diagnostics, service, and repair. The center also sponsors a mobile computer training center, which is a converted recreational vehicle donated by a local corporation.

Another goal of the RPD is to encourage collaboration between the department and the Richmond Public Schools. The RPD recognizes the critical role of education in preventing the involvement of youth in drug, gang, and gun activity that too often leads to violent crime, including homicide. There are two activities, among others, that represent a focus for the department's strategy concerning schools: enlisting officers in an adopt-an-elementary-school program and developing a middle school mentoring program involving DARE officers and high school students.

These officers meet regularly with teachers, conduct DARE programs, and develop reading and mentoring programs for middle schools. In addition, they conduct truancy roundups that return young people to the school system through a special program designed to deal with students who are frequently truant and at risk of dropping out of school. The truancy program is non-punitive with an emphasis on returning truants to school and involving parents. Continued violations can result in students being referred to the city's probation department for review and placement. The RPD believes that over the long term, truancy reduces the prospects that city youngsters will become involved in legitimate educational and employment opportunities and increases the likelihood that they will form criminal contacts and lifestyles. The key focus is identifying the path of potential violators, employing intervention strategies with the goal in mind of preventing a potential violator from committing a future crime of violence.

Conclusion: Richmond, California

In Richmond, this perspective has led to a multidisciplinary, multifaceted strategy that recognizes that homicide, and violence in general, must be addressed on fronts that encompass the needs of youth and adults in education, training, employment, and alternatives to drugs and guns. Perhaps most compelling in Richmond's experience is the natural extension of problem-oriented and community-policing approaches to the last bastion of traditional policing—the homicide unit.

Under the Comprehensive Homicide Initiative, homicide prevention and investigation are no longer isolated from the rest of policing and community crime problems. Richmond's initiative recognizes the critical role of the police-community relationship, both in solving current cases and in devising community strategies to reduce the likelihood of future homicides. Its early success shows that an effective strategy can be led by an effective police department, but not by the police working in isolation. The involvement of other agencies and an active community are key ingredients, without which the most inspired police approach will not succeed. In each phase of planning, implementation, and operation, surveys of citizen perceptions were conducted. For instance, when RPD was involved with schools, surveys were distributed to residents near the schools about street conditions and safety in and around participating schools.

These findings are congruent with a study that describes how community-oriented policing strategies were used to deal with criminal activity and quality-of-life issues in a large suburban apartment complex (Hill, 2000). A special

Uniformed Tactical Team was established to work on reducing crime in the neighborhood. The team met with residents, beat officers, resident managers, and a crime analyst to identify specific individuals and groups active in area criminal activities. Some residents had outstanding warrants, which police enforced. Charges of loitering were brought against nonresidents who were noted repeatedly and frequently in the area. The Team enforced anything that could legally force criminals off apartment property, including charges of illegally selling pit bull puppies. Flyers in English and Spanish—describing arrests made, explaining the anti-crime efforts, and encouraging citizen participation—were posted throughout the area. The public's trust and confidence in the police improved, and officers cooperated to make the community-policing effort a success.

Repeat Offender Programs

Repeat Offender Programs (ROP) and/or Targeted Offender Programs (TOP) represent special collaborative police and prosecutorial initiatives designed to selectively incapacitate career criminals using pre-arrest targeting and post-arrest case enhancement strategies.[17]

Studies support what police officers have suspected, that a relatively small number of offenders commit a disproportionate percentage of most of the crime in the United States (Gottfredson & Hirschi, 1990). Specifically, the most active 10 percent of offenders are responsible for over 50 percent of all reported crimes (Blumstein et al., 1986). This subpopulation of high-rate offenders is often referred to as *career criminals* (Chaiken & Chaiken, 1982; Tonry & Petersilia, 2000).

Traditional case-oriented strategies (i.e., case prioritization based on the perceived seriousness of the offense, the probability of arrest, and the likelihood of positive prosecutorial outcome) made it increasingly difficult for law enforcement agencies to respond to repeat offenders because those prosecutorial decisions, in general, were influenced by the seriousness of the immediate offense rather than by a defendant's prior record. Therefore, many law enforcement agencies collaborated with prosecutors in identifying, targeting, and selectively incapacitating the most active and dangerous repeat offenders.

Early Initiatives

Washington, DC ROP One of the best-known repeat offender programs, and, until 1990, the only ROP extensively researched (Martin & Sherman, 1986) was established in 1982 by the Metropolitan Police Department in the District of Columbia. The objective of the Washington, DC ROP unit was to increase the apprehension rate of targeted offenders based on informants, crime patterns, and other sources of police intelligence. However, according to Martin and Sherman (1986: 9):

---

[17]See Bureau of Justice Assistance, (1997). Strategies for reducing homicide: The comprehensive homicide initiative in Richmond, California. Washington, DC: U.S. Department of Justice. NCJ 168100.

Although officers were expected to select criminally active targets, ROP did not establish formal indicators of activity or any system for prioritizing among potential candidates. Selection was based on informal understandings about what makes a good target.

This lack of control in allowing ROP squads to largely develop their own criteria resulted in three types of ROP squads:

1. Hunters (focused on warrant service).
2. Trappers (specialized in surveillance, decoys, and other covert proactive operations).
3. Fishers (brought back whatever they found).

When initial attempts at direct surveillance proved too frustrating or too time consuming, the Washington, DC ROP unit shifted most of its attention to serving outstanding felony warrants. On the other hand, the activities of fishing squads widened the net. That is, they labeled individuals as a "repeat offender" despite enough evidence to support the label. As a consequence, prosecutors were deluged with cases that lacked sufficient evidence to gain a conviction. One result was that many individuals were released when the evidence appeared to be too trivial. Of course, the reverse held true as well. That is, prosecutors allowed many ROPs to slip through the net.

Phoenix Police Department   In 1991, the RAND corporation developed and implemented an explicit test concerning the impact of post-arrest enhancement strategies utilized by the Phoenix Police Department. The randomized field experiment lasted one year (1987 through 1988) ending with 480 cases (257 cases in the experimental group and 223 in the control group). Analysis of case dispositions revealed that, while there was no significant increase in conviction rates for the experimental cases (ROP), there were significant increases in the likelihood of commitment to prison and in the length of sentenced imposed.

What Was Learned   These early efforts suggested that ROP programs would be more efficient and effective if three problems were appropriately addressed:

1. Information problem.
2. Mobility problem.
3. Chain problem.

The information problem pertains to "turf" management and poor interdepartmental and intradepartmental communication and coordination, especially with the prosecutorial component of the justice system. Experienced offenders are often mobile. They travel from city to city, and state to state. Therefore, no single departmental unit (especially if geographically and administratively decentralized) could have complete information about an individual offender's activities. To identify, arrest, convict, and incapacitate serious repeat offenders, there must be police interdepartmental cooperation and collaboration. A feat easier said than done since many police departments restrict information to their jurisdiction for various reasons. Finally, in order for the criminal justice community (police, courts, and corrections) to function efficiently and effectively, they must cooperate and collaborate with each other. Again, due to shear numbers, resources, and various policy and regulations, the best way to characterize the criminal justice community is to say that it is fragmented and thus unlikely that agencies can or will collaborate with each other. If many agencies do collaborate, and a chronic offender tends to operate in a region of the country that is not part of the collaborative link, they could easily remain undetected. How likely would it be for a high profile offender to learn which jurisdictions and/or agencies were collaborating and which ones were not?

In an attempt to overcome some of the weaknesses and criticisms of earlier repeat-offender programs, the Police Executive Research Forum (PERF), in conjunction with the Bureau of Justice Assistance (BJA), designed a "model" repeat offender program that was responsive to these specific problems, yet general enough to allow adaptability at the local level by police, prosecutors, and correction officials. PERF researchers selected three jurisdictions (Kansas City, Missouri; Rochester, New York; and Eugene, Oregon) to implement and test the model. The resulting conceptual design focused on internal integration, horizontal integration, and vertical integration activities between criminal justice agencies. Spelman and Eck (1987) explain the model:

- **Internal integration:** Prior repeat offender programs were confined to special units, but information, expertise, and other resources were broadly distributed throughout the criminal justice agencies involved. Special units would be more effective if agency members outside the unit were involved in program development and operations.
- **Horizontal integration:** Most prior efforts were confined to a single police department or prosecutor's office, but repeat offenders often committed crimes in several jurisdictions. Thus, ROPs would be more effective if all municipal and county law enforcement agencies within the metropolitan area participated.
- **Vertical integration:** The prosecutor's participation in target selection decisions and in tactical operations would help to ensure that most, if not all, repeat offenders received special attention. Formal involvement of probation and/or parole officers could similarly ensure that repeaters were supervised more closely while they were on the street.

In all three cities, a successful ROP initiative was mounted with a modicum of specialization and centralization. As with other types of innovative police strategies, these ROPs have met with varying degrees of success. The key, as expected, was collaboration, within and between agencies, in each of these cases. Although these ROPs relied on different administrative structures and tactics, an integrated, system-wide approach was common among the agencies involved.

Repeat-Offender Programs in Texas

In 1992, a statewide survey of ROPs and TOPs operating in Texas in agencies with 150 or more sworn officers (N=30) found that only one-third or ten of them specialized in a career criminal unit. Most of those having career criminal units were from large metropolitan police departments, 13 percent from sheriffs departments, and 7 percent from small police departments.

San Antonio Police Department

Development   Steps were then taken by Captain Jimmy Kopeck of the San Antonio Police Department (SAPD), to implemented a repeat-offender program that would both meet the law enforcement needs of San Antonio and, at the same time, resemble the District of Columbia's ROP unit. Officers assigned to work for the ROP were selected based on their abilities and personal characteristics that would allow them to operate unobtrusively within all sections of the community.

Organization   Originally, the ROP unit was organizationally located in the Criminal Investigation Division and consisted of 47 sworn personnel. The ROP unit originally had two assistant district attorneys permanently assigned to it from the Career Offenders Unit of the San Antonio District Attorney's Office. These prosecutors were physically located in the same office space as the ROP unit in order to facilitate and enhance interagency collaboration.

In 1992, the ROP unit had only 24 patrol officers and was divided into two squads. It had no target committee, and no specially assigned prosecutors. The ROP unit lost the use of its special prosecutors over time due to changes in the personnel and goals of the District Attorney's Office. Cases filed by the ROP go through the same channels as all other divisions. Because of budgetary constraints, the patrol officers were reassigned back to patrol in 1994.

In 1998, the ROP unit did not use any formal criteria for selecting targeted offenders. The only criterion used by the ROP unit is that the offender(s) be involved in some type of property crime. The "target" does not have to be a "repeat" offender and the offense does not have to be a felony. Shoplifting, theft of any amount, and burglary all qualify for targeting and surveillance. Targets are selected by general consensus and agreement between the three sergeants. For example, there were targets wanted for theft of gas from a Shamrock Gas Station, shoplifting cigarettes from Kmart, and theft of two watches.

Surveillance is heavily used by the ROP but there is conflicting evidence as to its effectiveness and productivity. Because there is no crime analysis used to target certain offenders or certain geographical locations, SAPD's ROP personnel commented that targeting property offenders was difficult and more a function of being in the "right place at the right time," absent information from the use of paid confidential informants and snitches.

Observations The ROP has experienced severe program goal displacement. The unit functions as a property crimes task force. They do not use crime analysis or any pre-arrest criteria to identify highly active repeat felony offenders. For the most part, "career criminals" and/or "repeat offenders" are discovered after their arrest. This change in program emphasis is, in part, due to several external and internal factors such as personnel changes at the district attorney's office and personnel changes within the SAPD. Also, the decline of narcotics-related offenses due to multiple federal, state, and local narcotics task forces working in the area; the increase of crimes related to gangs, terrorism, work-place violence; and high-tech cyber crimes caused multiple narrow investigative units to be created (in part because federal monies were available for supporting such efforts). In light of these types of crimes (and criminals), the apprehension of "repeat offenders" (which for many was a highly speculative process to begin with) lost its momentum and elite status. Organizational decentralization of many police services also contributed to the ROP objectives.

Additionally, there were some internal factors that led to ROP's failure at the SAPD. The ROP unit tends to duplicate the efforts of several other investigative bureaus, resulting in inefficient use of resources and criticism. According to one member of the SAPD, many of the ROP unit's cases were the same cases as those handled by other divisions. There was also a failure of the ROP to develop a close working relationship with other investigative units resulting in criticisms of elitism, numerical prioritizing, and political expediency. Additionally, the ROP unit's paperwork made it appear as though the ROP officers did all the work, when in fact, it was another bureau detective (e.g., burglary) that identified the suspect and issued the warrant. The ROP assisted in the apprehension of the offender through surveillance. Making the ROP unit autonomous and separate from the rest of the department led in part to its downfall.

Then, too, there was a failure to adequately train or prepare officers for program implementation. According to one ROP supervisor, from 1985 to 1989 they had no clue how to target "repeat offenders," how to conduct moving surveillance, or how to operate elaborate undercover operations. They were just "muddling" through. Even though those originally selected to staff the ROP were seasoned police officers, they had little or no experience with the type of tasks necessary to properly implement the objectives of the ROP. After attending several training seminars in 1989 on covert operations and moving surveillance, the ROP became more successful and efficient. Unfortunately, by this time, old habits (like not using crime analysis) had become the norm. Lastly, the ROP unit relied on the media rather than solid program implementation and results. That is, they took media along on targeting, surveillance, warrant executions, and other apprehension operations. This media coverage gave the unit a high "proactive" crime-fighting profile. However, one result was that ROP became isolated from the other units, which in turn made it a potentially dangerous "political issue" for those wishing to modify or discontinue it.

Dallas Police Department

Development   The Dallas Police Department's (DPD) ROP was a departmental, self-initiated, "pre-arrest targeting" program that was implemented in August 1986. In October 1993, the ROP was discontinued and reorganized as a Public Integrity Investigations Unit.

Organization   Originally, the Dallas ROP was roughly half the size of the San Antonio ROP and was organizationally located under the Intelligence Division. The ROP unit consisted of 19 officers and operated under the "team concept" with four or five officers assigned to each sergeant. Dallas' ROP unit was operated independently of other divisional policing efforts. Currently, the tasks of identifying and targeting habitual offenders have been decentralized to individual patrol division "deployment" units. These deployment units primarily consist of plain-clothes officers who target "hot spots" within the geographical operational boundaries of the patrol division.

Targeting Criteria   Deployment units vary extensively in terms of enforcement and apprehension tactics, use of crime analysis, and use of target selection criteria. Some deployment units do not use any crime analysis, while others use it extensively. Although all of the deployment units loosely use the targeting criteria, they are, in reality, an offense-driven, reactive investigative unit. Actually, deployment unit efforts are administratively directed by individuals who utilize these units to focus on community problems and thus is offense-specific rather than offender-specific. That is, whenever there is a significant increase in the number of auto thefts, or residential burglaries, or robbery offenses, departmental administrators will ask the deployment unit to use surveillance and undercover or covert operations to target the emerging problem.

Additionally, these deployment units do not have access to specially appointed prosecutors, and are limited in their ability to increase or enhance post-arrest case incarceration sentences. Deployment officers are therefore required to hand-deliver each set of charges through the central intake office of the district attorney's office. The officer must brief the assistant district attorney on duty and the assistant district attorney will decide whether to accept the charges. If accepted, the officer then "walks the charges through" the system. Afterward, at the trial court stage, an assistant district attorney and judge are chosen at random. The police file is stamped "Targeted Offender" on the case jacket and the defendant is, theoretically, given more prosecutorial consideration. In reality however, according to deployment officers, many apprehended targets are given light sentences due, in part, to the complacency of many assistant district attorneys who do not agree philosophically, ethically, or operationally with the deployment goals and objectives.

Recommendations   Targeted offender programs, if implemented correctly, tend to be resource-intensive. A great deal of time is spent in selecting appropriate targets and apprehension surveillance. While producing better quality arrests that lead to a conviction, the quantity of arrests is lower. This becomes problematic for those supervisors and administrators that place an emphasis on arrest rates.

Crime analysis seems to be the first program element ignored or neglected. Over time, most repeat-offender programs begin to rely less on crime analysis and eventually develop very loose, if any, selection criteria.

If targeted offender programs are to be productive and successful, they must be linked to careful crime analysis and information driven by narrowly defined selection criteria. Failure to do so precipitates program degeneration until the ROP is nothing more than an offense-specific task force. Furthermore, absent the targeting of specific violent repeat offenders, the ROP unit tends to duplicate the efforts of several other investigative bureaus, resulting in inefficient use of resources.

Programs that are initiated on the basis of grants should be more forward looking as to how the program will be continued once grant monies are exhausted. Personnel changes within the police department and the District Attorney's Office usually seriously impact the program.

In order to avoid criticisms of being elitists, the ROP should actively seek to collaborate with other investigative units within the department. A good relationship with the prosecutor's office must be diligently maintained if the program is to accomplish its objectives.

Summary

The fear of violent crime was demonstrated through the results of a study reporting that some participants obtained a weapon to protect themselves. One implication of these findings is that traditional policing is not as meaningful a deterrent to homicide as it might be to other crimes of violence. One police agency initiated a coordinated effort with their communities, city agencies, and school systems to address homicide in an untypical method. The rationale was that homicide prevention should be seen as a critical police responsibility.

An agency can identify the paths that frequently lead to homicide and closing those paths through intervention include community, probation, and school collaboration, and job skill training. Measuring the impact of the program was a big part of its success. A repeat-offender program discussed early police initiatives and current strategies, some of which worked and some that didn't work. Finally, recommendations were given to aid individuals to better understand the challenges presented to police agencies as agencies continue to provide quality police service in order to control crime, reduce the fear of crime, and enhance the life experiences of their constituents.

Do You Know?

1. Describe what is meant by a fear of crime. What role do you think fear of crime plays in the daily life decisions of different groups of people?
2. Under what conditions would you purchase a weapon?
3. Describe the primary types of criminal behavior that the Richmond Police Department believed were the most likely to lead to homicide.
4. Describe a typical repeat offender program. In your opinion, what are its strengths and its weaknesses?
5. Describe the early initiatives of the repeat offender program in Washington, DC and Phoenix, Arizona. What was learned from those early efforts?
6. Describe the Dallas Police Department's pre-arrest targeting program and include its organization and targeting criteria. What recommendations were offered and how well do you think those recommendations will do in Dallas and in your city?
7. Describe the repeat-offender programs in San Antonio and Dallas. In what way(s) do they differ?
8. Identify some of the recommendations made by the Dallas Police Department.
9. In what way does Joseph Stalin's statement fit this chapter? "A single death is a tragedy, a million deaths is a statistic."

15

Police Function and Change

"Man does not live by words alone, despite the fact that sometimes he has to eat them."

Adlai Stevenson (1900–1965)

Key Topics

- Neighborhood safety issues, social stability, and the fear of crime.
- Function of police and changes in policing practices.

Introduction

Based on observations of numerous police strategies, public records, and results from an investigation consisting of 2,010 surveys and 76 interviews in eight jurisdictions across America, the question remains: Does police practice enhance neighborhood safety issues and provide social order and stability? The premise was that community-policing strategies gave rise to crime control, reductions in the fear of crime, and enhancements in quality of life. However, despite the professional intervention strategies employed by police, there is reason to believe that community members, especially culturally diverse members, are fearful of becoming victims of violent crime, and are fearful of, or lack confidence in police intervention. Accordingly, their lifestyle experiences were not enhanced as expected through community-policing strategies.

Beliefs about police intervention are compounded by ideas held by many individuals about municipal services. Specifically, there is a general belief that municipal services are under the influence of police commanders and that those services are rewards or penalties, depending on community member cooperation with police directives.

It should be acknowledged that most community members, whether they attend community police meetings or not, do not influence police decision-making processes of hiring, training, disciplinary, and promotional activities, and/or police practice. Practice, according to the participants, included deployment, use of force limits, service priorities, investigative activity, and neighborhood problem-solving remedies. The belief that they lack influence over police or municipal services causes an intensity of fear. It could be argued that the effect from their fear of crime impacts their lifestyle choices more than actual crime rates.

As you recall from an chapter 5, one way to explain the behavior of the participants in the investigation for this text, or for that matter community members across the country, is that most of them seek stable environments, relationships, and jobs. People like to think they are in control of their lives. If their behavior adds to community instability, it is easier to change their attitude than their behavior. People try to reduce tension or contradiction in their lives and in their communities in several ways, and it appears that most often they adopt a new attitude that justifies their conduct.

One example used in Chapter 5 was about Monica who believed her community to be unsafe.[1] Consequently, she bought a handgun despite her attitude that violence is inappropriate. Although Monica felt that individuals who lacked appro-

---

[1]This example was used in Chapter 5 to demonstrate how cognitive dissonance can work.

priate training with a firearm might fall victim to a criminal in her community, she continued to carry her handgun every day to and from work in her pocketbook. The inconsistency between her attitude and her behavior creates *dissonance*,[2] an unpleasant state of arousal. When people feel uncertain about their neighborhood (or anything else for that matter), they might attend community meetings, but they do not participate at a competent level. Rather, they tend to give lip service to others. They might attend the meeting just for something to do on Tuesday night. They might select a host of lifestyle behaviors that reflect their fears. If police power were accepted, compliance to laws and trust would be greater and individuals would accept the direction of police more often. But let's not blame only the police since there are two parts to the equation: the cops and everybody else.

Changing a Way of Life

Many societal attributes, including every community member residing in a neighborhood, can affect a community's stability or social order. For instance, the sensationalism of crime as reported by the media and the politicalization of crime to advance interest groups and power brokers are factors that significantly impact the fear of crime in a community. For instance, after September 11, 2001, how many times have we all seen the replay of the commercial jets flying into the World Trade Center?

Other aspects that can change a way of life among community members include individual and collective historical, economic, and health experiences, and cultural and religious beliefs. Sometimes a tragic event can change the mood of a nation in seconds. Technology, politics, and the weather (including the fullness of the moon) can alter social stability levels, too. Sporting events and municipal and state services such as water, zoning, and licensing, as well as availability and quality of health care also play major roles in public order.

Evidence in police records celebrating law enforcement practices and embracing the use of force and information gathered in this investigation support the compelling argument that police service largely maintains the interests of the dominant class. In America, that dominant class is linked to Western European ideas about safety, control, and social order.

Eurocentric

American police service can be characterized through its primary emphasis on methods of social control that include strict law enforcement and harsh punitive sanctions. But, all through the history of policing (or for that matter the history of humankind), control and stability depend on whose definition is used. The evidence suggests that Eurocentric perspectives define standards of social order in the United States.

[2]See Cognitive Dissonance as discussed in Chapter 5.

Today, many Americans find Eurocentric perspectives obsolete and inappropriate. Instead of regarding American police as providers of safety and leaders of democracy, many people experience something else. Many have found isolation, discrimination, and fear to be more commonplace than safety. A curious note in the jurisdictions investigated where a person of color held a top police position (i.e., Columbia, Columbus, Miami-Dade County, Sacramento) and other jurisdictions used as models such as Chicago, Washington, DC, Nashville, St. Petersburg, many residents reported they were neglected and discriminated by both police services and municipal services.

Function of the American Police

What is the function of the American police? Are they "crime fighters" and through "get tough policies" such as zero-tolerance strategies, which marshal a magic bullet, do they deliver a crime-free America? The evidence suggests that social order and stability are not as strongly linked to strict enforcement policies with constituents, many of whom work hard at remaining law-abiding and resent intrusions. Understandably, there is frustration on the part of most police officers who want to put the bad guy out of business. That should be everyone's goal. However, in a democratic society, the truth is that no matter what police techniques are used to keep the public safe, it can only be accomplished through Constitutional practices.

Function of the American Police

The primary function of the American police is to safeguard the Constitution of the United States and to exercise due process guarantees to all individuals whom they encounter.

Yes, crime must be reduced; but without resorting to crime-fighting strategies that violate the basic social fabric of freedom and the principles of a world-class nation. Most assuredly, the bad guys cannot do whatever they want. However, a police state can only enhance social disorder as historical accounts have demonstrated time and again in third-world nations and elsewhere. It was about 225 years ago that the United States went to war over governmental strategies resembling zero-tolerance remedies. The point is that desired results such as public order cannot sanction just any method get it. Think of it this way: you want a college degree. You receive an authentic-looking degree through the mail for one hundred bucks. You mount your college degree above your desk with pride hoping to astonish everybody. Are you proud of your new knowledge or are you celebrating ignorance? The end never justifies the means.[3] As Albert Einstein said, "We can't solve problems by using the same kind of thinking we used when we created them." We need a new way to think about police service otherwise we repeat the "same ole same ole."

[3]Karim Ismaili (2001) delivered a strong argument on this position at the 21st Academy of Criminal Justice Sciences conference at Washington, DC, March 2001.

Changes in Police Practice

The most obvious change in police practice must come through the concepts of community-policing strategies since those strategies emphasize an empowered constituents. This thought acknowledges that constituents must take responsibility for crime control, for reducing the fear of crime, and for enhancing lifestyle experiences of others. Therefore, community policing requires community participation, characterized by accountability and responsibility.

While most police agencies are managed by dedicated professionals, revisions to their organization and practice depends on embracing appropriate practices (with city government's help) that fit the needs of a specific agency located in a specific jurisdiction. Getting community members to accept change is another matter.[4] Thus, police must lead the way.

When changes in policing are discussed, there tends to be a conversation around principles of bureaucratic organizational features.[5] Advocates of this perspective want to enhance police bureaucracy and suggest that greater control of officers can be accomplished through more written rules and more evaluations of police practices. This is where some of the ideas about a division of labor through specialization, hierarchy, clear lines of authority, written rules and policies, come from. It's also where an officer talks about doing the job "by the book," which translates to complying with written agency rules.

The other school of thought attempts to "de-bureaucratize" police organizations. In either case, most police agencies, like most enterprises in the United States, operate with top-down authority. Furthermore, it is unlikely that a bureaucratic organization will disappear since the state bureaucracy monopolizes the justice community. As Max Weber pointed out some time ago, a bureaucratic organization is inevitable. Breaking a police agency out of its bureaucratic cage is no guarantee that the agency personnel will provide due process guarantees to the next person encountered. So, focusing on areas we know can change, might be the best way to look at the situation.

Why Change Police Practice

Traditional policing has served the United States well, but it's time to move on. Community policing is one way in which policing can advance the interests of the constituents they serve and reduce fear of crime in the process.

Police practice should change because as a public institution, police are no longer "crime fighters," and they no longer represent America's changing society or its culture. Frankly, in the twenty-first century, the function of the police must change or it will relegate itself to become primarily an inner-city enforcement unit disposing radicals who oppose the status-quo. One way of preventing police extinction as a worthy institution in a democratic society is to bring certainty to its constituents and respect to its contributions by aiding constituents through

---

[4]In Dennis J. Stevens, (2003). *Case Studies in Applied Community Policing,* there is a section that relates to this perspective.
[5]See Samuel Walker (1999). *The Police in America.* NY: McGraw Hill. pp. 362–364.

facilitative leadership that will educate community members and municipal personnel to make the right choices.

It makes good sense that if public funds support police practices, then public sentiment and reflection should help rule the day. Since American police are protectors of individual Constitutional mandates, policing as an institution must continue to rise to its challenge especially in this day of federal intervention in local and state business.

Federal responsibility for terrorist response through the U.S. Patriot Act temporarily sets aside basic due-process guarantees. And many questions arise from federal conduct. For instance, through the U.S. Patriot Act of 2001, the FBI was given new authority to investigate anyone.[6] Make a deposit at your local bank and if the clerk thinks you're suspicious or in violation of some state or federal law, the clerk can turn that information over to the FBI. Also, the FBI can ask a "secret court" for a warrant to monitor Internet activities of anyone suspected of terrorism. If that involves use of Internet connections at libraries or cybercafes, the FBI can collect all the e-mails and information on Internet sites visited, but to read that information they need to obtain another warrant.

During days of terrorist uncertainty, we might see that the FBI requires different authority, and if they cooperate with police agencies, that could make some sense. However, Baltimore's Police Commissioner Edward T. Norris told a panel of the House Committee on Government Reform that while the FBI has shared names, descriptions, and addresses of suspected terrorists, the agency has not provided photographs.[7] "While the FBI has done nothing to prevent us from doing this work on our own, they have not given us anything but a watch list to go," Norris said.[8] The head of the Philadelphia Police Department, Commissioner John F. Timoney, has also criticized the FBI for not being forthcoming with information. He said the information the FBI gave them was largely worthless.[9] Thus, it appears that the FBI is frustrating local agencies and utilizing techniques much like the secret police of foreign countries that you've read about. More than at any other time in American history, the American people need police intervention between individual rights and federal conduct.

How to Facilitate a Balance

Police should take charge without using lethal strategies. Police commanders need to become the professional leaders the public already thinks they are. Since the roots of crime are not necessarily police business, maybe police commanders should concentrate on restoring and maintaining public trust by becoming representatives of their constituents. While there is a prescribed process of resolving violator challenges including due process remedies, the philosophy of the twenty-first century for police service emphasizes that action be taken by police managers

[6]See Lance Gay, (2001, October 27–28). How anti-terrorism bill could affect you. *The Patriot Ledger*. p. 14.
[7]See Judy Holland, (2001, October 6–7). FBI frustrates police chiefs. *The Patriot Ledger*. p. 9.
[8]Ibid.
[9]Ibid.

as that of a facilitator, rather than that of a lethal enforcer as seen in traditional police organizations.[10]

Specifically, enhancing social order can result from developing and performing tasks produced through a facilitated decision-making processes involving community members and municipal personnel, who identify problems, arrange priorities, find solutions, act upon those solutions, and evaluate results—problem-solving strategies. Homicide and other violent crime prevention should become a critical police responsibility that can best be accomplished by identifying the paths that frequently lead to violent crime and closing those paths through early intervention through partnerships with community, probation, school collaboration, and job training.

As a community facilitator, a higher quality-of-life experience should result as opposed to an increase in frustration and discrimination of American residents. The products of frustration and discrimination are prolonged anger, isolation, and the acquisition of guns. And, as we already know, fearful people kill. The following sections discuss some practices that might help achieve stability, from the perspective of the 2086 participants in the study for this book.

Police Response to Quality Municipal Services

Since municipal services were as much a part of quality-of-life experiences among constituents polled as police services—and in some jurisdictions equal to and more important than police service—municipal services must be provided at quality levels equal to or exceeding quality police service. One unexpected finding was when municipal services were not provided at expected levels, failure of municipal service was seen as instigated by the police. Police agencies were generally seen as cure-alls and as an omnipotent agent of social change. Therefore, many civilians believed that police could alter zoning regulations, mend business license violations, and board up abandoned buildings. Some even thought that police could take a building owner into custody for an assumed building violation or a grocer for an overcharge.

Clearly, the implication is that lifestyles and the pursuit of happiness have more to do with personal comfort than an arrest. Another idea expressed by many participants is that they prefer their own cultural perspectives, sense of morality, and virtues in matters linked to public safety, supervision and education of their children, licensing of neighborhood businesses, and property outcomes. People dislike uncertainty, an imbalance in their lives, and in the lives of their children. One way to explain the understanding about police and their influence over municipal services is to say that a police officer tends to be viewed conceptually, as a "government bureaucrat."[11]

Additionally, the public can see and interact with an officer easier than other government or municipal personnel. Police leaders should help facilitate a bal-

---

[10]For more details, see Dubois and Hartnett (2001) and Stevens (2001c).

[11]See Carl B. Klockars (1999). The dirty Harry problem. In Victor E. Kappeler (Ed.) *The Police and Society*, (pp. 368–385). Prospect Heights, Illinois: Waveland Press.

ance for their constituents. Therefore, while police and municipal agencies are separate agencies, it is strongly recommended that police leadership should assume authority over all municipal services in order to provide social stability and efficiency.[12] Police commanders should become managers of public service as opposed to acting in a limited role of directing public safety. It is imperative that problem-solving sessions end in solving problems and in many cases, most of the problems that constituents have are with municipal service agencies. In their new role as chief of public service, one goal would be to provide municipal amenities (which include policing) through problem-solving resolutions, performance, and evaluations involving all municipal services in an effort to reduce the fear of crime and ultimately, crime itself.

Police Response to Meeting Avoiders

Meeting avoiders (residents who do not attend community meetings) report their most serious community problem as a fear or lack of trust of police and discrimination by police and the community they live in.[13] If the evidence supports the idea that few community meeting members actually influenced any police decision-making process, then it's equally likely that those individuals who never attend meetings are never heard. Consequently, services provided by both police and municipal agencies are of less quality to meeting avoiders than to those who attend meetings and are heard. The issues and problems of meeting avoiders may never come to the forefront of policing strategies or services since few crimes committed against them are ever reported. "The squeaky wheel gets the grease."

Although never polled for this investigation, there are other individuals who are meeting avoiders, for example those who are mentally or physically challenged. In what way does an autistic child or a blind adult get a change to influence police or city services he or she receives? Consider also the young, the elderly, the homeless, and those institutionalized (including those incarcerated). Who speaks for them? However, a safe bet is that if someone did, few would listen. Through professional management techniques, police leaders can reach those silent groups and ultimately help shape programs that heighten their participation. Because these individuals are not present in meetings, does not mean that quality police service should be unavailable to them. Agencies must find ways to enfranchise all groups.

Since newcomers tend to live in communities where others like them reside, community members and local businesses could also reach out to those individuals. Working through churches and schools could be profitable. Churches and schools could act as a buffer and the newcomer, for instance, would be more likely to accept their leadership role, helping the newcomer become part of the com-

---

[12]This thought might sound ridiculous at first glance, but recall when some individuals suggested county sheriff's office and city police should be merged. Certainly it won't work everywhere.

[13]See Dennis J. Stevens, (2003). *Case Studies in Applied Community Policing*. There were 76 individuals, many whom spoke a language other than English, interviewed primarily in Boston.

munity. Civilian police personnel could easily perform appropriate tasks required of community-policing representatives.

Police Response to Fear of Crime

Policymakers think that through more aggressive apprehension and arrest the fear of crime will be reduced in a community. A major incident must occur in order for law enforcement to respond. Victims must be produced before aggressive enforcement occurs. For instance, it took a catastrophic incident for federal law enforcement agencies to do their job of providing quality service at airports, overseeing food supplies, and deal with terrorists. The U.S. Patriot Act of 2001 represents enforcement activity as opposed to preventive activity. If federal law enforcement agencies were protecting American residents prior to September 11, 2001, would the World Trade Centers still be standing? Dealing with the fear of crime has little to do with enforcement activities. Reducing the fear of crime has to do with situations never happening or minimizing them. This type of policing is referred to as prevention.

The contradiction of police rhetoric versus police practice is well documented regardless of which law enforcement agency is under review. For instance, official rhetoric of most police agencies include the words "partnership" and "prevention," but most agencies largely interact with law violators as they previously had, and even when a few officers work on preventive issues such as DARE, they too still seek violators and make arrests.

One source of evidence comes from arrest data. Of approximately 14 million arrests, driving under the influence, drunkenness, and violations of liquor laws top the list, representing an estimated 21 percent of all arrests in 1999. Drug violations came in second. Officers busy themselves on alcohol- and drug-related violations, simple assaults, larceny/theft, and disorderly conduct, aside from traffic and patrol. What officers do, if we use arrest rates as the guide, is different from being engaged in a partnership with the community. The following three police agencies represent typical mission statements of most police agencies across the United States.

> **Boston, Massachusetts:** We dedicate ourselves to work in partnership with the community to fight crime, reduce fear, and improve the quality of life in our neighborhoods.
>
> **Midland, Texas:** We are committed to being responsive to our community in the delivery of quality service. Recognizing our responsibility to maintain order, while affording dignity and respect to every individual, our objective is to improve the quality of life through a community partnership, which promotes safe, secure neighborhoods. The values of the MPD evolve around people, leadership, service, and performance.
>
> **Alexandria, Virginia:** We maintain law and order, protect persons and property, apprehend persons suspected of crime, direct and control traffic, investigate traffic accidents, and enforce all state and city criminal laws. We are committed to community policing; a partnership of police officers and citizens working together to address crime and neighborhood quality-of-life issues.

If mission statements in many police agencies were similar, since their function and role are similar, it would appear that police practices might be different than indicated by their official statements or their official image. Consequently, the fear of crime is rarely addressed. Fear of crime can be accomplished by agencies keeping their word. Trust in a police agency is not as common an experience as it should be. Perhaps when agencies build trusting relationships with their constituents, fear of crime will be reduced. How do agencies build trust? Providing reliable information is one way.

Police Response to Communication

A perceived lack of information from police agencies to community members was considered a personal affront by many of the participants in the investigation. Many community members felt that police information was incomplete, inaccurate, or the agency never advised community members at meetings of all situations. As a result, some community members felt as though they were "dissed" (disrespected) by police, which in turn, compromised motivational levels of community members and their leaders. A typical case was found in Alexandria, Virginia. The following account, in part, appeared in the local newspaper:[14]

> The Afghan Restaurant has dodged a bullet with Alexandria City Council's decision to override city staff and Planning Commission recommendations to revoke the establishment's special-use permit. (A) party occurred on the night of May 5 and the following morning.... According to a memo from Alexandria Police Chief Charles E. Samarra to City Manager Philip G. Sunderland, a fight involved more than 100 restaurant patrons, one person was stabbed... (finally) was brought under control by 19 Alexandria police officers and 15 Arlington County police officers...

> "The saddest part is that no one would have even known about this if the restaurant had not come up for its Special Use Permit renewal," advised one neighborhood association president.[15] While the incident was described as severe, police left the incident off the crime report sent to local media and posted on the city's website. Amy Bertsch, Alexandria police spokesperson, characterized it as "a bar fight," adding that the incident did not meet the city's criteria of incidents meriting public reports. "The purpose of the crime report is to inform the public about crimes that affect the general public safety," she said. "The general public was not involved in the party and were therefore not endangered by it," she added.

> "This is our community," one neighborhood leader responded. "Where do the police get leaving us out of the loop."[16] When community members feel that police neglect to communicate adequately, trust between the police and the community is affected.

---

[14] *The Journal.* June 18, 2001. Restaurant can keep its special use permit, p. 1.
[15] Personal communication with principal investigator.
[16] Ibid.

Police Response to Community Advocacy

There is a suspicion that a number of participants have little knowledge about the justice system and/or public services in most of the jurisdictions investigated. How can people live a satisfying life if they know little or nothing about public services such as health care and education? Under those conditions, it is doubtful that an individual could make an informed decision if engaged in problem-solving strategies, when they know little of the system.[17]

There are four solutions to the question of how the police should respond to community advocacy: build relationships, organize communities, offer training, and address inequities.

- **Build Relationships.** This idea of building relationships is guided by looking at Chicago's ambitious program. For instance, researchers such as Jill DuBois and Susan M. Hartnett (2002) learned that community support must be won. That is, it cannot be assumed that community support is present just because a meeting date and time are selected. "Getting the community on board can be as difficult as engaging the rank and file," say DuBois and Hartnett (2002, p. 5). Many residents, especially those who may be poor or live in disenfranchised neighborhoods, have been disappointed in the past. For example, many of the Miami-Dade residents investigated for this text may cling to each other and their cultural perspectives for support instead of reaching out for municipal aid because, in part, city service formats changed frequently, they reported. It was difficult to keep up with the changes, and some participants felt those changes were intentionally made to keep services out of reach of disenfranchised community members. One suggestion is that public services must be accessible, community-friendly, and consistent in its presentation, including the agency forms that need to be completed to initiate services. Complicated forms that change often which lack phone numbers and other help-aids to complete can do more harm toward building relationships within a community than good.
- **Organize Communities.** Effective community involvement with police can depend on an organized community. Involving random people off the street is not effective.
- **Offer Training.** Training is critical for the community and all police personnel. For example, some Miami-Dade residents are as apprehensive and initially resistant to change as the police officers; therefore, they should not be expected to simply step into their new role without any guidance.

[17]One guiding thought relates to a 1,200 people poll completed June 20, 2001 suggesting that the economic boom of the 1990s helped the upper middle-class and wealthy, but had little impact on the outlook or financial condition of those who make less money. "The boom has passed these people by," said pollster Andrew Kohut, director of the Pew Research Center for the People & the Press. The number of people who think the country is divided between those who have enough and those who don't has grown steadily and as of June 21, 2001 is at 44%—up from 26% in 1988. Less than half say they are in good or excellent financial shape personally, a drop of 8% points from a year ago. For more information, see http://www.people-press.org

- **Address Inequities.** There is a real risk of inequitable outcomes. The best-off communities will take to community police strategies pretty well, but those who really need it may be last to come on board—if they come on at all. There are many reasons for these inequities; however, two primary thoughts stand out among them.
  1. Community members from poorer neighborhoods are not empowered at similar levels in the problem-solving process as are community members from affluent neighborhoods. One reason for this lack of shared power is that the police may have less confidence in decisions made by lower class individuals. The police may even be suspicious of input from poorer community members since there is evidence that a criminalization of poverty perspective exists among many justice professionals.
  2. Since community police strategies are often seen by lower-class community members as another way for police to gain access to a troubled neighborhood, it is believed that police engage in community police activities for the purpose of making more arrests in their community. In part, this perspective is supported by the idea that many justice professionals continually exploit lower-class members and lower-class crime more often than upper class members who commit upper-class crimes such as white collar crime and corporate crime. In both cases, white-collar crime and corporate crime's victims tend to be lower-class members.

Residents who basically support police efforts but struggle to get the attention of the police have also been disappointed too often by outbreaks of "nasty misconduct or corruption."[18] Those residents can never be certain that the latest smiles coming from police or municipal workers are sincere. They are being told, "This time it's for real!"

How can these inequalities be solved? Chief Charles Ramsey (2002, p. 38–39) has some helpful suggestions that might help restore inequalities.

"In preparing the community for community policing, police departments must be as thorough, as rigorous and as persistent as we have been in preparing our own members. That means applying to the community the same types of strategies we used internally: generating community understanding and buy-in; providing residents with the knowledge and skills they need to implement the concepts of community policing, making information available to residents through open, cooperative information technology projects; and encouraging community involvement in the new tools and tactics developed for community policing."

Equally important, the community must accept problem-solving responsibility. That is, community groups in concert with municipal services, provide permanent solutions—the ultimate goal of community efforts. The key to solving

---

[18]See DuBois and Hartnett (2002). Making the community side of community policing work. In D.J. Stevens. *Policing and community partnerships*, (pp. 1–17), Upper Saddle River, NJ: Prentice Hall.

community instability (and ensuring compliance) is efficient problem-solving strategies, and if the chief of police were also in charge of municipal services, the task of providing relevant public service could have a greater chance of being accomplished. Community members regardless of where they are located within the American social class structure have to see that they are empowered during the community decision making process. But, they have to know the limits of their powers before they pursue them. In fact, all individuals engaged in the decision making process must be trained, they must train other community members, and they all must be retrained during the process itself. Furthermore, the police agency has to demonstrate that it serves all individuals within its jurisdiction without regard for a constituent's social position, and all agency personnel must demonstrate that constitutional guarantees are practiced department-wide and jurisdiction-wide.

Police Response to Homeownership Issues

The police need to lead others through the homeownership issue since homeowners are largely more involved in the community and contribute at positive levels. One way to explain the benefits of homeownership might be to say that greater unity can be developed by individuals who own their homes than those who rent. Recall an earlier chapter where group dynamics were discussed.[19] There would be a greater "we" feeling or a belongingness among homeowners than among renters. Productive community groups are people who share many common characteristics and who believe that what they have in common is significant. Police agencies need to know that homeowners can be organized more easily and they tend to have a "collective consciousness" about community issues. This translates to a quality of cohesion or unity of a community group that can well determine behavioral outcome or at least offer some idea about social outcomes. Homeowners are productive since unity is often present.

There are many issues that require attention, including thoughts about middle-class America which is battling an economic squeeze that is challenging their very existence. And nowhere is this squeeze more obvious than in Boston, where housing values have increased by triple digits over the past five years (1997–2002). At least middle class America still has something to squeeze, but there are people in many cities with little or nothing; nevertheless, they too want a part of the American dream and work towards that goal. Some argue that economic rights are as essential to human dignity as are the political and civil freedoms guaranteed in the Bill of Rights.[20] Solving the low-income housing crisis and realizing the right to housing will not happen easily. However, some highlighted suggestions are as follows:[21]

[19]See Chapter 5: Thinking about Behavior, Consensus Theory, p. 88.
[20]See M.E. Stone, e. Werby, E. & D.H. Friedman, (2000). Report 2000: Meeting the needs of lower-income Massachusetts residents. The John W. McCormack Institute for Public Affairs, University of Massachusetts Boston. http://www.mccormack.umb.edu/
[21]See Stone, Werby, and Friedman, (2000). pp. 13–14.

- Expand nonprofit, public, and limited equity resident ownership and production of housing to ensure long-term affordability.
- Finance production and acquisition of non-speculative housing through direct public capital grants rather than debt.
- Require all private capital market participants to make below-market set-asides as a complement to capital grants for financing non-speculative housing and community development.
- Reform landlord-tenant law to facilitate tenant unionization and institutionalize collective bargaining rights, just cause for eviction, habitability standards and enforcement, dispute resolution, and resources for technical and organizing assistance.
- Establish employer accountability and financial responsibility for contributing to meeting the housing needs of their workers and communities.
- Enforce anti-discrimination laws fully and aggressively along with affirmative-action programs within communities of color and the larger society.
- Support community control and resident empowerment in the production and operation of housing.

There are many successful programs across the United States helping families get into homes. Some programs guide the arrangement with lenders whereby a family might save a specific dollar amount weekly and at the end of an agreed-upon period, those monies are used as a down payment. Other programs can be more in-depth. For instance, in Massachusetts the Community Land Trust of Cape Ann stands out. This one was conceived in the early 1990s. Total housing costs including mortgage, estimated taxes, and condo fees are less than the current high rental prices in Gloucester, MA and the homes are designed to stay affordable forever, through resale price restrictions defined in the ground lease. Eligible families must have lived or worked in one of the five Cape Ann communities for at least a year, earn less than 80 percent of the area median income, and qualify for a mortgage with one of the participating banks. Many units were sold to individuals with less than 50 percent of the area median income. New owners receive training in condominium management at monthly workshops during the first year. And the second year, the owner trustees take charge. The units are managed by the owners and the land trust has oversight responsibilities.

Police leadership should play a key role with housing issues since housing issues seem to be primary concerns of most of their constituents. The conditions under which people live have much to do with social stability.

Police Response to Traditional Police Practice

In most cases, leadership practices of police managers are typical of traditional policing practices as opposed to community-policing philosophy.[22] Due to the

---

[22]See Dennis J. Stevens, (2001). Community policing and managerial techniques: Total Quality Management Techniques. *The Police Journal*, 74(1), 26–41.

responses of the participants in the investigation for this book, it is plausible that many police middle managers, or at least their policies, direct behavior from an antiquated control, arrest, and command hierarchy with top-down dictates about deployment, tactical and use-of-force limits, and constituent conduct. In a sense, middle manager characteristics of traditional policing are strongly supported throughout the reports of the participants. A brief review of the media shows that police officers have high burnout rate, due in part to a lack of coping with family problems, occupational stress, little status, low public trust, and are more likely to be involved in a civil liability suit than any other occupation.[23] One explanation is that officers often interact with violators and people who generally have a different regard about social order and compliance than most law-abiding individuals. Moving away from traditional policing would cut into the burnout rate among officers.

Police Response to Political Interference

There is a general feeling that police officers, especially police managers, make all the decisions about police practice. Sometimes, establishing police policy is beyond the prerogative of a police agency or its managers. Officers, at every rank, cannot follow through with community problem-solving decisions if policy, regulations, and employment expectations dictate otherwise.[24] Community-policing models are different in different jurisdictions and even within those jurisdictions.[25]

Aside from expertise and history of police personnel, many factors shape police practice. For instance, power brokers and/or city officials have a great deal of input concerning the well being of an agency, including the continued employment of any officer (including a chief) who might oppose a political mandate.[26] Drawing on survey results from Midland, Texas (one of the jurisdictions surveyed for this text), participants reported their most serious community problem was a fear or lack of trust of police. However, those survey-takers gave police officers high marks for professional behavior. So why would residents be fearful of or have a lack of confidence in police when they have high regards for police personnel and their agency? One answer might relate to an implication that emerged from another investigation:

> Events that led to a less efficient community policing initiative were centered in the priorities of some or several city officials. ...some departments (Camden, NJ

[23]See Carter & Radelet, 1999; and Stevens, 2000b, 1999d, 1999e.

[24]Sometimes, it is hard to believe that the Political Era discussed in Chapter 1 is actually over since city hall's influence over police policy seems widespread. This thought includes legal rulings which seems to place more authority in the hands of the courts than in the hands of police managers concerning policy.

[25]See Dennis J. Stevens (2001a). *Case Studies in Community Policing*. NJ: Prentice Hall. pp. 1–16. And Dennis J. Stevens (2001c). Community policing and managerial techniques: Total Quality Management Techniques. *The Police Journal*, 74(1), 26–41. Also, Carter and Radelet (1999).

[26]Ibid.

and Fayetteville, NC) experienced continual involvement on the part of city officials in police matters whose conduct demonstrated a lack of concern for the welfare of the department (which might well be an appropriate position for officials assuming their priorities are their constituents). However, alienation flowed from the relationship between city hall and the police department because of those political priorities (or at least that's the perception of many commanders). Then, too, some of those officials and inexperienced police leaders supported programs which were standardized items pulled from a shelf much like prepackaged goods in a store, rather than tailored to the specific audience or specific problem.[27]

Midland might be suffering from a similar experience as Camden and Fayetteville. City counsel of those jurisdictions dictated police policy and interfered with police operations so much that those agencies failed to maintain order and failed the officers and the people, too. It was evident that professional managers and commanders were not in control of those police agencies (although they tried), but political agendas controlled those departments. Months after the above investigation was published, the state of New Jersey took control of Camden's municipal structure, including the police agency. In Fayetteville, many of the top police executives, including their chief, were squeezed from their jobs. Having a professional complement of sworn officers including top commanders, has less to do with crime control, fear of crime levels, and quality-of-life experiences than expected, if political agendas dictate policy.

The Camden police department remains a paramilitary operation with the politicians making police policy and the police dictating those policies of arrest, calls, and stops as a method of measuring its success.

Police Response to Managerial Practice

Police managerial practices must change too. Legally and morally, police services provide two distinct strategies: prevention through problem-solving partnerships and arrest and investigation through Constitutional mandates. A balance must be found between these two strategies because facilitating public order and reducing the fear of crime have little to do with controlling traffic, responding to emergency calls, and building a legitimate case that will shape legal outcomes against violators. Feeling safe and being safe require a different set of practices.

Just as police agencies are experiencing philosophical changes about police service and relationships with the community, the process in which police executives work must also change.[28] One of the better managerial strategies is Total Quality Management (TQM). There are four reasons police management should adapt Total Quality Management as a managerial style:

[27]See Dennis J. Stevens (2001a). *Case studies in community policing.* p. 259.
[28]See Dennis J. Stevens, (2001c). Community policing and managerial techniques: Total Quality Management Techniques. *The Police Journal,* 74(1), 26–41. Also, Carter and Radelet (1999).

1. Police critics suggest the authority of police managers at all levels are affected by a host of regulations and obstructions advanced by politicians, community leaders, and organizational leaders in both public and private sectors.
2. The public has a litigious nature and bringing civil suits against police departments and police management at all levels in record numbers often influences day-to-day, serve-and-protect decisions.
3. Community-policing strategies are at the core of future police services.
4. Community-policing strategies and TQM have similar ideals that promote each other.

Since all members within TQM are goal-directed and participate in goal attainment as opposed to fulfilling personal goals, it would appear to be a managerial tool that complements community-policing initiatives. It is thought that its adoption, or another form of it, by police agencies can help agencies achieve more professionalism than other strategies

Summary

American police are to be applauded for the job they have accomplished in light of the barriers they have confronted. Without their genuine support, consider the alternatives. However, since police have a moral and a legal imperative to protect Constitutional rights, an urgent recommendation is that police agencies accept the leadership role of their constituents—all their constituents—and facilitate social order through empowered partnerships that rely on problem-solving techniques in order to efficiently deliver quality municipal services. The suggestion is that municipal services must also initiate a philosophy of empowerment, facilitative leadership, partnerships, proactive solutions, and an evaluation process in order to serve their constituents in concert with and under the guidance of police leadership. The challenge is not with the American public or even those born elsewhere, but with skills and achievements required of professional leaders. Will police leaders accept their real challenge?

How can you enhance the growth of the police, a community, or an individual, if truth is ignored? Myths must be separated from reality about quality-of-life experiences and the link between policing and justice. The fact is that there are policymakers, organizations, and individuals who reject the realities of life experiences and crime control as they relate to the history of every known civilization. That is, a society can either honestly confront the realities of myths about quality-of-life issues and crime control or face decline. The function of the police must be a means to justice and to the sanctity of individual liberty.

Do You Know?

1. What was the primary finding produced from observations of numerous police strategies, public records, and results from an investigation of 2,010 surveys and 76 interviews?
2. What do municipal services have to do with neighborhood stability?
3. Describe dissonance and its relevance to the fear of crime.
4. Identify some of the societal attributes that affect neighborhood stability. In what way might the media impact the fear of crime? Do you have a current example you might share?
5. Characterize Eurocentrism and explain its primary role relative to policing. In what way do you agree or disagree with the author about this issue?
6. Identify the ultimate function of the police. In your opinion, in what way does this function support or not support traditional reactive practices demonstrated by some police personnel.
7. The author suggested that change for community members might be a greater challenge than for the police. In what way do you agree or disagree with the author's perspective?
8. Identify four reasons why American police should change their style of policing.
9. Identify the primary recommendation made in police response to quality municipal services. In what way do you agree or disagree with the author?
10. Identify the primary problem mentioned in police response to meeting avoiders. In what way do you agree or disagree with the author?
11. Can you explain why reducing the fear of crime is an important step for social stability?
12. Identify the four factors that could address the question of how the police should respond to community advocacy. How might a police agency accomplish two of the four?
13. Explain why homeownership impacts social stability.
14. Describe how political interference from outside a police department can hamper quality police service. In what way do you feel political interference can be advantageous for a department and/or its constituents?
15. What elements does TQM have that would benefit community-police strategies?

Websites

Sites Relating to Community Policing

Bureau of Justice Statistics
http://www.ojp.usdoj.gov/bjs.welcome.html

Statistics about crimes and victims, criminal victimization, characteristics of crime, characteristics of victims, drugs and crime, homicide trends, criminal offenders, firearms and crime, crime and justice data, FBI Uniform Crime Reports, juvenile justice statistics, international statistics, law enforcement: federal, state, and local, prosecution, courts and sentencing, pretrial release and detention, criminal case processing, criminal sentencing, corrections including capital punishment, jails, prisons, probation and parole, expenditure and employment.

Community Policing Consortium (CPC)
http://www.communitypolicing.org

The CPC is a partnership of five of the leading police organizations in the United States:

1. International Association of Chiefs of Police (IACP)
2. National Organization of Black Law Enforcement Executives (NOBLE)
3. National Sheriffs' Association (NSA)
4. Police Executive Research Forum (PERF)
5. Police Foundation

These five organizations play a principal role in the development of community-police research, training, and technical assistance, and each is firmly committed to the advancement of this policing philosophy. At this site you can research publications, a chat room, training information, bulletins, discussions, and material related to community police initiatives.

Community-Police Pages
http://web.indstate.edu/crim/index.html
http://msnhomepages.talkcity.com/LibraryLawn/devere_woods

Dedicated to continuing the work of Robert C. Trojanowicz, these sites publish pages to stimulate research and decision on policing issues. There are papers on community policing, an extensive bibliography, and a forum for comments.

U.S. Department of Justice
http://www.usdoj.gov

A great place to start: statistics, links, and research articles on all phases of the criminal justice community.

Federal Bureau of Investigation
http://www.fbi.gov

Contains links, crime statistics, job opportunities, most-wanted criminals, and major investigations.

Police Executive Research Forum (PERF)

http://www.policeforum.org

> The PERF is a national membership organization of progressive police executives from the largest city, county, and state law enforcement agencies. PERF is dedicated to improving policing and advancing professionalism through research and involvement in public policy debate. Incorporated in 1977, PERF's primary sources of operating revenues are government grants and contracts, and partnerships with private foundations and other organizations. On this site you will find research, resources, bulletin boards, and more.

National Criminal Justice Reference Service

http://www.ncjrs.org

> Information, statistics, links, and publications on corrections, courts, and police are available online at this site.

United States Census

http://www.census.gov

> Current statistics about populations in the United States such as numbers, age, race, education, crime rates, and projections.

Justice Information Center

http://www.ncjrs.org

> A service of the National Criminal Justice Reference Service Center. It is a search engine for government resources. Its search includes corrections, courts, crime prevention, criminal justice statistics, drugs and crime, international, juvenile justice, law enforcement, research and evaluation, victims, current highlights, and abstracts database. The National Criminal Justice Reference Service Abstracts Database contains summaries of more than 150,000 criminal justice publications, including federal, state, and local government reports, books, research reports, journal articles, and unpublished research.

The White House Office of National Drug Control Policy's Drug Policy Information Clearinghouse

http://www.whitehousedrugpolicy.gov

> A summary of correctional system statistics, research, and drug treatment information, as well as information regarding ongoing projects addressing drug abuse treatment in the criminal justice system.

Sites Relating to Family and Domestic Violence

Abuse Free—A Mail List for Recovering Spouse Abusers
http://blainn.cc/abuse-free/

American Bar Association Commission on Domestic Violence
http://www.abanet.org/domviol/home.html

American College of Obstetricians and Gynecologists
http://www.acog.org

American Institute on Domestic Violence, Inc.
http://www.aidv-usa.com

Battered Women and Their Children
http://cwolf.uaa.alaska.edu/~afrhm1/index.html

Call to Protect
http://www.cels.com/sets/june16.html

Communities Against Violence Network (CAVNET)
http://www.asksam.com/cavnet

Family Violence Prevention Fund
http://www.fvpf.org

National Clearinghouse on Marital and Date Rape
http://members.aol.com/ncmdr/index.html

National Coalition for Domestic Abuse Awareness
http://www.domesticabuseawareness.org

National Domestic Violence Hotline
http://www.usdoj.gov/vawo/newhotline.htm

National Domestic Violence Organizations
http://www.usdoj.gov/vawo/national.htm

National Latino Alliance for the Elimination of Domestic Violence
http://www.dvalianza.com

Victim Services Domestic Violence Shelter Tour
http://www.dvsheltertour.org/

Sites Relating to Rape

Center for Sex Offender Management
http://www.csom.org

Communities Against Violence Network (CAVNET)
http://www.asksam.com/cavnet

Men's Rape Prevention Project
http://www.mencanstoprape.org

Men Stopping Rape
http://tps.stdorg.wisc.edu/MGLRC/groups/MenStoppingRape.html

Rape, Abuse and Incest National Network
http://www.rainn.org

Rape Response & Crime Victim Center, Inc.
http://www.easternidaho.com/victims

Sexual Assault Information Page
http://www.cs.utk.edu/~bartley/saInfoPage.html

Voices in Action
http://www.voices-action.org

About the Author

Dr. Dennis J. Stevens holds a PhD from Loyola University of Chicago (1991) and is an Associate Professor of Criminal Justice at The University of Massachusetts Boston. In addition to teaching traditional and nontraditional students, he has taught and counseled sworn officers at police academies and police stations such as the North Carolina Justice Academy. He has conducted many investigations influencing policy for several state legislative bodies including North Carolina, South Carolina, New York, and Florida, on police corruption, police stress, prison gangs, prison drug trafficking, prison violence, and classification profiles; and at the request of the Provincial government on Canada he investigated their prison educational system and made recommendations on how to educate their educable prison populations with an eye on recidivism. He has written manuals for correctional systems and public and private law enforcement agencies such as the use of deadly force for Wachenhut International and the US Department of Energy.

Dr. Stevens has also taught and led group encounters among felons at maximum custody penitentiaries such as Attica in New York, Eastern and Women's Institute in North Carolina, Stateville and Joliet near Chicago, and CCI in Columbia, South Carolina. Most recently, he instructs male and female felons at high custody prisons in Massachusetts and has conducted extensive profile assessments among sexual offenders such as child molesters.

He has facilitated group encounters for a national nonprofit organization rendering assistance to parents in conflict with children. He has over seventy articles in national and international press on criminology, corrections, and policing. His books include *Perspective: Corrections* (Coursewise, 1997, editor), *Inside the Mind of the Serial Rapist* (Austin-Winfield, 1998), *Case Studies in Community Policing* (Prentice Hall, 2001), *Policing and Community Partnerships* (Prentice Hall, 2002), and *Case Studies in Applied Community Policing* (Allyn and Bacon, 2003).

Currently he is writing a text on corrections from a similar applied perspective as this work. Dr. Stevens would appreciate your comments and suggestions for the next edition of this book. He can be reached at dennis.stevens@umb.edu or dennis.stevens@att.net.

Bibliography

Albrecht, J.F. (2001). The police state in New York City: The impact of the zero tolerance initiative on racism, police brutality and corruption in the NYPD. Paper presented at the annual conference of the Academy of Criminal Justice Sciences, March, Washington DC.

Albritton, J.S. (1999). Simply inflated promises. In James Sewell and Steven Eggers (Eds.) *Controversial Issues*, (pp. 215–223). Needham Heights, MA: Allyn and Bacon.

Alpert, G., & Moore, M. (1997). *Critical issues in policing*. Prospect Heights, IL: Waveland Press.

APBnews.com (2000, December 20). McCaffrey looks back on his years as drug czar: Says money for education programs was well-spent. www.apbnews.com/newscenter/breakingnews/2000/12/22/mccaffrey1222_01.html

APBnews.com (1999, November 5). 34 nations to coordinate drug war: Promise to forge more cooperative effort. www.apbnews.com/newscenter/breakingnews/1999/11/05/drugs1105_01.html

Asante, M.K. (1988). *Afrocentricity*. Trenton, NJ: Africa World Press.

Ashley, K.E. (2001, November/December). School district, police divvy up chores to help cope with violence. *Community Policing Exchange*, VII(33), 7.

Babcock, L. (1996). The evolution of community policing in Newport News, VA. In Police Executive Research Forum. (pp. 37–46). Themes and variations in community policing: Case studies in community policing. Washington DC: Police Executive Research Forum.

Bash, C., Amato, M., & Sacks, M. (2000, January). Chelsea, Massachusetts: A city helps its diverse population get along. Practitioner Perspectives Bulletin. BJS. www.ncjrs.org/txtfiles1/bja/179866.tB

Bayley, D.H. (1991). Community policing: A report from the devil's advocate. In Jack R. Greene and Stephen D. Mastrofski (Eds.). *Community policing: Rhetoric or reality*, (pp. 126–237). NY: Praeger Publications.

Becker, H. (1993). *Outsiders: Studies in the Sociology of deviance*. NY: Free Press.

Beckett, K., & Sasson, T. (2000). *The politics of injustice: Crime and punishment in America*. Thousand Oaks, CA: Pine Forge Press.

Bender, P. (1994, June 12). Rand Study: Drug treatment more effective than enforcement. *Gannet News Service*, pp. A1, A2. www.elibrary.com

Berger, P.L. (1963). *Invitation to sociology: A humanistic perspective*. Garden City, NJ: Anchor Books.

Berhie, G., & Hailu, A. (2000). Study of knowledge and attitudes of public housing residents: Toward community policing in the City of Charleston, South Carolina. NIJ Research Review. NCJ 182434. www.ncjrs.org/rr/vol1_3/27.html

Berry, O. (1996). Community policing in Philadelphia. In Police Executive Research Forum. (pp. 47–56). *Themes and variations in community policing: Case studies in community policing*. Washington DC: Police Executive Research Forum.

Bittner, E. (1974). A theory of the police. In H. Jacob (Ed.), *Potential for reform of criminal justice*. (p. 17–44). Beverly Hills: Sage.

Blakely, C.R., & Bumphus, V.W. (2002). American criminal justice philosophy: What's old – what's new? In Wilson R. Palacios, Paul F. Cromwell, and Roger G. Dunham, (pp. 16–24), *Crime & justice in America*. Upper Saddle River, NJ: Prentice Hall.

Blumstein, A., Cohen, J., Roth, J., & Uisher, E. (Eds.) (1986). *Criminal careers and career criminals*. Washington, DC: National Academy Press.

BOTEC Analysis Corporation CCP Survey, 1998.

Bowen, L., & Green, C. (2001, Winter). Latino workers may feel impact of new workforce development act. *The Gaston Institute Report*. The Mauricio Gaston Institute for Latino Community Development and Public Policy,. p. 1.

Bridges, W. (1991). *Managing transitions: Making the most of changes*. Reading, MA: Addison-Wesley Publishing Company.

Brodeur, J.P. (1998). *How to recognize good policing: Problems and issues*. Thousand Oaks, CA: Sage.

Bucher, R.D. (2000). *Diversity consciousness: Opening our minds to people, cultures, and opportunities*. Upper Saddle River, NJ: Prentice Hall.

Buckeye State Poll, (1998). Columbus: The Ohio State University, College of Social and Behavioral Science, Survey Research Unit.

Bureau of Justice Assistance, (1997, December). *Strategies for reducing homicide: The comprehensive homicide initiative in Richmond, California*. Washington, DC: U.S. Department of Justice. NCJ 168100.

Bureau of Justice Assistance. (1994). www.ojp.usdoj.gov/BJA/

Bureau of Justice Statistics. (2000). *Sourcebook of Criminal Statistics 1999*. www.ojp.usdoj.gov/bjs/

Bureau of Justice Statistics. (2001). *Contacts between police and the public*. Washington, DC: US Department of Justice. NCJ 184957.www.ojp.usdoj.gov/bjs/

Butler, M. (1996). Community policing in Las Vegas: Back to the basics in a high stakes town. In Police Executive Research Forum. (pp. 25–36). *Themes and variations in community policing: Case studies in community policing*. Washington, DC: Police Executive Research Forum.

Buzawa, E., Hotaling, G.T., Klein, A., & Byrne J. (2000). Response to domestic violence in a pro-active court setting—Final Report. NIJ Research Review. NCJ 181427. www.ncjrs.org/rr/vol1_3/18.html

Cardarelli, A.P., McDevitt, J., & Baum, K. (1998). The rhetoric and reality of community policing in small and medium sized cities and towns. *Policing: An International Journal of Police Strategies & Management*, 21(3), 397–415.

Carter, D.L., & Radelet, L.A. (1999). *The police and the community*. 6th edition. Upper Saddle River, NJ: Prentice Hall.

Chaiken, J.M., & Chaiken, M.R. (1982). *Varieties of Criminal Behavior*. National Institute of Justice, U.S. Department of Justice. LA: Rand.

Chambliss, W. (1975). Toward a political economy of crime. *Theory and Society*, 2, 152–153.

Champion, D.J. (1993). *Research methods for criminal justice and criminology*. Upper Saddle River, NJ: Prentice Hall.

Cheurprakobkit, S. (2000). Police citizen contact and police performance: Attitudinal differences between Hispanics and non-Hispanics. *Journal of Criminal Justice, 28*, 325–336.

Cheurprakobkit, S., & Bartsch, R.A. (1999). Police work and the police profession: Assessing attitudes of city officials, Spanish speaking Hispanics and their English speaking counterparts. *Journal of Criminal Justice, 27*(2), 87–100.

Chicago Community Policing Evaluation Consortium. (2000, November). Chicago policing in Chicago, year seven: An interim report. Evanston, Illinois: Institute for Public Police, Northwestern University.

City of Columbia Police Department Multi-Year Plan, FY 1998/ 1999 through FY 2000/2001.

Community policing & domestic violence. (2000). policing.com/ articl/cpanddv.html

Cooper, J. (1980). *The police and the ghetto*. Port Washington, NY: National University Publication, Kennikat Press.

Cordner, G., & Jones, M. (1995). The effects of supplementary foot patrol on fear of crime and attitudes toward the police. In P. Kratcoski and D. Dukes (Eds.). *Issues in Community Policing* (pp. 189–198). Highland Heights, KY: Anderson Publishing.

Coventry, G., & Johnson, K. (2001, January). Building relationships between police and the Vietnamese community in Roanoke, Virginia. Bureau of Justice Assistance Bulletin. www.ncjrs.org/txtfiles1/bja/185778.txt

Cox, T.C., & White, M.F. (1988). Traffic citations and student attitudes toward the police: An examination of selected interaction dynamics. *Journal of Police Sciences and Administration*, 16, 105–121.

"Crime rate is dropping." (1999, August 19). But public's fear increases. Why? *The Charlotte Observer*. Charlotte, NC. newslibrary.krmediastream.com/cgi-bin/newslib

Currie, E. (1999). Reflections on crime and criminology at the millenium. *Western Criminology Review*, 1–15. wcr.sonoma.edu/ v2n1/currie.html

Dahrendorf, R. (1959). *Class and class conflict in industrial society*. Stanford, CA: Stanford University Press.

Dantzker, M.L. (2000). *Understanding today's police*. Upper Saddle River, NJ: Prentice Hall.

De Courtivron, I. (2000, July 7). Educating the global student, whose identity is always a matter of choice. Chronicle of Higher Education. chronicle.com/search97cgi/s97_cgi

De Leon-Granados, W. (1999). *Travels through crime and place*. Boston: Northeastern Press.

Diagnostic and Statistical Manual of Mental Disorders, (1994). (DSM IV). Fourth Edition Washington, DC: American Psychiatric Association.

Dicker, T.J. (1998). Tension on the thin blue line: Police officer resistance to community oriented policing. *American Journal of Criminal Justice, 23*(1), 59–82.

DuBois, J., & Hartnett, S.M. (2002). Making the community side of community policing work: What needs to be done. In Dennis J. Stevens (Ed.) *Policing and Community Policing*. Upper Saddle River, NJ: Prentice Hall.

Durkheim, E. (1933; 1984). *Durkheim: The division of labor in society*. Translated by W.D. Hall. NY: The Free Press.

Edward, N. (1994). The dynamics of the drug market. *Challenge*, 37, 13. www.elibrary.com

Egan, T. (1999, February 28). War on crack retreats. *The New York Times*. NY.

Erickson, R.V., & Haggerty, K.D. (1997). *Policing the risk society*. Toronto: University of Toronto Press.

Erikson, K.T. (1966). *Wayward Puritans: A study in the sociology of deviance*. NY: John Wiley & Sons.

Elshtain Bethke, J. (2000, April 21). Crisis in democratic authority. *Chronicle of Higher Education*. A14.

Excellence in problem-oriented policing. (2000). The 1999 Herman Goldstein Award Winners. US Department of Justice. Office of Justice Problems. www.ojp.usdoj.gov/nij

Faragher, J.M., Buhle, M.J., Czitrom, D., & Armitage, S.H. (2000). *Out of many. A history of the American people*. 3ʳᵈ edition. Upper Saddle River, NJ: Prentice Hall.

Finney, W.K. (2000, January/February). Providing proper police service in the 21st century. *Community Policing Exchange*, VII(30), 4.

Frank, A.G. (1969). *Capitalism and underdevelopment in Latin America*. NY: Monthly Review Press.

Fyfe, J. (1988). Police use of deadly force: Research and reform. *Justice Quarterly*, 5, 166–205.

Geberth, V. (2000, November). Domestic violence lust murder: A clinical perspective of sadistic and sexual fantasies integrated into domestic violence dynamics. *Law and Order*, 48(11), 45–51.

Gilbert, D., & Kahl, J.A. (1987). *The American class structure*. Belmont, CA: Wadsworth.

Glaser, D. (1997). *Profitable penalties: How to cut both crime rates and costs*. Thousand Oaks, CA: Pine Forge Press.

Goldstein, H. (1977). *Policing a free society*. Cambridge, MA: Ballinger.

Goldstein, H. (1990). *Problem-oriented policing*. NY: McGraw Hill.

Gottfredson, M.R., & Hirschi, T. (1990). *A general theory of crime*. Stanford. CA: Stanford University Press.

Griffiths, C.T., & Winfree, L.T. (1982). Attitudes toward the police: A comparison of Canadian and American adolescents. *Journal of Police Science & Administration*, 11, 127–141.

Hall, J.R., & Neitz, M.J. (1993). Culture: Sociological perspectives. Englewood Cliffs, NJ: Prentice Hall.

Hartnett, S. (1998, July). Community policing Chicago Style: Can it work? Paper presented at the Annual Conference on Criminal Justice Research and Evaluation, Washington, DC.

Haviland, W.A. (1999). *Cultural anthropology*. Ninth Edition. NY: Harcourt Brace College Publishers.

Hawkins, C. (1996). Ready, fire, aim: A look at community policing in Edmonton. Alberta, Canada. In Police Executive Research Forum, pp. 13–24. *Themes and variations in community policing: Case studies in community policing*. Washington, DC: Police Executive Research Forum.

Heinz, J. P., & Manikas, P. M. (1992). Networks Among Elites in a Criminal Justice System. Law and Society.

Henshel, R.L. (1990). *Thinking about social problems*. San Diego: Harcourt Brace Jovanovich Publishers.

Hill, R. (2000). Problem solving through community policing: Making the critics believers. *Problem Solving Quarterly*, 13(2), 5–9. NCJ 184985.

Hirschi, T. (1969). *Causes of delinquency*. Berkeley, CA: University of California Press.

Hunter, R.D. (1994). Who guards the guardians? Managerial misconduct in policing. In Thomas Barker and David L. Carter (Eds.). pp. 169–184. *Police Deviance*. Cincinnati, OH: Anderson Publishing Company

Huysamen, G K. 1993. *Metodologie vir die Sosiale en Gedragswetenskappe*. *Halfweghuis*: Southern.

Inciardi, J.A. (2002). *The war on drugs III*. Boston: Allyn & Bacon.

Irwin, J., Austin, J., & Baird, C. (1998). Fanning the flames of fear. *Crime & Delinquency*, 44(1), 32–48.

Ismaili, K. (2001). The social costs of urban crime reduction initiatives: Some lessons from New York City. Paper presented at the annual conference of the Academy of Criminal Justice Sciences, March, Washington, DC.

Jagwanth, S. 1994. Definition community policing in South Africa. *South African Journal for Criminal Justice.* 7(2):164–176.

Kabagarama, D. (1997). Breaking the ice: A guide to understanding people from other cultures. Boston: Allyn and Bacon.

Kalat, J.W. (1993). *Introduction to psychology.* Pacific Grove, CA: Brook/Cole Publishing.

Kansas City, Missouri Police Department. (1977). Response time analysis reports. Washington, DC: National Institute of Law Enforcement and Criminal Justice.

Kappeler, V.E. (1999). The police and society. Prospect Heights, IL: Waveland Press.

Karmen, A. (1996, November 30). What's driving New York's crime rate down? *Law Enforcement News,* John Jay College of Criminal Justice/CUNY. Khan, D. (1999, October 26). When voters want a crime fight. *Boston Globe.*

Kelling, G., Pate, T., Dieckman, D., & Brown, C. E. (1974). The Kansas City preventive patrol experiment: A technical report. Washington, DC: Police Foundation.

Kelling, G. (1998). Columbia's Comprehensive Communities Program: A Case Study.

Kelling, G.L., & Moore, M.H. (1999). The evolving strategy of policing. In Victor E. Kappeler (Ed.), *The police and society,* pp. 2–26. Prospect Heights, IL: Waveland Press.

Kerley, K.R. (2002). Perceptions of community policing across community sectors: Results from a regional survey. In Dennis J. Stevens (Ed.) *Policing and Community Partnerships,* pp. 93–110. Upper Saddle River, NJ: Prentice Hall.

Kirkland, R., & Glensor, R. (1992). Community oriented policing and problem solving department report. Reno, NV: Reno Police Department.

Klockars, C.B. (1988). The rhetoric of community policing. In J.R. Greene & S.D. Mastrofski (Eds.), *Community policing: Rhetoric or reality* (pp.239–258). NY: Pralger.

Klockars, C.B. (1986). Street justice. Some micro-moral reservations. *Justice Quarterly,* 3(4), 513–516.

Klockars, C.B. (1999). The dirty Harry problem. In Victor E. Kappeler (Ed.) *The Police and Society,* (368–385). Prospect Heights, IL: Waveland Press.

Knoke, D., & Kuklinski, J. H. (1982). Network Analysis. Beverly Hills, CA: Sage.

Kruskal, J. B., & Wish, M. (1978). *Multidimensional scaling.* Beverly Hills, CA: Sage.

Kruttschnitt, C., Ward, D., & Sheble, M.A. (1987). Abuse-resistant youth: Some factors that may inhibit violent criminal behavior. *Social Focus,* 66(2), 501–519.

Lasley, J.R., Vernon, R.L., & Dery III, G.M. (1995). Operation cul-de-sac: LAPD's total community program. In P. Kratcoski and D. Dukes (Eds.) *Issues in community policing* (pp. 51–67). Highland Heights, KY: Anderson Publishing Company.

Lee, W.L.M. (1901). *A history of police in England.* London: Methuen.

Liou, T.K., & Savage, E. (1996). Citizen perception of community policing impact. *Public Administration and Management: An Interactive Journal,* 1(1). www.pamij.com/liou1.html

Lipset, S.M., & Bendix, R. (1951). Social status and social structure. *British Journal of Sociology, II.*

Lively, K. (2000, September 10). Diversity increases among presidents: Survey finds that more women and members of minority groups are rising to the top. *Chronicle of Higher Education.* chronicle.com/weekly/v47/i03/03a03101.htm

Macionis, J.J. (2000). *Society: The basics.* Upper Saddle River, NJ: Prentice Hall.

Macionis, J.J., & Parrillo, V.N. (1998). *Cities and urban life.* Upper Saddle River, NJ: Prentice Hall.

Manning, P. K. (1997). *Police work: The social organization of policing.* Prospect Heights, IL: Waveland Press.

Marx, K., & Engels, F. (1972, originally 1848). Manifesto of the communist party. In Robert C. Tucker (Ed.) *The Marx-Engels Reader.* NY: Norton.

Marx, G. (1999). Ironies of social control: Authorities as contributors to deviance through escalation, nonenforcement, and convert facilitation. In Henry N. Pontell (Ed.) *Social deviance: Readings in theory and research,* pp. 7–19. Upper Saddle River, NJ: Prentice Hall.

Masterson, M., & Stevens, D.J. (2002). The value of measuring community policing performance in Madison, Wisconsin. In Dennis J. Stevens (Ed.) *Policing and community partnerships.* pp. 77–92. Upper Saddle River, NJ: Prentice Hall.

Masterson, M., & Stevens, D.J. (2001, December). Madison Speaks up: Measuring community policing performance. *Law and Order,* 49(10), 98–100.

Martin, S. E., & Sherman, L.W. (1986).Selective apprehension: a police strategy for repeat offenders. *Criminology* 24: pp. 55–72.

McCaffrey, B.R. (2000, December 14). White House Drug Czar says "Monitoring the future" results show cocaine and heroin use down among key youth age groups, but huge upsurge in ecstasy. National Drug Control Center.

McElroy, J.E., Cosgrove, C.A., & Sadd, S. (1993). *Community policing: The CPOP in New York.* Newbury Park, CA: Sage.

Meek, J.G. (2000, December). Customs chief calls for new drug strategy: Kelly urges renewed efforts at treatment prevention. APBnews.com. www.apbnews.com/newscenter/breakingnews/2000/12/29/customs1229_01.html

Milofsky, A. (2000, January/February). Examining police behavior under Nazi rule offers contemporary lessons on moral responsibility and civil liabilities. *Community Policing Exchange. VII(30),* 3.

Mink, O., Dietz, A.S., & Mink, J. (2000). Changing a police culture of corruption: Implications for the police psychologist. Paper presented at the 29th Annual Society of Policing and Criminal Psychology conference, Cleveland, OH.

Newland, K. (2000). Worldwide Refugee Information: Carnegie Endowment for International Peace. www.refugees.org/world/articles/wrs99_decadeinreview.htm

Nowicki, D.E. (1998). Mixed messages. In Geoffrey Alpert and Alex Piquero (Eds.) *Community Policing,* pp. 265–274, Prospect Heights, IL: Waveland Press.

Oettmeier, T.N., & Wycoff, M.A. (1997). Personnel performance evaluations in the community policing context. In Geoffrey Alpert and Alex Piquero (Eds.) *Community Policing,* pp. 275–306. Prospect Heights, IL: Waveland Press.

Orwin, C. (1996). All quiet on the western front. *The Public Interest, 123,* 3–9.

Peak, K.J., & Glensor, R.W. (1999). *Community policing and problem solving: Strategies and practices.* Upper Saddle River, NJ: Prentice Hall.

Peel Regional Police Survey of Attitudes and Opinions, (1994, March). Brampton, Ontario: Benchmark Study.

Perlman, J.E. (1976). *The myth of marginality: urban poverty and politics in Rio de Janeiro.* Berkeley, CA: University of California Press.

Planty, M., & Rennison, C. (2001). *Examining the decline in crime: The victim's perspective.* Bureau of Justice Statistics, US Department of Justice. Paper presented at the Academy of Criminal Justice Sciences 2001 annual meeting in Washington, DC.

Police Executive Research Forum. (1996). *Themes and variations in community policing.* Washington, DC: Police Executive Research Forum.

Popenoe, D. (2000). *Sociology.* Upper Saddle River, NJ: Prentice Hall.

Portes, A., & Rumbaut, R.G. (1996). *Immigrant America.* Berkeley, CA: University of California Press.

Reckless, W. (1973). *The crime problem.* 5th edition. NY: Appleton.

Redfield, R. (1959). *The folk culture of Yucatan.* Chicago: University of Chicago Press.

Reiman, J. (1995). *The rich get richer and the poor get prison.* 4th edition. Boston: Allyn and Bacon.

Reiner, R. (1998). Process or product? Problems of assessing individual police performance. In Jean-Paul Brodeur (Ed.), *How to recognize good policing: Problems and issues,* pp. 55–72. Thousand Oaks, CA: Sage.

Reisberg, L. (2000, August 11). A Professor's Controversial Analysis of Why Black Students Are Losing the Race: Berkeley scholar says their own anti-intellectualism prevents academic success. *The Chronicle of Higher Education.* A51.

Reno, J., Dwyer, J.C., Robinson, L., & Gist, N.E. (1997, September). Crime Prevention and Community Policing: A Vital Partnership. Washington, DC: Bureau of Justice Assistance, Justice Assistance: Crime Prevention and Community Policing: A Vital Partnership. NCJ 166819. www.ojp. usdoj.gov/BJA

Reno Police Department. (1992, July). Telephone poll. Reno, NV: Reno Police Department.

Rezendes, M. (1993, December 22). A dream dashed on the street crime rates fall, but fears rise. *Boston Globe.* Boston, MA. p. 1.

Ritzer, G. (1993). *The McDonaldization of society. An investigation into the changing character of contemporary social life.* Thousand Oaks, CA: Pine Forge Press.

Roeber, J., & Ranalli, R. (2000, August 17). 15 arrested, 1Mil in cocaine seized. B2.

Rodriguez, C. (2000, August 30). Birthrate of minorities outpaces white in hub. *Boston Globe,* p. 1, A16, A17.

Ryan, J.E. (2001). Police decisions to arrest in responses to domestic assault calls in Vermont. An analysis of qualitative factors. Paper presented at the annual conference of the Academy of Criminal Justice Sciences, March, Washington, DC.

Sacco, V.F. (1998). Evaluating satisfaction. In Jean-Paul Brodeur (Ed.), *How to recognize good policing: Problems and issues,* pp. 123–140. Thousand Oaks, CA: Sage.

Sadd, S., & Grinc, R. (1994). Innovative neighborhood oriented policing: An evaluation of community policing programs in eight cities. In D.P. Rosenbaum (Ed.), *The challenge of community policing: Testing the promises,* pp. 27–52. Newbury Park, CA: Sage.

Sampson, R.J., & Bartusch, D.J. (1999, June). Attitudes toward crime, the police, and the law: Individual and neighborhood differences. National Institute of Justice. Washington, DC. www.ojp.usdoj.gov/nij/pubs-sum/fs000240.htm

Sampson, R.J., & Raudenbush, S.W. (2000). Disorder in urban neighborhoods—does it lead to crime? National Institute of Justice. Washington, DC. www.ncjrs.org/txtfiles1/nij/186049.txt

Schmalleger, F. (1999). *Criminology today.* Upper Saddle River, NJ: Prentice Hall.

Schmalleger, F. (1999b). *Criminal justice today.* Upper Saddle River, NJ: Prentice Hall.

Sekulic, D., Massey, G, & Hodson, R. (1994). Who were the Yugoslavs? Failed sources of common identity in the former Yugoslavia. *American Sociological Review, 59*(1), 83–97.

Shelden, R.G. (2001). *Controlling the dangerous classes: A critical introduction to the history or criminal justice.* Boston: Allyn and Bacon.

Sherman, L.W. (1995). The police. In James Q. Wilson and Joan Petersilia (Eds.), *Crime,* pp. .327–348. San Francisco: Institute for Contemporary Studies.

Simmel, G. (1964). The metropolis and mental life. In K. Wolff (Ed.), *The sociology of Georg Simmel.* (pp. 409–424). Originally published in 1905. NY: The Free Press.

Simon, D.R. (1995). *Social problems and the sociological imagination.* NY: McGraw-Hill. Skogan, W.G. (1990). *Disorder and decline: Crime and the spiral of decay in American Neighborhoods.* NY: The Free Press.

Skogan, W.G. (1990). Disorder and decline: Crime and the spiral of decay in American cities. NY: Free Press.

Skogan, W.G. (1998). Community participation and community policing. In Jean-Paul Brodeur (Ed.), *How to recognize good policing: Problems and issues.* (pp. 88–106). Thousand Oaks, CA: Sage.

Skogan, W.G. Hartnett, S.M., DuBois, J., Comey, J.T., Kaiser, M., & Lovig, J.H. (1999). On the beat: Police and community problem solving. UK: Westview Press.

Skogan, W.G., & Hartnett, S.M. (1997). *Community policing: Chicago style.* NY: Oxford University Press. Skolnick, J.H. (1966). *Justice without trial: Law enforcement in democratic society.* NY: John Wiley & Sons.

Spelman, W., & Brown, D. K. (1984). Calling the police: Citizen reporting of serious crime. Washington, DC: National Institute of Justice.

Spelman, W. & Eck, J. (1987). Problem oriented policing: The Newport News experiment. Washington, DC: Police Executive Research Forum.

Stephens, D.W. (1996). *Community problem oriented policing: Measuring impact, quantifying quality in policing.* Washington, DC: Police Executive Research Forum.

Stevens, D.J. (2002a). *Policing and community partnerships.* (Ed.). NY:Prentice Hall.

(2002b). Civil liabilities and arrest decisions. In Jeffery T. Walker (Ed.), *Policing and the Law,* pp. 53–70, Upper Saddle River, NJ: Prentice Hall.

(2002c). Canadian prison education: For whom the bell tolls. (Chapter) In *Compendium of Effective Correctional Programming.* Correctional Service Canada.

(2002d). Pedophiles: A case study. *Journal of Police and Criminal Psychology.* Spring.

(2002e). *Inside the mind of sexual offenders: Predatory rapists, pedophiles, and criminal profiles.* NY: Authors Choice Press.

(2001a). *Case studies in community policing.* NY: Prentice Hall.

(2001b, May). Civil liabilities and selective enforcement. *Law and Order,* 49(5), 105–109.

(2001c). Community policing and managerial techniques: Total Quality Management Techniques. *The Police Journal,* 74(1), 26–41. (2001d). *Measuring performance: An easy guide to master the skills of a researcher.* NY: Authors Choice.

(2000a). A study of three generations of incarcerated sexual offenders. In Dennis J. Stevens (Ed.) *Perspectives: Corrections.* Madison, WI: Coursewise Publications.

(2000b). Identifying criminal predators, sentences, and criminal classifications. *Journal of Police and Criminal Psychology,* 15(1), 50–71.

(2000c). Education programming for offenders. *Forum on Corrections Research. Correctional Service of Canada,* 12(2), 29–31.

(2000d, October). Improving community policing: Using managerial style and Total Quality Management. *Law and Order,* 197–204.

(1999a). Do college educated officers provide quality police service? *Law and Order.* December, 47(12), 37–41.

(1999b). Corruption among narcotic officers: A study of innocence and integrity. *Journal of Police and Criminal Psychology.* Fall, 14(2), 1–11.

(1999c). American police resolutions. *Police Journal,* LXXII(2). 140–150.

(1999d). Stress and the American police officer. *Police Journal,* LXXII(3), 247–259.

(1999e). Research Note: Myers-Briggs Type Indicator—cops, convicts, and college students. *Police Journal,* LXXII(1). 59–64.

(1999f, September). Police officer stress. *Law and Order.* www.lawandordermag.com/index2.html

(1999g). *Perspective: Corrections* (Ed.). Madison, WI: Coursewise Publishers.

(1999h). *Inside the mind of the serial rapist.* Bethesda, MD: Austin & Winfield Publishers. www.amazon.com

(1999i, March). Police tactical units and community response. *Law and Order.* 47(3), 48–52.

(1999j). Interviews with women convicted of murder: Battered women syndrome revisited. *International Review of Victimology,* 6(2).

(1998a). What do law enforcement officers think about their work? *The Law Enforcement Journal,* 5(1), 60–62.

(1998b). Urban communities and homicide: Why American blacks resort to murder. *Police and Society,* 8, 253–267.

(1998c). Mandatory arrest, spouse abuse, & accelerated rates of victimization: Attitudes of victims and officers. *The Criminologist.*

(1998d). Narcotic officers: A study of inexperience, virtue, and corruption. *The Law Enforcement Journal,* 5(3), Summer/Fall, pp. 58–69.

(1998e). Arrest-conviction barriers of narcotic law enforcement officers. *Police Journal.* LXXI(3), 213–225.

(1998f). Correctional officer attitudes: Job satisfaction levels linked to length of employment. *Corrections Compendium: The National Journal for Corrections.* American Correctional Association, 23(7), 1–2.

(1998g). Incarcerated women, crime, and drug addiction. *The Criminologist,* 22(1), 3–14.

(1997a). Influences of early childhood experiences on subsequent criminology violent behaviour. *Studies on Crime and Crime Prevention,* 6(1), 34–50.

(1997b). Violence begets violence. *Corrections Compendium: The National Journal for Corrections.* American Correctional Association. 22(12), 1–2.

(1997c). Prisoner restrictions, inmate custodial, and inmate attitudes towards compliance. *Forum on Research and Statistics Branch of the Correctional Service of Canada.*

(1997e). Origins of prison gangs in North Carolina. *Journal of Gang Research,* 4(4), 23–35.

(1997g). Prison Regime and Drugs. *The Howard Journal of Criminal Justice,* 36(1), 14–27.

(1992a). Research note: The death sentence and inmate attitudes. *Crime & Delinquency,* 38.

(1992b). Examining inmate attitudes: Do prisons deter crime? *The State of Corrections—American Correctional Association: 1991.* 272–79.

Stevens, D.J., & Ward, C. (1997). College education and recidivism: Educating criminals is meritorious. *Journal of Correctional Education,* 48(3), 106–111.

Stevens, P., & Yach, D.M. (1996). *Community Policing in Action: A practitioner's guide.* Kenwyn : Juta.

Stewart-Brown, R., & Rosario, M. (2001, November/December). Mind your own business is bad advice. *Community Policing Exchange,* VII(33), 1&8.

Stone, M.E., Werby, E., & Friedman, D.H. (2000). Report 2000: Meeting the needs of lower-income Massachusetts residents. The John W. McCormack Institute for Public Affairs, University of Massachusetts Boston. [On-line], Available: www.mccormack..umb.edu/

Strecher, V.G. (1988). Stimuli of police education: Wickersham and LBJ's Commission. *The Justice Professional,* 3(2).

Straus, M.A. (1994). *Beating the devil out of them.* New York: Lexington Books. Surveys of citizens attitudes. (1995). Telemasp Bulletin. Huntsville, Texas: Texas Law Enforcement Management and Administrative Problem, Bill Blackwood Enforcement Management Institute of Texas.

The African People's Socialist Party, (1999). www.uhurumovement.org/bosp9.htm

Thio, A. (2000). *Sociology: A brief introduction.* Boston: Allyn and Bacon.

Trojanowicz, R.C. (1982). *An evaluation of the neighborhood foot patrol program in Flint, Michigan.* East Lansing: Department of Criminal Justice, Michigan State University.

Trojanowicz, R.C., & Carter, D.L. (1988). *The philosophy and role of community policing.* East Lansing: National Neighborhood Foot Patrol Center, Michigan State University.

Trojanowicz, R.C., & Dixon, S.L. (1974). *Criminal justice and the community.* Englewood Cliffs, NJ: Prentice Hall.

Thurman, Q., & McGarrell, E.F. (1995, June). Findings of the 1994 Spokane Police Department Citizen Survey: Final report, Washington State Institute for Community Oriented Policing, Spokane, Washington.

Tonry, M., & Petersilia, J., (2000). Prisons research at the beginning of the 21st century. National Institute of Justice. Washington, DC: U.S. Department of Justice.

Uchida, C.D. (2002). The development of the American police. In Wilson R. Palacios, Paul F. Cromwell, and Roger G. Dunham (Eds.), pp. 87–99). *Crime & justice in America.* Upper Saddle River, NJ: Prentice Hall.

Uchida, C.D. (1993). The development of two American police: An historical overview. In Dunham and Alpert (Eds.), pp. 125–141. *Critical issues in policing.* Prospect Heights, IL: Waveland Press.

Wallace, H. (1999). *Family violence: Legal, medical and social perspectives.* Boston: Allyn and Bacon.

Walker, S. (1999). *The police in America.* Boston: McGraw Hill College.

Walker, S., & Katz, T. (2001). *The police in America.* Boston: McGraw Hill College.

Warner, B.D., Rountree, P.W. (1997). Local social ties in a community and crime model: Questioning the systemic nature of informal social control. *Social Problems,* 44(4), 520–536.

Williams, H., & Murphy, P.V. (1999). The evolving strategy of police: A minority view. In Victor E. Kappeler (Ed.), *The police and society,* (p. 27–50). Prospect Heights, IL: Waveland Press.

Williams, M.R. (1985). *Neighborhood organizations: Seeds of a new urban life*. Westport, CN: Greenwood Press.

Wilson, J.Q., & Kelling, G.L. (2000). Broken windows: The police and neighborhood safety. In Willard M. Oliver (Ed.) *Community Policing: Classical Readings*, pp. 1–15. Upper Saddle River, NJ: Prentice Hall.

Wirth, L. (1933). Urbanism as a way of life. *American Journal of Sociology, 44*(7).

Wulff, D. (2000, January/February). Winning strategies offered for working with different cultures. *Community Policing Exchange, VII*(30), 1.

Zevitz, R.G., & Rettammel, R.J. (1990). Elderly attitudes about police service. *American Journal of Police, 9,* 25–39.

Zevitz, R.G., & Farkas, M.A. (2000, December). Sex offender community notification: Assessing the impact in Wisconsin. National Institute of Justice: Research in Brief. NCJ 179992. www.ojp.usdoj.gov/nij

Zimbardo, P.G. (1970). The human choice: Individuation, reason, and order versus deindividuation, implulse, and chaos. In W. Arnold and D. Levine (Eds.), *Nebraska Symposium on Motivation 1969*, pp. 237–307. Lincoln, NB: University of Nebraska Press.

Zola, J. (1996). *Why police organizations change: A study of community oriented policing*. Washington, DC: Police Executive Research Forum. Anechiarico, F., & Jacobs, J.B. (1996). *The pursuit of absolute integrity.* Chicago: The University of Chicago Press.

Index